*Rick* W9-CHT-306

# BARCELONA

Rick Steves

# CONTENTS

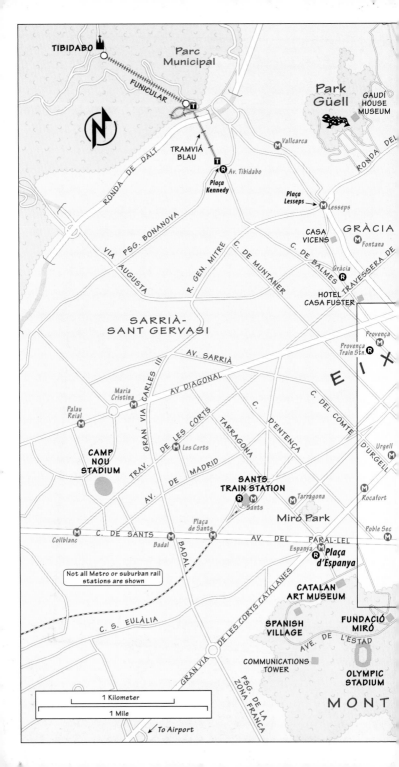

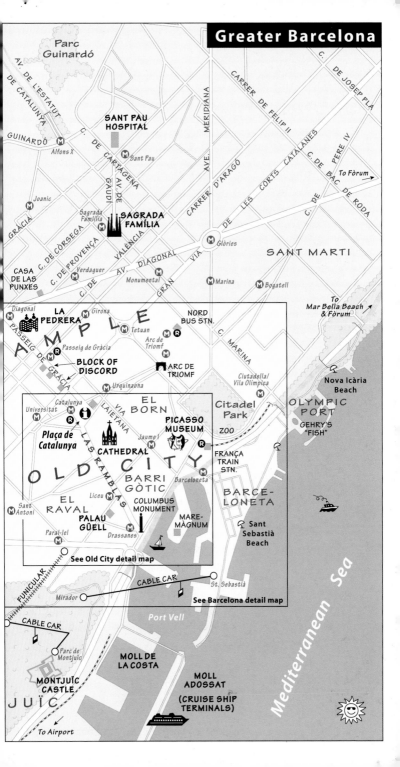

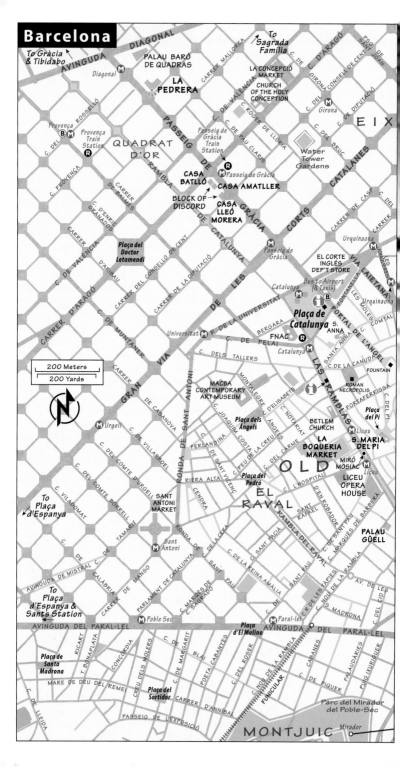

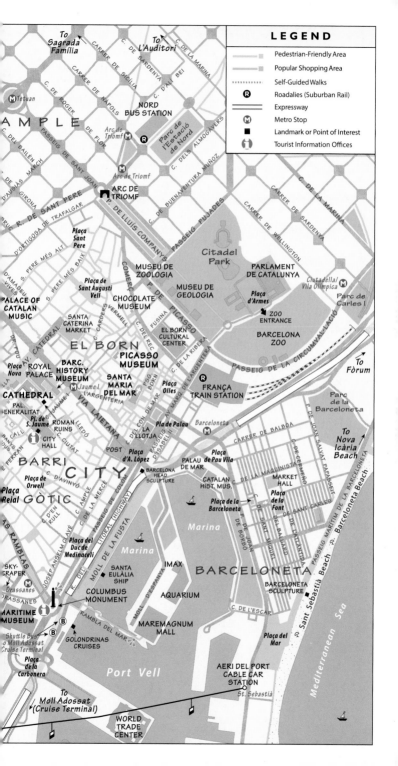

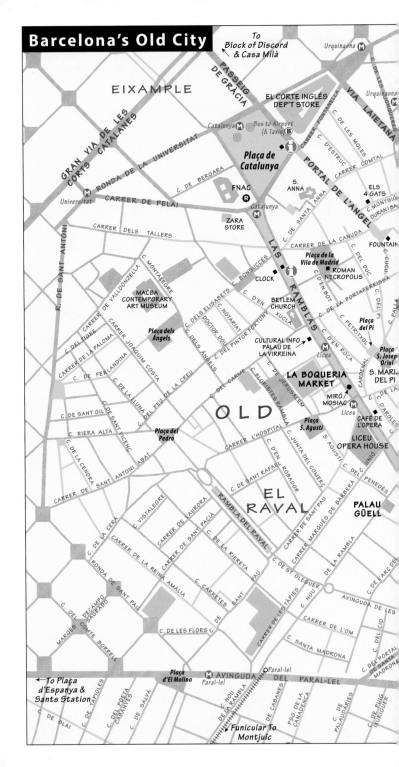

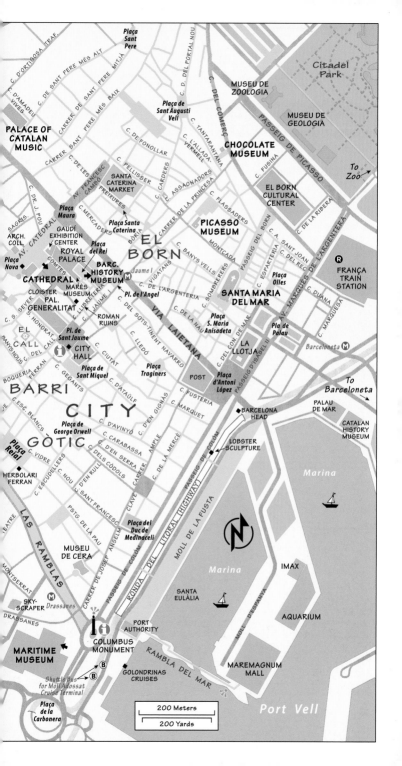

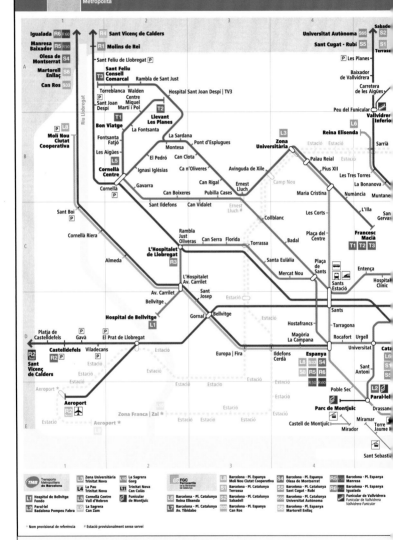

ATM | Àrea de Barcelona
Autoritat del Transport Metropolità

# Xarxa Ferroviària Integrada Central

\* Nom provisional de referència    # Estació provisionalment sense servei

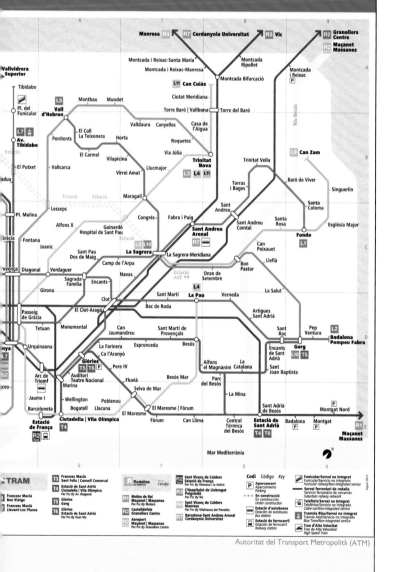

Autoritat del Transport Metropolità (ATM)

# *Rick Steves*®

# BARCELONA

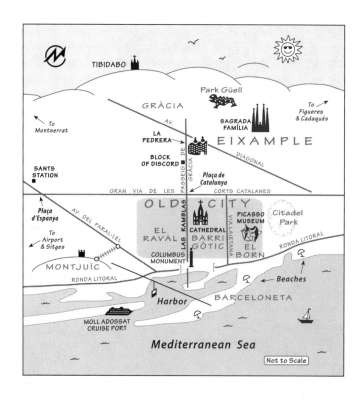

# INTRODUCTION

If you're in the mood to surrender to a city's charms, let it be in Barcelona. The capital of Catalunya and Spain's second city, Barcelona bubbles with life in its narrow Barri Gòtic alleys, along the pedestrian boulevard called the Ramblas, in the funky bohemian quarter of El Born, along the bustling beach promenade, and throughout the chic, grid-planned new part of town called the Eixample.

Barcelona's Old City is made for seeing on foot, full of winding lanes that emerge into secluded squares dotted with palm trees

and ringed with cafés and boutiques. The waterfront bristles with life, overlooked by the park-like setting of Montjuïc. Everywhere you go, you'll find the city's architecture to be colorful, playful, and unique. Rows of symmetrical ironwork balconies are punctuated with fanciful details: bay windows, turrets, painted tiles, hanging lanterns, flower boxes, and carved reliefs.

As the capital of the Catalan people, Barcelona is full of history. You'll see Roman ruins, a medieval cathedral, twisty Gothic lanes, and traces of Columbus and the sea trade. But by the late 19th century, the city had boomed into an industrial powerhouse and became the cradle of a new artistic style—Modernisme. Pablo Picasso lived in Barcelona as a teenager, just as he was on the verge of reinventing painting; his legacy is today's Picasso Museum. Catalan architects, including Antoni Gaudí, Lluís Domènech i Montaner, and Josep Puig i Cadafalch, forged the Modernista style and remade the city's skyline with curvy, playful fantasy buildings—culminating in Gaudí's over-the-top Sagrada Família, a church still under construction. Salvador Dalí and Joan

## Map Legend

| | | |
|---|---|---|
| ⅃ Viewpoint | ✈ Airport | )▨( Tunnel |
| ↑ Entrance | ⓣ Taxi Stand | ▨ Pedestrian Zone |
| ❶ Tourist Info | ⊤ Tram Stop | ⋯⋯ Railway |
| WC Restroom | ⓑ Bus Stop | ⋯⋯⋯⋯ Ferry/Boat Route |
| ⬤ Castle | Ⓜ Metro Stop | |
| ⬜ Church | Ⓡ Rodalies/Suburban Rail Stop | ⧾⧾⧾ Tram |
| ⬚ Synagogue | ⓟ Parking | ▥▥▥ Stairs |
| ▪ Statue/Point of Interest | ⬚ Park | • • • • • Walk/Tour Route |
| ⊠ Elevator | ◉ Fountain | ------- Trail |

*Use this legend to help you navigate the maps in this book.*

Miró join the long list of world-changing 20th-century artists with ties to this city.

Today's Barcelona is as vibrant as ever. Locals still join hands and dance the everyone's-welcome *sardana* in front of the cathedral every weekend. Neighborhood festivals jam the events calendar. The cafés are filled by day, and people crowd the streets at night, pausing to fortify themselves with a perfectly composed bite of seafood and a drink at a tapas bar. Barcelona's lively culture is on an unstoppable roll in Spain's most cosmopolitan and European corner.

## ABOUT THIS BOOK

*Rick Steves Barcelona* is a tour guide in your pocket.

In this book, you'll find the following chapters:

**Orientation to Barcelona** has specifics on public transportation, helpful hints, local tour options, easy-to-read maps, and tourist information. The "Planning Your Time" section suggests a schedule for how to best use your limited time.

**Sights in Barcelona** describes the top attractions and includes their cost and hours.

Four **Self-Guided Walks** cover Barcelona's most enjoyable neighborhoods: the Ramblas promenade, historic Barri Gòtic, trendy El Born, and a Modernista paradise, the Eixample.

The **Self-Guided Tours** lead you through Barcelona's most fascinating museums and sights: the Cathedral of Barcelona, the Picasso Museum, and two architectural gems, Gaudí's Sagrada Família and Park Güell.

**Sleeping in Barcelona** describes my favorite hotels, from good-value deals to cushy splurges.

# Key to This Book

## Updates

This book is updated regularly—but things change. For the latest, visit www.ricksteves.com/update.

## Abbreviations and Times

I use the following symbols and abbreviations in this book:

Sights are rated:

| | |
|---|---|
| ▲▲▲ | Don't miss |
| ▲▲ | Try hard to see |
| ▲ | Worthwhile if you can make it |
| **No rating** | Worth knowing about |

Tourist information offices are abbreviated as **TI,** and bathrooms are **WC**s. Accommodations are categorized with a **Sleep Code** (described on page 274); eateries are classified with a **Restaurant Price Code** (page 281). To indicate discounts for my readers, I include **RS%** in the listings.

Like Europe, this book uses the **24-hour clock.** It's the same as ours through 12:00 noon, then keeps going: 13:00, 14:00, and so on. For anything over 12, subtract 12 and add p.m. (14:00 is 2 p.m.).

When giving **opening times,** I include both peak-season and off-season hours if they differ. So, if a museum is listed as "May-Oct daily 9:00-16:00," it should be open from 9 a.m. until 4 p.m. from the first day of May until the last day of October (but expect exceptions).

A □ symbol in a sight listing means that sight is described in greater detail elsewhere—either with its own self-guided tour, or as part of a self-guided walk. A ∩ symbol indicates that a free, downloadable self-guided audio tour is available.

For **transit** or **tour departures,** I first list the frequency, then the duration. So, a train connection listed as "2/hour, 1.5 hours" departs twice each hour and the journey lasts an hour and a half.

**Eating in Barcelona** serves up a buffet of options, from inexpensive tapas bars to fancy restaurants.

**Barcelona with Children** includes my top recommendations for keeping your kids (and you) happy.

**Shopping in Barcelona** gives you tips on fun shopping areas to explore while staying within your budget.

**Nightlife in Barcelona** is your guide to fun, including classical concerts, flamenco performances, jazz clubs, bars, and other evening activities.

**Barcelona Connections** lays the groundwork for your smooth arrival and departure, covering transportation by train, plane, and bus (with detailed information on Barcelona's Sants train station and El Prat de Llobregat airport), plus the basics on the city's cruise ship docks.

**Day Trips from Barcelona** covers nearby sights: Montserrat, Figueres, Cadaqués, and Sitges.

**Barcelona: Past & Present** gives the background of this city and its region, including a timeline of Barcelona history, information about famous Catalans, and a rundown of contemporary events.

The **Practicalities** chapter near the end of this book is a traveler's tool kit, with my best advice about money, sightseeing, sleeping, eating, staying connected, and transportation.

The **appendix** has the nuts-and-bolts: useful phone numbers and websites, a holiday and festival list, recommended books and films, a climate chart, a handy packing checklist, and Spanish and Catalan survival phrases.

Throughout this book, you'll find money- and time-saving tips for sightseeing, transportation, and more. Some businesses—especially hotels and walking tour companies—offer special discounts to my readers, indicated in their listings.

Browse through this book and select your favorite sights. Then have a *meravellós* trip! Traveling like a temporary local, you'll get the absolute most out of every mile, minute, and dollar. As you visit places I know and love, I'm happy that you'll be meeting my favorite Catalans.

# Planning

This section will help you get started planning your trip—with advice on trip costs, when to go, and what you should know before you take off.

## TRAVEL SMART

Your trip to Barcelona is like a complex play—it's easier to follow and really appreciate on a second viewing. While no one does the same trip twice to gain that advantage, reading this book in its entirety before your trip accomplishes much the same thing.

Design an itinerary that enables you to visit sights at the best possible times. Note holidays, specifics on sights, and days when sights are closed or most crowded (all covered in this book). You can wait in line at the Sagrada Família, or get advance reservations and bypass the queue without breaking a sweat. Day-tripping to Figueres on an off-season Monday is a waste (you'll find the Dalí Theater-Museum to be closed). Be careful on the first Sunday of the month; sights such as Palau Güell and the Catalan Art Museum are jammed because they're free. To connect the dots smoothly, read the tips in Practicalities on taking trains and buses, or renting a car and driving. Designing a smart trip is a fun, doable, and worthwhile challenge.

Make your itinerary a mix of intense and relaxed stretches. Every trip—and every traveler—needs slack time (laundry, picnics, people-watching, and so on). Pace yourself. Assume you will return.

Even with the best-planned itinerary, you'll need to be flexible. Update your plans as you travel. Get online or call ahead to learn the latest on sights (special events, tour schedules, and so on), book tickets and tours, make reservations, reconfirm hotels, and research transportation connections.

Enjoy the friendliness of the Catalan people. Connect with the culture. Set up your own quest for the best square, cloister, tapas bar, or whatever. Slow down and be open to unexpected experiences. Ask questions—most locals are eager to point you in their idea of the right direction. Keep a notepad in your pocket for noting directions, organizing your thoughts, and confirming prices. Wear your money belt, learn the currency, and figure out how to estimate prices in dollars. Those who expect to travel smart, do.

## TRIP COSTS

Five components make up your trip costs: airfare to Europe, transportation in Europe, room and board, sightseeing and entertainment, and shopping and miscellany.

**Airfare to Europe:** A basic round-trip flight from the US to Barcelona can cost, on average, about $1,000-2,000 total, depending on where you fly from and when (cheaper in winter). If Barcelona is part of a longer trip, consider saving time and money in Europe by flying into one city and out of another; for instance, into Barcelona and out of Paris. Overall, Kayak.com is the best place to start searching for flights on a combination of mainstream and budget carriers.

**Transportation in Europe:** A 10-ride Metro card costs about $11. For round-trip train rides to day-trip destinations, allow about $25 for Montserrat and $45 for Figueres. To travel between El Prat airport and Barcelona, figure (one-way) $5-7 by public transportation, or $40 by taxi.

**Room and Board:** You can manage comfortably in Barcelona on $130 a day per person for room and board. This allows $5 for breakfast, $15 for lunch, $25 for dinner, and $85 for lodging (based on two people splitting the cost of a $170 double room). Students and tightwads can enjoy Barcelona for as little as $80 a day ($45 for a bed, $35 for meals and snacks).

**Sightseeing and Entertainment:** It's worth considering the $33 Articket BCN sightseeing pass, which admits you to six museums, including the recommended Picasso Museum, Catalan Art

## "You're Not in Spain, You're in Catalunya!"

This is a popular nationalistic refrain you might see on T-shirts or stickers around town. Catalunya is *not* the land of bullfighting and flamenco that many visitors envision when they think of Spain (best to visit Madrid or Sevilla for those).

The region of Catalunya, with Barcelona as its capital, has its own language, history, and culture. Its people—eight million strong—have a proud, independent spirit. Historically, Catalunya ("Cataluña" in Spanish, sometimes spelled "Catalonia" in English) has often been at odds with the central Spanish government in Madrid. The Catalan language and culture were discouraged or even outlawed at various times in history, as Catalunya often chose the wrong side in wars and rebellions against the kings in Madrid. In the Spanish Civil War (1936-1939), Catalunya was one of the last pockets of democratic resistance against the military coup of the fascist dictator Francisco Franco, who punished the region with four decades of repression. During that time, the Catalan flag was banned—but locals vented their national spirit by flying their football team's flag instead.

Three of Barcelona's monuments are reminders of royal and Franco-era suppression. Citadel Park (Parc de la Ciutadella) was originally a much-despised military citadel, constructed in the 18th century to keep locals in line. The Castle of Montjuïc, built for similar reasons, has been the site of numerous political executions, including hundreds during the Franco era. The Sacred Heart Church atop Tibidabo, completed under Franco, was meant to atone for the sins of Barcelonans during the civil war—the main sin being opposition to Franco. Today, many Catalans favor breaking away from Spain, but the central government has vowed to block any referendum on independence (see page 261).

To see real Catalan culture, look for the *sardana* dance or an exhibition of *castellers* (both described on page 45). The main symbol of Catalunya is the dragon, which was slain by St. George ("Jordi" in Catalan)—the region's patron saint. You'll find dragons all over Barcelona, along with the Catalan flag—called

Museum, and Fundació Joan Miró (for more information, see page 24). Otherwise, figure $10-25 per major sight (Picasso Museum-$13, La Pedrera-$23, Sagrada Família-$20 and up), and $10 for others. An evening concert at the Palace of Catalan Music costs about $25-50 per person. An overall average of $40 a day works for most people. Don't skimp here. After all, this category is the

the Senyera—with four horizontal red stripes on a gold field. Nineteenth-century Catalan Romantics embraced a vivid story about the origins of their flag: In the ninth century, Wilfred the Hairy—a count of Barcelona and one of the founding fathers of Catalunya—was wounded in battle. A grateful neighboring king rewarded Wilfred's bravery with a copper shield and ran Wilfred's four bloody fingers across its surface, leaving four red stripes. While almost certainly false, this legend hints at the nostalgic mood in 19th-century Barcelona, when the Renaixença (Catalan cultural revival) prodded historians to dig deeply into their medieval past to revive obscure historical figures and lend legitimacy to the resurgent Catalan nation.

The Catalan language is irrevocably tied to the history and spirit of the people here. After the end of the Franco era in the mid-1970s, the language made a huge comeback. Schools are now required by law to conduct all classes in Catalan; most school-age children learn Catalan first and Spanish second. While all Barcelonans still speak Spanish, nearly all understand Catalan, three-quarters speak Catalan, and half can write it.

Most place names in this book are listed in Catalan. Here's how to pronounce the city's major landmarks:

| | |
|---|---|
| Plaça de Catalunya | PLAH-sah duh kah-tah-LOON-yah |
| Eixample | eye-SHAM-plah |
| Passeig de Gràcia | PAH-sehj duh GRAH-see-ah |
| Catedral | KAH-tah-dral |
| Barri Gòtic | BAH-ree GOH-teek |
| El Born | el BORN |
| Montjuïc | mohn-jew-EEK |

When finding your way, these terms will be useful:

| | | |
|---|---|---|
| exit | *sortida* | sor-TEE-dah |
| square | *plaça* | PLAH-sah |
| street | *carrer* | kah-REHR |
| boulevard | *passeig* | PAH-sehj |
| avenue | *avinguda* | ah-veen-GOO-dah |

For more Catalan words, see the survival phrases on page 323.

driving force behind your trip—you came to sightsee, enjoy, and experience Barcelona.

**Shopping and Miscellany:** Figure roughly $3 per coffee, ice-cream cone, or soft drink. Shopping can vary in cost from nearly nothing to a small fortune. Good budget travelers find that this

## 🎧 Rick Steves Audio Europe 🎧

My free **Rick Steves Audio Europe app** is a great tool for en-joying Europe. This app makes it easy to download my audio tours of top attractions, plus hours of travel interviews, all or-ganized into destination-specific playlists.

My self-guided **audio tours** of major sights and neighbor-hoods across Europe are free, user-friendly, fun, and informa-tive. My Barcelona City Walk audio tour covers parts of the Ramblas, Barri Gòtic, and El Born districts (marked in this book with the 🎧 symbol). These audio tours are hard to beat: Nobody will stand you up, your eyes are free to appreciate the sights, you can take the tour exactly when you like, and the price is right.

The Rick Steves Audio Europe app also offers a far-reach-ing library of insightful **travel interviews** from my public radio show with experts from around the globe—including many of the places in this book.

This app and all of its content are entirely free. (And new content is added about twice a year.) You can download Rick Steves Audio Europe via Apple's App Store, Google Play, or the Amazon Appstore. For more information, see www.ricksteves.com/audioeurope.

*Rick Steves*
**AUDIO**
**EUROPE**

category has little to do with assembling a trip full of lifelong mem-ories.

## WHEN TO GO

Sea breezes off the Mediterranean and a generally warm cli-mate make Barcelona pleasant for much of the year. Late spring and early fall offer the best combination of good weather, lighter crowds, long days, and plenty of tourist and cultural activities. You'll encounter hot, humid weather and the biggest crowds in July and August, and some shops and restaurants close down in August. Winter temperatures are far from freezing, but rainfall is abundant.

## KNOW BEFORE YOU GO

Your trip is more likely to go smoothly if you plan ahead. Check this list of things to arrange while you're still at home.

You need a **passport**—but no visa or shots—to travel in Spain. You may be denied entry into certain European countries if your passport is due to expire within six months of your ticketed date of return. Get it renewed if you'll be cutting it close. It can take up to six weeks to get or renew a passport (for more on passports and re-quirements for Spain, see www.travel.state.gov). Pack a photocopy of your passport in your luggage in case the original is lost or stolen.

**Book rooms well in advance** if you'll be traveling during

# Barcelona Almanac

**Population:** 1.6 million.

**Languages:** Spanish and Catalan are the two official languages of Catalunya, but Catalan is the preferred language in schools and offices. Catalan is not a dialect of Spanish, but an independent language.

**Currency:** Euro (€)

**City Layout:** The tangled Gothic Quarter (Barri Gòtic) lies at the heart of the city, edged by the connected boulevards of the Ramblas. The more orderly Eixample district spreads north of the Old City, while unassuming Barceloneta spills along the seafront. Looking down over it all is the big Montjuïc hill.

**Tourist Tracks:** More than 7.5 million people visit Barcelona each year. The Ramblas sees more than 150,000 people daily. Avinguda del Portal de l'Angel is Spain's most walked street, trod upon by 3,500 pairs of feet every hour.

**Architecture:** Barcelona is home to the Modernista style championed by Catalan architect Antoni Gaudí, whose most famous work is the Sagrada Família church. Nearly 30 of his buildings are scattered throughout the greater Barcelona area.

**Fun in the Sun:** Until 1992, when the city hosted the Olympic Games, Barcelona had only one small beachfront area, in Barceloneta. Other waterfront property was taken up by industrial purposes. For the Olympics, the seaside was reconstructed, and the city shoreline is now spanned by nine beaches along a three-mile stretch.

**Soccer:** Futbol Club (FC) Barcelona has the largest privately owned stadium in the world, with a seating capacity of 100,000. Every year, more than 1.5 million people visit its museum.

**The Average Jordi:** The average Barcelonan is 41 years old, will live to age 81, and is likely Catholic. The majority (62 percent) of Barcelona's residents were born in Catalunya.

Barcelona's peak season (April-Oct) or on any major holidays or festivals (see page 314).

Call your **debit- and credit-card companies** to let them know the countries you'll be visiting, to ask about fees, to request your PIN if you don't already know it, and more. See page 267 for details.

Do your homework if you're considering **travel insurance.** Compare the cost of the insurance to the cost of your potential loss. Also check whether your existing insurance (health, homeowners, or renters) covers you and your possessions overseas. For more tips, see www.ricksteves.com/insurance.

If you're taking an **overnight train,** especially to internation-

## How Was Your Trip?

Were your travels fun, smooth, and meaningful? You can share tips, concerns, and discoveries at www.ricksteves.com/feedback. To check out readers' hotel and restaurant reviews—or leave one yourself—visit my travel forum at www.ricksteves.com/travel-forum. I value your feedback. Thanks in advance.

al destinations, and need a sleeping berth *(litera)*—and you must leave on a certain day—consider booking it in advance through a US agent (such as www.ricksteves.com/rail), even though it may cost more than buying it in Spain. All high-speed trains in Spain require a seat reservation, but it's usually possible to make arrangements in Spain just a few days ahead unless it's a holiday weekend. (For more on train travel, see Practicalities.)

If you're planning on **renting a car** for travels beyond Barcelona, bring your driver's license and get an International Driving Permit (see page 304).

You'll need **reservations** to visit Barcelona's Palace of Catalan Music or the Salvador Dalí House near Cadaqués (see page 248). To minimize your time in lines, reservations are recommended for these Barcelona sights, especially in peak season: Picasso Museum, Sagrada Família, Casa Batlló, La Pedrera, Palau Güell, and Park Güell's Monumental Zone. Casa Lleó Morera and Casa Amatller are viewable by guided tour only—it's smart to check tour times and buy tickets in advance. You'll find more information in the individual sight listings.

If you plan to hire a **local guide,** reserve ahead by email. Popular guides can get booked up.

If you're bringing a **mobile device,** consider signing up for an international plan for cheaper calls, texts, and data (see page 291). Download any apps you might want to use on the road, such as translators, maps, transit schedules, and Rick Steves Audio Europe (see page 8).

Check for recent **updates** to this book at www.ricksteves.com/update.

## Traveling as a Temporary Local

We travel all the way to Spain to enjoy differences—to become temporary locals. You'll experience frustrations. Certain truths that we find "God-given" or "self-evident," such as cold beer, ice in drinks, bottomless cups of coffee, "the customer is king," and bigger being better, are suddenly not so true. One of the benefits of travel is the eye-opening realization that there are logical, civil, and even better alternatives. A willingness to go local ensures that you'll enjoy a full dose of Spanish hospitality.

Europeans generally like Americans. But if there is a negative aspect to the Spanish image of Americans, it's that we are loud, wasteful, ethnocentric, too informal (which can seem disrespectful), and a bit naive.

While Spaniards look bemusedly at some of our Yankee excesses—and worriedly at others—they nearly always afford us individual travelers all the warmth we deserve.

Judging from all the happy feedback I receive from travelers who have used this book, it's safe to assume you'll enjoy a great, affordable vacation—with the finesse of an independent, experienced traveler.

Thanks, and *bon viatge!*

# Back Door Travel Philosophy

### From *Rick Steves Europe Through the Back Door*

Travel is intensified living—maximum thrills per minute and one of the last great sources of legal adventure. Travel is freedom. It's recess, and we need it.

Experiencing the real Europe requires catching it by surprise, going casual..."Through the Back Door."

Affording travel is a matter of priorities. (Make do with the old car.) You can eat and sleep—simply, safely, and enjoyably—anywhere in Europe for $100 a day plus transportation costs. In many ways, spending more money only builds a thicker wall between you and what you traveled so far to see. Europe is a cultural carnival, and time after time, you'll find that its best acts are free and the best seats are the cheap ones.

A tight budget forces you to travel close to the ground, meeting and communicating with the people. Never sacrifice sleep, nutrition, safety, or cleanliness to save money. Simply enjoy the local-style alternatives to expensive hotels and restaurants.

Connecting with people carbonates your experience. Extroverts have more fun. If your trip is low on magic moments, kick yourself and make things happen. If you don't enjoy a place, maybe you don't know enough about it. Seek the truth. Recognize tourist traps. Give a culture the benefit of your open mind. See things as different, but not better or worse. Any culture has plenty to share. When an opportunity presents itself, make it a habit to say "yes."

Of course, travel, like the world, is a series of hills and valleys. Be fanatically positive and militantly optimistic. If something's not to your liking, change your liking.

Travel can make you a happier American, as well as a citizen of the world. Our Earth is home to seven billion equally precious people. It's humbling to travel and find that other people don't have the "American Dream"—they have their own dreams. Europeans like us, but with all due respect, they wouldn't trade passports.

Thoughtful travel engages us with the world. It reminds us what is truly important. By broadening perspectives, travel teaches new ways to measure quality of life.

Globetrotting destroys ethnocentricity, helping us understand and appreciate other cultures. Rather than fear the diversity on this planet, celebrate it. Among your most prized souvenirs will be the strands of different cultures you choose to knit into your own character. The world is a cultural yarn shop, and Back Door travelers are weaving the ultimate tapestry. Join in!

# ORIENTATION TO BARCELONA

Bustling Barcelona is geographically big and culturally complex. Plan your time carefully, carving up the metropolis into manageable sightseeing neighborhoods. Use my day plans to help prioritize your time, and make advance reservations for sights (or get a sightseeing pass) to save time waiting in lines. For efficiency, learn how to navigate Barcelona by Metro, bus, and taxi. Armed with good information and a thoughtful game plan, you're ready to go. Then you can relax, enjoy, and let yourself be surprised by all that Barcelona has to offer.

## BARCELONA: A VERBAL MAP

Like Los Angeles, Barcelona is a basically flat city that sprawls out under the sun between the sea and the mountains. It's huge

(1.6 million people, with about 5 million people in greater Barcelona), but travelers need only focus on four areas: the Old City, the harbor/Barceloneta, the Eixample, and Montjuïc.

A large square, **Plaça de Catalunya,** sits at the center of Barcelona, dividing the older and newer parts of town. Below Plaça de Catalunya is the Old City, with the boulevard called the Ramblas running down to the harbor. Above Plaça de Catalunya is the modern residential area called the Eixample. The Montjuïc hill overlooks the harbor. Outside the Old City, Barcelona's sights are widely scattered, but with a map and a willingness to figure out public transit (or take taxis), all is manageable.

ORIENTATION

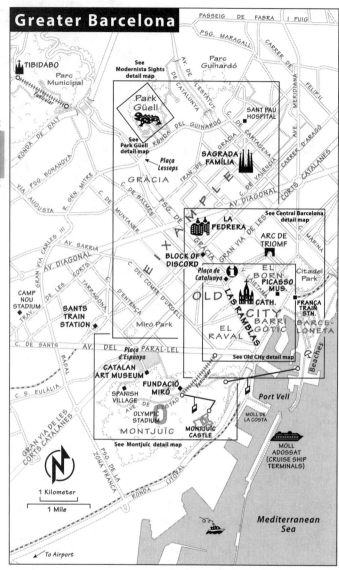

# Greater Barcelona

PASSEIG DE FABRA I PUIG

TIBIDABO

Parc Municipal

*See Modernista Sights detail map*

Parc Guinardó

Park Güell

*See Park Güell detail map*

SANT PAU HOSPITAL

Plaça Lesseps

GRÀCIA

SAGRADA FAMÍLIA

LA PEDRERA

*See Central Barcelona detail map*

ARC DE TRIOMF

BLOCK OF DISCORD

Plaça de Catalunya

EL BORN

PICASSO MUS.

CAMP NOU STADIUM

SANTS TRAIN STATION

Miró Park

OLD CITY

CATH.

BARRI GÒTIC

FRANÇA TRAIN STN.

BARCE-LONETA

EL RAVAL

LAS RAMBLAS

Plaça d'Espanya

PARAL·LEL

*See Old City detail map*

CATALAN ART MUSEUM

FUNDACIÓ MIRÓ

SPANISH VILLAGE

OLYMPIC STADIUM

MONTJUÏC

MONTJUÏC CASTLE

*See Montjuïc detail map*

Beaches

Port Vell

MOLL DE LA COSTA

MOLL ADOSSAT (CRUISE SHIP TERMINALS)

N

1 Kilometer

1 Mile

To Airport

*Mediterranean Sea*

Here are overviews of the major neighborhoods:

**Old City** (Ciutat Vella): This is the compact core of Barcelona—ideal for strolling, shopping, and people-watching—where you'll probably spend most of your time. It's a labyrinth of narrow streets that once were confined by the medieval walls. The lively pedestrian drag called the **Ramblas** goes through the heart of the Old City from Plaça de Catalunya to the harbor. The Old City is

# Barcelona Neighborhood Overview

TIBIDABO

Park Güell

GRÀCIA

BEYOND THE EIXAMPLE

SAGRADA FAMÍLIA

LA PEDRERA

PASSEIG DE GRÀCIA

E I X A M P L E

BLOCK OF DISCORD

CAMP NOU STADIUM

Plaça de Catalunya

OLD CITY

EL BORN

VIA LAIETANA

Citadel Park

PICASSO MUSEUM

CATHEDRAL

BARRI GÒTIC

SANTS STATION

GRAN VIA DE LES CORTS CATALANES

LES RAMBLAS

EL RAVAL

BARCELONETA & BEACHES

AV. DEL PARAL·LEL

To Airport

Plaça d'Espanya

CATALAN ART MUSEUM

MONTJUÏC

Port Vell

CRUISE PORT

Not to Scale

Mediterranean Sea

**ORIENTATION**

divided into thirds by the Ramblas and another major thoroughfare (running roughly parallel to the Ramblas), Via Laietana. Between the Ramblas and Via Laietana is the characteristic **Barri Gòtic** (BAH-ree GOH-teek, Gothic Quarter), with the cathedral as its navel. Locals call it "El Gòtic" for short. To the east of Via Laietana is the trendy **El Born** district (a.k.a. "La Ribera"), a shopping, dining, and nightlife mecca centered on the Picasso Museum and the Church of Santa Maria del Mar. To the west of the Ramblas is the **Raval** (rah-VAHL), enlivened by its university and modern-art museum. The Raval is of least interest to tourists (while some parts of the neighborhood are becoming trendy, others are quite dodgy and should be avoided).

**Harborfront:** The old harbor, **Port Vell,** gleams with landmark monuments and new developments. A pedestrian bridge links the Ramblas with the modern Maremagnum shopping/aquarium/entertainment complex. On the peninsula across the quaint sailboat harbor is **Barceloneta,** a traditional fishing neighborhood with gritty charm and some good seafood restaurants. Beyond Barceloneta, a gorgeous man-made **beach** several miles long leads east to the commercial and convention district called the **Fòrum.**

**Eixample:** Above the Old City, beyond the bustling hub of Plaça de Catalunya, is the elegant Eixample (eye-SHAM-plah) district, its grid plan softened by cut-off corners. Much of Barcelona's Modernista architecture is found here—especially along the swanky artery Passeig de Gràcia, an area called **Quadrat d'Or**

# Barcelona: From Small to Sprawl

The city of Barcelona has grown with its history. The original Roman town from the time of Christ was contained inside the knot of streets clustered around today's cathedral and enclosed by an oval-shaped ring of Roman walls (stretching basically southeast from the square in front of the cathedral).

When Rome fell (around A.D. 476), the Christian Visigoths made the cathedral the center of town, and the populace remained huddled inside the Roman walls. During the Dark Ages, the city was ruled briefly by Moors (714-801) and Franks (ninth century). When the Counts of Barcelona unified Catalunya (10th century), the city began expanding. They built churches outside the Roman walls (or *extra muro*), each a magnet gathering a small community. By 1250, they needed to build a larger wall to contain these new settlers. This medieval wall stretched from Plaça de Catalunya to the sea, embracing the whole Old Town. The hilltop of Montjuïc—outside the residential area—was topped with a harbor-guarding fortress.

Barcelona is a good example of how a city's architectural heritage rises and falls with economic times. In the 14th century, when the Mediterranean was the epicenter of trade, Barcelona thrived. That's why there are a lot of Gothic buildings here. After 1492, when the Age of Discovery opened up new sea routes, trade shifted to the Atlantic and away from Mediterranean ports. The following centuries saw little grand building in Barcelona.

Then, in the 19th century, Barcelona bounced back, powered by the Industrial Revolution. By 1850, the city was bursting at the seams. The outer wall was torn down and replaced by circular boulevards (named Rondas, meaning "to go around"). The city expanded in a regimented grid of modern boulevards—an urban waffle known as the Eixample. With affluence came big shots with big egos and plenty of money to finance the Modernista architectural wonders that now grace the city.

In 1992, Barcelona hosted the Summer Olympics, which quickly accelerated modernization and stoked Barcelona's economy. In a brilliant move, organizers of the games housed much of the one-time rush of visitors on huge cruise ships. It seems this helped jump-start a thriving cruise ship industry. In 1992, 70 cruise ships called here. Today Barcelona is one of the leading cruise ports in Europe, and last year the city hosted over 800 (much bigger) ships.

A big issue for the character of the city today is the end of rent control for landowners and their tenants in the city center. Now that the ceiling has been lifted, many of the charming shops that add so much character to the old quarter have been driven out of business, replaced by branches of much mightier corporate retailers. But the rising affluence and trendiness of the city have worked to keep the town vibrant and colorful.

Today, Barcelona's population sprawls beyond city maps, creating a greater metropolitan area of some 5 million people—more than half of all the people in Catalunya.

("Golden Quarter"). Beyond that is the **Gràcia** district and Antoni Gaudí's **Park Güell.**

**Montjuïc:** The large hill overlooking the city to the southwest is Montjuïc (mohn-jew-EEK), home to a variety of attractions, including some excellent museums (Catalan Art, Joan Miró) and the Olympic Stadium. At the base of Montjuïc, stretching toward Plaça d'Espanya, are the former **1929 World Expo Fairgrounds,** with additional fine attractions (including the CaixaForum art gallery and the bullring-turned-mall, Las Arenas).

Apart from your geographical orientation, it's smart to orient yourself linguistically to a language distinct from Spanish. Although Spanish ("Castilian"/*castellano*) is widely spoken, the native tongue in this region is Catalan—nearly as different from Spanish as Italian (see the sidebar on page 6).

## PLANNING YOUR TIME

Barcelona is easily worth two days, and no one would regret having a third day (or more). If you can spare only one full day for the city, it will be a scramble, but a day you'll never forget.

When planning your time, be aware that many top sights are closed on Monday—making them especially crowded on Tuesday and Sunday (for itinerary considerations on a day-by-day basis, see the "Daily Reminder," later). Some of Barcelona's major sights can have long lines, such as the Picasso Museum, Sagrada Família, and La Pedrera; it's smart to get advance tickets.

### Barcelona in One Day

For a relaxing day, stroll the Ramblas, see the Sagrada Família, add the Picasso Museum if you're a fan, and have dinner in the trendy El Born district.

To fit in much more, try the following ambitious but doable plan. You'll have to rush through the big sights (cathedral, Picasso Museum, Sagrada Família), having just enough time to visit each one but not to linger.

| | |
|---|---|
| 9:00 | From Plaça de Catalunya (with its handy TI), follow my Barri Gòtic Walk and Cathedral of Barcelona Tour. |
| 11:00 | Circle back to Plaça de Catalunya and follow my self-guided Ramblas Ramble to the harborfront. |
| 12:30 | Walk along the harborfront to El Born, grabbing a quick lunch. |
| 14:00 | Take my Picasso Museum Tour. |
| 16:00 | Hop a taxi or the Metro to the Sagrada Família. |
| 18:00 | Taxi, bus, or walk to Passeig de Gràcia in the Eixample to see the exteriors of Gaudí's La Pedrera |

ORIENTATION

ORIENTATION

(a.k.a. Casa Milà) and the Block of Discord. Stroll back down toward Plaça de Catalunya.

19:00   Wander back into the Barri Gòtic at prime paseo time. Enjoy an early tapas dinner along the way, or a restaurant dinner later in the Old City.

## Barcelona in Two or More Days

With at least two days, divide and conquer the town geographically: Spend one day in the Old City (Ramblas, Barri Gòtic/cathedral area, Picasso Museum/El Born) and another on the Eixample and Gaudí sights (La Pedrera, Sagrada Família, Park Güell). If you have a third day, visit Montjuïc and/or side-trip to Montserrat.

With extra time on any day, consider taking a hop-on, hop-off bus tour for a sightseeing overview (for example, the Tourist Bus blue route links most Gaudí sights and could work well on Day 2).

### Day 1: Old City

9:00   Follow my Barri Gòtic Walk and Cathedral of Barcelona Tour.

11:00   Head to the Ramblas using the route described in my "Barri Gòtic Shopping Walk," then follow my Ramblas Ramble down to the harborfront.

13:00   Grab lunch in El Born or the Barri Gòtic.

14:00   Tour the Palace of Catalan Music in El Born (advance reservation required).

15:00   Follow my El Born Walk, including a visit to the Picasso Museum. Afterwards shop to your heart's content.

Evening   For an early dinner, sample tapas at several bars in El Born (or the Eixample or Barri Gòtic); to dine at a restaurant, go when locals do, around 21:00. Evening activities include sightseeing (for sights open late, see page 219); performances of Spanish guitar, flamenco, or jazz; concerts at La Pedrera or the Palace of Catalan Music; or hanging out at a *chiringuito* beach bar in Barceloneta.

Another fun evening activity is to zip up to Montjuïc for the sunset and a drink on the Catalan Art Museum's terrace, then head down to the Magic Fountains (Fri-Sat, plus Sun and Thu in summer). For more ideas, see the Nightlife in Barcelona chapter.

### Day 2: Modernisme

9:00   Take my Eixample Walk, touring La Pedrera and/or one of the Block of Discord houses: Casa Batlló, Casa Lleó Morera, or Casa Amatller (last two by guided tour only).

12:00   Eat an early lunch in the Eixample, then
        Sagrada Família.

15:00   Choose among these options: Taxi or bus ____ ᴀʀᴋ
        Güell for more Gaudí. Or take the bus to Montjuïc
        (if you're not going to Montjuïc on Day 3) to enjoy
        the city view and your pick of sights. Or explore the
        harborfront La Rambla de Mar and Old Port (unless
        you already did this on Day 1, at the end of the
        Ramblas Ramble).

Evening   Choose among the evening activities listed earlier.

## Day 3: Montjuïc and Barceloneta

Tour Montjuïc from top to bottom (both physically and in order of
importance), stopping at these sights: Catalan Art Museum, Fundació Joan Miró, and CaixaForum. If the weather is good, take the
scenic cable-car ride down from Montjuïc to the port, and spend
the rest of the day at Barceloneta—stroll the promenade, hit the
beach, and find your favorite *chiringuito* (beach bar) for dinner.

## Day 4

Consider these options: Visit the markets (La Boqueria and Santa
Caterina—both closed Sun). Tour more sights (Palau Güell's Modernista interior, Barcelona History Museum, Frederic Marès Museum, Chocolate Museum, and more). Take a walking or bike tour.
Relax or rent a rowboat in Citadel Park.

## Days 5-7

With more time, choose among several day trips, including the
mountaintop monastery of Montserrat, the beach resort town of
Sitges, and the Salvador Dalí sights at Figueres and Cadaqués (see
the Day Trips from Barcelona chapter).

## Connecting with the Rest of Spain

Located in the far northeast corner of Spain, Barcelona makes
a good first or last stop for your trip. With the high-speed AVE
train, Barcelona is three hours away from Madrid—faster and
more comfortable than flying. Or you could sandwich Barcelona
between flights. From the US, it's as easy to fly into Barcelona as it
is to land in Madrid, Lisbon, or Paris. Those who plan on renting a
car later in their trip can start here, take the train or fly to Madrid,
and sightsee Madrid and Toledo, all before picking up a car—cleverly saving on several days' worth of rental fees. For more on train
travel and car rentals in Spain, see the Practicalities chapter.

# Daily Reminder

**Sunday:** Most sights are open, but Casa Lleó Morera and the Boqueria and Santa Caterina markets are closed. Some sights close early today, including the Roman Temple of Augustus (at 14:00); Fundació Joan Miró, Olympic and Sports Museum, and Camp Nou Stadium (14:30); and the Chocolate Museum and Catalan Art Museum (15:00). The Frederic Marès Museum and Barcelona History Museum are open late (until 20:00). Informal performances of the *sardana* national dance take place in front of the cathedral at noon (none in Aug).

Some museums are free at certain times: Catalan Art Museum and Palau Güell (free on first Sun of month); Maritime Museum (free after 15:00); Picasso Museum, Barcelona History Museum, Frederic Marès Museum, and Barcelona 1700 exhibit at the El Born Cultural Center (free on first Sun of month plus other Sun from 15:00).

The Magic Fountains come alive on summer evenings (May-Sept).

**Monday:** Many sights are closed, including the Picasso Museum, Catalan Art Museum, Palau Güell, Barcelona History Museum, Casa Lleó Morera, *Santa Eulàlia* schooner (part of the Maritime Museum), Fundació Joan Miró, Frederic Marès Museum, El Born Cultural Center, and Olympic and Sports Museum. But most major Modernista sights are open today, including the Sagrada Família, La Pedrera, Park Güell, Casa Batlló, and Casa Amatller.

**Tuesday:** All major sights are open.

**Wednesday:** All major sights are open.

**Thursday:** All major sights are open. These sights are open late year-round: the Picasso Museum (until 21:30) and Fundació Joan Miró (until 21:00; two-for-one tickets from 18:00). The Magic Fountains spout on summer evenings (May-Sept).

**Friday:** All major sights are open. The Magic Fountains light up Montjuïc year-round.

**Saturday:** All major sights are open. Barcelonans occasionally dance the *sardana* on Saturdays at 18:00 in front of the cathedral. The Magic Fountains dance all year. The Catalan Art Museum is free after 15:00.

**Late-Hours Sightseeing:** For a list of sights open late, see the sidebar on page 219).

# Overview

## TOURIST INFORMATION

Barcelona's TI has several branches (central tel. 932-853-834, www.barcelonaturisme.cat). The primary TI is beneath the main square, **Plaça de Catalunya** (daily 8:30-20:30, entrance just across from El Corte Inglés department store—look for red sign and take stairs down, tel. 932-853-832).

There's a TI kiosk near the top of the **Ramblas** (daily 8:30-20:30, at #115). You'll also find branches on **Plaça de Sant Jaume,** just south of the cathedral (Mon-Fri 8:30-20:30, Sat 9:00-19:00, Sun 9:00-14:00, in the Barcelona City Hall at Ciutat 2); inside the base of the harborside **Columbus Monument** (Mon-Sat 8:30-19:30, Sun 9:00-15:00); at the **airport** in terminals 1 and 2B (both daily 8:30-20:30); and at the **Sants train station** (daily 8:00-20:00).

Smaller info kiosks pop up in touristy locales: on **Plaça d'Espanya,** in the park across from the **Sagrada Família** entrance, near the **Columbus Monument** (where the shuttle bus from the cruise port arrives), at the **Nord bus station,** at the various **cruise terminals** along the port, and on **Plaça de Catalunya.** In addition, throughout the summer, young red-jacketed tourist-info helpers appear in the most touristy parts of town; although they work for the hop-on, hop-off Tourist Bus, they are happy to answer questions.

At any TI, pick up free handouts such as the monthly *Barcelona Planning.com* guidebook (with basic tips on sightseeing, shopping, events, and restaurants; also available online) and the quarterly *See Barcelona* guide (with more in-depth practical information on museums and a sightseeing rundown by neighborhood). Also free, the monthly *Time Out BCN Guide* offers a concise but thorough day-by-day list of events; the monthly *Barcelona Metropolitan* magazine has timely coverage of local topics and events. The free El Corte Inglés map provided by most hotels is better than the TI's map.

TIs are handy places to buy tickets for the Tourist Bus (see page 33) or for TI-run walking tours (see page 31). You can also buy line-skipping tickets for La Pedrera, Casa Batlló, and Camp Nou Stadium, among other sights. And they sell tickets to FC Barcelona soccer games.

**Modernisme Route:** Inside the Plaça de Catalunya TI is the privately run **Ruta del Modernisme** desk, which gives out a handy map showing all 116 Modernista buildings and offers a sightseeing discount package (€12 for a great guidebook and 20-50-percent discounts at many Modernista sights—worthwhile if going beyond the biggies I cover in depth; for €18 you'll also get a guidebook to Modernista bars and restaurants; www.rutadelmodernisme.com).

ORIENTATION

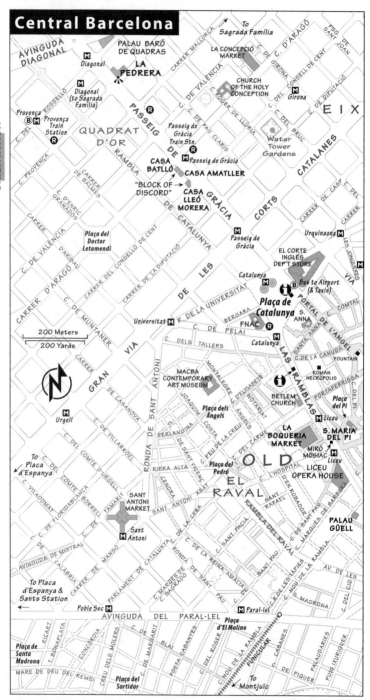

# Central Barcelona

AVINGUDA DIAGONAL

To Sagrada Família

PALAU BARÓ DE QUADRAS

LA CONCEPCIÓ MARKET

Diagonal

LA PEDRERA

CARRER MALLORCA

C. DE VALÈNCIA

CHURCH OF THE HOLY CONCEPTION

Diagonal (to Sagrada Família)

PASSEIG DE

C. DE ROGER DE LLÚRIA

C. DE PAU CLARIS

C. DEL CONSELL DE CENT

Girona

C. DE BRUC

EIX

Provença

Provença Train Station

QUADRAT D'OR

RAMBLA

Passeig de Gràcia Train Stn.

Passeig de Gràcia

Water Tower Gardens

CATALANES

C. PROVENÇA

CARRER DE BALMES

C. D'ENRIC GRANADOS

CASA BATLLÓ

CASA AMATLLER

"BLOCK OF DISCORD"

CASA LLEÓ MORERA

DE

GRÀCIA

CORTS

C. DE CASP

CARRER

Plaça del Doctor Letamendi

DE CATALUNYA

Passeig de Gràcia

CARRER

C. DE VALÈNCIA

C. D'ARIBAU

CARRER DEL CONSELLO DE CENT

CARRER DE LA DIPUTACIÓ

DE

Urquinaona

CARRER D'ARAGÓ

C. DE MUNTANER

LES

EL CORTE INGLÉS DEP'T STORE

VIA

LES JONQUERES

200 Meters

200 Yards

GRAN

CARRER

DE CASANOVA

C. DE VILLARROEL

R. DE LA UNIVERSITAT

Catalunya

Plaça de Catalunya

Bus to Airport (& Taxis)

S. ANNA

Universitat

R. DE LA UNIVERSITAT

Bergara

FNAC

C. DE PELAI

Catalunya

PORTAL DE L'ÀNGEL

COMTAL

Urgell

DE

C. DELS TALLERS

MACBA CONTEMPORARY ART MUSEUM

Plaça dels Àngels

MONTALEGRE

C. D'ELISABETS

NOTARIAT

BETLEM CHURCH

SANTA ANNA

C. DE LA CANUDA

FOUNTAIN

ROMAN NECROPOLIS

LAS RAMBLAS

FORTAFERRISSA

Plaça del Pi

C. DEL

To C. DEL Plaça d'Espanya

C. DEL COMTE D'URGELL

RIERA ALTA

JOAQUIM COSTA

PERLANDINA

DE SANT VICENÇ

Plaça del Pedró

C. PEU DE LA CREU

OLD

C. DEL CARME

EL

RAVAL

C. DE L'HOSPITAL

LA BOQUERIA MARKET

SANT RAFAEL

MIRÓ MOSAIC

LICEU OPERA HOUSE

Liceu

S. MARIA DEL PI

Liceu

C. VILADOMAT

C. DE FLORIDABLANCA

C. DE TAMARIT

SANT ANTONI MARKET

SENDRA

SANT ANTONI ABAT

C. DE LA GERA

C. SANT PÀGIA

RAMBLA DEL RAVAL

C. DE SANT PAU

C. DE L'EST

C. MARQUÈS DE BARBERÀ

PALAU GÜELL

Sant Antoni

C. DE

AVINGUDA DE MISTRAL

CARRER DE MANSO

RONDA DE SANT PAU

C. DE LA REINA AMÀLIA

SANT HAU

C. DE LES TÀPIES

AV. DE LES

C. DEL CID

To Plaça d'Espanya & Sants Station

CALABRIA

PARLAMENT DE CATALUNYA

C. SAGRADO

C. MARQUÈS DE SANT PAU

C. NOU DE LA RAMBLA

C. DE S. MADRONA

PALAUDARIES

PUIG IXURIGUER

Poble Sec

AVINGUDA     DEL     PARAL·LEL

Paral·lel

Plaça d'El Molino

FUNICULAR

Plaça de Santa Madrona

RICART

T. BONAPLATA

CONCÒRDIA

CREU DELS MOLERS

DE

C. DE MARGARIT

BLAI

POETA CABANYES

C. DEL ROSER

C. NOU DE LA RAMBLA

CABANES

DE

DE PIQUER

MARE DE DÉU DEL REMEI

Plaça del Sortidor

To Montjuïc

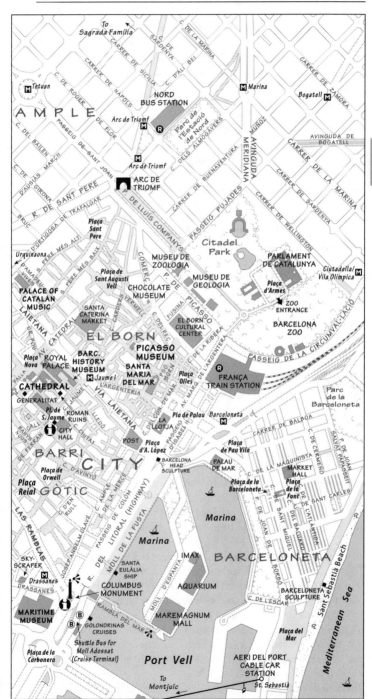

ORIENTATION

**Regional Catalunya TI:** The all-Catalunya TI can help with travel and sightseeing tips for the entire region, and even Madrid (Mon-Sat 10:00-19:00, Sun 10:00-14:00, in Palau Robert building near the intersection of Passeig de Gràcia and Diagonal, Passeig de Gràcia 107, tel. 932-388-091, www.catalunya.com).

**Sightseeing Passes:** The **Articket BCN** pass covers admission to six art museums and their temporary exhibits, letting you skip the ticket-buying lines. Sights include the recommended Picasso Museum, Catalan Art Museum, and Fundació Joan Miró (€30, valid three months; sold at participating museums and the TIs at Plaça de Catalunya, Plaça de Sant Jaume, and Sants Station; www.articketbcn.org). If you're planning to go to three or more covered museums, this ticket will save you money and time, especially at sights prone to long lines, such as the Picasso Museum. Just show your Articket BCN (to the ticket taker, at the info desk, or at a special Articket window), and you'll get your ticket, which you can use to enter at any time (especially useful for Picasso Museum).

I'd skip the **Barcelona Card** (€45/3 days, €55/4 days, €60/5 days) and the **Barcelona Card Express** (€20/2 days). These cover public transportation (buses, Metro, Montjuïc funicular, and *golondrinas* harbor tour) and include free admission to mostly minor sights and small discounts on many major sights (sold at TIs and El Corte Inglés department stores, www.barcelonaturisme.com).

## ARRIVAL IN BARCELONA

For more information on getting to or from Barcelona by train, plane, bus, or cruise ship, see the Barcelona Connections chapter.

## HELPFUL HINTS

**Exchange Rate:** €1 = about $1.20

**Country Calling Code:** 34 (see page 294 for dialing instructions)

**Advance Tickets and Passes:** In busy Barcelona, you can avoid long lines and ensure you'll get in to popular sights when you want by buying timed-entry tickets in advance for the following: Picasso Museum (see page 48), Sagrada Família (page 58), Casa Batlló (page 145), La Pedrera (page 150), Palau Güell (page 37), and Park Güell's Monumental Zone (page 59).

It's smart to plan ahead and buy advance tickets to go inside Casa Lleó Morera (see page 149) and Casa Amatller (page 148), as both are viewable by guided tour only. Advance tickets are required to tour the Palace of Catalan Music (page 49). If you plan to visit several art museums, consider the Articket BCN pass, which can save you money and lets you skip ticket-buying lines (especially helpful at the Picasso Museum; see page 48).

**Theft and Scam Alert:** You're more likely to be pickpocketed here—especially on the Ramblas—than about anywhere else in Europe. Most crime is nonviolent, but muggings do occur. Leave valuables in your hotel and wear a money belt. Whenever you pay with cash, count your change carefully.

Street scams are easy to avoid if you recognize them. Most common is the too-friendly local who tries to engage you in conversation by asking for the time or whether you speak English. If a super-friendly man acts drunk and wants to dance because his soccer team just won, he's a pickpocket. Beware of thieves posing as lost tourists who ask for your help. Don't fall for any street-gambling shell games. Beware of groups of women aggressively selling flowers, people offering to clean off a stain from your shirt, and so on. If you stop for any commotion or show on the Ramblas, put your hands in your pockets before someone else does. Assume any scuffle is simply a distraction by a team of thieves. Don't be intimidated...just be smart.

**Personal Safety:** Some areas feel seedy and can be unsafe after dark. I'd avoid the southern part of the Barri Gòtic (basically the two or three blocks directly south and east of Plaça Reial—though the strip near the Carrer de la Mercè tapas bars is better); and I wouldn't venture too deep into the Raval (just west of the Ramblas). One block can separate a comfy tourist zone from the junkies and prostitutes.

**Festivals:** Barcelona erupts with festivals all year long. For a list of the major ones, see the sidebar on the next page.

**Language Barrier:** In posted information throughout the city (such as museum descriptions), you'll see Catalan first, followed by Spanish (Castellano), and English. Young people, the well-educated, and people in tourism generally speak English in this very touristy city. You might notice a little political tension showing itself in a tendency to favor English over Castellano.

**Web Addresses:** Note that many businesses here use ".cat" in their web links—the web suffix for Catalunya—rather than ".com" or ".es".

**Wi-Fi:** The free city network, Barcelona WiFi, has hundreds of hotspots; look for the blue diamond-shaped sign with a big "W" (www.bcn.cat/barcelonawifi). You can also log onto the Apple Store network on Plaça de Catalunya (look for groups of teenagers milking the free Wi-Fi).

**Baggage Storage: Locker Barcelona** is located near the recommended Hotel Denit. You can pay for the day and access your locker as many times as you want, and can even leave bags overnight (daily 9:00-21:00, €3.50-12 depending on locker size, Carrer Estruc 36, tel. 933-028-796, www.lockerbarcelona.com).

ORIENTATION

# City of Festivals

Barcelona celebrates more festivals, markets, and street fairs than your average city. They dance the *sardana* (a circle dance), build human pyramids, parade colorful *gegants* (giant puppets), and light up the night with fireworks displays called *correfoc* (fire run). Here's a rundown of Barcelona's most lively festivals, listed roughly in chronological order.

**Les Festes de Santa Eulàlia:** Celebrating the patron saint of the city, this four-day festival features parades, dancing, *correfocs*, and many kid-friendly activities (mid-Feb, www.bcn.cat/santaeulalia).

**El Día de Sant Jordi:** This celebration of St. George, the patron saint of Catalunya, is also Barcelona's version of Valentine's Day, when lovers exchange books and flowers, and the streets are draped with the red-and-gold Catalan flag (April 23).

**Corpus Christi:** This festival, dating to 1320, contains tradition-  al elements such as processions, music, and "dancing" eggs. The eggs, placed in flower-decorated fountains, spin ("dance") atop jets of water (late May/early June, go to http://barcelonacultura.bcn.cat and click on "Festivals and Traditions").

**Grec Festival de Barcelona:** The city's premier summer arts festival has dance, theater, and music, with several events at Teatre Grec—a Greek-style amphitheater (usually July, http://grec.bcn.cat).

**Música als Parcs:** Jazz and classical music fill the air in this popular series of evening concerts at city parks (June-Aug).

**La Festa Catalana:** The city hosts a little spectacle of local folk traditions—human towers *(castells)*, giant puppets *(gegants)*, folk music and dancing—in spring and summer on the square in front of the cathedral (Saturdays at 19:30, May through Sept, ask at TI or your hotel for more details).

**Festes de Sant Roc:** The Barri Gòtic's biggest street party is filled with *gegants*, *sardana* dancing, street games, and fireworks (mid-Aug, go to http://barcelonacultura.bcn.cat and select "Festivals and Traditions").

**Festa Major de Gràcia:** For eight days and nights, this festival features live music, *sardana* dancing, human pyramids, and traditional food and drinks (mid-Aug, www.festamajordegracia.cat).

**La Mercè:** Barcelona's main street festival is named after the city's patron saint, the Virgen de la Mercè. During the five-day festival the city is filled with fireworks, music, an air show, human pyramids, a parade, and much more (late Sept, http://lameva.barcelona.cat/merce/en).

**Pharmacy:** A 24-hour pharmacy is across from La Boqueria Market at #98 on the Ramblas. Another is on the corner of Passeig de Gràcia #90 and Provença, just opposite the entrance to La Pedrera.

**Laundry:** Several self-service launderettes are located around the Old City. The clean-as-a-whistle **LavaXpres** is centrally located near recommended Plaça de Catalunya and Ramblas hotels (self-service-€8/load, instructions in English, daily 8:00-22:00, Passatge d'Elisabets 3, www.lavaxpres.com). **Wash 'n Dry,** just off the Ramblas, is in a seedier neighborhood just down the street past Palau Güell (self-service-€6.50/load, full service-€14.50/load, daily 9:00-22:00, Carrer Nou de la Rambla 19, tel. 934-121-953). For both locations, see the map on page 174.

**Bike Rental:** Biking is a joy in Citadel Park, the Eixample, and along the beach (suggested route on page 76), but it's stressful in the city center, where pedestrians and cars rule. There are bike-rental places in just about every part of the city; I've listed just a few (all prices include helmets and locks). Handy **Bike Tours Barcelona,** near the Church of Santa Maria del Mar (50 yards behind the flame memorial), rents bikes and gives out maps and suggested biking routes (€5/hour, €10/4 hours, €15/24 hours, daily 10:00-19:00, leave €250 or photo ID as deposit, Carrer de l'Esparteria 3—see map on page 174, tel. 932-682-105, www.biketoursbarcelona.com); they also lead bike tours (see "Tours in Barcelona," later).

To rent a bike on the Barceloneta beach, consider the following shops (see map on page 75 for locations): **Biciclot,** on the sand 300 yards from Olympic Village towers (€5/hour, €10/3 hours, €17/24 hours, daily in summer 10:00-20:00, shorter hours off-season, Passeig Maritime 33, tel. 932-219-778, www.bikinginbarcelona.net), and **Barcelona Rent-A-Bike,** about four blocks from the Barceloneta Metro stop (€6/2 hours, €10/4 hours, €15/24 hours, daily 10:00-20:00, Passeig de Joan de Borbó 35, tel. 932-212-790, www.barcelonarentabike.com). Barcelona Rent-A-Bike also has a city-center location three blocks from Plaça de Catalunya (daily 9:30-20:00, inside the courtyard at Carrer dels Tallers 45—see map on page 174, tel. 933-171-970).

You'll see racks of government-subsidized "Bicing" **borrow-a-bikes** around town, but these are only for locals, not tourists.

ORIENTATION

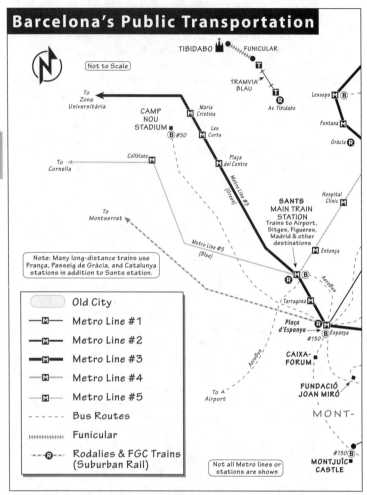

# Barcelona's Public Transportation

Not to Scale

TIBIDABO ●♦♦♦ FUNICULAR

TRAMVIA BLAU

To Zona Universitària

CAMP NOU STADIUM ■  Ⓑ #50

Maria Cristina Ⓜ

Les Corts Ⓜ

Lesseps Ⓜ Ⓑ

Fontana Ⓜ

Gràcia Ⓡ

Av. Tibidabo Ⓡ

To Cornellà

Collblanc Ⓜ

Plaça del Centre Ⓜ

Metro Line #5 (Green)

SANTS MAIN TRAIN STATION
Trains to Airport, Sitges, Figueres, Madrid & other destinations

Hospital Clínic

Ⓜ Entença

To Montserrat

Metro Line #5 (Blue)

Note: Many long-distance trains use França, Passeig de Gràcia, and Catalunya stations in addition to Sants station.

Tarragona Ⓜ

Ⓡ Ⓜ Ⓑ

AeroBus

Plaça d'Espanya →
Ⓡ Ⓜ
Ⓑ Espanya
#150

CAIXA-FORUM ■

FUNDACIÓ JOAN MIRÓ ■

MONT-

AeroBus

To Airport

#150
MONTJUÏC ■ Ⓑ
CASTLE

Old City

——Ⓜ——  Metro Line #1

——Ⓜ——  Metro Line #2

——Ⓜ——  Metro Line #3

·······Ⓜ·······  Metro Line #4

——Ⓜ——  Metro Line #5

- - - - -  Bus Routes

ⱵⱵⱵⱵⱵ  Funicular

·—Ⓡ—·  Rodalies & FGC Trains (Suburban Rail)

Not all Metro lines or stations are shown

# GETTING AROUND BARCELONA

Barcelona's Metro and bus system is run by **TMB**—Transports Metropolitans de Barcelona (tel. 902-075-027, www.tmb.cat). It's worth asking for TMB's excellent Metro/bus map at the TI, larger stations, or the TMB information counter in the Sants train station (not always available).

## By Metro

The city's Metro, among Europe's best, connects just about every place you'll visit. A single-ride ticket *(bitllet senzill)* costs €2.15. The T10 Card—€9.95 for 10 rides—is a great deal (cutting the per-ride cost more than in half). The card is shareable, even by

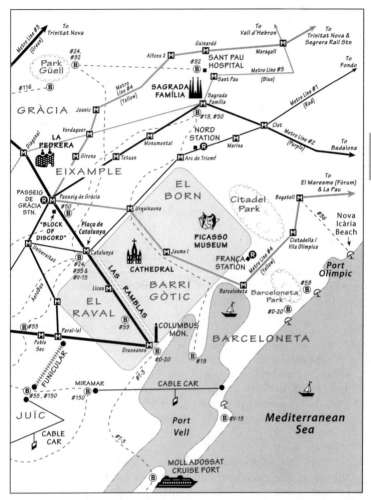

companions (insert the card in the machine per passenger). The back of your T10 card will show how many trips were taken, with

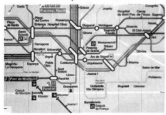

the time and date of each ride. One "ride" covers you for 1.25 hours of unlimited use on all Metro and local bus lines, as well as local rides on the RENFE and Rodalies de Catalunya train lines (including the ride to the train station) and the suburban FGC trains. Transfers made within your 1.25-hour limit are not counted as a new ride, but you still must revalidate your T10 Card whenever you transfer.

Multiday "Hola BCN!" travel cards are also available (€14/2 days, €20.50/3 days, €26.50/4 days, €32/5 days). Machines at the Metro entrance have English instructions and sell all types of tickets (most machines accept credit/debit cards as well as cash).

Whatever type of ticket you use, keep it until you have exited the subway. You don't need the ticket to go through the exit, but inspectors occasionally ask riders to show it.

Barcelona has several color-coded Metro lines. Most useful for tourists is the **L3 (green)** line. Handy city-center stops on this line include (in order):

**Sants Estació:** Main train station

**Espanya:** Plaça d'Espanya, with access to the lower part of Montjuïc and trains to Montserrat

**Paral-lel:** Funicular to the top of Montjuïc

**Drassanes:** Bottom of the Ramblas, near Maritime Museum and Maremagnum mall

**Liceu:** Middle of the Ramblas, near the heart of the Barri Gòtic and cathedral

**Plaça de Catalunya:** Top of the Ramblas and main square with TI, airport bus, and lots of transportation connections

**Passeig de Gràcia:** Classy Eixample street at the Block of Discord; also connection to L2 (purple) line to Sagrada Família and L4 (yellow) line (described below)

**Diagonal:** Gaudí's La Pedrera

The **L4 (yellow)** line, which crosses the L3 (green) line at Passeig de Gràcia, has a few helpful stops, including **Joanic** (bus #116 to Park Güell), **Jaume I** (between the Barri Gòtic/cathedral and El Born/Picasso Museum), and **Barceloneta** (at the south end of El Born, near the harbor action).

Before riding the Metro, study a map (available at TIs, posted at entrances, and printed on some tourist city maps and in the front of this book) to get familiar with the system. Look for your line number and color, and find the end stop for your direction of travel. Enter the Metro by inserting your ticket into the turnstile (with the arrow pointing in), then reclaim it. Follow signs for your line and direction. On board, most trains have handy lighted displays that indicate upcoming stops. Because the lines cross one another multiple times, there can be several ways to make any one journey. (It's a good idea to keep a general map with you—especially if you're transferring.)

Watch your valuables. If I were a pickpocket, I'd set up shop along the made-for-tourists L3 (green) line.

## By Bus

Given the excellent Metro service, it's unlikely you'll spend much time on **local buses** (also €2.15, covered by T10 Card, insert ticket in machine behind driver). However, buses are useful for reaching Park Güell, connecting the sights on Montjuïc, and getting to the beach. For information on **hop-on, hop-off bus tours,** see "Tours in Barcelona," later.

## By Taxi

Barcelona is one of Europe's best taxi towns. Taxis are plentiful (there are more than 11,000) and honest, whether they like it or not. A green light on the roof indicates that a taxi is available. Cab rates are reasonable (€2.10 drop charge, about €1/kilometer, these *"Tarif 2"* rates are in effect 8:00-20:00, pay higher *"Tarif 1"* rates off-hours, €2.10 surcharge to/from train station, €3.10 surcharge for airport or cruise port, other fees posted in window). Save time by catching a cab (figure €10 from Ramblas to Sants station).

# Tours in Barcelona

## ON FOOT
### TI Walking Tours
The TI at Plaça de Sant Jaume offers great guided walks through the **Barri Gòtic.** You'll learn the medieval story of the city as you walk from Plaça de Sant Jaume through the cathedral neighborhood (€16, daily at 9:30, 2 hours, groups limited to 35, buy ticket 15 minutes early at the TI desk—not from the guide, in summer stop by the office a day ahead to reserve, tel. 932-853-832, www.barcelonaturisme.cat).

The TI at Plaça de Catalunya offers a **Picasso** walk, taking you through the streets of his youth and early career and finishing in the Picasso Museum (€22, includes museum entry, runs Tue-Sat at 15:00, 2 hours including museum visit). There are also walks for **gourmets** (€22, Mon-Fri at 10:30, 2 hours) and fans of **Modernisme** (€16; Mon, Wed, and Fri at 18:00; Nov-March Wed and Fri at 15:30; 2 hours). Other themes include literary Barcelona, the Spanish Civil War, and a medieval tour for children (drop by the office for a full list). It's always smart to reserve in advance and double-check departure times with the TI.

The Ruta del Modernisme desk inside the Plaça de Catalunya TI offers tours of specific **Modernista buildings** that are otherwise not open to the public (see page 21).

### Discover Walks
Discover Walks offers two daily walking tours, both two hours and €19: **Gaudí** (10:30, also at 17:00 April-Oct, meet in front of Casa Batlló), and the **Ramblas and Barri Gòtic** (15:00, meet in front of Liceu Opera House on the Ramblas). They also have a Gaudí tour for €49, which includes entry to Casa Batlló (skipping the line).

The company distinguishes itself by using exclusively native-born guides—no expats (tel. 931-816-810, www.discoverwalks.com).

### "Free" Walking Tours

A dozen or so companies offer "free" walks that rely on—and expect—tips to stay in business. Though led by young people who've basically memorized a clever script (rather than trained historians), these walks can be a fun, casual way to get your bearings. **Runner Bean Tours,** run by Gorka, Ann-Marie, and a handful of local guides, is reliable and well-established. They offer two 2.5-hour, English-only walks, one covering the Old City and the other covering Gaudí (both tours depart from Plaça Reial daily at 11:00, also at 16:30 April-mid-Oct, mobile 636-108-776, www.runnerbeantours.com). They also do night tours, family walks, and more. Groups can range from just a couple of people up to 30.

### Local Guides

The **Barcelona Guide Bureau** is a co-op with about 35 local guides who give themed group tours as well as private, customized tours (check website for prices of group walks; customized tours cost €230/4 hours on weekdays, €275 on weekends; Via Laietana 50, tel. 932-682-422 or 933-107-778, www.barcelonaguidebureau.com).

**José Soler** is a great and fun-to-be-with local guide who enjoys tailoring a walk through his hometown to your interests (€250/half-day per group, mobile 615-059-326, www.pepitotours.com, info@pepitotours.com). He and his driver can take small groups by car or van on a four-hour Barcelona Highlights tour (€450-475) and can meet you at your hotel, the cruise port, or airport.

**Cristina Sanjuán** of Live Barcelona is another good, professional guide who leads walking tours and can also arrange cruise excursions (€155/2 hours, €20/each additional hour; €195 extra for a car for up to 2 people, €220 extra for up to 6; tel. 936-327-259, mobile 609-205-844, www.livebarcelona.com, info@livebarcelona.com).

## ON WHEELS

### Guided Bus Tours

The **Barcelona Guide Bureau** offers several sightseeing tours leaving from Plaça de Catalunya. Tours include most sight admissions and are designed to end at a major sight in case you'd like to spend more time there. The Gaudí tour visits Casa Batlló and Sagrada Família, as well as the facade of La Pedrera (€68, daily at 9:00, 3.5 hours). Other tours offered year-round include Montjuïc (€33, daily at 12:30, 2.5 hours); Barcelona Highlights (€64, daily at 10:00, also Mon-Sat at 12:30, 5 hours); and Montserrat (€49, Mon-Sat at 15:00, 4 hours—a convenient way to get to this mountaintop monastery if you don't want to deal with public transportation). During high season, there are additional itineraries. You can get details and book tickets at a TI, on their website, or simply by showing up at their departure point on Plaça de Catalunya in front of the Deutsche Bank (next to Hard Rock Café—look for guides holding orange umbrellas; tel. 933-152-261, www.barcelonaguidebureau. com).

**Catalunya Tourist Bus** also runs excursions to nearby destinations, including some that are difficult to reach by public transportation. Trips include **Montserrat** (€70, Tue-Sun at 8:30, 8 hours, includes Gaudí's unfinished Colònia Güell development), **Easy Montserrat** (€48, mid-March-Oct Tue-Sat at 10:00, 6 hours, includes the Rack Railway), and **Salvador Dalí sights** in Figueres and Girona (€78, Wed and Sat at 8:30, 11 hours). All itineraries depart from Plaça de Catalunya in front of El Corte Inglés (live trilingual commentary in Catalan, Spanish, and English; €5 extra for a more in-depth English audioguide; book at TIs, by phone, or online—10 percent web discount; tel. 932-853-832, www. catalunyabusturistic.com).

### Hop-On, Hop-Off Buses

The handy hop-on, hop-off **Tourist Bus** (Bus Turístic) offers three multistop circuits in colorful double-decker buses that go topless in sunny weather and are useful as a once-over-lightly tour or simply to get around. The two-hour blue route covers north Barcelona (most Gaudí sights); the two-hour red route covers south Barcelona (Barri Gòtic and Montjuïc); and the shorter, 40-minute green route covers the beaches and modern Fòrum complex (this route runs April-Oct only). All have headphone commentary and free Wi-Fi (daily 9:00-

20:00 in summer, off-season until 19:00, buses run every 10-25 minutes, most frequent in summer, www.barcelonabusturistic.cat). Ask for a brochure (includes city map) at the TI or at a pickup point. One-day (€28) and two-day (€39) tickets, which you can buy on the bus, at the TI, or online, offer 10 to 20 percent discounts on the city's major sights and walking tours, which will likely save you about the equivalent of half the cost of the Tourist Bus. From Plaça de Catalunya, the blue northern route leaves from El Corte Inglés; the red southern route leaves from the west—Ramblas—side of the square. A different company, **Barcelona City Tour,** offers a nearly identical service (same price and discounts, two loops instead of three, www.barcelonacitytour.cat).

## Bike Tours

**Bike Tours Barcelona** offers three-hour English-only bike tours, during which you'll ride from sight to sight, mostly on bike paths and through parks, with stop-and-go commentary (€23, daily at 11:00, also Fri-Mon at 16:30 April-mid-Sept, no reservations needed, includes one drink, tours meet just outside TI on Plaça Sant Jaume in Barri Gòtic—or, 15 minutes later, at their bike shop in El Born near the Church of Santa Maria del Mar; for contact info see their bike-rental listing on page 27).

## SPECIALTY TOURS AND ACTIVITIES

### Spanish Civil War Tours

Nick Lloyd is the author of *Forgotten Places: Barcelona and the Spanish Civil War*. Both he and his partner, Catherine Howley, are passionate teachers, taking small groups on highly regarded walks through the Old Town to explain the social context and significance of the Spanish Civil War (1936-1939) in Barcelona. History buffs absolutely love this tour (€25/person, Mon-Tue and Thu-Sat mornings, 4 hours, English only, www.iberianature.com, nick.iberianature@gmail.com).

### Cooking Classes and Food Tours

**Cook & Taste** offers private and group cooking classes in which you'll make and eat four traditional dishes paired with local wines (group classes daily at 11:00 and 17:00, €65/person, €13 extra for guided La Boqueria or Santa Caterina visit offered Tue-Sat morning or Fri afternoon; private class for 2 people-€215/person, less per person for larger groups, includes market visit, meal, and wine; Carrer Paradís 3, tel. 933-021-320, www.cookandtaste.net, info@cookandtaste.net). They also offer a gastronomic tour guided by a chef who shows you gourmet food and wine shops and takes you to La Boqueria.

At **The Barcelona Taste,** Joe Littenberg and Jo Marvel, American ex-pat foodie guides and long-time Barcelona residents, take small groups on guided walks, making three or four stops in roughly three hours. They enthusiastically introduce you to lots of local taste treats and drinks. You can choose from a tour of the Barri Gòtic or the Poble Sec neighborhood at the foot of Montjuïc (€85/person, Tue-Sat at 19:00, reserve early in season, www.thebarcelonataste.com, contact@thebarcelonataste.com).

Nuria and Margherita at **Food Lovers Company** carefully choose four atmospheric spots where, over four hours, you can sample local and seasonal specialties as they share insights on Barcelona and its cuisine (€99/person, daily at 12:00 and 18:00, max 8 people, mobile 617-710-624, www.foodloverscompany.com, hello@foodloverscompany.com).

## TOUR PACKAGES FOR STUDENTS

Andy Steves (Rick's son) runs **Weekend Student Adventures** (WSA Europe), offering 3-day and 10-day budget travel packages across Europe including accommodations, skip-the-line sightseeing, and unique local experiences. Locally guided and DIY unguided options are available for student and budget travelers in 12 of Europe's most popular cities, including Barcelona (guided trips from €199, see www.wsaeurope.com for details).

# SIGHTS IN BARCELONA

The sights listed in this chapter are primarily arranged by neighborhood for handy sightseeing. When you see a 📖 in a listing, it means the sight is covered in much more depth in one of my walks or self-guided tours. A 🎧 means the neighborhood is also covered by my free Barcelona City Walk audio tour (via my Rick Steves Audio Europe app—see page 8).

For tips on sightseeing, see page 270 in the Practicalities chapter. For some sights, it's either required or highly recommended that you make advance reservations (see "Advance Tickets and Passes," on page 24).

## ON OR NEAR THE RAMBLAS
### ▲▲The Ramblas

Meandering through the heart of the Old City is the Ramblas, Barcelona's most famous boulevard. Named for the long-gone stream

*(rambla)* whose course it followed, the Ramblas flows from Plaça de Catalunya, past the core of the Barri Gòtic, to the harborfront Columbus Monument. Boasting a generous pedestrian strip down the middle, the Ramblas feels like a long street festival packed with people—mostly tourists—out browsing. Though it was once vibrant with flowers, a bird market, and newspaper stands, those businesses don't work with the international crowd, so today it's mostly just a big, fun, international promenade with a fabled history. Halfway down is the booming La Boqueria Market.

📖 For a self-guided walk down this pedestrian boulevard, see

The Ramblas Ramble chapter; 🎧 part of the Ramblas is also covered by my free Barcelona City Walk audio tour.

### ▲La Boqueria Market

Barcelona has many characteristic market halls, but this is the most central—and the most crowded. Housed in a cool glass-and-steel structure, La Boqueria features a wide variety of produce and Catalan edibles that you'll pay a premium for. For less touristy markets, consider Santa Caterina in El Born (with avant-garde architecture; see page 119) or La Concepció in the Eixample (with a neighborhood vibe; see page 144). Still, La Boqueria's handy location right in the heart of the Old City makes it well worth a visit.

**Cost and Hours:** Free, Mon-Sat 8:00-20:00, best mornings after 9:00, closed Sun, Rambla 91, tel. 933-192-584, www.boqueria.info.

For a self-guided walk through the market, see page 85 in 📖 The Ramblas Ramble chapter.

### ▲Palau Güell

Just as the Picasso Museum reveals a young genius on the verge of a breakthrough, this early building by Antoni Gaudí (completed

in 1890) shows the architect taking his first tentative steps toward what would become his trademark curvy style. Dark and masculine, with castle-like rooms, Palau Güell (pronounced "gway") was custom-built to house the Güell clan and gives an insight into Gaudí's artistic genius. The rooftop has his signature colorful tile mosaic chimneys and offers a fantastic panorama of the city. While some people will find this redundant if also visiting La Pedrera, others will appreciate this exquisite building for its delightfully loopy rooftop and far fewer crowds.

**Cost and Hours:** €12 for timed-entry ticket, includes good audioguide, free first Sun of the month; open Tue-Sun 10:00-20:00, Nov-March until 17:30, closed Mon year-round; last entry one hour before closing, rooftop closes when raining; best to buy tickets in advance on-site or online to avoid lines or a wait for your entry time; a half-block off the Ramblas at Carrer Nou de la Rambla 3, Metro: Liceu or Drassanes, tel. 934-725-775, www.palauguell.cat.

**Visiting the House:** The parabolic-arch **entryways,** viewable from the outside, are the first clue that this is not a typical townhouse. For inspiration, Gaudí hung a chain to create a U-shape, then flipped it upside-down. The wrought-iron doors were cleverly designed so that those inside could see out, and light from the outside could get in—but not vice versa.

# Barcelona at a Glance

▲▲▲**Picasso Museum** Extensive collection offering insight into the brilliant Spanish artist's early years. **Hours:** Tue-Sun 9:00-19:00, Thu until 21:30, closed Mon. See page 48.

▲▲▲**Sagrada Família** Gaudí's remarkable, unfinished church—a masterpiece in progress. **Hours:** Daily 9:00-20:00, Oct-March until 18:00. See page 58.

▲▲**Ramblas** Barcelona's colorful, gritty, tourist-filled pedestrian thoroughfare. **Hours:** Always open. See page 36.

▲▲**Palace of Catalan Music** Best Modernista interior in Barcelona. **Hours:** Fifty-minute English tours daily every hour 10:00-15:00, plus frequent concerts. See page 49.

▲▲ **La Pedrera (Casa Milà)** Barcelona's quintessential Modernista building and Gaudí creation. **Hours:** Daily 9:00-20:00, Nov-Feb until 18:30. See page 56.

▲▲**Park Güell** Colorful Gaudí-designed park overlooking the city. **Hours:** Paid Monumental Zone open daily 8:00-21:30, Nov-March 8:30-18:00. See page 59.

▲▲**Catalan Art Museum** World-class showcase of this region's art, including a substantial Romanesque collection. **Hours:** Tue-Sat 10:00-20:00 (Oct-April until 18:00), Sun 10:00-15:00, closed Mon year-round. See page 69.

▲▲**CaixaForum** Modernista brick factory, now occupied by cutting-edge cultural center featuring excellent temporary art exhibits. **Hours:** Daily 10:00-20:00. See page 72.

▲**La Boqueria Market** Colorful but touristy produce market, just off the Ramblas. **Hours:** Mon-Sat 8:00-20:00, best mornings after 9:00, closed Sun. See page 37.

▲**Palau Güell** Exquisitely curvy Gaudí interior and fantasy rooftop. **Hours:** Tue-Sun 10:00-20:00, Nov-March until 17:30, closed Mon year-round. See page 37.

▲**Maritime Museum** A sailor's delight, housed in a medieval shipyard (but permanent collection not likely on display). **Hours:** Temporary exhibits daily 10:00-20:00. See page 41.

▲**Cathedral of Barcelona** Colossal Gothic cathedral ringed by distinctive chapels. **Hours:** Generally open to visitors Mon-Fri 8:00-19:30, Sat-Sun 8:00-20:00. See page 44.

▲*Sardana* **Dances** Patriotic dance in which proud Catalans join hands in a circle. **Hours:** Every Sun at 12:00, sometimes also Sat at 18:00, no dances in Aug. See page 46.

▲**The Gaudí Exhibition Center** Fine exhibit about the man who made Barcelona what it is today. **Hours:** Daily 10:00-20:00, winter until 18:00. See page 46.

▲ **Frederic Marès Museum** Quirky museum highlighted by Marès' collection of bric-a-brac from 19th-century Barcelona. **Hours:** Tue-Sat 10:00-19:00, Sun 11:00-20:00, closed Mon. See page 46.

▲**Barcelona History Museum** One-stop trip through town history, from Roman times to today. **Hours:** Tue-Sat 10:00-19:00, Sun 10:00-20:00, closed Mon. See page 47.

SIGHTS

▲**Santa Caterina Market** Fine market hall built on the site of an old monastery and updated with a wavy Gaudí-inspired roof. **Hours:** Mon-Sat 7:30-15:30, Tue and Thu-Fri until 20:30, closed Sun. See page 51.

▲**Church of Santa Maria del Mar** Catalan Gothic church, built by wealthy medieval shippers. **Hours:** Generally open to visitors Mon-Fri 9:00-20:30, Sat-Sun 10:00-20:30. See page 51.

▲**Casa Batlló** Gaudí-designed home topped with fanciful dragon-inspired roof. **Hours:** Daily 9:00-21:00. See page 53.

▲**Casa Lleó Morera** One of the best-preserved Modernista interiors in the city, viewable by guided tour (may be closed when you visit). **Hours:** Tue-Sun 10:00-13:30 & 15:00-19:00, closed Mon. See page 55.

▲**Fundació Joan Miró** World's best collection of works by Catalan modern artist Joan Miró and his contemporaries. **Hours:** Tue-Sat 10:00-20:00 (Nov-March until 18:00), Thu until 21:00, Sun until 14:30, closed Mon year-round. See page 65.

▲**Magic Fountains** Lively fountain spectacle near Plaça d'Espanya. **Hours:** May-Sept Thu-Sun 21:00-23:00, Oct-April Fri-Sat 19:00-20:30. See page 72.

▲**Las Arenas** Bullfighting-arena-turned-mall with rooftop terrace sporting great views. **Hours:** Daily 10:00-22:00. See page 74.

▲**Barcelona's Beaches** Fun-filled, man-made beaches reaching from the harbor to the Fòrum. **Hours:** Always open. See page 74.

Once inside, an engaging 24-stop audioguide, included with your admission, fills in the details. The Neo-Gothic **cellar**, with its mushroom pillars, was used as a stable—notice the rings on some of the posts used to tie up the horses (WCs are in the far corner).

A grand staircase leads to the **living space**, including a family room, dining room, and so on. Photos show how the Güell fam-

ily—with their textile wealth—originally furnished the place. The intricacy of Gaudí's design work evokes the impossibly complex patterns that decorate great Moorish palaces. Step onto the terrace out back, and take a look at the bay window, elaborately decorated in a sort of industrial fantasy.

The tall, skinny, atrium-like **central hall** fills several floors under a parabolic dome. Behind the grand, gilded doors is a personal chapel, which made it easy to instantly convert the hall from a secular space to a religious one.

**Upstairs** are Isabel Güell's bedrooms, rooms with period furniture, and a film telling the story of the two men behind this building: Gaudí and his patron, the building's resident and namesake, Eusebi Güell. At a time when most wealthy urbanites were moving to the Eixample, Güell decided to stay in the Old City.

The most dramatic space is the **rooftop**; Gaudí slathered the 20 chimneys and ventilation towers with bits of stained glass, ceramic tile, and marble to create a forest of giant upside-down ice-cream cones. Move around the rooftop, which follows the form of the parabolic dome

you just saw inside, and admire the view of Barcelona from this high perch.

## Plaça Reial

This genteel-feeling square, with palm trees and a pair of Gaudí-designed lampposts, is a welcoming open space in the otherwise claustrophobic Old City. You can sit down for a drink at one of the touristy bars, or just lean up against the fountain and take it all in.

For more on Plaça Reial, see page 88 in 📖 The Ramblas Ramble chapter. For food and drink recommendations nearby, see page 190.

## THE LOWER RAMBLAS AND HARBORFRONT
### ▲Maritime Museum (Museu Marítim)

Barcelona's medieval shipyard, the best preserved in the entire Mediterranean, is home to an excellent museum near the bottom of the Ramblas. Its permanent collection is closed for renovation, but the museum hosts a series of worthwhile temporary exhibits.

**Cost and Hours:** €7, free Sun from 15:00, open daily 10:00-20:00, nice café with seating inside or out on the museum courtyard

(free to enter), Avinguda de la Drassanes, Metro: Drassanes, tel. 933-429-920, www.mmb.cat.

**Visiting the Museum:** The building's cavernous halls evoke the 14th-century days when Catalunya was a naval and shipbuilding power, cranking out 30 huge galleys a winter. As in the US today, military and commercial ventures mixed and mingled as Catalunya built its trading empire. When the permanent collection reopens, it'll cover the salty history of ships and navigation from the 13th to the 20th century. In the meantime, a highlight is the impressively huge and richly decorated replica of the royal galley Juan de Austria, which fought in the 1571 Battle of Lepanto.

If you just want to view the building and appreciate its history, you can walk around the outside and look into the big glass windows. Or you can go inside the main entrance (around the back of the museum, facing the water) and into a long hallway, which often holds interesting and free exhibits; from here you can also glimpse the building's interior.

**Nearby:** Your ticket includes entrance to the *Santa Eulàlia*, an early 20th-century schooner docked a short walk from the Columbus Monument (€3 for entry without museum visit, Tue-Sun 10:00-20:30 except Sat from 14:00, Nov-March until 17:30, closed Mon year-round). On Saturday mornings, you can ride along as the schooner sets sail around the harbor for three hours—reserve well in advance (Sat 10:00-13:00, €12 for adults, €6 for kids 6-14, tel. 933-429-920, reserves.mmaritim@diba.cat).

### Columbus Monument (Monument a Colóm)

Located where the Ramblas hits the harbor, this 200-foot-tall monument was built for the 1888 world's fair and commemorates Columbus' visit to Barcelona following his first trip to America. A tight four-person elevator takes you to a glassed-in observation area at the top for congested and average views (for better options, see the "Barcelona's Best Views" sidebar on page 50). There is a

**SIGHTS**

SIGHTS

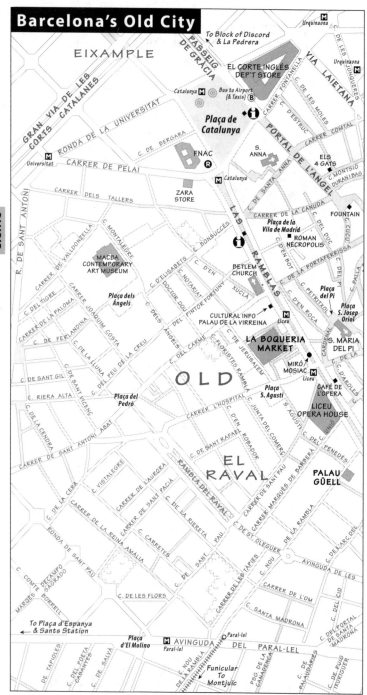

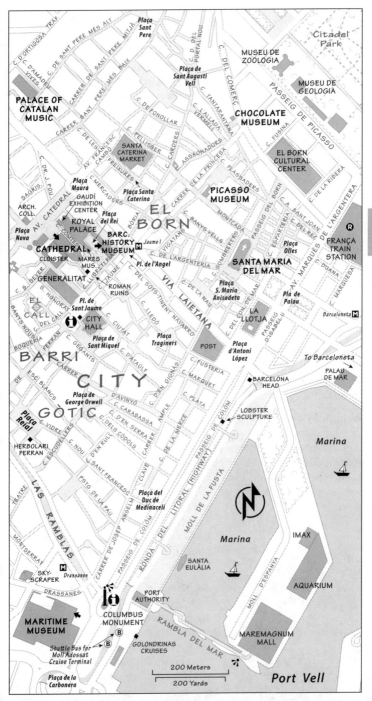

small and usually uncrowded TI inside the base of the monument.

**Cost and Hours:** Elevator-€6, daily 8:30-20:30, Oct-Feb until 19:30, last ride 30 minutes before closing, when crowded they may close the line up to an hour early, Plaça del Portal de la Pau.

For more details on the monument, see page 90 of 📖 The Ramblas Ramble chapter.

### Golondrinas Cruises

At the harbor near the Columbus Monument, tourist boats called *golondrinas* offer two different unguided trips, giving you a view of Barcelona's (not particularly striking) skyline from the water. The shorter version goes around the harbor in 40 minutes (€7.40, daily about 11:30-19:00, more in summer, fewer in winter, tel. 934-423-106, www.lasgolondrinas.com). The 1.5-hour trip goes up the coast to the Fòrum complex and back (€15, can disembark at Fòrum in summer only, daily 11:30-19:30, shorter hours off-season).

## THE BARRI GÒTIC

For more details on this area and several of the following sights, see my 📖 Barri Gòtic Walk or 🎧 download my free Barcelona City Walk audio tour.

### Avinguda del Portal de l'Angel

This broad, traffic-free boulevard, which connects the modern Plaça de Catalunya to its historic cathedral district, is Barcelona's most well-trodden street. Although overrun with Spanish and international chain stores, its circa-1888 remodel has left it with a certain dignified air. Just off this drag, you'll discover humble old churches and the famous bar called Els Quatre Gats, where a young Picasso got his start. For tips on shopping along this street, see page 215.

### ▲Cathedral of Barcelona

The city's 14th-century, Gothic-style cathedral (with a Neo-Gothic facade) has played a significant role in Barcelona's history—but as far as grand cathedrals go, this one is relatively unexciting. Still, it's worth a

# Circle Dances in Squares and Castles in the Air

From group circle dancing to human towers, Catalans have

some interesting and unique traditions. A memorable Barcelona experience is watching (or participating in) the patriotic **sardana** dances. Locals of all ages seem to spontaneously appear. For some it's a highly symbolic, politically charged action representing Catalan unity—but for most it's just a fun chance to kick up their heels. All are welcome, even tourists cursed with two left feet. The dances are held in the square in front of the cathedral on Sundays at noon (and occasionally on Saturdays at 18:00).

Participants gather in circles after putting their things in the center—symbolic of community and sharing (and the ever-present risk of theft). Holding hands, dancers raise their arms—slow-motion, *Zorba the Greek*-style—as they hop and sway gracefully to the music. The band *(cobla)* consists of a long flute, tenor and soprano oboes, strange-looking brass instruments, and a tiny bongo-like drum *(tambori)*. The rest of Spain mocks this lazy circle dance, but considering what it takes for a culture to survive within another culture's country, it is a stirring display of local pride and patriotism. During 36 years of Franco dictatorship, the *sardana* was forbidden.

Another Catalan tradition is the **castell,** a tower erected solely of people. *Castells* pop up on special occasions, such as the Festa Major de Gràcia in mid-August and La Mercè festival in late September. Towers can be up to 10 stories high. Imagine balancing 50 or 60 feet in the air, with nothing but a pile of flesh and bone between you and the ground. The base is formed by burly supports called *baixos;* above them are the *manilles* ("handles"), which help haul up the people to the top. The *castell* is capped with a human steeple—usually a child—who extends four fingers into the air, representing the four red stripes of the Catalan flag. A scrum of spotters (called *pinyas*) cluster around the base in case anyone falls. *Castelleres* are judged both on how quickly they erect their human towers and how fast they can take them down. Besides during festivals, you can usually see this spectacle in front of the cathedral on spring and summer Saturdays at 19:30 (as part of the Festa Catalana; see page 26).

One thing that these two traditions have in common is their communal nature. Perhaps it's no coincidence, as Catalunya is known for its community spirit, team building, and socialistic bent.

**SIGHTS**

visit to see its richly decorated chapels, finely carved choir, tomb of Santa Eulàlia, and restful cloister with gurgling fountains and resident geese.

**Cost:** Free to enter Mon-Sat before 12:45, Sun before 13:45, and daily after 17:15, but during free times you must pay €3 each to visit the choir or the terrace (the museum is closed during these hours). The church is open to tourists for several hours each afternoon (Mon-Sat 13:00-17:00, Sun 14:00-17:00), but you must pay €7 (covers admission to choir, terrace, and museum).

**Hours:** Cathedral generally open to visitors Mon-Fri 8:00-19:30, Sat-Sun 8:00-20:00. The cathedral's three minor sights are open Mon-Sat (with different hours) and closed Sun: choir 9:00-19:00, terrace 9:00-18:00, museum 12:45-17:15. Both the choir and terrace may close earlier on slow days. Tel. 933-151-554, www. catedralbcn.org.

☐ See the Cathedral of Barcelona Tour chapter.

### ▲*Sardana* Dances

If you're in town on a weekend, you can see the *sardana*, a patriotic dance in which Barcelonans link hands and dance in a circle (see sidebar on previous page).

**Cost and Hours:** Free, Sun at 12:00, sometimes also Sat at 18:00, no dances in Aug, event lasts 1-2 hours, in the square in front of the cathedral.

### ▲The Gaudí Exhibition Center

This center fills the stony complex of ancient and medieval buildings immediately to the left of the cathedral with a thoughtful, beautifully lit, and well-described exhibit (via the included audioguide). With plenty of actual historic artifacts, it provides the best introduction to Antoni Gaudí—the man and the architect. You'll spend about an hour following the audioguide through six rooms on three floors.

**Cost and Hours:** €15, daily 10:00-20:00, until 18:00 in winter, Pla de la Seu 7, Metro: Jaume I, tel. 932-687-582, www. gaudiexhibitioncenter.com.

### ▲Frederic Marès Museum (Museu Frederic Marès)

This delightful little museum, adjacent to the cathedral, features the eclectic collection of Frederic Marès. The museum, which sprawls through several old Barri Gòtic buildings around a peaceful courtyard, offers a fascinating look at ancient Roman statues from this region, an exquisite warehouse of Romanesque and

Gothic Christian art from Catalonia, and a glimpse at life in 19th-century Barcelona through Marès' fascinating "Collector's Cabinet"—an entire floor stacked with curiosities. And it's all well-described with the essential audioguide.

Marès (1893-1991) was a local sculptor and packrat. His quirky and intimate "Collector's Cabinet" features a dozen rooms of scissors, keys, irons, fans, nutcrackers, stamps, pipes, snuffboxes, opera glasses, pocket watches, bicycles, toy soldiers, dolls, and other bric-a-brac. And in Marès' study are several sculptures by the artist himself. The tranquil courtyard café offers a pleasant break, even when the museum is closed (café open in summer only, until 22:00).

**Cost and Hours:** €4.20, free first Sun of the month and other Sun from 15:00; open Tue-Sat 10:00-19:00, Sun 11:00-20:00, closed Mon; audioguide-€1, Plaça de Sant Iu 5, Metro: Jaume I, tel. 932-563-500, www.museumares.bcn.cat.

### Plaça de Sant Jaume

This open-feeling square (a rarity in the tight Barri Gòtic) is flanked by the two most important administrative buildings in Catalunya: the Palau de la Generalitat (home of the autonomous Catalan government) and the Barcelona City Hall.

For details, see page 104 of the ▢ Barri Gòtic Walk chapter.

### Roman Temple of Augustus (Temple Roma d'August)

Tucked inside a small medieval courtyard, four columns from an ancient temple of Augustus are a reminder of Barcelona's Roman origins. The temple, dating from the late first century B.C., stood at one corner of the ancient forum quarter.

**Cost and Hours:** Free, daily 10:00-19:00 except Mon until 14:00, Carrer del Paradís 10, tel. 933-152-311.

For more on the temple, see page 105 of the ▢ Barri Gòtic Walk chapter.

### Plaça del Rei

Perhaps the best place in town to get a feel for Barcelona's faint connection to Old World royalty, this "Square of the Monarch" offers a good view of the Royal Palace, where both Spanish kings and Catalan counts once resided. Although the palace complex is mostly closed to tourists, parts of the building are used for exhibits for the Barcelona History Museum.

### ▲Barcelona History Museum
### (Museu d'Història de Barcelona: Plaça del Rei)

At this main branch of the city history museum (MUHBA for short), you can literally walk through the history of Barcelona, including an underground labyrinth of excavated Roman ruins.

**Cost and Hours:** €7; ticket includes audioguide and other

ches; free all day first Sun of month and other Sun
but no audioguide during free times; open Tue-Sat
10:00-19:00, Sun 10:00-20:00, closed Mon; Plaça del Rei, enter on
Carrer del Veguer, Metro: Jaume I, tel. 932-562-122.

**Visiting the Museum:** Though the museum is housed in part
of the former Royal Palace complex, you'll see only a bit of that
grand space. Instead, the focus is on the exhibits in the cellar. The
included audioguide provides informative, if dry, descriptions of
the exhibits; you'll also find abundant English handouts.

Start with the 10-minute introductory video in the theater (at
the end of the first floor to the left). Then take an elevator down 65
feet (and 2,000 years—see the date spin back as you descend) to
stroll the streets of Roman Barcino—founded by Emperor Augustus around 10 B.C.

The history is so strong here, you can smell it. This was a
working-class part of town. The archaeological route leads through
areas used for laundering clothes and dyeing garments, the remains
of a factory that salted fish and produced garum (a fish-derived
sauce used extensively in ancient Roman cooking), and facilities for
winemaking. Next, wander through bits of a seventh-century early
Christian church and an exhibit in the 11th-century count's palace
that shows Barcelona through its glory days in the Middle Ages.
The final section downstairs takes you through Visigothic remains,
including a baptistery.

Finally, head upstairs (or ride the elevator to floor 0) to see a
model of the city from the early 16th century. From here, you can
enter **Tinell Hall** (part of the Royal Palace), with its long, grace-
ful, rounded vaults. The nearby 14th-century **Chapel of St. Agatha**
sometimes hosts free temporary exhibits.

## EL BORN

Despite being home to the Picasso Museum, El Born (also known
as "La Ribera") feels wonderfully local, with a higher ratio of Barcelonans to tourists than most other city-center zones (Metro:
Jaume I). Narrow lanes sprout from the neighborhood's main artery, Passeig del Born—the perfect springboard for exploring artsy
boutiques, inviting eateries, funky shops, and rollicking nightlife.
For a tour of this neighborhood, see the ☐ El Born Walk or ∩
download my free Barcelona City Walk audio tour. For tips on
shopping here, see page 211.

### ▲▲▲Picasso Museum (Museu Picasso)

Pablo Picasso may have made his career in Paris, but the years he
spent in Barcelona—from age 14 through 23—were among the
most formative of his life. It was here that young Pablo mastered
the realistic painting style of his artistic forebears—and it was also

here that he first felt the freedom that allowed him to leave that all behind and give in to his creative, experimental urges. When he left Barcelona, Picasso headed for Paris...and revolutionized art forever.

The pieces in this excellent museum capture that priceless moment just before this bold young thinker changed the world. While you won't find Picasso's famous later Cubist works here, you will enjoy a representative sweep of his early years, from the careful crafting of art-school pieces to the gloomy hues of his Blue Period to the revitalized cheer of his Rose Period. You'll also see works from his twilight years, including dozens of wild improvisations inspired by Diego Velázquez's seminal *Las Meninas,* as well as a roomful of works that reflect the childlike exuberance of an old man playing like a young kid on the French Riviera. It's the top collection of Picassos here in his native country and the best anywhere of his early years.

**Cost and Hours:** €11 for timed-entry ticket to permanent collection, €14 ticket includes temporary exhibits, free every Thu evening from 18:00 and all day on the first Sun of the month; open Tue-Sun 9:00-19:00, Thu until 21:30, closed Mon; audioguide-€5, Carrer de Montcada 15, tel. 932-563-000, www.museupicasso.bcn.cat.

**Crowd-Avoiding Tips:** You can skip the line either with an Articket BCN (which you can purchase around town or on-site) or by buying a timed-entry ticket in advance online. If you just show up, expect to wait in line, sometimes for more than an hour (in peak season, you may end up with an entry that's much later in the day, or tickets may sell out altogether). For details and more crowd-beating tips, see page 126.

&#x2610; See the Picasso Museum Tour chapter.

### ▲▲Palace of Catalan Music (Palau de la Música Catalana)

This concert hall, built in just three years and finished in 1908, features an unexceptional exterior but boasts my favorite Modernista interior in town (by Lluís Domènech i Montaner). Its inviting arches lead you into the 2,138-seat hall, which is accessible only with a tour (or by attending a concert). A kaleidoscopic skylight features a

choir singing around the sun, while playful carvings and mosaics celebrate music and Catalan culture. If you're interested in Mod-

# Barcelona's Best Views

Barcelona's delightful architecture is best seen up close, but to fully appreciate the city's scenic beauty, take advantage of one of many panoramic viewpoints. Many require an admission fee, but some are free, such as the castle at Montjuïc. When deciding between viewpoints, target the ones that are already on your sightseeing route.

**Cable Car:** Although it's pricey and slow to load, the Aeri del Port cable car between Montjuïc and Barceloneta (in either direction) offers a dramatic moving panorama of the city. See page 64.

**Park Güell:** Inviting, curvy benches along a spectacular terrace offer sweeping views of Barcelona from this foothills park (ticket required). Climb even higher to the Calvary for a free, bird's-eye view of the park and city below. See the Park Güell Tour chapter.

**Sagrada Família Towers:** Two different elevators take you up to the towers for a good view of the city and a unique angle on this fascinating church (tickets required). See the Sagrada Família Tour chapter.

**Montjuïc:** Overlooking the port, this hill-top affords free city views from its castle ramparts and Miramar viewpoint park, as well as from the Catalan Art Museum's terrace and stylish restaurant. See page 60.

**El Corte Inglés:** The gigantic department store on Plaça de Catalunya has a great view cafeteria on its ninth floor. See page 215.

**La Pedrera:** The rooftop of this Gaudí masterpiece offers up-close views of fairytale chimneys plus a vista of the Eixample and the distant spires of the Sagrada Família. See page 56.

**Las Arenas:** Take a pay glass elevator or escalate/elevate for free (from inside the building) to the restaurant-ringed roof terrace atop this former bullring—now a mall—for some of the best views of the World Expo Fairgrounds and Montjuïc.

**Tibidabo:** The city's highest peak offers almost limitless (but distant) city and Mediterranean views—if the weather and air quality cooperate. See page 60.

**Cathedral of Barcelona:** A pay elevator takes you up to a view terrace for an expansive city view from the heart of the Barri Gòtic.

**Columbus Monument:** A tiny pay elevator rides up to a glass-enclosed deck with ho-hum views of the waterfront and Ramblas. See page 41.

ernisme, taking this tour (which starts with a relaxing 12-minute video) is one of the best experiences in town—and helps balance the hard-to-avoid focus on Gaudí as "Mr. Modernisme."

**Cost and Hours:** €18, 50-minute tours in English run daily every hour 10:00-15:00, tour times may change based on performance schedule, about 6 blocks northeast of cathedral, Carrer Palau de la Música 4, Metro: Urquinaona, tel. 902-442-882, www.palaumusica.cat.

**Advance Reservations Required:** You must buy tickets in advance to get a spot on an English guided tour (tickets available up to 4 months in advance—purchase yours at least 2 days before, though they're sometimes available the same day or day before—especially Oct-March). You can buy tickets in person at the concert hall box office or at its Modernista ticket window to the left of the main concert hall entrance (box office open Mon-Sat 9:30-21:00, Sun 10:00-15:00, less than a 10-minute walk from the cathedral or Picasso Museum). You can also purchase tickets over the phone (no extra charge, tel. 902-475-485) or on the concert hall website (€1 fee).

**Concerts:** An excellent way to see the hall is by attending a concert (300 per year, €20-50 tickets, see website for details and to buy tickets, box office tel. 902-442-882).

## ▲Santa Caterina Market

This eye-catching market hall was built on the ruins of an old monastery, then renovated in 2006 with a wildly colorful, swooping, Gaudí-inspired roof and shell built around its original white walls (a good exhibition at the far corner provides a view of the foundations and English explanations). The much-delayed construction took so long that locals began calling the site the "Hole of Shame." Come for the outlandish architecture, but stay for a chance to shop for a picnic without the tourist logjam of La Boqueria Market on the Ramblas.

**Cost and Hours:** Free, open Mon-Sat 7:30-15:30, Tue and Thu-Fri until 20:30, closed Sun, Avinguda de Francesc Cambó 16, www.mercatsantacaterina.cat.

For more on the market, see page 119 of the 📖 El Born Walk chapter.

## ▲Church of Santa Maria del Mar

This so-called "Cathedral of the Sea" was built entirely with local funds and labor, in the heart of the wealthy merchant El Born quarter. Proudly independent, the church features a purely Catalan Gothic interior that was forcibly uncluttered of its Baroque decor by civil war belligerents.

**Cost and Hours:** Free to all during worship times: Mon-Fri 9:00-13:00 & 17:00-20:30, Sat-Sun 10:00-14:00 & 17:00-20:30;

SIGHTS

otherwise, entry is with a €5 ticket Mon-Fri 13:00-17:00, Sat-Sun 14:00-17:00 (interior is illuminated, includes access to choir and crypt); €8 guided rooftop tours on the hour during paid entry times; Plaça Santa Maria, Metro: Jaume I, tel. 933-102-390.

For more information on the church, see page 123 of the 🕮 El Born Walk chapter.

### El Born Cultural Center
### (El Born Centre de Cultura i Memòria)

Occupying the cast-iron structure of a 19th-century market, El Born Cultural Center is a multipurpose space. It hosts an exhibition devoted to Barcelona in the 18th century, an active medieval archaeological site, temporary exhibits, and a café.

**Cost and Hours:** Center—free and open Tue-Sun 10:00-20:00, Oct-Feb until 19:00, closed Mon year-round; Barcelona 1700 exhibit—€4.40, free all day first Sun of month and other Sun from 15:00, includes audioguide, same hours; Plaça Comercial 12, http://elbornculturaimemoria.barcelona.cat.

For more information on the center, see page 121 of the 🕮 El Born Walk chapter.

### Chocolate Museum (Museu de la Xocolata)

This museum—operated by the local confectioners' guild—tells the story of chocolate from Aztecs to Europeans via the port of Barcelona, where it was first unloaded and processed. But the history lesson is just an excuse to show off a series of remarkably ornate candy sculptures. These works of edible art—which change every year but often include such themes as Don Quixote or Gaudí's dragon from Park Güell—begin as store-window displays for Easter or Christmas. Once the holiday passes, the confectioners bring the sculptures here to be enjoyed.

**Cost and Hours:** €5, Mon-Sat 10:00-19:00, summer until 20:00, Sun 10:00-15:00 year-round, between Picasso Museum and Citadel Park at Carrer del Comerç 36, Metro: Jaume I, tel. 932-687-878, www.museuxocolata.cat.

## THE EIXAMPLE

For many visitors, Modernista architecture is Barcelona's main draw. And one name tops them all: Antoni Gaudí (1852-1926). Barcelona is an architectural scrapbook of Gaudí's galloping gables and organic curves. A devoted Catalan and Catholic, he immersed himself in each project, often living on-site. At various times, he called Park Güell, La Pedrera (Casa Milà), and the Sagrada Família home. For more on Gaudí and some of his contemporaries, see the sidebar on page 146. To learn about Modernisme, see page 139.

At the heart of the Modernista movement was the Eixample,

a carefully planned "new town," just beyond the Old City, with wide sidewalks, hardy shade trees, and a rigid grid plan cropped at the corners to create space and lightness at each intersection. Conveniently, all of this new construction provided a generation of Modernista architects with a blank canvas for creating boldly

experimental designs. At the edge of the Eixample is Gaudí's greatest piece of work, the yet-to-be-finished Sagrada Família.

In this section, I've focused on the big Modernista sights in the Eixample, starting at the center of this neighborhood with the **Block of Discord,** where three colorful

Modernista facades compete for your attention: Casa Batlló, Casa Amatller, and Casa Lleó Morera (all on Passeig de Gràcia—near the Metro stop of the same name—between Carrer del Consell de Cent and Carrer d'Aragó). All were built by well-known Modernista architects at the end of the 19th century. Because the mansions look as though they are trying to outdo each other in creative twists, locals nicknamed the noisy block the "Block of Discord." By the way, if you're tempted to snap photos from the middle of the street, be careful—Gaudí died after being struck by a streetcar. If deciding between Casa Batlló, Casa Amatller, and Casa Lleó Morera, consider this: A combo-ticket that covers express tours of both Casa Amatller and Casa Lleó Morera is less expensive than crowded Casa Batlló's regular entry price.

From the Block of Discord, you're four blocks from Gaudí's **La Pedrera,** and a quick subway ride from his **Sagrada Família.**

Even though Modernisme revolved around the Eixample, traces of this style can also be found elsewhere. Other Modernista highlights include Gaudí's **Park Güell,** where he put his colorful stamp on 30 acres of greenery (see page 59), and his **Palau Güell,** just off the Ramblas (see page 37); Lluís Domènech i Montaner's **Palace of Catalan Music** in El Born (page 49); and Josep Puig i Cadafalch's **CaixaForum,** at the base of Montjuïc (page 72). For information on more Modernista sights, you can visit the Plaça de Catalunya TI, where a special desk is set aside just for Modernisme seekers (see page 21). For a tour of the Eixample, including a route that connects some of these sights, see my 🕮 Eixample Walk.

#### ▲Casa Batlló

While the highlight of this Gaudí-designed residence is the roof, the interior is also interesting—and much more over-the-top than La Pedrera's. Paid for with textile industry money, the house features a funky mushroom-shaped fireplace nook on the main floor, a

SIGHTS

## Modernista Sights

blue-and-white-ceramic-slathered atrium, and an attic with parabolic arches. There's barely a straight line in the house. You can also get a close-up look at the dragon-inspired rooftop. The ticket includes a good (if long-winded) videoguide that shows the rooms as they may have been.

**Cost and Hours:** €22.50 includes videoguide, €27.50 fast pass ticket (see next); open daily 9:00-21:00, may close early for special events—closings posted at entrance; Passeig de Gràcia 43, tel. 932-160-306, www.casabatllo.cat.

**Buying Tickets:** You can purchase timed-entry tickets from the website, but you'll still wait in a line with other e-ticket holders to get in. The pricey fast pass ticket lets you skip all of the lines. If you don't purchase a ticket online, you'll likely face big lines at the ticket office, which are especially fierce in the morning.

### Casa Amatller

The middle residence of the Block of Discord, Casa Amatller was designed by Josep Puig I Cadafalch in the late 19th century for the

Amatller chocolate-making family. Opened to the public in 2015, the Modernista interior—viewable via guided tour—features mostly original furniture, placed just as the owners had it when they lived there.

Without a ticket, you can still admire the home's Neo-Catalan Gothic facade, with tiles and *esgrafiado* decoration, or step inside the foyer (free during open hours) to see the Modernista stained-glass door and ceiling, and an elaborate staircase. Past the foyer is a café and chocolate shop, where you can taste Amatller hot chocolate with toast. From the café, you can catch a tiny peek of the back of Casa Batlló if you strain your neck.

**Cost and Hours:** €15 for 1-hour English tour, €12 for express 30-minute tour (in a mix of English, Spanish, and Catalan), €21.60 combo-ticket (Mansana de la Discordia Card) covers express tours for both Casa Amatller and Casa Lleó Morera—purchase through Lleó Morera's website; open daily 10:30-18:00, English tours at 11:00 and 15:00, advance tickets available online, Passeig de Gràcia 41, tel. 934-617-460, www.amatller.org.

### ▲Casa Lleó Morera

This house, designed by Lluís Domènech i Montaner and finished in 1906, has one of the finest Modernista interiors in town. Unfortunately, it may no longer be open to the public by the time you visit. If not, you can still

admire the outside. The architect rebuilt the facade, embellishing it with galleries and balconies on the different floors. To create the sculptural ornamentation, he hired the city's best craftsmen. Look for the recurring references to mulberries in the decoration—an allusion to the family name (which means mulberry in Spanish).

**Cost and Hours:** If open—€15 for 1-hour English tour, €12 for express 30-minute tour (in a mix of English, Spanish, and Catalan), €21.60 combo-ticket (Mansana de la Discordia Card) covers express tours for both Casa Amatller and Casa Lleó Morera; open Tue-Sun 10:00-13:30 & 15:00-19:00, closed Mon; tour times change, so check website; on-site box office is credit card only—it's best to purchase tickets in advance, either online at www.casalleomorera.com or in person at the Palau de la Virreina cultural center (Ramblas 99, tel. 933-161-000, www.lavirreina.bcn.cat). The house itself is at Passeig de Gràcia 35, tel. 936-762-733.

## ▲▲La Pedrera (Casa Milà)

One of Gaudí's trademark works, this house—built between 1906 and 1912—is an icon of Modernisme. The wealthy industrialist Pere Milà i Camps commissioned it, and while some still call it Casa Milà, most call it La Pedrera (The Quarry) because of its jagged, rocky facade. While it's fun to ogle from the outside, it's also worth going inside, as it's arguably the purest Gaudí interior in town—executed at the height of his abilities (unlike his earlier Palau Güell)—and contains original furnishings. While Casa Batlló has a Gaudí facade and rooftop, these were appended to an existing building; La Pedrera, on the other hand, was built from the ground up according to Gaudí's plans. Your ticket includes entry to the interior and to the delightful rooftop, with its forest of tiled chimneys.

**Cost and Hours:** €20.50 timed-entry ticket includes good audioguide, €27 premium ticket allows you to skip all lines (see below); open daily 9:00-20:00, Nov-Feb until 18:30; roof may close when it rains; at the corner of Passeig de Gràcia and Provença (visitor entrance at Provença 261), Metro: Diagonal; info tel. 902-400-973, www.lapedrera.com.

**Avoiding Lines:** As lines can be long (up to a 1.5-hour wait to get in), it's best to reserve ahead at www.lapedrera.com. Without a ticket, the best time to arrive is right when it opens. The pricey premium ticket allows you to arrive whenever you wish (no entry time, valid 6 months from date of purchase) and skip all lines, including

those for audioguides and the elevator to the apartment and r
(often up to a 30-minute wait).

**Nighttime Visits:** After-hour visits dubbed "Gaudí's Pedrera: The Origins" include a guided tour of the building (but not the apartment), with the lights turned down low and images projected onto the chimneys, along with a glass of *cava* (€34; daily mid-May-Oct from 21:00, Nov-mid-May from 19:00, check changeable schedule and offerings online). There's also the "La Pedrera Day and Night" ticket for €39.50, which combines a normal day visit with "The Origins" nighttime experience.

**Concerts:** On summer weekends, an evening rooftop concert series, "Summer Nights at La Pedrera," features live jazz and the chance to see the rooftop illuminated (€27, late June-early Sept Thu-Sat at 22:30, book advance tickets online or by phone, tel. 902-101-212, www.lapedrera.com).

**Visiting the House:** A visit covers three sections—the apartment, the attic, and the rooftop. Enter and head upstairs to the apartment. If it's near closing time, continue up to the attic and rooftop first, to make sure you have enough time to enjoy Gaudí's works and the views.

The typical bourgeois **apartment** is decorated as it might have been when the building was first occupied by middle-class urbanites (a seven-minute video explains Barcelona society at the time). Notice Gaudí's clever use of the atrium to maximize daylight in all of the apartments.

The **attic** houses a sprawling multimedia exhibit tracing the history of the architect's career, with models, photos, and videos of his work. It's all displayed under distinctive parabola-shaped arches. While evocative of Gaudí's style in themselves, the arches are formed this way partly to support the multilevel roof above. This area was also used for ventilation, helping to keep things cool in summer and warm in winter. Tenants had storage spaces and did their laundry up here.

From the attic, a stairway leads to the undulating, jaw-dropping **rooftop,** where 30 chimneys and ventilation towers play volleyball with the clouds.

Back at the **ground level** of La

...to the dreamily painted original entrance court-

### Família (Holy Family Church)

Gaudí's grand masterpiece sits unfinished in a residential Eixample neighborhood 1.5 miles north of Plaça de Catalunya. An icon of  the city, the Sagrada Família boasts bold, wildly creative, unmistakably organic architecture and decor inside and out—from its melting Glory Facade to its skull-like Passion Facade to its rainforest-esque interior. Begun under Gaudí's careful watch in 1883, the project saw some setbacks in the mid-20th century, but recent progress has been remarkable. The city has set a goal of finishing by 2026, the centennial of Gaudí's death. Visitors get a close-up view of the dramatic exterior flourishes, the chance to walk through the otherworldly interior, and access to a fine museum detailing the design and engineering behind this one-of-a-kind architectural marvel.

**Cost and Hours:** Basic ticket-€18 (church only), Guided Experience ticket-€29 (church and live guide), Audio Tour ticket-€26 (church and audioguide), Top Views ticket-€35 (church, audioguide, and tower elevator), Gaudí's Work and Life ticket-€31 (church, audioguide, and Gaudí House Museum at Park Güell—see page 170). All options are cheaper if you buy online. Open daily 9:00-20:00, Oct-March until 18:00. Metro: Sagrada Família, exit toward Plaça de la Sagrada Família, tel. 932-073-031, www.sagradafamilia.cat.

**Avoiding Lines:** Lines of up to 45 minutes—and occasionally much longer—are possible at peak times. To skip the line, buy advance tickets, take a tour, or hire a private guide (for details, see page 153). If just showing up, arrive right at 9:00 (when the church opens) or after 16:00 to minimize waiting.

**Connecting with Park Güell:** For information on getting to Park Güell from the Sagrada Família, see page 164.

📖 See the Sagrada Família Tour chapter.

### Hospital de la Santa Creu i Sant Pau

This distinctive Modernista-style hospital complex was designed by Lluís Domènech i Montaner (for more about him, see page 146). A short walk from the Sagrada Família and on the bus line to Park Güell, the hospital's interior and courtyards are worth a look if you're in the area...and a Modernista fan.

**Cost and Hours:** €10, €16 guided tour; Mon-Sat 10:00-18:30, Nov-March until 16:30, Sun 10:00-14:30 year-round; English tours offered daily at 12:00, 13:00, but check as times may vary; tel. 932-682-444, www.visitsantpau.com.

## BEYOND THE EIXAMPLE
### ▲▲Park Güell

Gaudí fans enjoy the artist's magic in this colorful park, located on the outskirts of town. While it takes a bit of effort to get here, Park Güell (Catalans pronounce it "gway") offers a unique look at Gaudí's style in a natural rather than urban context.  Designed as an upscale housing development for early 20th-century urbanites, the park is home to some of Barcelona's most famous symbols, including a dragon guarding a whimsical staircase and a wavy bench bordering a panoramic view terrace supported by a forest of columns. Gaudí used vivid tile fragments to decorate much of his work, creating a playful, pleasing effect. Much of the park is free, but the part visitors want to see, the **Monumental Zone**—with all the iconic Gaudí features—has an admission fee and timed-entry ticket. Also in the park is the **Gaudí House Museum,** where Gaudí lived for a time (separate ticket required). Although he did not design the house, you can see a few examples of his furniture here. Even without its Gaudí connection, Park Güell is simply a fine place to enjoy a break from a busy city, where green space is relatively rare.

**Cost and Hours:** Monumental Zone—€8 at the gate, €7 online, smart to reserve timed-entry tickets in advance (as much as three months early), open daily 8:00-21:30, Nov-March 8:30-18:00, www.parkguell.cat; Gaudí House Museum—€5.50, €31 combo-ticket includes Sagrada Família and its audioguide (but no towers), open daily 10:00-20:00, Oct-March until 18:00, www.casamuseugaudi.org.

**Getting There:** To reach Park Güell—about 2.5 miles from Plaça de Catalunya—it's easiest to take a taxi, though you can also get there by bus or a Metro plus bus combo. For details, see page 166. For instructions on linking the Sagrada Família to Park Güell, check page 164.

📖 See the Park Güell Tour chapter.

## Tibidabo

Tibidabo comes from the Latin for "to thee I shall give," the words the devil used when he was tempting Christ. It's still an enticing offer: At the top of Barcelona's highest peak, you're offered the city's oldest fun-fair, a great spot for kids, and—if the weather and air quality are good—an almost limitless view of the city and the Mediterranean.

**Cost and Hours:** €28.50, cheaper for kids under 4 feet tall, hours depend on season—generally July-Aug Wed-Sun 12:00-23:00, closed Mon-Tue, weekends only in off-season, lockers, café, tel. 932-117-942, www.tibidabo.cat.

**Getting There:** The direct "Tibibus" (#T2A) runs from Plaça de Catalunya to the park about every 20 minutes starting at 10:15 on days the park is open (€2.95, board in front of Caja Madrid bank).

Otherwise, the trip involves several steps. First, get to the Tibidabo stop by taking the Rodalies train L7 (brown) line from the Plaça de Catalunya Metro station (under Café Zürich; use T10 Card or buy individual ticket) or the blue Tourist Bus. From the Tibidabo station exit, cross the street to Plaça John F. Kennedy and catch bus #196 (3-4/hour, runs until 22:00) or Barcelona's only remaining trolley, Tramvía Blau (possibly Sat-Sun only, 2-4/hour until 19:30, €5.50 one-way, buy ticket on board). Get off at Plaça Dr. Andreu, where you'll see a handful of bars and restaurants (see page 224). From there, take the funicular to the top (€7.70 round-trip, €4.10 if paying park admission, tel. 906-427-017).

## Camp Nou Stadium

The home turf of FC Barcelona is a mecca for soccer fans. A tour takes you into the press room, by the box seats, through the trophy room, and past the warm-up bench, ending in a ground-level view of the field and, of course, a big shop to buy official "Barça" gear. You'll also tour a museum tracing the highlights of Barça history, with interactive touch screens and the six championship cups that the team won in a single season ("the sextuple," 2009-2010)—a feat, they say, that will never be repeated. For more on this team and its significance to Barcelona and Catalunya, see page 83.

**Cost and Hours:** €23 for Camp Nou Experience (includes tour and museum); mid-April-early Oct Mon-Sat 9:30-19:30 (off-season until 18:30), Sun 10:00-14:30, shorter hours on game days and sometimes the day before, Metro: Maria Cristina or Collblanc, tel. 902-189-900, www.fcbarcelona.cat.

# MONTJUÏC

Montjuïc (mohn-jew-EEK, "Mount of the Jews"), overlooking Barcelona's hazy port, has always been a show-off. Ages ago, it was capped by an impressive castle. When the Spanish enforced their rule, they built the imposing fortress that you'll see the shell of today. The hill has also played an integral role in the construction of Barcelona's great structures—significant parts of the historic city, the cathedral, the Sagrada Família, and much more were all built with stones quarried from Montjuïc.

Montjuïc has also been prominent during the last century. In 1929, it hosted an international fair, from which many of today's sights originated. And in 1992, the Summer Olympics directed the world's attention to this pincushion of attractions once again. While Montjuïc lacks one knockout, must-see attraction, it is home to a variety of good sights. For art lovers, the most worthwhile destinations are the Fundació Joan Miró, Catalan Art Museum, and CaixaForum.

**Sightseeing Strategies:** I've listed these sights by altitude, from the hill-topping castle down to the 1929 World Expo Fairgrounds at the base of Montjuïc (described in the next section). If you're visiting all of my listed sights, ride to the top by bus, funicular, or taxi, then visit them in this order so that most of your walking is downhill. However, if you want to visit only the Catalan Art Museum and/or CaixaForum, you can take the Metro to Plaça d'Espanya and ride the escalators up (with some stair-climbing as well).

**Getting to Montjuïc:** You have several choices. The simplest is to take a **taxi** directly to your destination (about €8 from downtown).

**Buses** also take you up to Montjuïc. From Plaça de Catalunya, bus #55 goes as far as Montjuïc's cable-car station/funicular. If you want to get higher (to the castle), ride the Metro or bus #9 or #50 from Plaça de Catalunya to Plaça d'Espanya, then make the easy transfer to bus #150 to ride all the way up the hill. Alternatively, the red Tourist Bus will get you to the Montjuïc sights.

Another option is by **funicular** (covered by Metro ticket, runs every 10 minutes 9:00-22:00). To reach it, take the Metro to the

Paral-lel stop, then follow signs for *Parc Montjuïc* and the little funicular icon—you can enter the funicular without using another ticket. The funicular closes annually in winter for maintenance; during those times a bus takes you up instead and drops you at the funicular exit (don't be disappointed if you end up on the bus— you'll get great views of the industrial and cruise ports and the sea). From the top of the funicular, turn left and walk gently downhill (4 minutes to Miró museum, 8 minutes to Olympic Stadium, 12

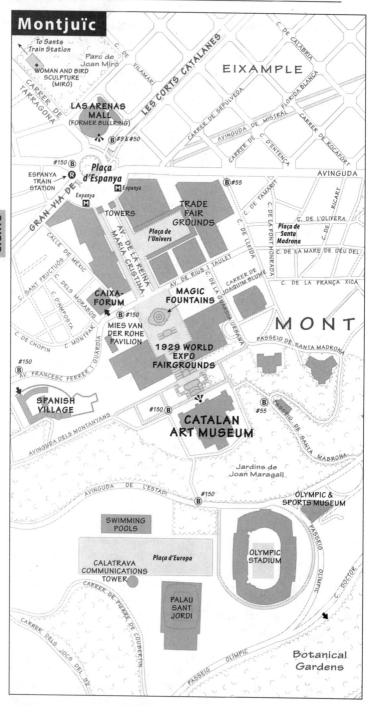

# Montjuïc

To Sants Train Station

Parc de Joan Miró

WOMAN AND BIRD SCULPTURE (MIRÓ)

EIXAMPLE

C. DE CALABRIA

C. DE VILAMARÍ

LES CORTS CATALANES

CARRER DE TARRAGONA

LAS ARENAS MALL (FORMER BULLRING)

B #9 & #50

CARRER DE SEPÚLVEDA

AVINGUDA DE MISTRAL

FLORIDA BLANCA

CARRER DE ROCAFORT

CARRER DE D'ENTENÇA

#150 B

ESPANYA TRAIN STATION

R

Plaça d'Espanya

Espanya M

M Espanya

AVINGUDA

B #55

C. DE TAMARIT

C. DE L'OLIVERA

C. DE RICART

Plaça de Santa Madrona

TOWERS

TRADE FAIR GROUNDS

Plaça de l'Univers

C. DE LLEIDA

C. DE LA FONT HONRADA

C. DE LA MARE DE DÉU DEL

GRAN VIA DE

CALLE DE MEXIC

AV. DE LA REINA MARIA CRISTINA

AV. DE RIUS I TAULET

C. DE LA GUARDIA URBANA

CARRER DE JOAQUIM BLUME

C. DE LA FRANÇA XICA

C. SANT FRUCTUÓS

C. DELS MORABOS

C. D'AMPOSTA

CAIXA-FORUM

B #150

MAGIC FOUNTAINS

MONT

C. DE CHOPIN

C. MONTFAR

MIES VAN DER ROHE PAVILION

1929 WORLD EXPO FAIRGROUNDS

PASSEIG DE SANTA MADRONA

#150 B

AV. FRANCESC FERRER I GUARDIA

SPANISH VILLAGE

#150 B

CATALAN ART MUSEUM

B #55

PASSEIG DE SANTA MADRONA

AVINGUDA DELS MONTANYANS

Jardins de Joan Maragall

AVINGUDA DE L'ESTADI

#150 B

OLYMPIC & SPORTS MUSEUM

SWIMMING POOLS

Plaça d'Europa

OLYMPIC STADIUM

PASSEIG

OLIMPIC

CALATRAVA COMMUNICATIONS TOWER

CARRER DE PIERRE DE COUBERTIN

PALAU SANT JORDI

C. DOCTOR

CARRER DELS JOCS DEL 92

PASSEIG OLIMPIC

Botanical Gardens

SIGHTS

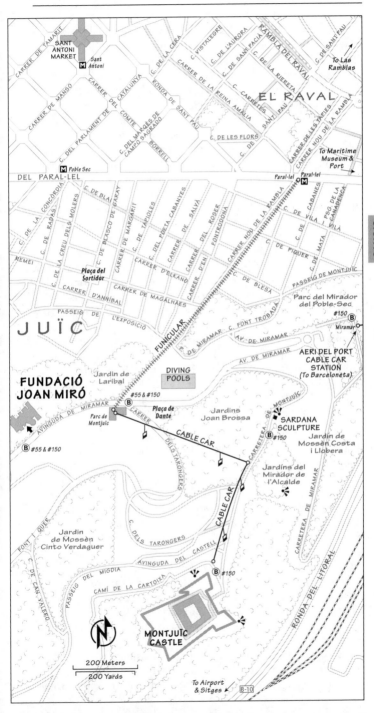

minutes to Catalan Art Museum). If you're heading all the way up to the castle, you can catch a bus or cable car from the top of the funicular (see castle listing, later).

For a scenic (if slow) approach to Montjuïc, you can ride the fun circa-1929 Aeri del Port **cable car** *(telefèric)* from the tip of the Barceloneta peninsula (across the harbor, near the beach) to the Miramar viewpoint park in Montjuïc. (Another station, along the port near the Columbus Monument, is currently closed.) The cable car is expensive, loads excruciatingly slowly (especially coming from the beach), and goes between two relatively remote parts of town, so it's really not an efficient connection. It's only worthwhile for its sweeping views over town or to head back down to Barceloneta at the end of the day, as lines are shorter if you board in Montjuïc (€11 one-way, €16.50 round-trip, 3/hour, daily 11:00-17:30, June-Sept until 20:00, closed in high wind, tel. 934-414-820, www.telefericodebarcelona.com).

**Getting Around Montjuïc:** Up top, it's easy and fun to walk between the sights—especially downhill. You can also connect the sights using the red Tourist Bus or one of the public buses: Bus #150 does a loop around the hilltop and is the only bus that goes to the castle; on the way up, it stops at or passes near the Caixa-Forum, Mies van der Rohe Pavilion, Spanish Village, Catalan Art Museum, Olympic Stadium, Fundació Joan Miró, the lower castle cable-car station/top of the funicular, and finally, the castle. On the downhill run, it loops by Miramar, the cable-car station for Barceloneta. Bus #55 connects only the funicular/cable-car stations, Fundació Joan Miró, and the Catalan Art Museum.

### Castle of Montjuïc (Castell de Montjuïc)

The castle, while just an empty brick-and-concrete shell today, offers great city views from its ramparts...and some poignant history. It was built in the 18th century with a Vauban-type star fortress design by the central Spanish government to keep an eye on Barcelona and stifle citizen revolt. Until the late 20th century, the place functioned more to repress the people of Barcelona than to defend them. Being "taken to Montjuïc" meant you likely wouldn't be seen again. When the 20th-century dictator Franco was in power, the castle was the site of hundreds of political executions. But in 2010, Spain's Prime Minister José Luis Rodríguez Zapatero, keeping a campaign promise, turned over control of the castle from Spain's national government to the city of Barcelona. These days it serves as a park, jogging destination, and host to a popular summer open-air cinema.

Beefy civil war-vintage cannons point visitors to grand Mediterranean vistas. Survey the boats in the harbor: Ships belonging to Grimaldi Lines, an Italian company, sail off to Genoa, Rome,

and Sardinia; Mallorca ferries make the eight-hour trip to Barcelonans' big party escape; and the cruise-ship terminal busily hosts 800 ships a year (Barcelona is one of the main ports of embarkation for Mediterranean cruises). The seafront stretching far to the left was part of an Olympics project that turned a derelict industrial zone into a swanky stretch of promenades, beaches, and fancy condos. At the far right is Spain's leading port; you'll see containers stretching all the way to the airport.

**Cost and Hours:** €5, daily 10:00-20:00, Nov-March until 18:00; €10 English tours Mon-Fri at 12:30 and 17:00 in summer (11:00 and 15:00 in winter), Sat-Sun at 12:00 and 16:00 year-round; www.bcn.cat/castelldemontjuic.

**Getting There:** To spare yourself the hike up, ride bus #150 to the base of the castle, catching it from Plaça d'Espanya, the top of the Montjuïc funicular, or various other points on Montjuïc. Or if the lines aren't too long, consider the much pricier **cable car** (Telefèric de Montjuïc), which departs from near the upper station of the Montjuïc funicular and offers excellent views (€8 one-way, €12 round-trip, runs daily June-Sept 10:00-21:00, shorter hours off-season).

### ▲Fundació Joan Miró

This museum has the best collection anywhere of works by Catalan artist Joan Miró (ZHOO-ahn mee-ROH, 1893-1983). Born in Barcelona, Miró divided his time between Paris and Catalunya (including Barcelona and his favorite village, Mont-roig del Camp). This building—designed in 1975 by Josep Lluís Sert, a friend of Miró and a student of Le Corbusier—was purpose-built to show

off Miró's art. The museum displays an always-changing, loosely chronological overview of Miró's oeuvre (as well as generally excellent temporary exhibits of 20th- and 21st-century artists). Consider renting the wonderful videoguide, which is well worth the extra charge.

If you don't like abstract art, you'll leave here scratching your head. But those who love this place are not faking it...they understand the genius of Miró and the fun of abstraction. Children

## Joan Miró: The Freedom of Simplicity

Miró believed that everything in the cosmos is linked—colors, sky, stars, love, time, music, dogs, men, women, dirt, and the void. He mixed simple symbols of these things creatively, as a poet uses words. It's as liberating for the visual artist to be abstract as it is for the poet: Both can use metaphors rather than being confined to concrete explanations. Miró would listen to music and paint. It's interactive, free interpretation. He said, "For me, simplicity is freedom."

COPA DEL MUNDO DE FUTBOL ESPAÑA 82

Here are some tips to help you enjoy and appreciate Miró's art: First meditate on it, then read the title (for example, *The Smile of a Tear*), then meditate on it again. Repeat the process until you have an epiphany. There's no correct answer—it's pure poetry. Devotees of Miró say they fly with him and don't even need drugs. Psychoanalysts liken Miró's free-for-all canvases to Rorschach tests. Is that a cigar in that star's mouth?

probably understand it the best. Eavesdrop on what they say about the art; you may learn something.

**Cost and Hours:** €12, 2-for-1 tickets Thu from 18:00; open Tue-Sat 10:00-20:00 (Nov-March until 18:00), Thu until 21:00, Sun until 14:30, closed Mon year-round; great videoguide-€5; 200 yards from top of funicular, Parc de Montjuïc, tel. 934-439-470, www.fundaciomiro-bcn.org. The museum has a restaurant, café, and bookshop (all accessible without museum ticket).

**Visiting the Museum:** From the entrance, pass through the temporary exhibits or walk through the outdoor courtyard to reach the permanent collection, starting on the main floor. Look for the following highlights, but note that some of the pieces mentioned below may no longer be in these locations, following a reinstallation of its permanent collection.

**Room 11:** The massive 400-square-foot *Tapestry of the Foundation,* which Miró designed for this space in 1979, has real texture—like a painting with thick brushstrokes. Notice Miró's trademark star and moon high above. (A different tapestry, which Miró custom-made for New York City's World Trade Center around this same period, was lost in the 9/11 terrorist attacks.)

In the hallway to the next room, look through the window to find the *Mercury Fountain,* by American sculptor Alexander Calder. This piece was created for the same 1937 exhibition at which Picasso premiered his seminal *Guernica*. Like Picasso's canvas, Calder's fountain was created to honor victims of the Spanish Civil War—in this case, the residents of Almadén, a mercury-mining town. Watch the liquid do its unpredictable thing as it drips and drops.

**Room 12 (Sculpture Gallery):** This gallery features several small bronze pieces by Miró. Ascend the ramp for a different angle. Nearby, find the stairs down to the Espai 13 installation space. Or continue to the end of the hall and downstairs to a room filled with pieces by other artists paying homage to Miró, plus a 15-minute film about Miró.

**Room 16 (Sala Joan Prats):** The collection in this room loosely traces Miró's artistic development. Young Miró is a sponge of different styles—Fauvism, Cubism, Catalan folk art, Impressionism (see the canvases of beaches and countryside), Orientalism *(Portrait of a Young Girl)*—and whatever else he is exposed to. In 1920, he goes to Paris, dabbles in Dada, and socializes with Surrealists. Is Miró himself a Surrealist? Sort of. They share the same goal: circumventing the viewer's preconceptions about art and reality by juxtaposing unlikely items in order to short-circuit the brain.

Miró's early work does resemble Dalí's. But as his own idiosyncratic style evolves, Miró adds more and more abstraction to the mix. In his Green Paintings series (1925-1927), instead of placing photorealistic items against an otherworldly background (as Dalí would have), Miró arranges highly abstract symbols against a flat background. By 1925, Miró has left the figurative world behind and leaps wholeheartedly into the abyss—pushing the boundaries of abstraction. He paints a completely uninterpretable canvas...and then, just to be cheeky, titles it *Painting*.

**Second Floor:** With the 1930s and the advent of the civil war, Miró temporarily becomes more figurative with his Wind Paintings. Recognizable monsters lurk threateningly. In the early 1940s, Miró flees the Nazi takeover of France and retreats to Spain. He becomes fixated on the heavens and produces his Constellations series—23 paintings of stars, moons, and other brightly colorful items cast against bright backgrounds.

By the late 1940s, Miró is becoming internationally appreciated and within a few years, begins to do more public commissions. But corporatization doesn't tame Miró, as the Sixties Gallery demonstrates. If anything, he continues to refine his trademark style and strip everything down to basics. Star. Moon. Bird. Woman. Increasingly, Miró's works are intended as something to meditate on. Some of his best-known and most appreciated works date from this period and can't be found in any museum, but are scattered around the streets of Barcelona—in the middle of the Ramblas (see page 87), in the park behind the nearby Las Arenas bullring mall (see page 74), and elsewhere.

**The Rest of the Museum:** Gallery K contains works from the 1960s and 1970s. Return to earth with a visit to the terrace, where you'll find a modern sculpture gallery and views of the surrounding area.

### Olympic and Sports Museum (Museu Olímpic i de l'Esport)

This museum rides the coattails of the stadium across the street. You'll twist down a timeline-ramp that traces the history of the Olympic Games, interspersed with random exhibits about various sports. Downstairs you'll find exhibits designed to test your athleticism, a play-by-play rehash of the '92 Barcelona Olympiad, a commemoration of Juan Antonio Samaranch (the influential Catalan president of the IOC for two decades), a sports media exhibit, and a schmaltzy movie collage. High-tech but hokey, the museum is worth the time and money only for those nostalgic for the '92 Games.

**Cost and Hours:** €5.10, Tue-Sat 10:00-20:00 (Oct-March until 18:00), Sun 10:00-14:30, closed Mon year-round, unnecessary audioguide-€2, Avinguda de l'Estadi 60, tel. 932-925-379, www.museuolimpicbcn.cat.

### Olympic Stadium (Estadi Olímpic)

Aside from the memories of the medals, Barcelona's Olympic Stadium offers little to see today. But if the doors are open, you're welcome to step inside. History pan-els along the railings overlooking the playing field tell the stadium's dynamic story and show the place in happier times—filled with fans as Bon Jovi, the Rolling Stones, and Madonna pack the place.

The stadium was originally built for the 1929 World Expo, but soon thereafter, it played a big part in Barcelona's plan to host the "People's Olympiad." These were to take place in July of 1936 as an alternative to Hitler's Fascist Olympics, which were scheduled for that same summer in Berlin (and which Spain had planned to boycott). But just days before the Barcelona games were to begin, civil war broke out in Spain, and the event was cancelled.

Fifty-something years later, the stadium was updated and expanded in preparation for the 1992 Summer Olympics. It was officially named for Catalan patriot Lluís Companys i Jover, the left-wing leader who was president when Spain's Civil War began.

Companys had pushed for the democratic alternative to Hitler's games; he was later arrested and executed by Franco.

The memorable XXV Olympiad kicked off here on July 25, 1992. At the opening ceremonies, an archer dramatically lit the Olympic torch—which still stands high at the end of the stadium overlooking the city skyline—with a flaming arrow. Over the next two weeks, Barcelona played host to the thrill of victory—most notably at the hands of Michael Jordan, Magic Johnson, Larry Bird, and the rest of the US basketball "Dream Team"—and the agony of defeat (i.e., the nightmares of the Dream Team's opponents). These Olympics also coincided with several turning points in global geopolitics. It was the first Olympiad after the fall of the Soviet Union (and the first since 1972 without boycotts). Twelve newly independent states sent their athletes as one big Unified Team. These were also the first Games in which the post-Apartheid South African team was invited to participate; the first Games after the breakup of Yugoslavia (with four teams from that region instead of one); and the first to feature a reunified German team.

**Nearby:** Hovering over the stadium is the futuristic **Montjuïc Communications Tower** (designed by prominent Spanish architect Santiago Calatrava), originally used to transmit Olympic highlights and lowlights around the world.

## ▲▲Catalan Art Museum (Museu Nacional d'Art de Catalunya)

The big vision for this wonderful museum is to showcase Catalan art from the 10th century through about the mid-20th century.

Often called "the Prado of Romanesque art" (and "MNAC" for short), it holds Europe's best collection of Romanesque frescoes and offers a good sweep of modern Catalan art—fitting, given Catalunya's astonishing contribution to the Modern. It's all housed in the grand Palau Nacional, an emblematic building from the 1929 World Expo, with magnificent views over Barcelona, especially from the building's rooftop terrace.

**Cost and Hours:** €12, valid for 2 days entry within 30 days, includes temporary exhibits and rooftop terrace, €18 combo-ticket includes Spanish Village, free Sat from 15:00 and first Sun of month; open Tue-Sat 10:00-20:00 (Oct-April until 18:00), Sun 10:00-15:00, closed Mon year-round; audioguide-€3.50; in massive National Palace building above Magic Fountains, near Plaça d'Espanya—take escalators up; tel. 936-220-376, www.museunacional.cat.

**Rooftop Terrace:** You can visit the rooftop with your museum ticket; without a ticket, it's €2 to access the rooftop. To reach the terrace from the main entrance, walk past the bathrooms on the left and show your ticket to get on the elevator. You'll ride up nearly to the viewpoint, and from there hike up a couple of flights of stairs to the terrace. To take an elevator the whole way, go to the far end of the museum, through the huge dome room, to the far-right corner.

**Visiting the Museum:** As you enter, pick up a map. The left wing is Romanesque, and the right wing is Gothic, exquisite Renaissance, and Baroque. Upstairs is more Baroque, plus modern art, photography, coins, and more.

The MNAC's rare, world-class collection of **Romanesque** (Romànic) art came mostly from remote Catalan village church-

es (most of the pieces were moved to the museum in the early 1920s to save them from scavenging art dealers). A series of videos shows the process of extracting the frescoes from the churches to move them to the museum. The Romanesque wing features a remarkable array of 11th- to 13th-century frescoes, painted wooden altar fronts, and ornate statuary. This classic Romanesque art—with flat 2-D scenes, each saint holding his symbol, and Jesus (easy to identify by the cross in his halo)—is impressively displayed on replicas of the original church ceilings and apses.

Go back to the main hall and enter the **Gothic** wing, opposite where you entered the Romanesque collection. Fresco murals give way to vivid 14th-century wood-panel

paintings of Bible stories. A roomful of paintings (Room 26) by the Catalan master Jaume Huguet (1412-1492) deserves a look, particularly his *Consecration of St. Agustí Vell.* Also on the ground floor is a selection of **Renaissance** works covering Spain's Golden Age (Zurbarán, heavy religious scenes, and Spanish royals with their endearing under-bites) and examples of Romanticism (dewy-eyed Catalan landscapes). In addition, you'll find minor works by major—if not necessar-ily Catalan—names (Velázquez, El Greco, Goya, Tintoretto, Rubens, and so on).

For a break, go to the right from the Gothic exit to glide under the huge **dome,** which once housed an ice-skating rink. This was the prime ceremony room and dance hall for the 1929 World Expo.

From the big ballroom, you can ride the glass elevator upstairs to the **Modern Art** section, which takes you on an enjoyable walk from the late 1800s to about 1950. It's kind of a Catalan Musée d'Orsay, offering a big chronological clockwise circle covering Symbolism, Modernisme, fin de siècle fun, Art Deco, and more. Find the early 20th-century paintings by Catalan artists Santiago Rusiñol and Ramon Casas, both of whom had a profound impact on a young Picasso

(and, through him, on all of modern art). Casas was also one of the financiers of Els Quatre Gats, the hangout of Modernista artists (see page 190); his fun Toulouse-Lautrec-esque works, including a whimsical self-portrait on a tandem bicycle, are crowd-pleasers. Crossing over to the "Modern 2" section, you'll find more furniture (pieces that complement some of the empty spaces you may see if you visit Gaudí's buildings—including Gaudí-designed wooden chairs and a sofa), Impressionism, the shimmering landscapes of Joaquim Mir, and several distinctly Picasso portraits of women.

The museum also has a coin collection, seductive sofas scattered about, the chic and pricey Oleum restaurant (with vast city views), and a comfy outdoor terrace café (serving snacks with more city views).

## 1929 WORLD EXPO FAIRGROUNDS AND NEARBY

With the World Expo in 1929, Montjuïc morphed into an extravagant center for fairs, museums, and festivals. Nearly everything you see here dates from 1929 (the exceptions are CaixaForum and Las Arenas mall). The expo's theme was to demonstrate how electricity was about more than lightbulbs: Electricity powered the

funicular, the glorious expo fountains, the many pavilion displays, and even the flame atop the fountain marking the center of Plaça d'Espanya (and celebrating the electric company that sponsored the show). If Barcelona is known for growing through big events, this certainly is a good example.

Standing at Plaça d'Espanya (or, better yet, on the rooftop terrace of the bullring mall—described later), look through the double-brick-tower gate, down the grand esplanade, and imagine it alive with fountains and lined by proud national pavilions showing off all that was modern in 1929. Today the site is home to the Fira de Barcelona convention center. The Neo-Baroque fountain provides a brilliant centerpiece for Plaça d'Espanya.

**Getting There:** The fairgrounds sprawl at the base of Montjuïc, from the Catalan Art Museum's doorstep to Plaça d'Espanya. It's easiest to see these sights on your way down from Montjuïc. Otherwise, ride the Metro to Espanya, then use the series of stairs and escalators to climb up through the heart of the fairgrounds (eventually reaching the Catalan Art Museum).

## ▲Magic Fountains (Font Màgica)

Music, colored lights, and huge amounts of water make an artistic and coordinated splash in the evening near Plaça d'Espanya.

**Cost and Hours:** Free, 20-minute shows start on the half-hour; almost always May-Sept Thu-Sun 21:00-23:00, no shows Mon-Wed; Oct-April Fri-Sat 19:00-20:30, no shows Sun-Thu; from the Espanya Metro stop, walk toward the towering National Palace.

## ▲▲CaixaForum

The CaixaForum Social and Cultural Center (sponsored by the leading Catalan bank) is housed in one of Barcelona's most impor-

tant Art Nouveau buildings. In 1911, Josep Puig i Cadafalch (a top architect often overshadowed by Gaudí) designed the Casaramona textile factory, which showed off Modernista design in an industrial rather than a residential context. It functioned as a factory for less than a decade, then later served a long stint as a police station under Franco. Beautifully refurbished in 2002, the facility reopened as a great center for bringing culture and art to the people of Barcelona.

**Cost and Hours:** Free entrance to building, exhibits-€4, daily 10:00-20:00, Avinguda de Francesc Ferrer i Guàrdia 6, tel. 934-768-600, http://obrasocial.lacaixa.es—click on "Culture."

**Visiting the Center:** From the lobby, signs point to *Sala 2, 3,*

*4,* and *5;* each hosts different (and typically outstanding) temporary exhibitions. Ride the escalator to the first floor, which features a modest but interesting exhibit about the history and renovation of the building, including a model and photos. Then head into the appealing red-brick courtyard, from which you can access the various exhibition halls. (The sight features generally limited English descriptions.)

Take the stairs or elevator up to the Modernista Terrace (*Planta 2,* or follow signs to *Aula 1*), boasting a wavy floor, bristling with fanciful brick towers, and offering views over the complex and to Montjuïc. Enjoy the genius of Puig i Cadafalch's Modernista design, which provided state-of-the-art working conditions—natural light, good ventilation, and even two trademark towers filled with water (which could be broken to put out any factory fires). The various buildings (designed to be separate from each other to reduce the risk of fire) were built on terraces to level out the Montjuïc slope. Notice that there's no smokestack. This was one of the first electric-powered factories in town.

### Mies van der Rohe Pavilion (Pabellón Mies van der Rohe)

Architecture pilgrims enjoy the pavilion that Ludwig Mies van der Rohe designed for the German exhibits at the 1929 expo. Although it was dismantled at the end of the fair, the building was heralded as a seminal example of modern architecture, and in the 1980s, the city reconstructed it on the original site. It's small and stripped-down—a strictly functional "Modernist" (i.e., decidedly *not* Modernista) structure. Unless you're a huge fan, skip the entry fee and simply walk around the pavilion to get a peek inside (including views of the "Barcelona Chair," the tubular steel and leather-cushioned chair that's become an icon of 20th-century furniture design).

**Cost and Hours:** €5, daily 10:00-20:00, Oct-Feb until 18:00, Avinguda de Francesc Ferrer i Guàrdia 7, tel. 934-234-016, www.miesbcn.com.

### Spanish Village (Poble Espanyol)

This five-acre model village was built as part of the expo to show off the cultural and architectural diversity in Spain. Replicating traditional architecture from all over the country, the village was mostly a shell to contain gift shops—and today it still serves the same purpose. Craftspeople do their clichéd thing, and friendly shopkeepers offer plenty of tasty samples of traditional and local edibles. I think it's tacky and overpriced, but if you never expect to visit an authentic Spanish village (this place is popular with cruise groups), here's a pale substitute.

**Cost and Hours:** €12, €7 Tue-Sun from 20:00, €18 combo-ticket includes Catalan Art Museum; open Mon 9:00-20:00,

Tue-Sun 9:00-24:00, Jan-Feb closes earlier, €4.50 videoguide explains all the buildings, www.poble-espanyol.com.

**Getting There:** It's best to take bus #150, as it's a long hike up from the main World Expo esplanade.

### ▲Las Arenas (Bullring Mall)

What do you do with a big bullfighting arena that's been sitting empty for decades? Make a mall. The grand Neo-Moorish Modernista *plaça de toros* functioned as an arena for bullfights from around 1900 to 1977, and then reopened in 2011 as a mall. It now

hosts everything you'd expect in a modern shopping center: brand-name shops, a food-court basement, a 12-screen cinema complex, and a rock-and-roll museum.

The **rooftop terrace,** with stupendous views of Plaça d'Espanya and Montjuïc, is ringed with eateries (reachable by external glass elevator for €1 or from inside escalators/elevators for free). Besides getting a bird's-eye perspective of the fairgrounds, you can gaze down at Parc de Joan Miró, which includes the giant sculpture *Woman and Bird (Dona i Ocell).* This was one of the works (along with the mosaic on the Ramblas—see page 87) that the city commissioned from the artist to welcome visitors. Miró's sense of humor is evident—if the sculpture seems phallic, keep in mind that the Catalan word for "bird" is also slang for "penis."

**Cost and Hours:** Free, daily 10:00-22:00, restaurants serve until 24:00, Gran Via de les Corts Catalanes 373, Metro: Espanya, www.arenasdebarcelona.com.

## THE BEACHES AND NEARBY

### ▲Barcelona's Beaches

Barcelona has created a summer tourist trade by building a huge stretch of beaches east of the town center. From Barceloneta, an uninterrupted band of sand tumbles three miles northeast to the Fòrum. Before the 1992 Olympics, this area was an industrial wasteland nicknamed the "Catalan Manchester." Not anymore. The industrial zone was demolished and dumped into the sea, while sand was dredged from the seabed to make the pristine beaches locals enjoy today. Looking out to sea, you can't miss the W Hotel, shaped like a windblown sail, dominating a small peninsula.

The overall scene is great for sunbathing and for an evening paseo before dinner. It's like a resort island—complete with lounge chairs, volleyball, showers, WCs, bike paths, and inviting beach bars called *chiringuitos.* Each beach segment has its own vibe: Sant

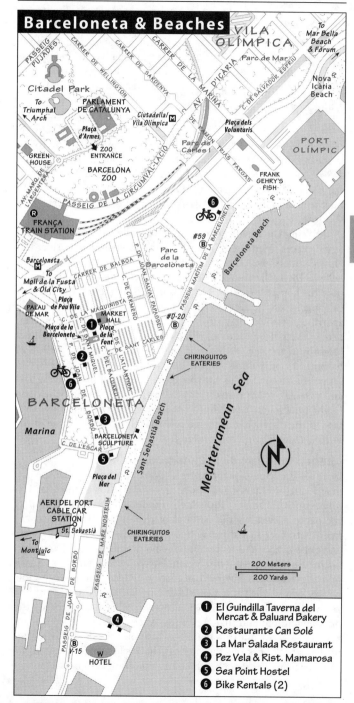

# Barceloneta & Beaches

**VILA OLÍMPICA**

To Mar Bella Beach & Fòrum

PASSEIG PUJADES

CARRER DE WELLINGTON

CARRER DE SARDENYA

CARRER DE LA MARINA

AV. D'ICÀRIA

Parc de Mar

C. DE SALVADOR ESPRIU

Nova Icària Beach

Citadel Park

PARLAMENT DE CATALUNYA

Ciutadella/ Vila Olímpica Ⓜ

AV. DE RAMON TRIAS FARGAS

Plaça dels Voluntaris

To Triumphal Arch

Plaça d'Armes

PORT OLÍMPIC

GREEN-HOUSE

AV. MARC DE L'ARGENTERA

ZOO ENTRANCE

BARCELONA ZOO

Parc de Carles I

FRANK GEHRY'S FISH

PASSEIG DE LA CIRCUMVAL·LACIÓ

Ⓡ FRANÇA TRAIN STATION

**6** 🚲

#59 Ⓑ

Barceloneta Ⓜ

Parc de la Barceloneta

PASSEIG MARÍTIM DE LA BARCELONETA

Barceloneta Beach

To Moll de la Fusta & Old City

CARRER DE BALBOA

P. DE JOAN SALVAT PAPASSEIT

Plaça de Pau Vila

C. DE LA MAQUINISTA

C. DE CERMEÑO

PALAU DE MAR

MARKET HALL

Plaça de la Barceloneta

**1** Plaça de la Font

C. DE SANT MIQUEL

C. DE SANT CARLES

C. DE L'ATLÀNTIDA

C. DEL BALUARD

#D-20 Ⓑ

CHIRINGUITOS EATERIES

**2**

**6** 🚲

C. DE JOAN

**BARCELONETA**

**3**

Marina

BARCELONETA SCULPTURE

C. DE L'ESCAR

C. DE BORBÓ

Sant Sebastià Beach

**Mediterranean Sea**

**5**

Plaça del Mar

AERI DEL PORT CABLE CAR STATION

St. Sebastià

To Montjuïc

CHIRINGUITOS EATERIES

PASSEIG DE MARE NOSTRUM

Ⓝ

200 Meters
200 Yards

PASSEIG DE JOAN DE BORBÓ

V-15

**4**

W HOTEL

**1** El Guindilla Taverna del Mercat & Baluard Bakery
**2** Restaurante Can Solé
**3** La Mar Salada Restaurant
**4** Pez Vela & Rist. Mamarosa
**5** Sea Point Hostel
**6** Bike Rentals (2)

**SIGHTS**

Sebastià (closest, popular with older beachgoers and families), Barceloneta (with many seafood restaurants), Nova Icària (pleasant family beach), and Mar Bella (attracts a younger crowd, clothing-optional).

**Getting There:** The Barceloneta Metro stop leaves you a long walk from the sand. To get to the beaches without a hike, take the bus. From the Ramblas, bus #59 will get you as far as Barceloneta Park; bus #D20 leaves from the Columbus Monument and follows a similar route. Bus #V15 runs from Plaça de Catalunya to the tip of Barceloneta (near the W Hotel).

**Biking the Beach:** For a break from the city, rent a bike (for rental places, see page 27) and take the following little ride: Explore Citadel Park, filled with families enjoying a day out (described below). Then roll through Barceloneta. This artificial peninsula was once the home of working-class sailors and shippers. From the Barceloneta beach, head up to the Olympic Village, where the former apartments for 13,000 visiting athletes now house permanent residents. The village's symbol, Frank Gehry's striking "fish," shines brightly in the sun. A bustling night scene keeps this stretch of harborfront busy until the wee hours. From here you'll come to a series of man-made crescent-shaped beaches, each with trendy bars and cafés. If you're careless or curious (down by Mar Bella), you might find yourself pedaling past people working on an all-over tan. In the distance is the huge solar panel marking the site of the Fòrum shopping and convention center.

### Citadel Park (Parc de la Ciutadella)

In 1888, Barcelona's biggest, greenest park, originally the site of a much-hated military citadel, was transformed for a Universal Exhibition (world's fair). The stately Triumphal Arch at the top of the park, celebrating the removal of the citadel, was built as the main entrance. Inside you'll find wide pathways, plenty of trees and grass, a zoo, and museums of geology and zoology. Barcelona, one of Europe's most densely populated cities, suffers from a lack of real green space. This park is a haven and is especially enjoyable on weekends, when it teems with happy families (for more on the zoo and kids' activities in Citadel Park, see page 206). Enjoy the ornamental fountain that the young Antoni Gaudí helped design, and consider a jaunt in a rental rowboat on the lake in the center of the park. Check out the tropical Umbracle greenhouse and the Hivernacle winter garden, which has a pleasant café-bar (Mon-Sat

10:00-14:00 & 17:00-20:30, Sun 10:30-14:00, shorter hours off-season).

**Cost and Hours:** Park—free, daily 10:00 until dusk, north of França train station, Metro: Arc de Triomf, Barceloneta, or Ciutadella/Vila Olímpica.

## The Fòrum

The original 1860 vision for Barcelona's enlargement would have extended the boulevard called Diagonal right to the sea. Developers finally realized this goal nearly a century and a half later, with the opening of the Fòrum neighborhood. Go here for a taste of today's Barcelona: nothing Gothic, nothing quaint, just big and modern—a mall, waterfront esplanade, and a convention center.

Among the modern structures here, you can't miss the triangular **Edifici Fòrum.** Built for a 2004 Universal Forum of Cultures conference and exhibition, the eccentric building was initially controversial, but it's since become a well-regarded landmark. Among other things, the Fòrum tries to be an inspiration for environmental engineering. Waste is burned to produce heat, and a giant solar panel creates perfectly clean and sustainable energy.

**Getting There:** You can get out to the Fòrum by bike, bus, or taxi via the long and impressive beach. Or the Metro zips you there in just a few minutes from the center (Metro: Fòrum).

# THE RAMBLAS RAMBLE

*From Plaça de Catalunya to the Waterfront*

For more than a century, this walk down Barcelona's main boulevard has been a magnet for visitors. It's a one-hour stroll that goes from Plaça de Catalunya gently downhill to the waterfront, with an easy return by Metro.

Sadly, the charm of the Ramblas has not survived the advent of mass tourism in Barcelona. Back when locals enjoyed strolling here, there was plenty of business to keep characteristic flower stalls, bird markets, and newspaper stands healthy. Today, the crowds are mostly tourists, locals are few and far between, and the street is lined not with cultural attractions, but with tacky souvenir trinkets and lousy eateries. Still, if you come to Barcelona...you've got to ramble the Ramblas.

The word "Ramblas" is plural; the street is actually a succession of five separately named segments. But street signs and addresses treat it as a single long street—"La Rambla," singular. This walk will help you see beyond the tourist crowds and enjoy the essence of the area. On the wide central sidewalk, you'll raft the river of tourism as you pass plenty of historic bits and pieces of this great city.

## Orientation

**Length of This Walk:** Allow an hour. If you have less time, focus on the stretch between the Fountain of Canaletes and the Miró mosaic at Liceu. With more time, dip into La Boqueria Market.

**When to Go:** The Ramblas is two different streets by day and by night. To fully experience its yin and yang, walk it once in the evening and again in the morning, grabbing breakfast on a stool in a market café. Note that the Ramblas can be rowdy and off-putting late at night. Saturday is the best time to see

La Boqueria Market (it's also open weekdays, but closed on Sun); Palau Güell and *Santa Eulàlia* are both closed on Monday.

**Getting There:** This walk begins at the Plaça de Catalunya end of the Ramblas, across the square from El Corte Inglés department store (Metro: Plaça de Catalunya).

**La Boqueria Market:** Mon-Sat 8:00-20:00, best mornings after 9:00, quiet after 16:00, closed Sun, Rambla 91.

**Palau Güell:** €12 timed-entry ticket, includes audioguide, free first Sun of the month; open Tue-Sun 10:00-20:00, Nov-March until 17:30, closed Mon year-round, last entry one hour before closing; Carrer Nou de la Rambla 3.

**Columbus Monument:** Elevator—€6, daily 8:30-20:30, Oct-Feb until 19:30, Plaça del Portal de la Pau.

*Santa Eulàlia:* €3, Tue-Sun 10:00-20:30 except Sat from 14:00, Nov-March until 17:30, closed Mon year-round, Moll de la Fusta quay.

**Tours:** ∩ My free Barcelona City Walk audio tour covers part of the Ramblas.

**Pickpockets:** The Ramblas is prime hunting ground for pickpockets. Keep only today's spending money in your front pocket; secure your credit/debit cards, extra cash, and passport in your money belt.

**Eating:** The eateries here are tourist traps: Don't eat or drink on the Ramblas. But just off the street you'll find a few handy lunch spots, and the stalls of La Boqueria Market invite grazing. For details, see page 184.

# The Walk Begins

• *Start your ramble on Plaça de Catalunya, at the top of the Ramblas.*

## ❶ Plaça de Catalunya

Dotted with fountains, statues, and pigeons, and ringed by grand Art Deco buildings, this plaza is Barcelona's center. The square's

stern, straight lines are a reaction to the curves of Modernisme (which predominates in the Eixample district, just above the square). Plaça de Catalunya is the hub for the Metro, bus, airport shuttle, and Tourist Bus. More than half of the eight million Catalans live in greater Barcelona, and for the inhabitants of this proud nation, this is their Times Square.

Geographically, the 12-acre square links the narrow streets

RAMBLAS RAMBLE

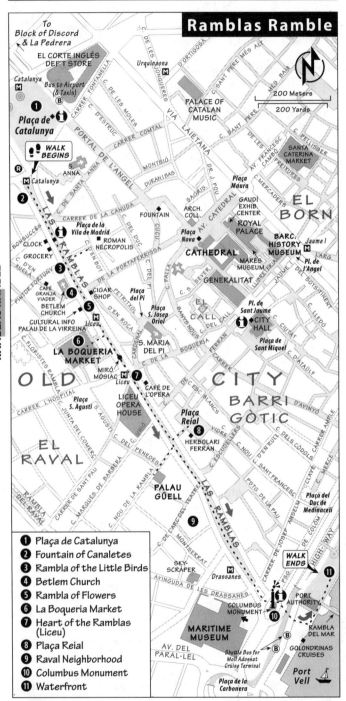

# Ramblas Ramble

To Block of Discord & La Pedrera

EL CORTE INGLÉS DEP'T STORE

Catalunya

Bus to Airport (& Taxis)

**❶ Plaça de Catalunya**

WALK BEGINS

❷ Catalunya

Urquinaona

PALACE OF CATALAN MUSIC

SANTA CATERINA MARKET

EL BORN

PORTAL DE L'ANGEL

CARRER FONTANELLA

C. DE LES MOLES

C. D'ESTRUC

CARRER COMTAL

MONTSIÓ

DURAN I BAS

S. ANNA

Plaça Maura

GAUDÍ EXHIB. CENTER

CARRER DE SANTA ANNA

CARRER DE LA CANUDA

❶ Plaça de la Vila de Madrid

FOUNTAIN

ARCH. COLL.

ROYAL PALACE

ROMAN NECROPOLIS

Plaça Nova

BARC. HISTORY MUSEUM

Jaume I

BONSUCCÉS

CLOCK

GROCERY

C. D'EN XUCLÀ

CATHEDRAL

MARÈS MUSEUM

Pl. de l'Àngel

❸

CIGAR SHOP

GENERALITAT

CAFÉ GRANJA VIADER

❹

Plaça del Pi

EL CALL

BETLEM CHURCH

❺

Plaça S. Josep Oriol

Pl. de Sant Jaume

CITY HALL

CULTURAL INFO PALAU DE LA VIRREINA

Liceu

S. MARIA DEL PI

Plaça de Sant Miquel

❻ LA BOQUERIA MARKET

OLD

MIRÓ MOSAIC

Liceu

❼

CITY

CARRER DE LA BOQUERIA

BARRI GÒTIC

CARRER L'HOSPITAL

Plaça S. Agustí

LICEU OPERA HOUSE

CAFÉ DE L'OPERA

Plaça Reial

❽

EL RAVAL

HERBOLARI FERRAN

PALAU GÜELL

❾

SKY-SCRAPER

Drassanes

AVINGUDA DE LES DRASSANES

WALK ENDS

❿ COLUMBUS MONUMENT

PORT AUTHORITY

⓫

MARITIME MUSEUM

AV. DEL PARAL·LEL

Shuttle Bus for Moll Adossat Cruise Terminal

RAMBLA DEL MAR

GOLONDRINAS CRUISES

Plaça de la Carbonera

Port Vell

❶ Plaça de Catalunya
❷ Fountain of Canaletes
❸ Rambla of the Little Birds
❹ Betlem Church
❺ Rambla of Flowers
❻ La Boqueria Market
❼ Heart of the Ramblas (Liceu)
❽ Plaça Reial
❾ Raval Neighborhood
❿ Columbus Monument
⓫ Waterfront

200 Meters
200 Yards

of old Barcelona with the broad boulevards of the newer city. Four great thoroughfares radiate from here. The Ramblas is the popular tourist promenade. Passeig de Gràcia, Barcelona's answer to Paris' Champs-Elysées, has fashionable shops and cafés (and noisy traffic). Rambla de Catalunya is equally fashionable but cozier and more pedestrian-friendly. Avinguda del Portal de l'Angel (shopper-friendly and traffic-free) leads to the Barri Gòtic.

Historically, Plaça de Catalunya links the modern city with its past. In the 1850s, when Barcelona tore down its medieval walls to expand the city, this square on the edge of the walls was one of the first places to be developed.

At the Ramblas end of the square, the odd, inverted-staircase **monument** represents the shape of Catalunya and honors one of

its former presidents, Francesc Macià i Llussà, who declared independence for the breakaway region in 1931. (It didn't quite stick.) Sculptor Josep Maria Subirachs, whose work you'll see at the Sagrada Família (see page 161), designed it.

The venerable Café Zürich, just across the street from the monument, was once a popular downtown rendezvous spot (before cell phones made such places less important). These days, young locals hang out opposite at the giant Apple Store (for the free Wi-Fi). Homesick Americans might prefer the nearby Hard Rock Café. And the giant El Corte Inglés department store towering above the square (on the northeast side) has just about anything you might need.

• *Cross the street and start heading down the Ramblas. To get oriented, pause 20 yards down, at the ornate lamppost with a fountain as its base (on the right, near #129).*

### ❷ Fountain of Canaletes

The black-and-gold **fountain** has been a local favorite for more than a century. When Barcelona tore down its medieval wall and transformed the Ramblas from a drainage ditch into an elegant promenade, this fountain was one of its early attractions. Legend says that a drink from the fountain ensures that you'll come back to Barcelona one day. Watch

the tourists—eager to guarantee a return trip—struggle with the awkwardly high water pressure. It's still a popular let's-meet-at-the-fountain rendezvous spot and a gathering place for celebrations and demonstrations. Fans of the Barcelona soccer team party here after winning a big match; the fountain has been toppled many times by happy revelers climbing it. It's also a good spot to fill up your water bottle.

As you survey the Ramblas action, get your bearings for our upcoming stroll. You'll see the following features here and all along the way:

**Wavy Tile Work:** The pavement decorations represent the stream that once flowed here. *Rambla* means "stream" in Arabic, and this used to be a drainage ditch along the medieval wall of the Barri Gòtic (to the left). Many Catalan towns, established where rivers approach the sea, have streets called "Ramblas." Today Barcelona's "stream" has become a river of humanity.

**Skinny Balconies:** Look up to see the city's characteristic shallow balconies. They're functional as well as decorative, with windows opening from floor to ceiling to allow more light and air into the tight, dark spaces of these cramped old buildings.

**Hardy Plane Trees:** The deciduous trees lining the boulevard are known for their peeling bark and toughness in urban settings. They're ideal for the climate, letting in maximum sun in the winter and providing maximum shade in the summer.

**Fixed Chairs:** Nearby, notice the chairs fixed to the sidewalk at jaunty angles. It used to be that you'd pay to rent a chair here to look at the constant parade of passersby. Seats are now free, and it's still the best people-watching in town. Enjoy these chairs while you can—you'll find virtually no public benches or other seating farther down the Ramblas, only cafés that serve beer and sangria in just one (expensive) size: *gigante*.

**ONCE Booths:** Across from the fountain and a few steps down, notice the first of many ONCE booths along this walk (pronounced OHN-thay, the Spanish "11"). These sell lottery tickets that support Spain's organization of the blind, a powerful advocate for the needs of people with disabilities.

• *Continue strolling.*

A generation ago the Ramblas had a different kind of commerce. Locals came here for their newspapers, flowers, and even domestic pets like birds and hamsters. Today, these businesses have vanished and the commerce that remains is trinkets and drinks for hordes of tourists.

Among the souvenirs, you'll see soccer paraphernalia, especially the scarlet-and-blue of FC Barcelona (known as "Barça"). The team is owned by its more than 170,000 "members"—fans who buy season tickets, which come with a share of ownership (the team's healthy payroll guarantees that they're always in contention). Their motto, "More than a club" *(Mes que un club)*, suggests that Barça represents not only athletic prowess but also Catalan cultural identity. This comes to a head during a match nicknamed "El Clásico," in which they face their bitter rivals, Real Madrid (whom many Barça fans view as stand-ins for Castilian cultural chauvinism).

Walk 100 yards farther to #115 and the venerable **Royal Academy of Science and Arts building** (it's now home to a performing-arts theater)—its fine facade struggling to be noticed above the Ramblas ruckus. This is a city of striking and creative architecture from the late 1900s—an industrial boom time that brought with it lots of construction. Look up: The clock high on the facade marks official Barcelona time—synchronize. The **Carrefour** supermarket just behind has cheap groceries (at #113).

• *You're now standing at what was the...*

## ❸ Rambla of the Little Birds (RIP)

Traditionally, kids brought their parents here to buy pets, especially on Sundays. But the clientele stopped coming and animal-rights groups lobbied to cut back on the stalls, claiming that many families were making impulse buys with no serious interest in taking care of these cute little critters. Today, none of the traditional pet kiosks survive—and there's not a bird in sight. Nowadays only the locals—and you—know the story behind the name, and ice-cream and souvenir shops line this stretch.

• *At #122 (the big, modern Citadines Hotel on the left), take a 100-yard detour through a passageway marked* Passatge de la Ramblas *to a restored...*

**Roman Necropolis:** Look down and imagine a 2,000-year-old tomb-lined road. In Roman cities, tombs (outside the walls)

typically lined the roads leading into town. Emperor Augustus spent a lot of time in modern-day Spain conquering new land, so the Romans were sure to incorporate Hispania into the empire's infrastructure. This road, Via Augusta, led into the Roman port of Barcino (today's highway to France still follows the route laid out by this Roman thoroughfare). Looking down at these ruins, you can see how Roman Barcino was about 10 feet lower than today's street level. For more on this city's Roman chapter, follow my Barri Gòtic Walk, later.

• *Return to the Ramblas and continue 100 yards or so to the next street, Carrer de la Portaferrissa (across from the big church). Turn left a few steps and look right to see the* **decorative tile** *over a fountain still in use by locals. The scene shows the original city wall with the gate that once stood here and the action on what is today's Ramblas. Study the merchants and their wares. Now cross the boulevard to the front of the big church.*

## ❹ Betlem Church

This imposing church is dedicated to Bethlehem, and for centuries locals have flocked here at Christmastime to see Nativity scenes.

The church is 17th-century Baroque: Check out the sloping roofline, ball-topped pinnacles, corkscrew columns, and scrolls above the entrance. The Baroque and also Renaissance styles are relatively unusual in Barcelona because it missed out on several centuries of architectural development. Barcelona enjoyed two heydays: during the medieval period (before the Renaissance) and during the turn of the 20th century (after Baroque). In between those periods, from about 1500 until 1850, the city's importance dropped—first, New World discoveries shifted lucrative trade to ports on the Atlantic, and then the Spanish crown kept unruly Catalunya on a short leash. The church interior is stark—having been burnt during the civil war back in the 1930s.

For a sweet treat, head around to the narrow lane on the far side of the church (running parallel to the Ramblas) to the recommended **Café Granja Viader,** which has specialized in baked and dairy delights since 1870. Step inside to see Viader family photos and early posters advertising Cacaolat—the local chocolate milk Barcelonans love.

• *Continue down the boulevard, through the stretch called the...*

## ❺ Rambla of Flowers

This colorful block, until recent years lined with a lot more flower stands, is the Rambla of Flowers.

Besides admiring the blossoms on display, gardeners will covet the seeds sold here for varieties of radishes, greens, peppers, and beans seldom seen in the US—including the iconic green Padrón pepper of tapas fame (if you buy seeds, you're obligated to declare them at US customs when returning home).

On the left, at #100, **Tabacs Gimeno** has been selling cigars since the 1920s. Step inside and appreciate the dying art of cigar boxes. Go ahead, buy a Cuban (little singles for €1). Tobacco shops sell stamps and phone cards, plus bongs and marijuana gear—the Spanish approach to pot is very casual. While people can't legally sell marijuana, they're allowed to grow it for personal use and consume it.

If you'll want to visit Casa Lleó Morera later on (described on page 55), you can buy the advance, required tickets at the **cultural center** in Palau de la Virreina at Ramblas 99, on your right (easier to buy here than at the actual sight).

• *Across the street (opposite the Erotic Museum) is the arcaded entrance to Barcelona's great covered market, La Boqueria.*

## ❻ La Boqueria Market

This lively market hall is an explosion of chicken legs, bags of live snails, stiff fish, delicious oranges, and odd odors. The best day for

a visit is Saturday, when the market is thriving. It's closed on Sundays.

Since as far back as 1200, Barcelonans have bought their animal parts here. The market was originally located just outside the walled city's entrance, as many medieval markets were (since it was more expensive to trade within the walls). It later expanded into the colonnaded courtyard of a now-gone monastery before being covered with a colorful arcade in 1850.

While tourists are drawn to the area around the main entry, locals know that the stalls up front pay the highest rent—and therefore inflate their prices and cater to out-of-towners. For example, the juices along the main drag just inside the entrance are

tempting, but if you venture to the right a couple of aisles, the clientele gets more local and the prices drop dramatically.

Stop in at the **Pinotxo Bar**—it's just inside the market, under the sign—and snap a photo of Juan. Animated Juan and his family are always

busy feeding shoppers. Getting Juan to crack a huge smile and a thumbs-up for your camera makes a great shot...and he loves it. The stools nearby are a fine perch for enjoying both your coffee and the people-watching.

The market and adjacent lanes are busy with tempting little eateries (several are listed on page 188). Drop by a café for an *espresso con leche* or breakfast *tortilla española* (potato omelet). Once you get past the initial gauntlet, do some exploring. The small square on the north (uphill) side of the market hosts a farmers market in the mornings. Wander around—as local architect Antoni Gaudí used to—and gain inspiration. Go on a scavenger hunt for some of these items:

**Produce stands** show off seasonal fruits and vegetables that you'll see on local menus. ("Market cuisine" is big at Barcelona restaurants—chefs come to markets like this each morning to rustle up ingredients.) The tubs of little green peppers that look like jalapeños are lightly fried for the dish called *pimientos de Padrón*. In a culinary form of Russian roulette, a few of these mild peppers sometimes turn out to be hot—greeting the eater with a  fiery jolt. In the fall, you'll see lots of mushrooms; in the winter, artichokes.

Full legs of *jamón* (ham) abound. The many varieties of *jamón serrano* are distinguished by the type of pig they come from and what that pig ate. Top quality are *ibérico* (Iberian type) and *bellota* (acorn eaters)—even by the slice these are very expensive, but gourmets pay €200 or more to go whole hock (see the "Sampling *Jamón*" sidebar on page 283).

You'll see many types of the Catalan specialty sausage *botifarra*. Some can be eaten as-is, while others must be cooked. You'll also find *chorizo*, the red Spanish sausage that's sometimes spicy (a rare bit of heat in an otherwise tame cuisine). Also keep an eye out for a few meats that are uncommon in American dishes—rabbit and suckling pig. Beware: *Huevos de toro* means bull testicles—surprisingly inexpensive...and oh so good.

The **fishmonger** stalls could double as a marine biology lab; in this Mediterranean city, people have come up with endless ways to harvest the sea. Notice that fish is sold whole, not filleted—local shoppers like to look their dinner in the eye to be sure it's fresh. Count the many different types of shrimp (*gamba, langostino*, clawed *cigala*). One of the weirdest Spanish edibles is the tubular razor clam *(navaja)*, with something oozing out of each end.

Some stalls specialize in dried **salt cod** *(bacalao)*. Historically, codfish—preserved in salt and dried—provided desperately needed protein on long sea voyages and was critical in allowing seafaring cultures like that of Catalunya to venture farther from their home ports. Before it can be eaten, salt cod must be rehydrated. Fish stalls sell it either covered in salt or submerged in water, to hasten the time between market and plate.

Certain food items are associated with a particular town—for example, anchovies from L'Escala, shrimp from Palamos, and so on. Among Catalans, this is a sort of code designating quality (like "Idaho potatoes" or "Washington apples" in the US).

Olives are a keystone of the Spanish diet. Take a look at the 25 kinds offered at Graus Olives i Conserves shop (straight in, near the back).

• *Head back out to the street and continue down the Ramblas.*

You're skirting the western boundary of the old Barri Gòtic neighborhood. As you walk, glance to the left through a modern cutaway arch for a glimpse of the medieval church tower of **Santa Maria del Pi,** a popular venue for guitar concerts (see the Nightlife in Barcelona chapter). This also marks Plaça del Pi and a great shopping street, Carrer Petritxol, which runs parallel to the Ramblas (see the Shopping in Barcelona chapter).

Now look across to the other side of the Ramblas. At the corner, find the highly regarded **Escribà** bakery, with its fine Modernista facade and interior (look for the *Antigua Casa Figueras* sign arching over the doorway). Notice the beautiful mosaics of twining plants, the stained-glass peacock displaying his tail feathers, and the undulating woodwork. In the sidewalk in front of the door, a plaque dates the building to 1902 (plaques like this identify historic shops all over town).

• *After another block, you reach the Liceu Metro station, marking the...*

## ❼ Heart of the Ramblas

At the Liceu Metro station's elevators, the Ramblas widens a bit into a small, lively square (Plaça de la Boqueria). Liceu marks the

midpoint of the Ramblas, halfway between Plaça de Catalunya and the waterfront.

Underfoot in the center of the Ramblas, find the much-trod-upon red-white-yellow-and-blue **mosaic** by abstract artist Joan Miró, a local boy who was born and grew up right here in the Gothic Quarter. The mosaic's black arrow represents an anchor, a reminder of the city's attachment to the ocean and a welcome to visitors arriving by sea (one of three Miró works welcoming visitors: There's also a mural at the airport and a sculpture at Sants train station). Miró's simple, colorful designs are found all over the city, from murals to mobiles to the La Caixa bank logo. The best place to see his work is in the Fundació Joan Miró at Montjuïc (see page 65).

The surrounding buildings have playful ornamentation typical of the city. The **Chinese dragon** holding a lantern (at #82) deco-

rates a former umbrella shop (notice the fun umbrella mosaics high up). While the dragon may seem purely decorative, it's actually an important symbol of Catalan pride for its connection to the local patron saint, St. George (Jordi).

Hungry? Swing around the back of the umbrella shop to the recommended **Taverna Basca Irati** tapas bar (a block up Carrer del Cardenal Casanyes). This is one of many user-friendly, Basque-style tapas bars in town; instead of ordering, you can just grab or point to what looks good on the display platters, then pay per piece.

Back on the Ramblas, a few steps down (on the right) is the **Liceu Opera House** (Gran Teatre del Liceu), which hosts world-class opera, dance, and theater (box office around the right side, open Mon-Fri 9:30-20:00). Opposite the opera house is Café de l'Opera (#74), an elegant stop for an expensive beverage. This bustling café, with Modernista decor and a historic atmosphere, boasts that it's been open since 1929, even during the Spanish Civil War.

• *We've seen the best stretch of the Ramblas; to cut this walk short, you could catch the Metro back to Plaça de Catalunya. Otherwise, let's continue to the port. The wide, straight street in another 30 yards (Carrer de Ferran) leads left to Plaça de Sant Jaume, the government center. Enjoy the view (even though flanked by KFC and McDonald's) of elegant lamps, facades, and balconies as it leads to the capital of Catalunya.*

*Head down the Ramblas another 50 yards (to #46), and turn left down an arcaded lane (Carrer de Colom) to the square called...*

## ❽ Plaça Reial

Dotted with palm trees, surrounded by an arcade, and ringed by yellow buildings with white Neoclassical trim, this elegant square has a colonial ambience. It comes complete with old-fashioned taverns, modern bars with patio seating, and a Sunday coin-and-stamp market (10:00-14:00). Completing the picture are Gaudí's first public works (the two colorful helmeted lampposts). While this used to be a seedy and dangerous part of town, recent gentrification efforts have given it new life, making it inviting and accessible. (The small streets stretching toward the water from the square remain a bit sketchier.) It's a lively hangout by day or by night (for nightlife options, see page 221). Big spaces like this (as well as the site of La Boqueria Market) often originated as monasteries. When these were dissolved in the 19th century and the government confiscated the land for secular usage, their fine colonnaded squares were incorporated into useful public spaces. To just relax over a drink and enjoy the scene, the **Ocaña cocktail bar** is a good bet.

• *Head back out to the Ramblas.*

Across the boulevard, a half-block detour down Carrer Nou de la Rambla brings you to **Palau Güell,** designed by Antoni Gaudí (on the left, at #3). Even from the outside, you get a sense of this innovative apartment, the first of Gaudí's Modernista buildings. As this is early Gaudí (built 1886-1890), it's darker and more Neo-Gothic than his more famous later work. The two parabolic-arch doorways and elaborate wrought-iron work signal his emerging nonlinear style. Completely restored in 2011, Palau Güell offers an informative look at a Gaudí interior (see listing on page 37).

• *Proceed along the Ramblas.*

## ❾ Raval Neighborhood

The neighborhood on the right-hand side of this stretch of the Ramblas is El Raval. Its nickname was Barri Xines—the world's only Chinatown with nothing even remotely Chinese in or near it. Named for the prejudiced notion that Chinese immigrants went hand-in-hand with poverty, prostitution, and drug dealing, the neighborhood's actual inhabitants were poor Spanish, North African, and Roma (Gypsy) people. At night, the Barri Xines was frequented by prostitutes, many of them transvestites, who catered to sailors wandering up from the port. Today, it's becoming gentrified, but it's still a pretty rough neighborhood.

At about this part of the Ramblas, you may see the first of the drag's surreal and goofy **human statues.** These performers—with creative and elaborate costumes—must audition and register with the city government. To enliven your Ramblas ramble, stroll with a pocketful of small change. As you wander downhill, drop coins into their cans (the money often kicks the statues into entertaining gear). Warning: Wherever people stop to gawk, pickpockets are at work.

All along the Ramblas you'll find *mantas,* sheets stretched out on the sidewalk with knockoffs of designer goods for sale. While police are supposed to run these vendors off and confiscate their merchandise, enforcement is lenient. It's almost a game: Police officers arrive, and vendors yank up on strings attached to the four corners of their sheets, bundling their wares as they scatter. The police leave, and the vendors return.

Near the bottom of the Ramblas, take note of the Drassanes Metro stop, which can take you back to Plaça de Catalunya when this walk is over. The skyscraper to the right of the Ramblas is the Edificio Colón. When built in 1970, the 28-story structure was Barcelona's first high-rise. Near the skyscraper is the Maritime Museum, housed in what were the city's giant medieval shipyards (see listing on page 41).

• *Up ahead is the...*

## ⑩ Columbus Monument

The 200-foot **column** honors Christopher Columbus, who came

to Barcelona in 1493 after journeying to America. This Catalan answer to Nelson's Column on London's Trafalgar Square (right down to the lions, perfect for posing with at the base) was erected for the 1888 Universal Exposition, an international fair that helped vault a surging Barcelona onto the world stage.

The base of the monument, ringed with four winged victories (taking flight to the four corners of the earth), is loaded with symbolism: statues and reliefs of mapmakers, navigators, early explorers preaching to subservient Native Americans, and (enthroned just below the winged victories) the four regions of Spain. The reliefs near the bottom illustrate scenes from Columbus' fateful voyage. It's ironic that Barcelona celebrates this explorer; the discoveries of Columbus started 300 years of decline for the city, as Europe

began to face West (the Atlantic and the New World) rather than East (the Mediterranean and the Orient). Within a few decades of Columbus, Barcelona had become a depressed backwater, and didn't rebound until events like the 1888 Expo cemented its status as a comeback city. A tiny elevator ascends to the top of the monument, lifting visitors to an observation area for fine panoramas over the city (entrance/ticket desk in TI inside the base of the monument; see page 21 for details).

• *Scoot across the busy traffic circle to survey the...*

## ⓫ Waterfront

Stand on the boardwalk (between the modern bridge and the kiosks selling harbor cruises), and survey Barcelona's bustling maritime zone. Although the city is one of Europe's top 10 ports, with

many busy industrial harbors and several cruise terminals, this low-impact stretch of seafront is clean, fresh, and people-friendly.

As you face the water, the frilly yellow building to your left is the fanciful Modernista-style port-authority

building. The wooden pedestrian **bridge** jutting straight out into the harbor is a modern extension of the Ramblas. Called La Rambla de Mar ("Rambla of the Sea"), the bridge swings out to allow boat traffic into the marina; when closed, the footpath leads to an entertainment and shopping complex. Just to your right are the *golondrinas* **harbor cruise** boats (for details, see page 44).

• *Turn left and walk 100 yards along the promenade between the port authority and the harbor.*

This delightful promenade is part of Barcelona's **Old Port** (Port Vell), stretching from the Columbus Monument to the Barceloneta neighborhood. The port's pleasant sailboat marina is completely enclosed by La Rambla del Mar's shopping and entertainment zone (notice that La Rambla del Mar connects back around to the mainland at the far end of the port, creating a handy pedestrian loop). Its attractions include the Maremagnum shopping mall, an IMAX cinema, a huge aquarium, restaurants, and piles of people. Late at night, it's a rollicking youth hangout. Along the promenade is a permanently moored historic schooner, the *Santa Eulàlia* (part of the Maritime Museum—see page 41).

Imagine: A little more than two decades ago, this was a gloomy, depressed warehouse zone. But to spiff up its front door for the 1992 Olympics, city leaders refurbished the port area, routing a busy highway underground to create this fine walkway sprinkled with palm trees and eye-pleasing public art. On a sunny day, it's fun to walk the length of the promenade to the iconic *Barcelona Head* sculpture (by American Pop artist Roy Lichtenstein, not quite visible from here), which puts you right at the edge of El Born, one of the city's most enjoyable shopping and restaurant areas. (For details, ◻ see the El Born Walk chapter.)

From here, you can also pick out some of Barcelona's more distant charms. The triangular spit of land across the harbor is **Barceloneta.** This densely populated community was custom-built to house fishermen and sailors whose traditional neighborhood in El Born was razed so Philip V could build a military citadel there in the 18th century. Today's Barceloneta is a little gritty but charming, popular for its relatively low real-estate prices (given its handy proximity to the town center) and its easy access to a gorgeous and inviting stretch of broad, sandy beaches (on the other side of the Barceloneta peninsula). From Barceloneta, beaches and boardwalks lead all the way to the modern Fòrum development (see page 77).

Looking back toward the Columbus Monument, you'll see in the distance the majestic, 570-foot bluff of **Montjuïc,** a parklike setting dotted with a number of sights and museums (see page 60; to get there, ride the Metro from Drassanes one stop to the Paral-lel stop, then take the funicular or bus up).

• *Your ramble is over. If it's a nice day, consider strolling the harborfront promenade and looping back around on La Rambla del Mar, dipping into El Born, or walking through Barceloneta to the beach.*

*To get to other points in town, your best bet is to backtrack to the Drassanes Metro stop, at the bottom of the Ramblas. Alternatively, you can catch bus #59 from along the top of the promenade back to Plaça de Catalunya, or hop in a cab.*

# BARRI GÒTIC WALK

*From Plaça de Catalunya to
Plaça del Rei*

Barcelona's Barri Gòtic (Gothic Quarter) is a bustling world of shops, bars, and nightlife packed into narrow, winding lanes and undiscovered courtyards. This is Barcelona's birthplace—where the ancient Romans built a city, where medieval Christians built their cathedral, where Jews gathered together, and where Barcelonans lived within a ring of protective walls until the 1850s, when the city expanded.

Today, this area of atmospheric tight lanes—nicknamed simply "El Gòtic"—is Barcelona's most historic neighborhood. It's a tangled-yet-inviting grab bag of grand squares, schoolyards, Art Nouveau storefronts, musty junk shops, classy antique shops (especially along Carrer de la Palla), street musicians strumming Catalan folk songs, and balconies with domestic jungles behind wrought-iron bars.

Treat this self-guided walk from Plaça de Catalunya to Plaça del Rei as a historical scavenger hunt. You'll focus on the earliest chunk of Roman Barcelona, right around the cathedral, and explore some legacy sights from the city's medieval era. For a more contemporary flavor, explore the shopping streets nearby (see page 211) or head to El Born 📖 (see the El Born Walk chapter).

## Orientation

**Length of This Walk:** Figure 1.5 hours, not including entering sights such as the cathedral.

**When to Go:** To visit the cathedral when admission is free, take this walk in the morning or late afternoon. If you plan to enter the museums mentioned on this walk, avoid Monday, when some sights are closed.

**Getting There:** Start at the southeast corner of the Plaça de Catalunya (Metro: Plaça de Catalunya).

**Church of Santa Anna:** €2, usually Mon-Sat 11:00-14:00 & 16:00-19:00, Sun 11:00-13:00, Plazoleta de Santa Anna.

**Cathedral of Barcelona:** Generally free except in afternoon (€7 to enter Mon-Sat 13:00-17:00, Sun 14:00-17:00), open Mon-Fri 8:00-19:30, Sat-Sun 8:00-20:00, Plaça de la Seu. (For details, see the Cathedral Tour chapter.)

**Old Main Synagogue:** €2.50, Mon-Fri 10:30-18:30, Sat-Sun 10:30-15:00, shorter hours off-season, Carrer Marlet 5, tel. 933-170-790, www.calldebarcelona.org.

**Roman Temple of Augustus:** Free, daily 10:00-19:00 except Mon until 14:00, Carrer del Paradís 10.

**Barcelona History Museum:** €7, Tue-Sat 10:00-19:00, Sun 10:00-20:00, closed Mon, off Plaça del Rei.

**Tours:** ∩ My free Barcelona City Walk audio tour covers the Barri Gòtic.

**Eating:** For restaurants and tapas bars along the way, see page 190.

# The Walk Begins

• *Start on Barcelona's grand main square,* **Plaça de Catalunya** *(described on page 79 of The Ramblas Ramble chapter). From the northeast corner (between the giant El Corte Inglés department store and the Banco de España), head down the broad pedestrian boulevard called...*

## ❶ Avinguda del Portal de l'Angel

For much of Barcelona's history, this was a major city gate. A medieval wall enclosed the city, and there was an entrance here—the "Gate of the Angel" that gives the street its name. An angel statue atop the gate purportedly kept the city safe from plagues and bid voyagers safe journey as they left the security of the city. Imagine the fascinating scene here at the Gate of the Angel, where Barcelona stopped and the Iberian wilds began.

Much later, this same boulevard (and much of the city) got a facelift in preparation for the 1888 Universal Exposition, the first international fair held in Spain. (The same event prompted the construction of the Columbus Monument at the bottom of the Ramblas.) The improvements to the Gate of the Angel are a good example of Barcelona's habit of spiffing itself up for big events. The city dressed up for another exposition in 1929 (Plaça d'Espanya fairgrounds) and again for the 1992 Olympic Games (sports facilities on Montjuïc and rejuvenated waterfront).

Picture the traffic congestion here in the 1980s, before this street was closed to most motorized vehicles (if you visit in the morning you'll still dodge the many delivery trucks supplying this street's Spanish and international chains). Today, you're elbow to elbow with shoppers cruising through some of the most expensive retail space in town. You'll notice branches of Zara, Oysho, Bershka, and Massimo Dutti, all owned by the same man (Amancio Ortega Gaona, the third-richest person in the world, according to locals). He gets the best locations for his shops, each targeted to a different market segment (for a rundown, see page 215 in the Shopping in Barcelona chapter).

Although today this street has been globalized and sanitized, a handful of businesses with local roots survive. On the right at the first corner (at #25), a green sign and particularly appetizing display window mark **Planelles Donat**—long appreciated for its ice cream, sweet *turró* (or *turrón*, almond-and-honey candy), refreshing *orxata* (or *horchata*, almond-flavored drink), and *granissat* (or *granizado*, ice slush). Imagine how historic shops like this one started, with artisans from villages camping out here in a vestibule of some big building, selling baskets of their homemade goodies—and eventually evolving into real shops. Planelles Donat's *turrón*

originated in the town of Xixona, in the coastal Alicante province.

• *A block farther down, pause at Carrer de Santa Anna to admire the Art Nouveau awning at another* **El Corte Inglés** *department store. From here, take a half-block detour to the right on Carrer de Santa Anna. At #32 go through a large entryway to a pleasant, flower-fragrant courtyard of the...*

## ❷ Church of Santa Anna

This 12th-century gem was an *extra muro* ("outside the walls") church; look for its marker cross still standing outside. This austere Catalan Gothic church was part of a convent. It has a fine cloister—an arcaded walkway around a leafy courtyard (viewable to the left of the church). Climb the modern stairs across from the church for views of the bell tower. Inside the church you'll find a bare Romanesque interior and Greek-cross floor plan, topped with an octagonal wooden roof. At

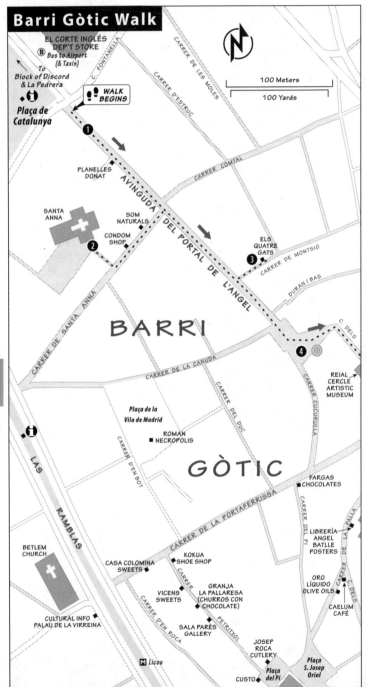

# Barri Gòtic Walk

EL CORTE INGLÉS DEP'T STORE
B Bus to Airport (& Taxis)

To Block of Discord & La Pedrera

Plaça de Catalunya

WALK BEGINS

CARRER DE LES MOLES

CARRER D'ESTRUC

C. FONTANELLA

100 Meters
100 Yards

PLANELLES DONAT

AVINGUDA DEL PORTAL DE L'ANGEL

CARRER COMTAL

SANTA ANNA

SOM NATURALS

CONDOM SHOP

ELS QUATRE GATS

CARRER DE MONTSIÓ

DURAN I BAS

CARRER DE SANTA ANNA

BARRI

CARRER DE LA CANUDA

C. DELS

REIAL CERCLE ARTISTIC MUSEUM

CARRER DEL DUC

Plaça de la Vila de Madrid

ROMÁN NECROPOLIS

GÒTIC

CARRER D'EN BOT

CARRER CUCURULLA

FARGAS CHOCOLATES

CARRER DE LA PORTAFERRISSA

LAS RAMBLAS

BETLEM CHURCH

CASA COLOMINA SWEETS

KOKUA SHOE SHOP

CARRER DEL PI

LIBRERÍA ANGEL BATLLE POSTERS

CARRER DE LA PALLA

ORO LÍQUIDO OLIVE OILS

VICENS SWEETS

GRANJA LA PALLARESA (CHURROS CON CHOCOLATE)

CAELUM CAFÉ

CULTURAL INFO PALAU DE LA VIRREINA

CARRER D'EN ROCA

SALA PARÉS GALLERY

PETRITXOL

JOSEP ROCA CUTLERY

Plaça S. Josep Oriol

M Liceu

CUSTO

Plaça del Pi

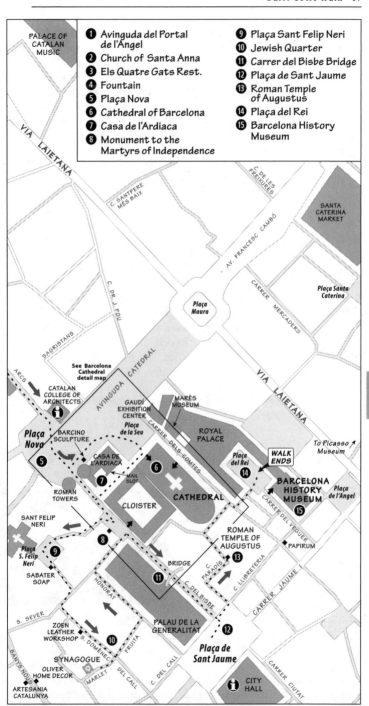

1 Avinguda del Portal de l'Àngel
2 Church of Santa Anna
3 Els Quatre Gats Rest.
4 Fountain
5 Plaça Nova
6 Cathedral of Barcelona
7 Casa de l'Ardiaca
8 Monument to the Martyrs of Independence
9 Plaça Sant Felip Neri
10 Jewish Quarter
11 Carrer del Bisbe Bridge
12 Plaça de Sant Jaume
13 Roman Temple of Augustus
14 Plaça del Rei
15 Barcelona History Museum

PALACE OF CATALAN MUSIC

VIA LAIETANA

C. SANTPERE MES BAIX

C. DE LES FREIXURES

SANTA CATERINA MARKET

AV. FRANCESC CAMBÓ

CARRER MERCADERS

Plaça Santa Caterina

Plaça Maura

C. DR. J. POU

SAGRISTANS

ARCS

See Barcelona Cathedral detail map

CATALAN COLLEGE OF ARCHITECTS

AVINGUDA CATEDRAL

GAUDÍ EXHIBITION CENTER
Plaça de la Seu

MARÈS MUSEUM

CARRER DELS COMTES

ROYAL PALACE

VIA LAIETANA

Plaça Nova

BARCINO SCULPTURE

CASA DE L'ARDIACA

MAIL SLOT

6 CATHEDRAL

Plaça del Rei
14

WALK ENDS

To Picasso Museum

BARCELONA HISTORY MUSEUM
15

Plaça de l'Àngel

5

ROMAN TOWERS

7

CLOISTER

SANT FELIP NERI

Plaça S. Felip Neri
9

8

ROMAN TEMPLE OF AUGUSTUS
13

CARRER DEL VEGUER

SABATER SOAP

HONORAT

BRIDGE
11

C. PARADIS

PAPIRUM

C. LLIBRETERIA

S. SEVER

ZOEN LEATHER WORKSHOP

S. DOMENEC

10

PALAU DE LA GENERALITAT

C. DEL BISBE

CARRER JAUME

SYNAGOGUE

FRUITA

12

Plaça de Sant Jaume

BANYS NOUS

OLIVER HOME DECOR

MARLET

DEL CALL

C. DEL CALL

ARTESANIA CATALUNYA

CITY HALL

CARRER CIUTAT

BARRI GÒTIC WALK

the back of the nave, the recumbent-knight tomb is of Miguel de Boera, renowned admiral of Charles V. The door at the far end of the nave leads to the peaceful cloister.

As you head back to the main drag, you'll pass—a few doors down—a **condom shop** on your left. It advertises (to men with ample self-esteem): *Para los pequeños placeres de la vida* ("For the little pleasures in life"). This sign is in Spanish, because the letter *ñ* doesn't exist in Catalan. Instead, Catalans write "ny" for this sound (as in "Catalunya"—which elsewhere in Spain is written "Cataluña").

Spain (especially its feisty nations without states—Catalunya and the Basque country) was kept in a moralistic time-warp under the extremely conservative dictator Francisco Franco, who ruled from 1939 to 1975. In the generation since the country won its freedom, the major Catholic issues (contraception, abortion, divorce, cohabitation, and so on) have swung to the liberal extreme.

Take a moment here on Carrer de Santa Anna to look around and notice little details. Look up at pulleys (handy in buildings with no elevators), and note the ironwork, ugly buildings with fine old entrances, cheaper facades with plasterwork showing fake columns, and how the buildings all maxed out on their late-19th-century height limits. Here (and around town), you may see the *estelada* flag—red-and-gold with a blue triangle and white star—a symbol of Catalan separatists (see page 6 for more about Catalunya vs. Spain).

• *Backtrack to Avinguda Portal de l'Angel. At Carrer de Montsió (on the left), opposite the Zara store, side-trip half a block to...*

## ❸ Els Quatre Gats

This restaurant (at #3) is a historic monument, tourist attraction, nightspot, and recommended eatery. It's famous for being the circa-1900 bohemian-artist hangout where Picasso nursed drinks with friends and had his first one-man show (in 1900). The building itself, by prominent architect Josep Puig i Cadafalch, represents Neo-Gothic Modernisme. Stepping inside, you feel the turn-of-the-century vibe. Rich Barcelona elites and would-be avant-garde artists looked to Paris, not Madrid, for cultural inspiration. Consequently, this place was clearly inspired by the Paris scene (especially Le Chat Noir cabaret/café, the hangout of Montmartre intellectuals). Like Le Chat Noir, Els Quatre Gats even published its own artsy magazine for a while. The story of the name? When the proprietor told his friends that he'd stay open 24 hours a day, they said, "No one will come. It'll just be you and four cats" (Catalan slang for "just a few people"). While you can have a snack, meal, or drink here, you're also welcome to pop in, check out the circa-1900 photos on the wall, and take a quick look around (ask *"Solo mirar, por favor?"*).

• *Return to and continue down Avinguda del Portal de l'Àngel. You'll soon reach a fork in the road and a building with a...*

## ❹ Fountain

The blue-and-yellow tilework, a circa-1918 addition to this even-older fountain, depicts ladies carrying jugs of water. In the 17th

century, this was the last watering stop for horses before leaving town. As recently as 1940, about 10 percent of Barcelonans still got their water from fountains like this.

• *Shoppers will feel the pull of wonderful little shops down the street to the right. But be strong and take the left fork, down Carrer dels Arcs.*

Just past the corner, you'll pass the **Reial Cercle Artistic Museum,** a private collection of Dalí's work—sculptures, prints, and several hundred lithographs—that'll curl the moustaches of Surrealism fans. Don't miss the additional artwork in smaller rooms behind the red curtains (€10, daily 10:00-22:00).

• *Enter the large square called...*

## ❺ Plaça Nova

Two bold **Roman towers** flank the main street. These once guarded the entrance gate of the ancient Roman city of Barcino. The big stones that make up the base of the (reconstructed) towers are actually Roman. Near the base of the left tower, **modern bronze letters** spell out "BARCINO." The city's name may have come from Barca, one of Hannibal's generals, who is said to have passed through during Hannibal's roundabout invasion of Italy. At Barcino's peak, the **Roman wall** (see the section stretching to the left of the towers) was 25 feet high and a mile around, with 74 towers. It enclosed a population of 4,000.

One of the towers has a bit of

reconstructed **Roman aqueduct** (notice the streambed on top). In ancient times, bridges of stone carried fresh water from the distant hillsides into the walled city.

Opposite the towers is the modern **Catalan College of Architects** building (Collegi d'Arquitectes de Barcelona, TI inside), which is, ironically for a city with so much great architecture, quite ugly. The frieze was designed by Picasso (1962) in his distinctive simplified style, showing (on three sides) Catalan traditions: shipping, music, the *sardana* dance, bullfighting, and branch-waving kings and children celebrating a local festival. Picasso

spent his formative years (1895-1904, age 14-23) here in the old town. He drank with fellow bohemians at Els Quatre Gats (which we just passed) and frequented brothels a few blocks from here on Carrer d'Avinyó ("Avignon")—which inspired his influential Cubist painting *Les Demoiselles d'Avignon*. Picasso's hunger to be on the cutting edge propelled him from the Barri Gòtic to Paris, where he eventually remade modern art.

• *Immediately to the left as you face the Picasso frieze,* **Carrer de la Palla** *is an inviting shopping street (and the starting point of my "Barri Gòtic Shopping Walk"; see page 211). But let's head left through Plaça Nova and take in the mighty facade of the...*

## ❻ Cathedral of Barcelona

While this location has been a center of Christian worship since the 4th century, what you see today dates (mainly) from the 14th century, with a 19th-century Neo-Gothic facade. The facade is a virtual catalog of Gothic motifs: a pointed arch over the entrance, robed statues, tracery in windows, gargoyles, and bell towers with winged angels. This Gothic variation is called French Flamboyant (meaning "flame-like"), and the roofline sports the prickly spires meant to give the impression of a church flickering with spiritual fires. The area in front of the cathedral is where Barcelonans dance the *sardana* (see page 45).

The cathedral's interior—with its vast size, peaceful cloister, and many ornate chapels—is worth a visit (□ see the Cathedral of Barcelona Tour chapter). If you interrupt this tour to visit the cathedral now, you'll exit the cloister a block down Carrer del Bisbe. From there you can circle back to the right, following the wall of the cathedral to visit stop #7—or skip #7 and step directly into stop #8.

• *As you stand in the square facing the cathedral, look far to your left to see the multicolored, wavy canopy marking the roofline of the **Santa Caterina Market**. The busy street between here and the market—called Via Laietana—is the boundary between the Barri Gòtic and the funkier, edgier **El Born** neighborhood. (My El Born Walk starts at the Santa Caterina Market; see page 119.)*

> *For now, return to the Roman towers. Pass between the towers to head up Carrer del Bisbe, and take an immediate left, up the ramp to the entrance of...*

## ❼ Casa de l'Ardiaca

It's free to enter this mansion, which was once the archdeacon's residence and now functions as the city archives. The elaborately carved doorway is Renaissance.

To the right of the doorway is a carved mail slot by 19th-century Modernista architect Lluís Domènech i Montaner. Enter a small courtyard with a fountain. Notice how the century-old palm tree seems to be held captive by urban man.

Next, step inside the air-conditioned lobby of the city archives, where—along the back of the ancient Roman wall—there are often free temporary exhibits. At the left end of the lobby, go through the archway and look down into the stairwell for a peek at more impressive Roman stonework. Back in the courtyard, climb to the balcony for views of the cathedral steeple and gargoyles. From this vantage point, note the small Romanesque chapel on the right (the only surviving 13th-century bit of the cathedral) and how it's dwarfed by the towering cathedral.

• *Return to Carrer del Bisbe and turn left. After a few steps, you reach a small square with a bronze statue ensemble.*

## ❽ Monument to the Martyrs of Independence

Five Barcelona patriots—including two priests—calmly receive their last rites before being garroted (strangled) for resisting Napoleon's occupation of Spain in the early 19th century. They'd been outraged by French atrocities in Madrid (depicted in Goya's famous *Third of May* painting in Madrid's Prado Museum). According to the plaque marking their mortal remains, these martyrs to independence gave their lives in 1809 *"por Dios, por la Patria, y por el Rey"*—for God, country, and king.

Tiles flanking the monument tell the story: On the far left, the patriots receive their last communion in prison. On the near left, they're escorted out of the citadel—that hated symbol of foreign occupation. On the near right is the execution scene. Priests, considered privileged, were strangled, while the common people were hung; see ropes and a ladder on the right above the three doomed men huddled with their priests. (The French last used the guillotine in 1977, and Spain last used the garrote in 1974. Europe is generally appalled that the US still executes people.) All the martyrs are buried across the way in the cathedral cloister.

The plaza offers interesting views of the cathedral's towers. Opposite the square is the "back door" entrance to the cathedral (through the cloister; relatively uncrowded and open during hours when the church is free).

• *Exit the square down tiny Carrer de Montjuïc del Bisbe (to the right as you face the martyrs). This leads to the cute...*

## ❾ Plaça Sant Felip Neri

This shaded square serves as the playground of an elementary school and is often bursting with energetic kids speaking Catalan (just a couple of generations ago, this would have been illegal and they would be speaking Spanish). The Church of Sant Felip Neri, which Gaudí attended, is still pocked with bomb damage from the Spanish Civil War. As a stronghold of democratic, anti-Franco forces, Barcelona saw a lot of fighting. The shrapnel that damaged this church was meant for the nearby Catalan government building (Palau de la Generalitat, which we'll see later on this walk).

Just as the Germans practiced their new air force technology in Guernica in the years leading up to World War II, the fascist friends of Franco (both German and Italian) also helped bomb Barcelona from the air. As was the fascist tactic, a second·bombing followed the first as survivors combed the rubble for lost loved ones. A plaque on the wall (left of church door) honors the 42 killed—mostly children—in that 1938 aerial bombardment.

In the medieval tangle of the Barri Gòtic, people gathered densely within the city's protective walls, leaving very few open spaces—except for cemeteries clustering around churches. Many squares, like this one, started out as cemeteries. They later became open spaces when, with the Enlightenment (c. 1800) and modern concern for hygiene, graveyards were moved outside of town.

The buildings here were paid for by the guilds that powered the local economy (notice the carved reliefs high above). On the corner where you entered the square, look for shoe reliefs above the windows—this is the former home of the shoemakers' guild. Also fronting the square is the fun **Sabater Hermanos** artisanal soap shop (see page 213).

• *Exit the square down Carrer de Sant Felip Neri. At the T-intersection, turn right onto Carrer de Sant Sever, then immediately left on Carrer de Sant Domènec del Call (look for the blue* El Call *sign). You've entered the...*

## ❿ Jewish Quarter (El Call)

In Catalan, a Jewish quarter goes by the name El Call—literally "narrow passage," for the tight lanes where medieval Jews were forced to live, under the watchful eye of the nearby cathedral. (Or some believe El Call comes from the Hebrew *kahal*, which means congregation.) At the peak of Barcelona's El Call, some 4,000 Jews were crammed into just a few alleys in this neighborhood.

Walk down Carrer de Sant Domènec del Call, passing the Zoen leather workshop and showroom, where everything is made on the spot (may be closed). Pass through the charming little square (a gap in the dense tangle of medieval buildings cleared by another civil war bomb), where you will find a rust-colored sign displaying a map of the Jewish Quarter. Take the next lane to the right (Carrer de Marlet). On the right is the low-profile entrance to what was likely Barcelona's **main synagogue** during the Middle Ages (Antigua Sinagoga Mayor, €2.50 entry includes a little tour by the attendant if you ask). The structure dates from the third century, but it was destroyed during a brutal pogrom in 1391. The city's remaining Jews were expelled in 1492, and artifacts of their culture—including this synagogue—were forgotten for centuries. In the 1980s, a historian tracked down the synagogue using old tax-collection records. Another clue that this was the main synagogue: In accordance with Jewish traditions, it stubbornly faces east (toward Jerusalem), putting it at an angle at odds with surrounding structures. The sparse interior includes access to two small subterranean rooms with Roman walls topped by a medieval Catalan vault. Look through the glass floor to see dyeing vats used for a later shop on this site (run by former Jews who had been forcibly converted to Christianity).

• *From the synagogue, start back the way you came but then continue straight ahead, onto Carrer de la Fruita. Pause and look around. Imagine the medieval city with carriages banging on the stony corners and these tight lanes filled with life in the shade for all but about 15 minutes a day. At the T-intersection, turn left, then right, to find your way back to the* Martyrs *statue. From here, turn right down Carrer del Bisbe, likely passing a street musician (the city gives permits for quality buskers to perform at set points like this one) to the...*

## ⓫ Carrer del Bisbe Bridge

This structure—reminiscent of Venice's Bridge of Sighs—connects the Catalan government building (on the right) with what was the

Catalan president's ceremonial residence (on the left). Though the bridge looks medieval, it was constructed in the 1920s by Catalan architect Joan Rubió (a follower of Gaudí), who also did the carved ornamentation on the buildings.

Check out the carved decor on the bridge—jutting angels, monsters, skulls, goddesses, old men with beards, climbing vines, and coats of arms. The delicate facade a few steps farther down on the right is much older. It marks the 15th-century entry to the government palace.

• *Continue along Carrer del Bisbe to...*

## ⓬ Plaça de Sant Jaume

This stately central square of the Barri Gòtic takes its name from the Church of St. James (in Catalan: Jaume, JOW-mah) that once stood here. After the church was torn down in 1823, the square was fixed up and rechristened "Plaça de la Constitució" in honor of the then-decade-old Spanish constitution. But the plucky Catalans never embraced the name, and after Franco, they went back to the original title—even though the namesake church is long gone.

Set at the intersection of ancient Barcino's main thoroughfares, this square was once a Roman forum. In that sense, it's been the seat of city government for 2,000 years. Today it's home to the two top governmental buildings in Catalunya: Palau de la Generalitat and, across from it, the Barcelona City Hall.

For more than six centuries, the **Palau de la Generalitat** (to your immediate right as you enter the square) has housed the offices of the autonomous government of Catalunya. It always flies the Catalan flag next to the obligatory Spanish one. Above the building's doorway is Catalunya's patron saint—St. George (Jordi), slaying the dragon. The dragon (which you'll see all over town) is an important Catalan symbol. From these balconies, the nation's leaders (and soccer heroes) greet the people on momentous days. The square is often the site of demonstrations, from a single aggrieved citizen with a megaphone (the phone company billed me twice!) to riotous thousands (demanding independence from Spain, for instance).

Facing the Generalitat across the square is the **Barcelona City Hall** (Casa de la Ciutat). It sports a statue (in the niche to the left

of the door) of a different James—"Jaume el Conqueridor." The 13th-century King Jaume I is credited with freeing Barcelona from French control, granting self-government, and setting it on a course to become a major city. He was the driving force behind construction of the Royal Palace (which we'll see shortly).

Locals treasure the independence these two government buildings represent. In the 20th century, Barcelona opposed the dictator Francisco Franco, and Franco retaliated. He abolished the regional government and (effectively) outlawed the Catalan language and customs. Two years after Franco's death in 1975, joyous citizens packed this square to celebrate the return of self-rule.

Look left and right down the main streets branching off the square; they're lined with ironwork streetlamps and balconies draped with plants. Carrer de Ferran, which leads to the Ramblas, is classic Barcelona.

In ancient Roman days, when Plaça de Sant Jaume was the town's central square, two main streets converged here—the Decumanus (Carrer del Bisbe—bishop's street) and the Cardus (Carrer de la Llibreteria/Carrer del Call). The forum's biggest building was a massive temple of Augustus, which we'll see next.

• *Facing the Generalitat, exit the square going up the second street to the right of the building, on tiny Carrer del Paradís. Follow this street as it turns right. When it swings left, pause at #10, the entrance to the...*

## ⑩ Roman Temple of Augustus

You're standing at the summit of Mont Tàber, the Barri Gòtic's highest spot. A plaque on the wall reads: "Mont Tàber, 16.9 meters" (elevation 55 feet). A millstone inlaid in the pavement at the doorstep of #10 also marks the spot. It was here that the ancient Romans founded the town of Barcino around 15 B.C. They built a *castrum* (fort) on the hilltop, protecting the harbor.

Go inside for a peek at the last vestiges of an imposing Roman temple (Temple Roma d'August). All that's left now are four columns and some fragments of the transept and its plinth (good English info on-site). The huge columns, dating from the late first

century B.C., are as old as Barcelona itself. They were part of the ancient town's biggest structure, a temple dedicated to the Emperor Augustus, who was worshipped as a god. These Corinthian columns (with deep fluting and topped with leafy capitals) were the back corner of a 120z-foot-long temple that extended from here to Barcino's forum.

• *Continue down Carrer del Paradís one block. When you bump into the back end of the cathedral, pause to notice how amazingly well-preserved the cityscape is here—under an assembly of gargoyles and a unicorn. This spot is a popular movie location.*

*Take a right, and go downhill about 100 yards (down Carrer de la Pietat/Baixada de Santa Clara) until you emerge into a square called...*

## ⓮ Plaça del Rei

The buildings enclosing this square exemplify Barcelona's medieval past. The central section (topped by a five-story addition) was the core of the **Royal Palace** (Palau Reial Major). A vast hall on its ground floor once served as the throne room and reception room. From the 13th to the 15th century, the Royal Palace housed Barcelona's counts as well as the resident kings of Aragon. In 1493, a triumphant Christopher Columbus, accompanied by six New World natives (whom he called *"indios"*) and several pure-gold statues, entered the Royal Palace. King Ferdinand and Queen Isabella rose to welcome him home and honored him with the title "Admiral of the Oceans."

To the right is the palace's church, the 14th-century **Chapel of Saint Agatha,** which sits atop the foundations of a Roman wall (entrance included in Barcelona History Museum admission; see page 47.)

To the left is the **Viceroy's Palace** (Palau del Lloctinent, for the ruler's right-hand man). This 16th-century building currently serves as the archives of the Crown of Aragon. After Catalunya became part of Spain in the late 15th century, Toledo became its capital. The Royal Palace was demoted and became a small regional residence, and the Viceroy's Palace became the headquarters of the local Inquisition. Step inside to see the delightful Renaissance courtyard. To the right, gaze up at a staircase and fine coffered wood ceilings. Among the archive's treasures (though it's rarely on display) is the 1492 Santa Fe Capitulations, a contract between Columbus and the monarchs about his upcoming sea voyage. (See the poster of the yellowed document on the wall outside, with an English explanation.) Ironically, Columbus' discovery of new trade routes (abandoning the Mediterranean for the Atlantic) made Barcelona's port less important.

• *Return to the square, go downhill onto Carrer del Veguer, where you'll find the entrance to the...*

## ⑮ Barcelona History Museum

This museum primarily contains objects from archaeological digs around Barcelona. But the real highlight is underground, where

you can examine excavated Roman ruins. For a peek at the Roman streets without going in, look through the low windows lining the street. For details on visiting the museum, see page 47.

• *Your walk is over. It's easy to get your bearings by backtracking to either Plaça de Sant Jaume or the cathedral (where you can follow my "Barri Gòtic Shopping Walk," described on page 211). The Jaume I Metro stop is two blocks away (leave the square on Carrer del Veguer and turn left). From here, you could head over to the Santa Caterina Market to browse for lunch before tackling my ☐ El Born Walk. Or simply wander through more of this area, enjoying Barcelona at its Gothic best.*

BARRI GÒTIC WALK

# CATHEDRAL OF BARCELONA TOUR

Although Barcelona's cathedral doesn't rank among Europe's finest (and frankly, barely cracks the Top 20), it's important, easy to visit, and—most of the time—free to see. This quick tour introduces you to the cathedral's highlights: its vast nave, rich chapels, tomb of Santa Eulàlia, and the oasis-like setting of the cloister. Other sights inside (which have admission fees) are the elaborately carved choir, the elevator up to the view terrace, and the altarpiece museum.

## Orientation

**Cost:** The cathedral is free for worship and visits in both the morning (Mon-Sat before 12:45, Sun before 13:45) and late afternoon (after 17:15), but during those times, you have to pay €3 each to visit the choir or take the elevator to the terrace (the museum is closed during these hours).

The church is open for tourism for several hours in the afternoon (Mon-Sat 13:00-17:00, Sun 14:00-17:00), but you must pay €7 (which covers admission to the choir, terrace, and museum). Paying the afternoon admission can be worthwhile on a crowded day.

**Hours:** Cathedral generally open Mon-Fri 8:00-19:30, Sat-Sun 8:00-20:00. The cathedral's three minor sights are open Mon-Sat (with different hours) and closed Sun: choir (9:00-19:00), terrace (9:00-18:00), museum (12:45-17:15). Both the choir and terrace may close earlier on slow days.

**Dress Code:** The dress code is strictly enforced; don't wear tank tops, shorts, or skirts above the knee.

**Getting There:** The huge, can't-miss-it cathedral is in the center of the Barri Gòtic on Plaça de la Seu (Metro: Jaume I). For an interesting way to reach the cathedral from Plaça de Catalunya, □ see the Barri Gòtic Walk chapter.

**Getting In:** The main, front door is open most of the time. While it can be crowded, the line generally moves fast. You can also enter directly into the cloister (through the door facing the *Martyrs* statue on the small square along Carrer del Bisbe) or through the side door (facing the Frederic Marès Museum along Carrer dels Comtes).

**Information:** Tel. 933-151-554, www.catedralbcn.org.

**Length of This Tour:** Allow 30 minutes, not counting the optional sights (choir, view terrace, museum). With limited time, zip past the many side chapels, but be sure to linger in the cloister.

**Visitor Services:** A tiny WC is in the center of the cloister.

**Photography:** Allowed without a flash.

## BACKGROUND

This has been Barcelona's holiest spot for 2,000 years. The Romans built their Temple of Jupiter here. In A.D. 343, the pagan temple was replaced with a Christian cathedral. That building was supplanted by a Romanesque-style church (11th century). The current Gothic structure was started in 1298 and finished in 1450, during the medieval glory days of the Catalan nation. The facade was humble, so in the 19th century the proud local bourgeoisie (enjoying a second Golden Age) redid it in a more ornate, Neo-Gothic style. Construction was capped in 1913 with the central spire, 230 feet tall.

# The Tour Begins

• *Enter the main door and look up, letting your eyes adjust to the low light. (If you're entering through another door, loop around to start at the rear of the nave.)*

## ❶ The Nave

The spacious church is 300 feet long and 130 feet wide. Tall pillars made of stone blocks support the crisscross vaults. Each round key-

stone where the arches cross features a different saint. Typical of many Spanish churches, there's a choir—an enclosed area of wooden seats in the middle of the nave, creating a more intimate space for worship, and isolating the selected elite who could actually get close to the altar and hear the sermons. The Gothic church also has fine stained glass, ironwork chandeliers, a 16th-century organ

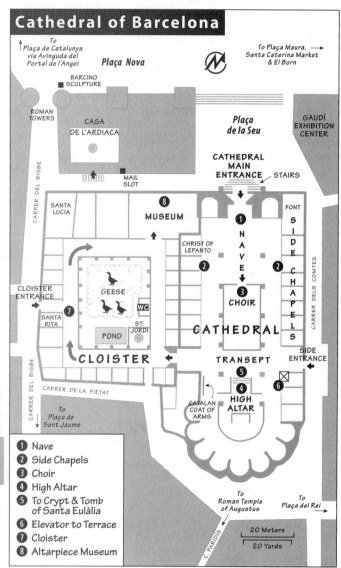

# Cathedral of Barcelona

To Plaça de Catalunya
via Avinguda del
Portal de l'Angel

To Plaça Maura, →
Santa Caterina Market
& El Born

**Plaça Nova**

BARCINO
SCULPTURE

ROMAN
TOWERS

CASA
DE L'ARDIACA

**Plaça
de la Seu**

GAUDÍ
EXHIBITION
CENTER

CARRER DEL BISBE

MAIL
SLOT

**CATHEDRAL
MAIN
ENTRANCE**  STAIRS

SANTA
LUCIA

**❽ MUSEUM**

FONT

**❶
N
A
V
E**

S
I
D
E

C
H
A
P
E
L
S

CHRIST OF
LEPANTO

**❷**

**❷**

CARRER DELS COMTES

CLOISTER
ENTRANCE

**GEESE**

WC

**❸
CHOIR**

SANTA
RITA

**❼**

ST.
JORDI

**CATHEDRAL**

POND

**CLOISTER**

**TRANSEPT**

SIDE
ENTRANCE

CARRER DEL BISBE

CARRER DE LA PIETAT

**❺**

**❻**

To
Plaça de
Sant Jaume

CATALAN
COAT OF
ARMS

**❹
HIGH
ALTAR**

**CATHEDRAL OF BARCELONA**

❶ Nave
❷ Side Chapels
❸ Choir
❹ High Altar
❺ To Crypt & Tomb
   of Santa Eulàlia
❻ Elevator to Terrace
❼ Cloister
❽ Altarpiece Museum

To
Roman Temple
of Augustus

To
Plaça del Rei

20 Meters

20 Yards

C. PARADIS

(left transept), tombstones in the pavement, and an "ambulatory"
floor plan, allowing worshippers to amble around to the chapel of
their choice.

## ❷ Side Chapels

The nave is ringed with 28 chapels. Besides creating worship spaces, the walls defining these chapels serve as interior buttresses sup-

porting the roof (which is why the exterior walls are smooth, without the normal Gothic buttresses outside). Barcelona honors many of the homegrown saints found in these chapels with public holidays.

From the 13th to 15th century, these side chapels were simply moneymakers for the church. After the Black Death ravaged the population—and the economy—the church rented chapels to guilds to function as private offices, which came with the medieval equivalent of safety-deposit boxes and notary public (documents signed here came with the force of God). Notice how the iron gates are more than decorative—they were protective. The rich ornamentation was sponsored by local guilds. Think of it: The church was the community's most high-profile space, and these chapels were a kind of advertising to illiterate worshippers.

The Church is still fund-raising. Candles, which aren't free, power your prayers. As you visit the chapels, employ one or more electronic candles. Pop in a coin and you'll get a candle for every €0.10 you donate. Try it—€0.50 turns on five candles. Or save your coins to light a real candle in the cloister's chapels.

• *We'll walk past a few of these chapels, just to get a sense of them. Begin by heading to the back-left corner (over your left shoulder as you enter the main door).*

The chapel at the back corner of the nave has an old **baptismal font** that once stood in the original fourth-century church. The Native Americans that Columbus brought to town were supposedly baptized here.

• *Work your way down the left aisle.*

The first chapel along the left wall is dedicated to **St. Severus,** the bishop here way back in A.D. 290.

The second chapel was by, for, and of the local **shoe guild.** Notice the two painted doors with shoes above them that lead to the back office. As the patron of shoemakers was St. Mark, there are plenty of winged lions in this chapel.

• *Cross the nave over to the large chapel in the back-right corner and work your way, one chapel at a time, down that side of the church.*

This chapel (reserved for worship) features the beloved **"Christ of Lepanto"** crucifix. They say the angular wooden figure of Christ, which swings to the left, leaned to dodge a cannonball during the history-changing Battle of Lepanto (1571), which stopped the Ottomans (and Islam) from advancing into Europe.

• *Now head down the right aisle.*

The next chapel has a statue of **St. Anthony** holding the Baby Jesus. His feast day (January 17) is one of many celebrated in the city with an appearance by the *gegants* (giant puppets), a street fair, horse races, and a blessing of pets.

The third chapel honors a 20th-century bishop, **San Josep Oriol,** who survived an assassination attempt in the cathedral cloister.

The golden fourth chapel is for **St. Roch** (at the top, pointing to his leg wound, above St. Pancraç), whose feast day is celebrated joyously in the Barri Gòtic in mid-August.

The fifth chapel has a black-and-white sideways statue of **St. Ramon (Raymond) of Penyafort** (1190-1275), the Dominican Bishop of Barcelona who heard Pope Gregory IX's sins and is the patron saint of lawyers (and, therefore, extremely busy). Ramon figures into the city's biggest festival, La Mercè, since he had a miraculous vision of the Virgin of Mercy.

The eighth chapel is worth a look for its over-the-top golden altarpiece decor nearly crowding out **Bishop Pacià**—considered one of the Church fathers (c. A.D. 310-391).

• *To visit the interior of the choir (described next), pay €3 or show your ticket at the choir entrance (straight ahead from the church's main doors). Otherwise, you can circle around to the far end and peer through the barrier.*

## ❸ Choir

The 15th-century choir *(coro)* features ornately carved stalls. During the standing parts of the Mass, the chairs were folded up, but VIPs still had those little wooden ledges to lean on. Each was creatively carved and—since you couldn't sit on sacred things—the artists were free to enjoy some secular and naughty fun here. In 1518, the stalls were painted with the coats of arms of Europe's nobility. They gathered here as members of the Knights of the Golden Fleece  to honor Charles V, King of Spain, who was making his first trip to the country he ruled. Like a proto-United Nations, they also discussed how to work together to defend Europe from the Turkish threat. Check out the detail work on the impressive wood-carved pulpit near the altar, supported by flying angels.

• *At the front of the church stands the...*

## ❹ High Altar

Look behind the altar (beneath the crucifix) to find the bishop's chair, or cathedra. As a cathedral, this church is the bishop's seat—hence its Catalan nickname of *La Seu*. To the left of the altar is the organ and the elevator up to the terrace. To the right of the altar, the wall is decorated with Catalunya's yellow-and-red coat of arms. Under that, the two wooden coffins on the wall are of two powerful Counts of Barcelona (Ramon Berenguer I and his third wife, Almodis), who ordered the construction of the 11th-century

Romanesque cathedral that preceded this structure.

• *Descend the steps beneath the altar, into the crypt, to see the...*

## ❺ Tomb of Santa Eulàlia

The marble-and-alabaster sarcophagus (1327-1339) contains the remains of Santa Eulàlia. The cathedral is dedicated to this saint.

Thirteen-year-old Eulàlia, daughter of a prominent Barcelona family, was martyred by the Romans for her faith in A.D. 304. Murky legends say she was subjected to 13 tortures. First she was stripped naked and had her head shaved, though a miraculous snowfall hid her nakedness. Then she was rolled down the street in a barrel full of sharp objects. After further torments failed to kill her, she was crucified on an X-shaped cross—a symbol you'll find carved into pews and seen throughout the church.

The relief on the coffin's side tells her story in three episodes: she preaches Christianity to the pagan Roman ruler; he orders her to die (while she pleads for mercy); and she's crucified on the X-shaped cross. As one of Barcelona's two patron saints, Eulàlia is honored with a festival (with *gegants*, fireworks, and human towers) in mid-February.

• *The ❻ elevator in the left transept takes you up to the rooftop terrace, made of sturdy scaffolding pieces, for an expansive city view (€3). Otherwise, exit through the right transept to enter the...*

## ❼ Cloister

The cloister's arcaded walkway surrounds a lush circa-1450 courtyard. Ahhhh. It's a tropical atmosphere of palm, orange, and magnolia trees; a fish pond; trickling fountains; and squawking geese.

From within the cloister, look back at the **arch** you just came through, an impressive mix of Romanesque (arches with chevrons, from the earlier church) and Gothic (pointy top).

The nearby **fountain** has a tiny statue of St. Jordi (George) slaying the dragon. Jordi is one of the patron saints of Catalunya and by far the most popular boy's name here. During the Corpus Christi festival in June, kids come here to watch a hollow egg dance atop the fountain's spray.

As you wander the cloister (clockwise), check out the **coats of arms** as well as the **tombs** in the pavement. These were for rich merchants who paid good money to be buried as close to the altar as possible. Notice the symbols of their trades: scissors, shoes, bakers, and so on. The cloister had a practical, economic purpose. The church sold out its chapel space, and this opened up an entire new wing to donors. A second floor was planned (look up) but not finished.

The resident **geese** have been here for at least 500 years. There are always 13, in memory of Eulàlia's 13 years and 13 torments. Other legends say they're white as a symbol of her virginity. Before modern security systems, they acted as alarms. Any commotion would get them honking, alerting the monk in charge. Faithful to tradition, they honk to this very day.

Farther along the cloister, next to the door, the **Chapel of Santa Rita** (patron saint of impossible causes) usually has the most candles. In the next corner of the cloister is the barrel-vaulted **Chapel of Santa Lucía,** a small 13th-century remnant of the earlier Romanesque cathedral. It's quite dark, as churches were before the advent of Gothic style. People hoping for good eyesight (Santa Lucía's specialty) pray here. Notice the nice eyes in the modern restoration of the altar painting.

• *At the far end of the cloister, you'll find the...*

## ❽ Altarpiece Museum (Museu Capitular)

The little museum (entry possible only during paid visiting hours)

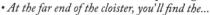

**CATHEDRAL OF BARCELONA**

has the six-foot-tall 14th-century Great Monstrance, a ceremonial display case for the communion wafer. Made of gold and studded with jewels, it's really three separate parts: a church-like central section, topped with a crown canopy, standing on a golden chair. This huge monstrance with its wafer is paraded through the streets during the Corpus Christi festival. Nearby is a gold-plated silver statue of Santa Eulàlia, carrying the X-shaped cross she was crucified on. An 11th-century baptismal font from the Romanesque church is also on view.

The next room, the Sala Capitular, has several altarpieces, including a pietà (*Desplà*) by Bartolomé Bermejo (1490). An anguished Mary cradles a twisted Christ against a bleak, stormy landscape. It's unique in Spanish art for its Italianesque, Renaissance 3-D. Rather than your basic gold backdrop, this has a strong foreground (the mourners), middle distance (the cross), and background (the city and distant hills). The kneeling donors who paid for the painting are photorealistic, complete with reading glasses and five o'clock shadows.

• *Our tour is over. Go in peace.*

CATHEDRAL OF BARCELONA

# EL BORN WALK

*From Via Laietana to the Waterfront*

The neighborhood called El Born (a.k.a. "La Ribera") is bohemian-chic, with funky shops, upscale cafés and wine bars, a colorful market hall, unique boutiques, gritty bars and nightclubs, and one of Barcelona's top museums (exhibiting the early works of Picasso). Anchored by the Church of Santa Maria del Mar and just a short stroll from the waterfront, El Born is a rewarding neighborhood to explore and a welcome escape from the sightseeing grind.

Back when Barcelona was Barcino—a walled Roman town—this area was farmland. As the city sprawled beyond its walls, El Born was "born" into a neighborhood with a main square that, over the years, hosted jousting tournaments, festivals, Inquisition-era heretic-burnings, and other public spectacles. Later, during the medieval city's trading heyday, El Born housed the wealthiest shippers and merchants. Its streets are lined with their grand mansions—which, like the much-appreciated Church of Santa Maria del Mar, were built with shipping wealth. All of that came crashing down in 1714, when the Spanish crown crushed Catalan hopes and razed a big chunk of this district to erect an imposing citadel (now a delightful park). The focus of the city shifted west, to the Barri Gòtic, and El Born became a largely forgotten backwater.

But in recent years, as the Barri Gòtic has become overrun by tourism, El Born has retained its pleasantly rough-around-the-edges appeal. While it's gentrifying and becoming one of the city's most in-demand residential areas, its tight lanes are lined not with chain stores, but with innovative one-off shops that, very often, make what they sell. Although we'll cover some history, this walk is designed to take you past some enticing boutique streets and provide a route for you to venture off and make your own discoveries.

# Orientation

**Length of This Walk:** About one hour, not including shopping stops. With limited time, focus on the core of El Born: Passeig del Born, the Monument of Catalan Independence, Church of Santa Maria del Mar, and the characteristic shopping lanes.

**Getting There:** This walk begins at Plaça d'Antoni Maura, where the pedestrian area in front of the Cathedral of Barcelona meets Via Laietana. The closest Metro stop is Jaume I.

**Name Game:** This neighborhood (between the Barri Gòtic to the west and Citadel Park to the east) goes by several names. The traditional name, **La Ribera,** generally implies the entire area. **El Born,** the name locals tend to use, technically refers to the southern half of this area (below Carrer de la Princesa—basically the zone covered by this walk), although it's sometimes also used to describe the entire neighborhood. Complicating matters, the city's official title for this district is "Sant Pere, Santa Caterina i la Ribera."

**Santa Caterina Market:** Open Mon-Sat 7:30-15:30, Tue and Thu-Fri until 20:30, closed Sun, Avinguda de Francesc Cambó 16.

**El Born Cultural Center:** Center—free and open Tue-Sun 10:00-20:00, Oct-Feb until 19:00, closed Mon year-round; Barcelona 1700 exhibit—€4.40, free all day first Sun of month and other Sun from 15:00, includes audioguide, same hours; Plaça Comercial 12.

**Picasso Museum:** €11 for timed-entry ticket to permanent collection, €14 also includes temporary exhibits, free every Thu evening from 18:00 and all day on the first Sun of the month; open Tue-Sun 9:00-19:00, Thu until 21:30, closed Mon; Carrer de Montcada 15.

**Church of Santa Maria del Mar:** Free to all during worship times: Mon-Fri 9:00-13:00 & 17:00-20:30, Sat-Sun 10:00-14:00 & 17:00-20:30; otherwise, pay €5 to visit Mon-Fri 13:00-17:00, Sat-Sun 14:00-17:00; Plaça Santa Maria.

**Tours:** ∩ My free Barcelona City Walk audio tour covers El Born.

# The Walk Begins

• *Our walk starts in front of the Cathedral of Barcelona. As you stand facing the cathedral, head left toward the Santa Caterina Market. You'll see its colorful, undulating roof in the distance. To get there, you'll cross...*

## ❶ Via Laietana

This traffic-choked street slices through Barcelona's Old City. It marks the boundary between the Barri Gòtic (behind you) and El Born (in front of you). When the road was built in 1908, Barcelona

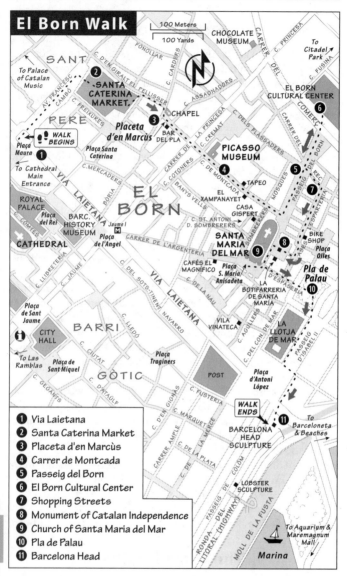

# El Born Walk

100 Meters
100 Yards

1 Via Laietana
2 Santa Caterina Market
3 Placeta d'en Marcùs
4 Carrer de Montcada
5 Passeig del Born
6 El Born Cultural Center
7 Shopping Streets
8 Monument of Catalan Independence
9 Church of Santa Maria del Mar
10 Pla de Palau
11 Barcelona Head

**EL BORN WALK**

was turning its back on its Gothic past and racing into its Modernista future—and hundreds of historic buildings were torn up to create this new artery.

When you cross the street, you're in the neighborhood called Sant Pere. While less colorful and gentrified than El Born, just to the south (or right), Sant Pere is home to a thriving residential population of mostly immigrants. A few short blocks to your left is one of the city's architectural treasures—Lluís Domènech i Montaner's Modernista-style **Palace of Catalan Music** (see listing on page 49).

• *Across Via Laietana and ahead, on the right, you can't miss what looks like a market wearing a giant, colorful sunhat, the...*

## ❷ Santa Caterina Market

While tourists swarm the more famous La Boqueria Market on the Ramblas, Santa Caterina Market is a lively dose of local color, still

primarily serving its neighborhood. This is the place to buy *jamón* and cheese without the crowds or tourist markup.

The market, built on the ruins of an old monastery (see the exhibit at the far corner for a view of the foundations with English explanations), was finally renovated in 2006 with a swooping roof and shell built around its original white walls. The roof's bright colors evoke Gaudí and the colorful fruit within.

The much-delayed construction took so long that locals began calling the site the "Hole of Shame." Its Catalan architect, Enric Miralles, is best known for designing the Scottish Parliament Building in Edinburgh—an unlikely connection that's also oddly fitting, since both the Catalans and the Scots consider themselves "nations without states."

Inside are beautifully lit produce stalls with mouthwatering presentations and surprising variety (one stall displays 20 kinds of tomatoes). There are lots of tempting eateries—locals eat before shopping so as not to overbuy. For tips on exploring the market, see the description on page 85 for La Boqueria, which offers similar products.

• *Walk through the market from one end to the other—keeping an eye out for those monastery ruins. (If the market is closed, you can simply loop around the left side to the far end.) Exiting through the back of the market, angle left to the corner of the square and find the tiny Carrer d'en Giralt el Pellisser. Going down this lane, you'll pop out facing a chapel and, on the right, the tiny square that seems more like a street called...*

## ❸ Placeta d'en Marcùs

On this square is a humble Romanesque chapel, Capella d'en Marcùs, from the 1100s, supposedly the oldest church in town. In medieval times, this is where locals would pause to share the news. Across the street from the chapel's front door, above the plaque for #1, notice the sign with the horse and the word *entrada* (entrance). This is an old-fashioned way of marking the direction of one-way streets in this tight tangle of lanes so carriages could circulate with-

out creating traffic jams. Across the tiny square past the chapel, find the sign's twin, *salida* (exit), above the street sign for Carrer dels Assaonadors. You'll spot signs like these all over El Born and the Barri Gòtic.

• *Passing between the chapel and the recommended Bar del Pla, continue straight down the lane called...*

## ❹ Carrer de Montcada

Follow this street one block until you reach the busy, bar-lined **Carrer de la Princesa.** If you turned right here, you'd go to the Jaume I Metro stop, Barri Gòtic, and cathedral area. Instead, cross Princesa and continue straight, noticing that Carrer de Montcada has suddenly become the most touristy street in El Born—thanks to the Picasso Museum, which lies just ahead. The street is named for the Montcada family, who owned the buildings that now house the museum (which consists of five mansions laced together). Because it connected the wealthy merchant district right near the waterfront with the tradesmen's quarter farther north, this drag attracted an elite class of homeowner during its 15th-century heyday and is lined to this day with many noble palaces.

A block down is the **Picasso Museum,** focused on the artist's early, formative works. If you don't already have a ticket, it's worthwhile to swing by to check available entry times (◻ see page 126 of the Picasso Museum Tour chapter for ticket details). In addition to the museum, Carrer de Montcada is lined with other art galleries, cafés, shops, and restaurants. While some are good (such as the recommended El Xampanyet and Tapeo bars, just down the street), most cater decidedly to tourist tastes. Browse the entire length of Carrer de Montcada.

• *At the end of the street, you'll pop out onto...*

## ❺ Passeig del Born

This long boulevard is the neighborhood center. Formerly a jousting square (as its Roman circus-esque shape indicates), it got its name, "El Born," from an old Catalan word for "tournament" (the name was eventually given to the entire neighborhood).

These days, Passeig del Born is a popular springboard for exploring tapas bars, fun restaurants, and nightspots in the narrow streets all around. Wandering around here at night, you'll find piles of inviting and intriguing little restaurants.

• *At the far end of Passeig del Born is the...*

## ❻ El Born Cultural Center

This vast, iron-and-glass construction was inspired by similar French market halls, which were the rage in the mid-19th century. Built in 1871 and the first such structure in town, **El Born Market** served as the city's main produce market hall until 1971, when it was relocated to the suburbs. The loss of the market led to the neighborhood's steep decline; only in the last decade or so has El Born become rejuvenated.

Today the market hall is open as the El Born Cultural Center, home to a permanent Barcelona 1700 exhibit as well as temporary displays. Enter for free to peruse the airy public space, look down at the medieval excavations, and read plaques about the history. You can also enjoy a drink in its modern café. The info point near the entry sells tickets to the Barcelona 1700 exhibit (ticket includes audioguide explaining the excavations).

The excavation below the market hall comes with a story poignant for locals. Before 1714, this neighborhood lost an uprising against the Spanish. Residents were forced to destroy their homes and use those very stones to build the citadel for their Spanish overlords—a fortress symbolic to this day of foreign control over Catalunya. The citadel came with a one-kilometer wide-open zone, so no buildings were allowed where the market stands today. Then, in the 19th century, a big marketplace was established here, thriving for a hundred years (1871-1971). The large hall had stood vacant since the market closed, but recent construction work revealed the medieval foundations of those pre-1714 buildings. From the railing you can look down at the pre-1714 street pavement stones and brick footprints of homes (well-described in English). The Barcelona 1700 exhibit brings that age to life with paintings, artifacts, and videos.

• *From the cultural center, return a block or so back into Passeig del Born and turn left on the arcaded Carrer del Rec. This part of El Born has a high concentration of...*

## ❼ Shopping Streets

Fashion boutiques populate the area around **Carrer del Rec.** And on the side streets, you can see local "fashions" flapping in the breeze from characteristic wrought-iron balconies. While strict building codes prohibit people from drying laundry outside their homes in most of the city, an exception is made for El Born—since this medieval quarter lacks interior courtyards.

Take the first right turn, down **Carrer de l'Esparteria**—another great shopping street. As elsewhere in El Born, most street names are tied to a particular craft or product; for example, the third street on the right, Carrer de la Formatgeria, was home to the cheesemakers.

Stick with the street as it passes a recommended bike rental shop, jogs slightly left, and becomes Carrer dels Ases. Pause at **Carrer del Malcuinat** (on the right), literally "the street of bad cooking." Looking left, you'll notice you're just a block off the port. In the Middle Ages, this lane was home to unpretentious eateries serving fill-the-tank meals to undiscerning sailors who were fresh off the boat. These days, no self-respecting restaurateur has the nerve to open an eatery along here (except, strangely, an Irish pub).

• *Turn right down the short Carrer del Malcuinat, emerging at a big square with the...*

### ❽ Monument of Catalan Independence

The square is called Plaça del Fossar de les Moreres ("The Burial Place of the Mulberry Trees"). The lone mulberry tree and mod-

ern monument honor a 300-year-old massacre that's still fresh in the Catalan consciousness. On September 11, 1714, the Bourbon King Philip V, ruling from Madrid, completed a successful 14-month siege of Barcelona (the "Catalan Alamo"). In retaliation for the local resistance to Bourbon rule, he massacred Catalan patriots. From that day on, the king outlawed Catalan language, culture, and institutions, kicking off more than two centuries of cultural suppression. For example, no university was allowed in Barcelona from 1720 to 1850. To establish his hold, the king demolished 20 percent of the homes in the nearby fishermen's quarter in order to build a gigantic citadel. These suddenly homeless seafarers were moved to the tightly grid-planned Barceloneta quarter, designed by a military architect, jutting out into the harbor just east of here. Meanwhile, the loss of a huge chunk of El Born contributed to this neighborhood's decline, as shipping shifted farther west, to the Barri Gòtic's harbor at Port Vell.

This square marks the site of a mass grave of the massacred Catalan patriots. The **eternal flame** burns atop this monument, and 9/11 remains a sobering anniversary for the Catalans, who still harbor a grudge. They say when heading to the toilet, "I'm going to Philip's house."

Here or elsewhere in El Born (which is a particularly feisty neighborhood), you may see displayed the *estelada* **flag,** the symbol of Catalan separatists: It features the typical red-and-gold horizontal stripes of the Catalunya flag, but with a blue triangle and white star on the hoist side. This design comes from the flag of a former Spanish colony that fought hard for its independence—Cuba. It's a provocative image to Spaniards who want to keep Catalunya in their country.

• *The hulking building dominating this square is the Church of Santa Maria del Mar. To reach its entrance, turn left and walk alongside it, until you get to the small square in front of the church.*

## ❾ Church of Santa Maria del Mar

This 14th-century church is the proud centerpiece of El Born. "Del Mar" means "of the sea," and that's where the money came from.

This is where shipwrights and merchants came to worship. The proud shippers built this church in less than 60 years, so it has a harmonious style that is considered pure Catalan Gothic. Located outside the city walls, this was a defiantly independent symbol of neighborhood pride; to this day, it's fully supported not by the Church or the city, but by the community.

On the big **front doors,** notice the figures of workers who donated their time and sweat to build the church. The stone for the church was quarried at Montjuïc and had to be carried across town on the backs of porters called *bastaixos*. Although they've always been celebrated by residents, their work is now more widely appreciated, following the release of the 2006 novel *Cathedral of the Sea*, which tells the story of the church's construction from the perspective of an ambitious *bastaixo*.

The largely unadorned **Gothic interior** used to be more highly decorated with Baroque frills, up until the Spanish Civil War (1936-1939). During the war, the Catholic Church sided with the conservative forces of Franco against leftists supporting the Spanish Republic. In retaliation, the working class took their anger out on this church, burning all of its wood furnishings and decor (carbon still blackens the ceiling). Today the church remains stripped down—naked in all its Gothic glory. The tree-like columns inspired Gaudí (their influence on the columns inside his Sagrada Família church is obvious). Sixteenth-century sailors left models of their ships at the foot of the main altar for Mary's protection. Even today, a classic old Catalan ship remains at Mary's feet. As within the Cathedral of Barcelona, here you can see the characteristic Catalan Gothic buttresses flying inward, defining the chapels that ring the nave. Brilliant stained glass—most notably the rose window over the main entry—floods the interior with soft light.

## Indulgences near the Church

Barcelona's most colorful bohemian quarter—this neighborhood around the Church of Santa Maria del Mar—offers plenty of inviting places to eat, drink, and shop (with recommended eateries nearby—see page 193). Explore!

For liquid and gourmet food souvenirs, try **Vila Vinateca,** a wine shop with (they claim) the widest selection in Barcelona (Mon-Sat 8:30-20:30, closed Sun, Carrer des Agullers 7—as you face the church it's buried about 100 yards away in the streets over your right shoulder, tel. 902-327-777). Across the lane is their gifty edibles shop with a wild cheese selection. To go with your wine and cheese, try the very Catalan sausage *botifarra* from **La Botifarreria de Santa Maria.** Take a number and join the locals in line; be sure to ask for *botifarra* that doesn't require cooking (Mon-Sat 8:30-14:30 & 17:00-20:30, closed Sun; Carrer Santa Maria 4; tel. 933-199-123).

A caffeine jolt awaits at **Cafés El Magnífico,** selling what's reputed to be the city's best coffee beans and takeout coffee (Mon-Sat 10:00-20:00, closed Sun, one block up Carrer de l'Argenteria at #64—immediately to the left as you face the church's front door, tel. 933-196-081). For a fragrant snack, head to **Casa Gispert,** which has been roasting nuts in the same wood-fired oven since 1851. Drop in to enjoy the aroma of fire-roasted nuts and pick up a snack (Mon-Sat 10:00-14:00 & 16:00-20:00, closed Sun; facing front door of church, circle around left side and walk almost all the way to the end—store is on the left at Carrer dels Sombrerers 23, tel. 933-197-535).

Near Casa Gispert is the start of an excellent shopping area. Head up the little lane just to the right of Gispert, Carrer de Sant Antoni dels Sombrerers. Follow this street as it jogs left, then (at the end), turn right onto Carrer dels Banys Vells. Follow this all the way up to Princesa—a bunch of great shops hide along the lanes branching off to the left. Many of them have workshops actually producing the goods for sale. The streets wedged between here and Carrer de l'Argenteria are particularly interesting and an easy place to score cool finds, including handmade clothing, accessories, and bags.

Outside, around the right side of the church is a poignant memorial to the "Catalan Alamo" of September 11, 1714 (described earlier, under "Monument of Catalan Independence").

• *If you've seen enough, you could end our walk now and give in to El Born's many buyable and edible temptations (see sidebar for ideas). To continue on to the* **waterfront,** *face the church, and turn right up Carrer d'Espaseria. You'll pop out at the square...*

## ❿ Pla de Palau

The hulking building on your right, at the end of the square, is **La**

**Llotja de Mar,** or fish exchange. Back when Barcelona was a major shipping center and El Born was its ritziest neighborhood, this was one of Europe's first stock exchanges. From the late 17th through the late 20th century, the building also housed the prestigious Barcelona Arts and Crafts School. The oldest design school in Spain (from 1715), this local institution has provided state-subsidized instruction to budding artists—including Pablo Picasso and Joan Miró.

• *Walk along the front of La Llotja de Mar, cross the wide street, and turn right to walk under the shaded arches of the big arcaded building. At the busy intersection, turn left around the corner and come face-to-face with the...*

## ⓫ Barcelona Head

This sculpture, created for the 1992 Summer Olympics by American Pop artist Roy Lichtenstein, instantly became an icon of the

city. It brings together the colors of Miró, the tiles of Gaudí, the Cubism of Picasso, and the comic-newsprint trademark of Lichtenstein. The grand Main Post Office stands across the main avenue.

Down the promenade from the head, look for the canopy with a giant, whimsical **lobster sculpture** waving from on top. This was designed by Javier Mariscal. While the restaurant that commissioned this work is long gone, the cheery lobster survives—one more piece of invigorating public art on Barcelona's fine waterfront, a veritable open-air contemporary art museum.

• *Barcelona's inviting waterfront beckons. From here, you can walk left, past the Catalan History Museum, to reach **Barceloneta** and the beach (or consider renting a bike at the recommended Bike Tours Barcelona shop for a pedal down the beach promenade to the Fòrum—see page 27 for rental details). Going right takes you along the delightful art-lined **promenade** next to the Old Port (bristling with sailboats) to the Columbus Monument at the bottom of the Ramblas. Another option is to head up busy **Via Laietana**, which we crossed at the beginning of this walk. Or if you haven't yet explored El Born's shopping streets (see sidebar on previous page), what better time than now?*

# PICASSO MUSEUM TOUR

*Museu Picasso*

This museum has the best collection in Spain of the work of Pablo Picasso (1881-1973), and the best collection anywhere of his earliest works. The Spaniard Picasso spent his formative years (from age 14 to 23) in Barcelona, and a visit to this museum intimately reveals the young man finding his way as an artist. By experiencing his youthful, realistic art, you can better understand his later, more challenging art and more fully appreciate his genius.

Picasso's personal secretary, Jaume Sabartés, amassed many examples of his friend's work and bequeathed them to Barcelona. The artist, happy to have a museum showing off his work in the city of his youth, added to the collection over the years. The museum and artworks are now housed in several connected Catalan Gothic palaces in the El Born neighborhood.

## Orientation

**Cost:** €11 for timed-entry ticket to permanent collection, €14 also includes special exhibits, free every Thu evening from 18:00 and all day on the first Sun of the month.

**Hours:** Tue-Sun 9:00-19:00, Thu until 21:30, closed Mon.

**Crowd-Avoiding Tips:** There's almost always a ticket-buying line, sometimes with waits of more than an hour. During peak season, tickets may sell out altogether. To get in when you want—without a wait—buy an **advance timed-entry ticket** online at www.museupicasso.bcn.cat (if the temperamental website won't work, try it on another device, such as your mobile phone), or use an **Articket BCN** (described on page 24). With the Articket, you can enter the galleries whenever you wish—but you must first go to the Articket window to show your pass and receive a ticket. (You can also buy an Articket at the window.)

For **day-of tickets,** go as early as possible, especially in peak season. Upon arrival, check the screen near the ticket office for available entry times (you can either try for immediate entry or buy tickets for later in the day). Day-of tickets are also sold online (must purchase at least two hours before you want to go). Off-season, you can probably just line up for tickets and get right in.

The museum's **busiest times** are mornings before 13:00, all day Tuesday, and during the free entry times on Sundays.

**Getting In:** The galleries sit one floor above a free-to-enter courtyard with several entrances. Tickets are sold at the center ground-floor entry; those with timed tickets can enter at either side. The Articket window is at the far right.

**Getting There:** It's at Carrer de Montcada 15; the ticket office is at #21. From the Jaume I Metro stop, it's a quick five-minute walk. Just head down Carrer de la Princesa (across the busy Via Laietana from the Barri Gòtic), turning right on Carrer de Montcada. It's a 10-minute walk from the cathedral and many parts of the Barri Gòtic; for an interesting approach from the cathedral area, ☐ take the El Born Walk.

**Information:** Tel. 932-563-000, www.museupicasso.bcn.cat.

**Tours:** The 1.5-hour audioguide costs €5 and offers ample detail about the collection. On Sundays only, free guided tours are offered at 11:00 (no tours in Aug); reserve a spot by emailing museupicasso_reserves@bcn.cat.

**Length of This Tour:** Allow at least an hour, or more time for lingering, especially in first part of the collection (through the Blue Period), with Picasso's formative early works.

**Services:** The ground floor, which is free to enter, has a required bag check, a bookshop, and WC.

**Photography:** Strictly forbidden.

**Cuisine Art:** Outside the museum, right along Carrer de Montcada in either direction, are several great recommended tapas bars: With your back to the museum, a few steps to the left are **El Xampanyet** and **Tapeo,** while to the right (across Carrer de la Princesa and up a block) is **Bar del Pla.** For details about these and other characteristic places nearby, see page 194.

# The Tour Begins

The Picasso Museum's collection of nearly 300 paintings is presented more or less chronologically. With good text panels in every room (and guards who don't let you stray), it's easy to follow the evolution of Picasso's work. This tour is arranged by the stages of

# Picasso Museum

Not to Scale

Room 11
**❸** Room 4
Room 3
**❷**
**❻**
Room 9
Room 10
Room 5
Room 2
Room 13
**❼**
Room 6
**❹**
Room 1
Room 14
Room 8
Room 7
**❶**
Room 12
**❺**
ELEV.
MAIN
HALLWAY
Stairs from
Ground Floor
**TOUR BEGINS**
Stairs to
Ground Floor
Room 16
B1
B2
A1
A4
Room 15
**TOUR ENDS**
**❽**
**❾**
N
A2
A3

TIMED-TICKET ENTRY
(GROUND LEVEL)

TICKET WINDOW
& ENTRY
(GROUND LEVEL)

ARTICKET WINDOW
& TIMED-TICKET ENTRY
(GROUND LEVEL)

CARRER DE MONTCADA

← To
Santa Caterina Market
(5 min. walk)

To Church of →
Santa Maria del Mar
(5 min. walk)

To Jaume 1 Ⓜ (5 min. walk)
& Cathedral (10 min. walk)

❶ Boy Wonder
❷ Developing Talent/Early Success
❸ Barcelona Freedom
❹ Paris
❺ Blue & Rose Periods
❻ Barcelona Redux/
   Synthetic Cubism
❼ Picasso & Velázquez
❽ French Riviera
❾ Ceramics/Sabartés Portraits

his life and art. If you don't see a specific piece, it may be out for restoration, on tour, or "sleeping," as local guides and museum guards say (the museum director likes to let certain paintings rest while putting other works up in their place). The art is rearranged every so often, but the themes and chronology remain constant.

• *Begin in Rooms 1 and 2.*

## ❶ Boy Wonder

Pablo's earliest art (in the first room) is realistic and earnest. His work quickly advances from childish pencil drawings (from about 1890), through a series of technically skilled **art-school works** (copies of plaster feet and arms), to oil paintings of impressive technique. Even at a young age, his **portraits** of grizzled peasants demonstrate surprising psychological insight. Because his dedicated father—himself a curator and artist—kept everything his son ever did, Picasso must have the best-documented youth of any great painter.

• *In Rooms 2 and 3, you'll find more paintings from Pablo's early years.*

## ❷ Developing Talent

During a summer trip to Málaga in 1896, Picasso dabbles in a series of fresh, Impressionistic-style landscapes (relatively rare in Spain at the time). As a 15-year-old, Pablo dutifully enters art-school competitions. His first big work, *First Communion,* features a pre-scribed religious subject, but Picasso makes it an excuse to paint his family. His sister Lola is the model for the communicant, and the features of the man beside her belong to Picasso's father. Notice Lola's ex-quisitely painted veil. This piece is heavily influenced by the academic style of local painters.

Picasso's relatives star in a number of portraits from this time. If it's on view, find the **portrait of his mother** (this and other family portraits are among the works that are frequently rotated). The teenage Pablo is working on the fine details and gradients of white in her blouse and the expression in her cameo-like face. Notice the signature. Spaniards keep both parents' surnames, with the father's first, followed by the mother's: Pablo Ruiz Picasso.

## Early Success

In the large, classically painted *Science and Charity* (1897), Picasso conveys the real feeling typical of the social realism move-ment of the late 19th century. The doctor (modeled on Pablo's father) represents science. The nun repre-sents charity and religion. From her hopeless face and lifeless hand, it seems that Picasso believes nothing will save this woman from death. Pablo painted a little perspective trick: Walk back and forth across the room to see the bed stretch and shrink. Three small studies for this

# Pablo Picasso
## (1881-1973)

Pablo Picasso was the most famous and, for me, the greatest artist of the 20th century. Always exploring, he became the master of many styles (Cubism, Surrealism, Expressionism) and of many media (painting, sculpture, prints, ceramics, assemblages). Still, he could make anything he touched look unmistakably like "a Picasso."

Born in Málaga, Spain, Picasso was the son of an art teacher. At a very young age, he quickly advanced beyond his teachers. Picasso's teenage works are stunningly realistic and capture the inner complexities of the people he painted. As a youth in Barcelona, he fell in with a bohemian crowd that mixed wine, women, and art.

In 1900, at age 19, Picasso started making trips to Paris. Four years later, he moved to the City of Light and absorbed the styles of many painters (especially Henri de Toulouse-Lautrec) while searching for his own artist's voice. His paintings of beggars and other social outcasts show the empathy of a man who was himself a poor, homesick foreigner. When his best friend, Spanish artist Carlos Casagemas, committed suicide, Picasso plunged into a **Blue Period** (1901-1904)—so called because the dominant color in these paintings matches their melancholy mood and subject matter (emaciated beggars, hard-eyed pimps).

In 1904, Picasso got a steady girlfriend (Fernande Olivier) and suddenly saw the world through rose-colored glasses—the **Rose Period.** He was further jolted out of his Blue Period by the "flat" look of the Fauve paintings being made around him. Not satisfied with their take on 3-D, Picasso played with the "building blocks" of line and color to find new ways to reconstruct the real world on canvas.

At his studio in Montmartre, Picasso and his neighbor Georges Braque worked together, in poverty so dire they often didn't know where their next bottle of wine was coming from. And then, at age 25, Picasso reinvented painting. Fascinated by the primitive power of African tribal masks, he sketched human faces with simple outlines and almond eyes. Intrigued by his girlfriend's body, he sketched Fernande from every angle, then experimented with showing several different views on the same canvas. A hundred paintings and nine months later, Picasso gave birth to a monstrous canvas of five nude, fragmented prostitutes with mask-like faces—*Les Demoiselles d'Avignon* (1907).

This bold new style was called **Cubism.** With Cubism, Picasso shattered the Old World and put it back together in a new way. The subjects are somewhat recognizable (with the help of the titles), but they're built with geometric shards (let's call them "cubes")—it's like viewing the world through a kaleidoscope of brown and gray. Cubism presents several different angles of the subject at once—say, a woman seen from the front and side simultaneously, resulting in two eyes on the same side of the nose. Cubism showed the traditional three dimensions, plus Einstein's new fourth dimension—the time it takes to walk around the subject to see other angles.

In 1918, Picasso married his first wife, Olga Kokhlova. He then traveled to Rome and entered a **Classical Period** (1920s) of more realistic, full-bodied women and children, inspired by the three-dimensional sturdiness of ancient statues. While he flirted with abstraction, throughout his life Picasso always kept a grip on "reality." His favorite subject was people. The anatomy might be jumbled, but it's all there.

Though he lived in France and Italy, Picasso remained a Spaniard at heart, incorporating Spanish motifs into his work. Unrepentantly macho, he loved bullfights, seeing them as a metaphor for the timeless human interaction between the genders. The horse—clad with blinders and pummeled by the bull—is just a pawn in the battle between bull and matador. To Picasso, the horse symbolizes the feminine, and the bull, the masculine. Spanish imagery—bulls, screaming horses, a Madonna—appears in Picasso's most famous work, *Guernica* (1937). The monumental canvas of a bombed village summed up the pain of Spain's brutal civil war (1936-1939) and foreshadowed the onslaught of World War II.

At war's end, Picasso left Paris, his wife, and his emotional baggage behind, finding fun in the **south of France**. Sun! Color! Water! Freedom! Senior citizen Pablo Picasso was reborn, enjoying worldwide fame. He lived at first with the beautiful young painter Françoise Gilot, mother of two of his children, but it was another young beauty, Jacqueline Roque, who became his second wife. Dressed in rolled-up white pants and a striped sailor's shirt, bursting with pent-up creativity, Picasso often cranked out a painting a day. Picasso's Riviera works set the tone for the rest of his life. They're sunny, lighthearted, and childlike; filled with motifs of the sea, Greek mythology (fauns, centaurs), and animals; and freely experimental in their use of new media. The simple drawing of doves Picasso made at this time become emblematic of the artist and an international symbol of peace.

Picasso made collages, built "statues" out of wood, wire, ceramics, papier-mâché, or whatever, and even turned everyday household objects into statues (like his famous bull's head made of a bicycle seat with handlebar horns). **Multimedia** works like these have become so standard today that we forget how revolutionary they once were. His last works have the playfulness of someone much younger. As it is often said of Picasso, "When he was a child, he painted like a man. When he was old, he painted like a child."

painting (on the right) show how this was an exploratory work. The frontier: light.

*Science and Charity* wins second prize at a fine-arts exhibition, earning Picasso the chance to study in Madrid. Stifled by the stuffy fine-arts school there, he hangs out instead in the Prado Museum and learns by copying the masters. An example of his impressive mimicry is sometimes displayed in this room—a nearly perfect copy of a **portrait of Philip IV** by the earlier Spanish master Diego Velázquez. (Near the end of this tour, we'll see a much older Picasso riffing on another Velázquez painting.)

Having absorbed the wisdom of the ages, in 1898 Pablo visits **Horta de San Joan,** a rural Catalan village. The small landscapes and scenes of village life he did there show him finding his artistic independence. But poor and without a love in his life, he returns to Barcelona.

• *Continue into Room 4.*

## ❸ Barcelona Freedom

Art Nouveau is all the rage in Barcelona when Pablo returns there in 1900. Upsetting his dad, he quits art school and falls in with the

avant-garde crowd. These bohemians congregate daily at Els Quatre Gats ("The Four Cats," a popular restaurant to this day—see page 190). Picasso even created the **menu cover** for this favorite hangout. Further establishing his artistic freedom, he paints **portraits** of his new friends (including one of Jaume Sabartés, who later became his personal assistant and donated the foundational works of this museum). Still a teenager, Pablo puts on his first one-man show at Els Quatre Gats in 1900.

• *The next few pieces are displayed in Rooms 5-7.*

## ❹ Paris

In 1900 Picasso makes his first trip to Paris, a city bursting with life, light, and love. Dropping the paternal surname Ruiz, Pablo establishes his commercial brand name: "Picasso." Here the explorer Picasso goes bohemian and befriends poets, prostitutes, and artists. He begins sampling the contemporary art styles around him: He paints **can-can dancers** like Toulouse-Lautrec,

**still lifes** like Paul Cézanne, brightly colored **Fauvist** works like Henri Matisse, and Impressionist **landscapes** like Claude Monet. In *The Waiting (Margot),* the subject—with her bold outline and strong gaze—pops out from the vivid, mosaic-like background. It is Cézanne's technique of "building" a figure with "cubes" of paint that will inspire Picasso to invent Cubism—soon.

• *Turn right into the hall, then—farther along—right again, to find Room 8 (and its side rooms), where you'll see hints of Picasso's Blue and Rose Periods.*

## ❺ Blue Period

Picasso travels to Paris several times (he settles there permanently in 1904). The suicide of his best friend, his own poverty, and the

influence of new ideas linking color and mood lead Picasso to abandon jewel-bright color for his Blue Period (1901-1904). He cranks out stacks of blue art just to stay housed and fed. With blue backgrounds (the coldest color) and depressing subjects, this period was revolutionary in art history. Now the artist is painting not what he sees, but what he feels. Look for the touching portrait of a mother and child, *Motherhood* (this very fragile pastel is only displayed intermittently), which captures the period well. Painting misfits and street people, Picasso, like Velázquez and Toulouse-Lautrec, sees the beauty in ugliness.

Back home in Barcelona, Picasso paints his hometown at night from **rooftops.** The painting is still blue, but here we see proto-Cubism...five years before the first real Cubist painting.

## Rose Period

Picasso is finally lifted out of his funk after meeting a new lady, Fernande Olivier. He moves out of the blue and into the happier Rose Period (1904-1907). For a fine example, see the portrait of a woman wearing a classic Spanish mantilla *(Portrait of Bernadetta Bianco).* Its soft pink and reddish tones are the colors of flesh and sensuality. (This is the only actual Rose Period painting in the museum, but don't be surprised if it is on loan elsewhere.)

• *Now move into Rooms 9-11.*

## ❻ Barcelona Redux

Picasso spent six months back in Barcelona in 1917 (yet another girlfriend, a Russian ballet dancer, had a gig in town). The paintings in these rooms demonstrate the artist's irrepressible versatility: He's already developed Cubism (with his friend Georges Braque; more on this below), but he also continues to play with other styles.

In **Woman with Mantilla,** we see a little Post-Impressionistic Pointillism in a portrait that is as elegant as a classical statue. Nearby, **Gored Horse** has all the anguish and power of his iconic *Guernica* (painted years later).

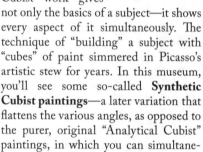

## Synthetic Cubism

Pablo's role in the invention of the revolutionary Cubist style is well known—at least I hope

so, since this museum has no true Cubist paintings. A Cubist work gives not only the basics of a subject—it shows every aspect of it simultaneously. The technique of "building" a subject with "cubes" of paint simmered in Picasso's artistic stew for years. In this museum, you'll see some so-called **Synthetic Cubist paintings**—a later variation that flattens the various angles, as opposed to the purer, original "Analytical Cubist" paintings, in which you can simultaneously see several 3-D facets of the subject.

• *Remember that this museum has very little from the most famous and prolific "middle" part of Picasso's career—basically, from his adoption of Cubism to his sunset years on the French Riviera. (To fill in the gaps in his middle career, see the "Pablo Picasso" sidebar in this chapter.) Skip ahead more than 30 years and into Rooms 12-14 (at the end of the main hallway, on the right).*

## ❼ Picasso and Velázquez

A series of Picasso's works relates to what many consider the greatest painting by anyone, ever: Diego Velázquez's *Las Meninas* (the 17th-century original is in Madrid's Prado Museum). Heralded as the first completely realistic painting, *Las Meninas* became an obsession for Picasso centuries later.

Picasso, who had great respect for Velázquez, painted more than **40 interpretations** of this piece. Picasso seems to enjoy a relationship of equals with Velázquez. Like artistic soul mates, the two Spanish geniuses spar and tease. Picasso deconstructs Velázquez and then injects light, color, and perspective as he improvises on the earlier masterpiece. In Picasso's big black-and-white canvas, the king and queen (reflected in the mirror in the back of the room) are hardly seen, while the painter towers above everyone. The two women of the court on the right look like they're in a tomb—but they're wearing party shoes. Browse the various studies, a playground of color and perspective. See the fun Picasso had playing paddleball with Velázquez's tour de force—filtering Velázquez's realism through the kaleidoscope of Cubism.

• *Head back down the hall and turn right, through Room 16, to find a flock of carefree white birds in Room 15.*

## ❽ The French Riviera (Last Years)

Picasso spends the last 36 years of his life living simply in the south of France. He said many times that "paintings are like windows open to the world." We see his sunny Riviera world: With simple black outlines and Crayola colors, Picasso paints sun-splashed nature, peaceful doves, and the joys of the beach. He's enjoying life with his second (and much younger) wife, Jacqueline Roque, whose portraits hang nearby.

• *Go back into the hallway and turn right into Rooms B1, N, and B2 to see Picasso's* ❾ *ceramic designs, including bowls and vases made in fun animal shapes and decorated with simple motifs. You'll also find portraits of Jaume Sabartés, whose initial donation made this museum possible.*

Picasso died with brush in hand, still growing as an artist. Picasso—who had vowed never to set foot in a fascist, Franco-ruled Spain—sadly never returned to his homeland...and never saw this museum (his death came in 1973—two years before Franco's). However, to the end, Picasso continued exploring and loving life through his art.

• *Our tour is finished. You're in the heart of the delightful El Born neighborhood. To explore this area further, 📖 see my El Born Walk.*

# EIXAMPLE WALK

*From Plaça de Catalunya to La Pedrera (and Beyond)*

Literally "The Expansion," L'Eixample is where Barcelona spread when it burst at the seams in the 19th century. Rather than allowing unchecked growth, city leaders thoughtfully funneled Barcelona's newfound wealth into creating a standardized yet refreshingly open grid plan—as if attempting to achieve the opposite of the claustrophobic Gothic lanes that had contained locals for centuries.

The creation of the Eixample also coincided with a burst in architectural creativity, as great Modernista minds such as Antoni Gaudí, Lluís Domènech i Montaner, and Josep Puig i Cadafalch were given both artistic license and seemingly limitless funds to adorn the new boulevards with fanciful facades. It was a perfect storm of urban planning, unbridled architectural innovation, Industrial Age technology, ample wealth, and Catalan cultural pride.

This walk takes you through the Eixample's "Golden Quarter" (Quadrat d'Or) to see two of the city's Modernista musts—the Block of Discord and La Pedrera (Casa Milà)—as well as several other sights. The roundabout route also winds you through some pleasant, relatively untouristy residential neighborhoods that showcase modern Barcelona's unusual street plan and everyday life in this elegant quarter.

## Orientation

**Length of This Walk:** Allow about 1.5 hours (more if you tour any of the sights). If you have less time, skip the first part of this walk and make a beeline for the Block of Discord and La Pedrera.

**Planning Your Time:** If you want to see the interiors, reservations are essential for Casa Lleó Morera, and advance purchase is smart for Casa Batlló and La Pedrera.

**Getting There:** This walk starts at Plaça de Catalunya (Metro: Plaça de Catalunya).

**Water Tower Garden:** €1.50 from late June-early Sept (when pool is open), open Mon-Sat 10:00-dusk.

**Church of the Holy Conception:** Free, daily 8:00-13:00 & 17:00-21:00, enter at Carrer de Roger de Llúria 70, through the cloister.

**La Concepció Market:** Free, Mon and Sat 8:00-15:00, Tue-Fri 8:00-20:00, closed Sun, Carrer de València 317, tel. 934-575-329.

**Casa Batlló:** €22.50 for timed-entry ticket, daily 9:00-21:00; for ticketing details, see page 53.

**Casa Amatller:** €15 for 1-hour English tour, €12 for 30-minute tour (in a mix of English, Spanish, and Catalan), daily 10:30-18:00, for tour times and ticketing details, see page 55.

**Casa Lleó Morera:** If open—€15 for 1-hour English tour, €12 for 30-minute tour (in a mix of English, Spanish, and Catalan); open Tue-Sun 10:00-13:30 & 15:00-19:00, closed Mon, tour times vary so check website; for reservations, see page 55.

**Fundació Antoni Tàpies:** €7, covered by Articket BCN, Tue-Sun 10:00-19:00, closed Mon, Carrer d'Aragó 255, tel. 934-870-315.

**La Pedrera (Casa Milà):** €20.50, daily 9:00-20:00, Nov-Feb until 18:30, for advance ticketing and crowd-beating tips, see page 56.

**Palau Baró de Quadras (Institut Ramón Llul):** Free, Mon-Thu 8:00-20:00, Fri 8:00-19:00, closed Sat-Sun, www.llull.cat.

**Eating:** Several fine tapas bars and restaurants are on or near the course of this walk. For details, see page 195.

## BACKGROUND

Barcelona boomed in the 1800s, with its population doubling (from a half-million to a million) over the course of one century. Before its roaring 19th century, Barcelona languished through centuries of stagnation: Columbus' discoveries had shifted trade from the Mediterranean to the Atlantic. Catalunya also suffered under the thumb of Madrid, which feared—perhaps rightfully—a Catalan uprising. Eventually, the Spanish Queen Isabella II loosened Madrid's grip on Barcelona. This land of abundant coal deposits and many rivers flowing from the Pyrenees to the Mediterranean provided the perfect resources for powering textile mills. Industrialization brought people from all over Spain (and beyond) to find work, and Barcelona's textile magnates powered a remarkably robust economy. Barcelona was back on the map.

But the upwardly mobile city had nowhere to grow. Because of the Madrid government's centuries-old restrictions, the city was forced to stay within its medieval walls. By the mid-19th century, 200,000 residents were crammed into the Old City. It was a slum of steep and crowded tenements where disease was rampant, the air was choked with coal soot, and the quality of life was miserable. It was clear that expansion was necessary.

Throughout Europe in the Industrial Age, cities (like Paris, Vienna, and Copenhagen) were dealing with similar growing pains: dense population and squalor needlessly corralled into tight quarters by antiquated defensive city walls. The solution: Tear down those walls. Use the land once taken by walls and moats for circular boulevards, parks, and lakes—and expand.

In 1854, Queen Isabella II allowed Barcelona to tear down the medieval wall and expand northward. Because very little existed outside the Old City, urban planners had a blank slate.

Civil engineer Ildefons Cerdà (1815-1876) proposed a carefully plotted, remarkably modern, and efficient grid of streets that would surround the convoluted tangle of Barcelona's Old City. Uptown Barcelona would be a unique variation on the common grid-plan city. By snipping off the building corners, light and spacious octagonal "squares" were created at every intersection.

Work began in 1860 on Cerdà's progressive Eixample plan, which envisioned a new town in which everything was made accessible to everyone. Each block-square district would have easy access to its own hospital, park, market, schools, and day-care centers. Restrictions on the height, width, and depth of buildings ensured that sunlight would reach every unit. The hollow space found inside each "block" of apartments would form a neighborhood park. Although parts of Cerdà's vision didn't quite pan out, the Eixample is an urban success.

The birth of the Eixample also coincided with two other important moments in the city's history: The revival of Catalan cultural pride (the Renaixença) and the emergence of Catalunya's own spin on Art Nouveau—Modernisme (see the sidebar).

Rich-and-artsy big shots bought plots along the Eixample grid and hired some of the best and brightest architects in the business, including Antoni Gaudí, Lluís Domènech i Montaner, and Josep Puig i Cadafalch. It's no accident that Modernista mansions come with big bay windows and outlandish decoration: The people who paid for them wanted both to be seen, and to be recognized for their forward-thinking embrace of the new art. The wealthiest landowners built as close to the center as possible—that's why the most distinctive buildings are near Passeig de Gràcia.

# Modernisme and the Renaixença

Modernisme is Barcelona's unique contribution to the Europe-wide Art Nouveau movement. Meaning "a taste for what is  modern"—things like streetcars, electric lights, and big-wheeled bicycles—this free-flowing organic style lasted from 1888 to 1906.

Broadly speaking, there were two kinds of Modernisme (Catalan Art Nouveau). Early Modernisme is a kind of Neo-Gothic, clearly inspired by medieval castles and towers—logically, since architects wanted to recall the days when Barcelona was at its peak. From that same starting point, Antoni Gaudí branched off on his own, adding the color and curves we most associate with Barcelona's Modernisme look.

The aim was to create objects that were both practical and decorative. To that end, Modernista architects experimented with new construction techniques. Their most important material was concrete, which they could use to make a hard stone building that curved and rippled like a wave. Then they sprinkled it with brightly colored glass and tile. The structure was fully modern, but the decoration was a clip-art collage of nature images, exotic Moorish or Chinese themes, and fanciful Gothic crosses and knights to celebrate Catalunya's medieval glory days.

It's ironic to think that Modernisme was a response against the regimentation of the Industrial Age—and that all those organic shapes were only made possible thanks to Eiffel Tower-like iron frames. As you wander through the Eixample looking at all those fanciful facades and colorful, leafy, flowing, blooming shapes in doorways, entrances, and ceilings, remember that many of these homes were built at the same time as the first skyscrapers in Chicago and New York City.

Underpinning Modernisme was the Catalan cultural revival movement, called the Renaixença. Across Europe, it was a time of national resurgence. It was the dawn of the modern age, and downtrodden peoples—from the Basques to the Irish to the Hungarians to the Finns—were throwing off the cultural domination of other nations and celebrating what made their own culture unique. Here in Catalunya, the Renaixença encouraged everyday people to get excited about all things Catalan—from their language, patriotic dances, and inspirational art to their surprising style of architecture.

Today's Eixample remains Barcelona's upscale and genteel up-town. It's also one center of the local gay community (especially a few blocks west of Passeig de Gràcia, around Carrer d'Aribau), earning it the nickname "Gayshample." The heart of the Eixample is the Quadrat d'Or, or "Golden Quarter," with the richest collection of Modernista facades...and the richest local residents. As you walk through the streets, peek into the big, ornate iron-and-glass doorways of almost any apartment building to see the eclectic decorative entrance halls and old-fashioned elevators. This remains one of the city's most desirable neighborhoods.

# The Walk Begins

• *Begin at Plaça de Catalunya. Head up the broad boulevard (Passeig de Gràcia) at the top end of the giant El Corte Inglés department store. Walk up two blocks (on the right side of this street) to the huge intersection with Gran Via de les Corts Catalanes; there's a big fountain in the middle.*

## ❶ Passeig de Gràcia

In the 500 feet between here and the Barri Gòtic, you've traveled 500 years—from the medieval Gothic vibe of the Barri Gòtic to the ambitiously modern late 19th-century Eixample.

In Catalan, *passeig* means "boulevard"—and this one leads to Gràcia, once a separate town but now overwhelmed by Barcelona's growth and a neighborhood within the city. As one of the first major thoroughfares of the Eixample, this was prime real estate. To this day, the boulevard remains the top street in town. Notice the extra-wide girth of this drag, the inviting park-like median strips, and the unique Modernista lampposts anchored by Gaudí-style benches slathered with broken white tile mosaics.

Originally Barcelona's wealthy class built elaborate residences along here. But within just a few decades, as the city continued to grow and real estate was at a premium, it became more lucrative to tear down those mansions and replace them with multistory apartment buildings. (One of the few surviving original mansions, now the Comedia theater, is kitty-corner across the inter-

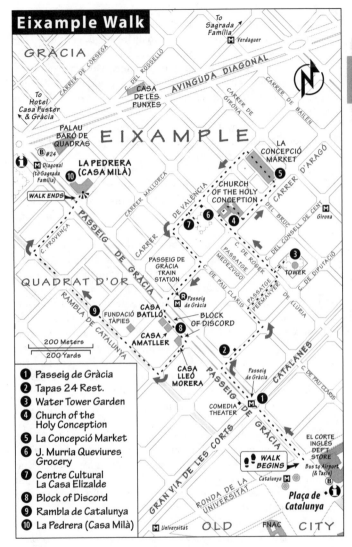

# Eixample Walk

GRÀCIA

To
Sagrada
Família
Ⓜ Verdaguer

CARRER DE CÒRSEGA

C. DEL ROSSELLÓ

CASA
DE LES
PUNXES

AVINGUDA DIAGONAL

CARRER DE GIRONA

CARRER DE BAILÈN

To
Hotel
Casa Fuster
& Gràcia

PALAU
BARÓ DE
QUADRAS

EIXAMPLE

LA
CONCEPCIÓ
MARKET

Ⓑ #24

Ⓜ Diagonal
(to Sagrada
Família)

LA PEDRERA
(CASA MILÀ)

⑩

CARRER D'ARAGÓ

CHURCH
OF THE HOLY
CONCEPTION

⑤

WALK ENDS

CARRER MALLORCA

DE VALÈNCIA

⑦ ⑥ ④

DEL BRUC

DEL CONSELL DE CENT

Ⓜ
Girona

PASSEIG DE GRÀCIA

CARRER

C. PROVENÇA

PASSATGE DE ROSER

C. DE ROGER

PASSEIG DE
GRÀCIA
TRAIN
STATION

C. DE PAU CLARIS

MEDEZVIGO

③

TOWER

C. DE DIPUTACIÓ

QUADRAT D'OR

Ⓡ Passeig
de Gràcia
Ⓜ

PASSATGE PERMANYER

DE LLÚRIA

RAMBLA DE CATALUNYA

⑨

FUNDACIÓ
TÀPIES

CASA
BATLLÓ

BLOCK
OF DISCORD

⑧

200 Meters
200 Yards

CASA
AMATLLER

CASA
LLEÓ
MORERA

②

Passeig
de Gràcia

CATALANES

C. DE PAU CLARIS

① Passeig de Gràcia
② Tapas 24 Rest.
③ Water Tower Garden
④ Church of the
   Holy Conception
⑤ La Concepció Market
⑥ J. Murria Queviures
   Grocery
⑦ Centre Cultural
   La Casa Elizalde
⑧ Block of Discord
⑨ Rambla de Catalunya
⑩ La Pedrera (Casa Milà)

COMEDIA
THEATER

PASSEIG DE GRÀCIA

①

 Ⓜ
Catalunya

WALK
BEGINS

EL CORTE
INGLÉS
DEP'T
STORE

Bus to Airport
(& Taxi)

Ⓑ

GRAN VIA DE LES CORTS

RONDA DE LA
UNIVERSITAT

Plaça de
Catalunya

Ⓜ Universitat

OLD

FNAC

CITY

section—just beyond the fountain.) Notice that, despite great architectural variation in their facades, most Eixample homes share an identical design: The entire building was owned by one family who lived in the middle and rented space above and below. Shops and businesses were on the ground floor; above that, a large first (our "second") floor, where the wealthy family lived; and, higher up, smaller floors for tenants. Throughout the Eixample, you'll see that the first floor is usually taller and more elaborate than the other floors—often with balconies or bay windows that higher floors are lacking. (Most of these houses predate the elevator; after that convenience was invented and widely installed, penthouse living became popular.) Many houses have two doors—one for the owners and another for the upstairs tenants. Most house blocks had an interior garden courtyard for ventilation and light, although over time many of these spaces have been covered over by one-story structures or parking lots.

Because the Eixample was developed during the Renaixença, you'll spot Catalan themes, such as St. George (Jordi)—the local patron saint—slaying the dragon.

See any flags? Catalunya's flag is a simple block of narrow red-and-gold stripes. But the version with the blue triangle with a white star is a call for independence from Spain inspired by the flag of Cuba (which successfully won its independence from Spain long ago).

Speaking of Catalan pride, imagine this street (and the ones around it) clogged with an estimated one million furious Catalans. It happened on July 10, 2010, after Spanish constitutional courts overturned key provisions of a Catalan statute for home rule (which had been approved by an overwhelming 73 percent of Catalan voters). These patriots of Catalunya—which considers itself a "nation without a state"—waved flags that read, *Som una nació. Nosaltres decidim.* (We are a nation. We decide.) This peaceful demonstration was a reminder that the Catalans—like the Basques and the Scots—take home rule very seriously. As locals here grumble for more autonomy and vote on self-rule, Spain will make economic concessions to keep the industrial powerhouse of Catalunya a part of Spain.

Continue one more block up Passeig de Gràcia (to the intersection with Carrer de la Diputació) to appreciate the delightfully airy street plan you'll find throughout the Eixample. Notice that the four corners are cropped off, creating a wide-open pleasant space at the intersection (which can be filled by café tables, inviting benches, or public art).

• *From here, turn right on Carrer de la Diputació. (If you're tight on time, you can continue directly ahead to stop #8 on this walk, the Block of Discord.)*

## ❷ Tapas 24

A few steps down on the left, you'll see the recommended Tapas 24, a popular and trendy Eixample tapas bar that also serves hot breakfasts (for tapas bar listings, see page 196). Continue one block down Carrer de la Diputació, noticing the distinctive paving stones (four squares with a circle in each one). This is one of a handful of distinctive patterns on mass-produced tiles that are a symbol of Barcelona.

• *At the corner, cross the street and turn left up Carrer de Pau Claris. Halfway up the block, notice the gated* **passage** *on the right (Passatge Permanyer, at #116). Cut through here for a peek at a fine residential strip buried in the middle of the block. Although such passageways were not a planned feature of the Eixample, here and there they've been carved out of the buildings' central courtyards, and make a pretty stroll. Popping out the other end, go right to cross the street and jog 30 yards to the left, then go down the passage at #56 (on the right, marked* Jardins de Torre de les Aigües*). This leads you to a...*

## ❸ Water Tower Garden

This tranquil (if somewhat sterile) courtyard has trees, benches, and a wading pool, all watched over by a brick water tower from

1867. In the summer, a temporary "beach" is created here for neighborhood families. Courtyards like this were part of the original vision for the Eixample. Each block was supposed to have a shared central patio, but over the last century, many of them have been converted to other purposes. More recently, as properties become available, the city of Barcelona has slowly begun restoring Cerdà's original public spaces. The *Serveis* sign indicates a public WC, which is occasionally open.

• *Exiting the garden the way you entered, turn right and head up Carrer de Roger de Llúria. Cross Carrer del Consell de Cent, passing under the pretty yellow Neo-Renaissance facade slapped onto a modern building.*

*Continue another block and cross another street (Carrer d'Aragó). Go straight up Carrer de Roger de Llúria a half-block, entering the delightful cloister with orange, magnolia, and palm trees at #70, on the right of the...*

## ❹ Church of the Holy Conception

Work your way through the cloister to the interior of the church.

This purely Gothic, 14th-century church with a 15th- and 16th-century cloister once stood in the Old City. But when the wall that once surrounded the Old City came down as part of Barcelona's expansion, a few historic churches like this one

were moved, brick by brick, to new locations in the 1870s. The bell tower came from a different Gothic church.

• *Exiting the church through its front door (or back through the cloister and left around to the front door), turn left, go one block, and cross Carrer del Bruc. Pass the detailed iron gate and columns of the entrance to the Seu del Districte Eixample—the Eixample's own "seat," or branch office, of City Hall. Continuing straight just beyond that, you'll reach (on the left)...*

## ❺ La Concepció Market

While it has many of the same features as La Boqueria (on the Ramblas) and the Santa Caterina Market (in El Born), this market (with a modern supermarket in the basement and a garage below that) has virtually zero tourists. Walk through the building, from one end to the other. It's a good place to sample local cheeses, buy olives, or pick up some fruit. At the far end, you'll emerge into a delightful flower market crowding the sidewalk.

• *Turn left and stroll along...*

## Carrer de València

As you walk, you'll pass many more flower stands and the turreted Municipal Conservatory of Barcelona on the corner, a city-

run music academy. Ponder the fact that in just a couple of blocks, we've passed a church, a municipal building, a market, and a school (just up the street next to the market). This is very much in keeping with the original vision for the Eixample: a series of self-sufficient neighborhood zones that give residents easy access to important services. A market like this serves each neighborhood here—part of the grand original plan.

Continuing straight on Carrer de València, you'll pass (at the corner, on the right) an unfortunate brick monstrosity that breaks up the Eixample harmony, followed by its antidote, at #293, a fine Modernista building with wrought-iron railings and twin bay windows. Cross the street. On your left, step into the Navarro flower shop. It's open daily 24 hours so there's just no excuse to miss it. Take a fragrant stroll, looping deep into the shop, noticing if there's a seasonal theme.

At the next intersection, cross the street to peek inside the classic Modernista grocery of ❻ **J. Murria Queviures.** This old-fashioned gourmet deli is stocked with pricey ingredients for a top-end picnic that may be a bit too classy for a park bench. Breathe deep to smell the cheese aging in the cellar. The vintage ad on the corner—dubbed *La Mona y el Mono (The Classy Lady and the Monkey)*—advertised anise liquor to Modernista-era clients.

Press ahead a half-block farther to the ❼ **Centre Cultural La Casa Elizalde** (Carrer de València 302, on the left). This cultural center, a facility of the city of Barcelona, is a hive of creative and personal growth activities. Head into the passage, noticing the community bulletin board listing classes and events. Continuing down the hall, you'll pop out into an appealing courtyard in the middle of the block with benches. Look up and around the buildings for a taste of the typical inner patios for the entire block of buildings, a quiet sanctuary from the busy Eixample streets. You'll find WCs inside the building: women, first floor; men, second floor.

• *Head back out to the street and turn left (the way you were going). At the end of the block, go left down Carrer de Pau Claris. After a block, turn right on the wide Carrer d'Aragó. Walk one block, stand on the corner, and you'll find yourself kitty-corner from the...*

## ❽ Block of Discord (Illa de la Discòrdia)

One block, three buildings, three astonishingly creative Modernista architects. Over a short span of time, the three big names of Catalunya's bold Art Nouveau architectural movement erected innovative facades along this one short stretch of Passeig de Gràcia. Although each of these architects has better works elsewhere in town, this is the most convenient place to see their sharply contrasting visions side by side. While these three buildings were done by famous, groundbreaking architects, the whole block is a jumble of delightful architectural whimsy. Reliefs, coats of arms, ironwork, gables, and bay windows adorn otherwise ordinary buildings.

• *Work your way down the block, beginning with the unmistakably Gaudí-style facade that's situated one building in from the corner.*

### Casa Batlló (#43)

The most famous facade on the block is that of the green-blue, ceramic-speckled Casa Batlló, designed by Antoni Gaudí. It's thought that Gaudí based the work on the popular legend of St. George (Jordi) slaying the dragon: The humpback roofline suggests a cresting dragon's back, and the smallest, top balcony is shaped like a rosebud (echoing the legend that a rose grew in the place where St. George spilled the dragon's blood). The building's tibia-like

# Modernista Masters: Gaudí and Beyond

Yes, you'll hear plenty about Gaudí, but he's merely one of many great minds who contributed to the architectural revolution of Modernisme. Here's a rundown of the movement's stars—great talents with names much harder to pronounce and remember than Gaudí's. For a sense of the historical context that gave rise to these talented architects, see the "Modernisme and the Renaixença" sidebar, earlier.

## The Stars of Modernisme

**Antoni Gaudí** (1852-1926), Barcelona's most famous Modernista artist, was descended from four generations of metalworkers—a lineage of which he was quite proud. He incorporated ironwork into his architecture and came up with novel approaches to architectural structure and space. Gaudí's work strongly influenced his younger Catalan contemporary, Salvador Dalí. Notice the similarities: While Dalí was creating unlikely and shocking juxtapositions of photorealistic images, Gaudí did the same in architecture— using the spine of a reptile for a bannister or a turtle shell design on windows. Entire trips (and lives) are dedicated to seeing the works of Gaudí, but on a brief visit in Barcelona, the ones most worth considering are his great unfin-

ished church, the Sagrada Família; several mansions in the town center, including La Pedrera, Casa Batlló, and Palau Güell; and Park Güell, his ambitious and never-completed housing development.

While Gaudí gets 90 percent of the tourists' attention, two other great Modernista architects were just as important: Lluís Domènech i Montaner and Josep Puig i Cadafalch. Gaudí was certainly a remarkable innovator, but these two were perhaps more purely representative of the Modernista style.

**Lluís Domènech i Montaner** (1850-1923), a professor and politician, was responsible for some major civic buildings, including his masterwork, the Palace of Catalan Music (described on page 49), and the Hospital de Sant Pau, a sprawling complex covering nine blocks (roughly between the Sagrada Família and Park Güell; see page 59). Domènech i Montaner also designed Casa Lleó Morera on the Block of Discord (described later) and Casa Fuster (now a luxury hotel—see page 151), along with several works in the towns of Canet de Mar, Comillas, and others.

**Josep Puig i Cadafalch** (1867-1956) was a city planner who oversaw the opening up of Via Laietana (through the middle of the Old City, see page 117), the redevelopment of Montjuïc for the 1929 World Expo, and a redesign of the monastery at Santa Maria de Montserrat. Later he flourished as a Modernista architect in his own right, best known for manor houses such as Casa de les Punxes (described on page 151) and Casa Amatller on the Block of Discord (described later). He designed the brick Casaramona factory complex, now the cutting-edge CaixaForum exhibition space (see page 72). Perhaps most importantly, Puig i Cadafalch de-signed Casa Martí, a home for the Modernista hangout bar Els Quatre Gats, which became a cradle of sorts for the whole movement. The bar still welcomes visitors today (see page 190).

## Supporting Cast

All architects worked with a team of people who, while not famous, made real contributions. For example, Gaudí's colleague **Josep Maria Jujol** (1879-1949) is primarily responsible for much of what Gaudí became known for—the broken-tile mosaic decorations (called *trencadís*) on Park Güell's benches and La Pedrera's chimneys.

**Joan Martorell i Montells** (1833-1906) was a professor, mentor, and employer of a young Antoni Gaudí. Although an accomplished architect in his own right, Martorell's most important role was as a facilitator of his prized student: He oversaw the committee that hired Gaudí to build the Sagrada Família, and introduced Gaudí to **Eusebi Güell,** who became Gaudí's most important benefactor.

Eusebi Güell (1846-1918) used his nearly $90 billion fortune to bankroll Gaudí and others, much as the Medici financed Michelangelo and Leonardo da Vinci. Güell's name still adorns two of Gaudí's most important works: Palau Güell and Park Güell (described on pages 37 and 59). The other Modernista architects also had deep-pocketed patrons who financed their works.

pillars and skull-like balconies evoke the dragon's victims. Look at the first-floor bay window. If you squint (and perhaps smoke some pot, the consumption of which is legal here, by the way), you might see a bat with outstretched wings, relating to a Catalunyan folk legend. Notice also the random broken tiles, a Gaudí trademark that only later became appreciated. The tiled roof has a soft-ice-cream-cone turret topped with a cross. But some see instead a Mardi Gras theme, with mask-like balconies, a facade flecked with purple and gold confetti, and the ridge of a harlequin's hat up top. The inscrutable Gaudí preferred to leave his designs open to interpretation (you can tour the interior—see listing on page 53).

Before moving on, turn 180 degrees and look across the boulevard to see the straight iron-framed apartment building at #52—structurally the same as Casa Batlló. In 1904, when Gaudí was hired to renovate Casa Batlló, it looked like that.

• *Next door is...*

## Casa Amatller (#41)

Josep Puig i Cadafalch completely remodeled this house for the Amatller family. The facade features a creative mix of three of Spain's historical traditions: Moorish-style pentagram-and-vine designs; Gothic-style tracery, gargoyles, and bay windows; and the step-gable roof from Spain's Habsburg connection to the Low Countries. Notice the many layers of the letter "A": The house itself (with its gable) forms an A, as does the decorative frieze over the bay window on the right side of the facade. Within that frieze, you'll see several more A's sprouting from branches (*amatller* means "almond tree"). The reliefs above the smaller windows show off the hobbies of the Amatller clan: Find the cherubs holding the early box camera, the open book, and the amphora jug (which

the family collected). Look through the second-floor bay window to see the corkscrew column. You can visit the interior via a guided tour (see page 55).

For another dimension of Modernisme, peek into the ground-floor windows of the Bagues Joieria jewelry shop and notice the slinky pieces by Spanish Art Nouveau jeweler Masriera.

• *Continue down the street to the end of the block. There, on the corner, you'll find...*

### Casa Lleó Morera (#35)

This paella-like mix of styles is the work of the architect Lluís
Domènech i Montaner, who also designed the Palace of Catalan
Music. The lower floors have classical
columns and a Greek-temple-like bay
window. (Notice the real marble column—supporting nothing but some
aristocrat's ego—placed for all to see
behind the bay window.) Farther up
are Gothic balconies of rosettes and
tracery, while the upper part has faux
Moorish stucco work. The whole thing
is ornamented with fantastic griffins,
angels, and fish. Flanking the third-
story windows are figures holding the
exciting inventions of the day—the
camera, lightbulb, and gramophone—
designed to demonstrate just how
modern the homeowners were in this age of Modern-isme. The
wonderful interior may be open to the public for limited guided
tours (see listing on page 55).

• *From here, it's four long blocks to Gaudí's Modernista masterpiece, La
Pedrera. While the easiest route is to simply turn around and plow back
up Passeig de Gràcia—passing top-end shops—it's more interesting to
detour around the block. From this corner, walk up Carrer del Consell de Cent, past galleries, high-end shops, and a Starbucks, to another
splashy Eixample boulevard—Rambla de Catalunya. When you hit this
delightful street, go into the park-like median strip and turn right.*

### ❾ Rambla de Catalunya

As you head up Rambla de Catalunya, you'll find a narrower, more
manageable street lined with inviting cafés and shops—boutiques
that are still upscale, but generally more local and unique than
those on the main drag.

 After one block, a half-block detour (to the right) on Carrer
d'Aragó gets you to the **Fundació
Antoni Tàpies,** dedicated to the
20th-century abstract artist from
Barcelona. The Montaner-designed
building sums up the Modernist
credo: modern brick, iron, and glass
materials; playful decorative motifs;
and a spacious, functional, and light-
filled interior. The tangled rooftop is
called "The Cloud and the Chair." The collection itself is pricey
to view (admission included with Articket BCN), yet fans of the

artist's work will enjoy seeing his distinct mud-caked canvases. Tàpies (1923-2012) laid the canvas on the floor, covered it with wet varnish, and sprinkled in dust, dirt, and paint. Then he drew simple designs in the still-wet goop, capturing the primitive power of cavemen tracing the first art in mud with a stick.

• *Continue up the median of Rambla de Catalunya. As you stroll three blocks, enjoy the variety of facades, and ahead, on the mountaintop, the 19th-century Church of the Sacred Heart. When you get to Carrer de Provença, turn right and make your way to...*

## ⓾ La Pedrera (a.k.a. Casa Milà)

This Gaudí exterior laughs down on the crowds filling Passeig de Gràcia. La Pedrera ("The Quarry") has a much-photographed

roller coaster of melting-ice-cream eaves. This is Barcelona's quintessential Modernista building and was Gaudí's last major work (1906-1910) before he dedicated his final years to the Sagrada Família.

The building has a steel structural skeleton to support its weight (a new construction technique at the time). Gaudí's planned statues of the Virgin Mary and archangels were vetoed by the owner. If you have time—and the line's not too long—consider touring the house's interior and rooftop (see listing on page 56).

• *From here, you can head back to Plaça de Catalunya—it's a straight shot, seven blocks down Passeig de Gràcia. The Diagonal Metro station near La Pedrera, on the L3 (green) line, has easy connections to Plaça de Catalunya and other key stops.*

*But for a finale to our walk, consider heading another two blocks up Passeig de Gràcia to the boundary of the Eixample. Continue up Passeig de Gràcia until you run into...*

## Avinguda Diagonal

This aptly named boulevard slashes diagonally through the middle of the Eixample, connecting the neighborhood to the port.

Diagonal marks the end of the Eixample; just across the street begins the neighborhood of **Gràcia.** Compared to the urban, upscale street plan of the Eixample, Gràcia feels like what it is—a onetime small town that's now part of a big city, with narrower streets and more character. Gràcia is known as an upper-middle-class, intellectual part of town, with many design schools and a youthful scene (see page 223 in the Nightlife in Barcelona chapter).

Cross over to the left side of Passeig de Gràcia and find the

Catalunya TI. Go through the gate to the left of the TI entrance to find your way to one of Barcelona's most enjoyable little parks—a tropical oasis in the heart of the city. Relax.

• *If you're a Modernista completist, it's just a short walk from here to three more fine buildings—"extra credit" for those fascinated by this era.*

## Modernista Detour

Cross Diagonal, continuing two long blocks on Passeig de Grà-cia. Where the street curves around the tree-lined median, you'll find the **Hotel Casa Fuster,** a fine Modernista building by Lluís Domènech i Montaner. This top-of-the-top luxury hotel is a favorite of Woody Allen (who has an affinity for Barcelona, featuring it in his film *Vicky Cristina Barcelona*). Seeking a place to play jazz in town, Allen prodded the hotel to sponsor jazz concerts. The hotel's Café Vienés now hosts a jazz night every Thursday (for details, see page 220).

Backtrack to Diagonal to reach two works by Josep Puig i Cadafalch. Take a left (go east) down the busy Diagonal boulevard. After a block, you reach the **Palau Baró de Quadras** (Diagonal 373, on the right across the street). Puig i Cadafalch's plateresque (Spain's medieval "silverwork" style of intricate decoration) facade celebrates a time when Catalunya was powerful, and the statues flanking the door—of St. George defeating the dragon—make the building's Catalan pride even more evident. Today the building houses Institut Ramón Llul, dedicated to promoting Catalan language and culture. As a public cultural center, it's a rare Modernista interior that's free to enter and explore (closed Sat-Sun).

Continuing another block and a half down Diagonal leads to the distinctively turreted Casa Terrades (at #416, on the left)—better known as **Casa de les Punxes** ("House of Spikes"). Here Puig i Cadafalch lassoed together what had been three separate buildings into one large complex, wrapping them in a fanciful Gothic castle cloak (no inside access). The turrets, spires, balconies, and ceramic tiles celebrate Catalan culture.

• *Back at Passeig de Gràcia (where it hits Diagonal), you have several options:*

*The* **Diagonal Metro stop** *(right in front of you) is on L3 (green), which zips you effortlessly to Plaça de Catalunya, Liceu (middle of the Ramblas), and Drassanes (bottom of the Ramblas).*

*You can also use the Metro to reach the pièce de résistance of Mod-*

*ernisme*, the **Sagrada Família:** *Head west one block on Carrer del Rosselló to find the entrance to the Diagonal stop for L5 (blue); take it to the Sagrada Família stop. (See the* 📖 *Sagrada Família Tour chapter.)*

*Or, to visit another great Modernista sight, hop on bus #24 to Gaudí's* **Park Güell** *(catch it on Passeig de Gràcia just south of Diagonal, same side of street as La Pedrera; get off at Ctra Carmel-Parc Güell stop;* 📖 *see the Park Güell Tour chapter).*

# SAGRADA FAMÍLIA TOUR

Architect Antoni Gaudí's most famous and awe-inspiring work is this unfinished, super-sized church. With its cake-in-the-rain facade and otherworldly spires, the church is not only an icon of Barcelona and its trademark Modernista style, but also a symbol of this period's greatest practitioner. As an architect, Gaudí's foundations were classics, nature, and religion. The church represents all three.

Nearly a century after his death, people continue to toil to bring Gaudí's designs to life. There's something powerful about a community of committed people with a vision, working on a church that won't be finished in their lifetime—as was standard in the Gothic age. The progress of this remarkable building is a testament to the generations of architects, sculptors, stonecutters, fund-raisers, and donors who've been caught up in the audacity of Gaudí's astonishing vision. After paying the steep admission price (becoming a partner in this building project), you will actually feel good. If there's any building on earth I'd like to see, it's the Basílica de la Sagrada Família...finished.

## Orientation

**Cost:** Basic ticket-€18 (church only), Guided Experience ticket-€29 (church and live guide), Audio Tour ticket-€26 (church and audioguide), Top Views ticket-€35 (church, audioguide, and tower elevator), Gaudí's Work and Life ticket-€31 (church, audioguide, and Gaudí House Museum at Park Güell—see page 59). All options are cheaper if you buy online.

**Hours:** Daily 9:00-20:00, Oct-March until 18:00.

**Advance Tickets:** To avoid the ticket-buying line and to save a few euros, you can reserve an entry time and buy tickets in advance at www.sagradafamilia.cat. You must decide if you want to add the audioguide, tower elevator, live guide, or Gaudí House Museum to your ticket at the time of purchase. (You can't buy any extras once inside the church.) Print tickets at home, and go to the main entrance on the Nativity Facade side for a security check before entering.

**Crowd-Beating Tips:** Though the line can seem long (often curving around the block), it generally moves quickly; you can ask for an estimate from the guards at the front of the line or find a sign giving wait times. Still, waits can be up to 45 minutes at peak times—and occasionally stretch much longer (most crowded in the morning). To minimize waiting, arrive right at 9:00 (when the church opens) or after 16:00. To skip the line, buy advance tickets.

**Getting There:** The church address is Carrer de Mallorca 401. The Sagrada Família Metro stop puts you right on its doorstep: Exit toward Plaça de la Sagrada Família.

**Getting In:** The ticket windows are on the west side of the church, at the Passion Facade. If you already have tickets, head straight for the Nativity Facade (in front of Plaça de Gaudí), where you'll find entry lines for individuals. Show your ticket to the guard, who will direct you to the right line.

**Information:** Tel. 932-073-031, www.sagradafamilia.cat.

**Tours:** The 50-minute English tours run May-Oct daily at 11:00, 12:00, 13:00, and 15:00 (no 12:00 tour Mon-Fri in Nov-April; choose tour time when you buy ticket). Or rent the good 1.5-hour audioguide.

**Tower Elevators:** Two elevators take you (for a fee) partway up towers on opposite sides of the Sagrada Família for great views of the city and a gargoyle's-eye perspective of the loopy church. You'll also get the opportunity to cross a dizzying bridge between towers. To get back down, you'll need to take the stairs.

The **Passion Facade elevator** takes you up a touch higher, and the stairs to come down are slightly wider than those you'd descend if you rode the **Nativity Facade elevator.** You can only ride the elevator back down if you don't feel well.

The elevators cost extra, and each ticket comes with an entry time. When you **reserve online** (see "Advance Tickets," earlier) you can try to get your tower entry time in sync with your church visit. You will only be able to ride one elevator, and you may not be able to choose which one.

No backpacks or bigger bags are allowed, but lockers are available at each elevator. The lockers, though intended for those riding the elevators, can be used by anyone.

**Length of This Tour:** Allow 1.5 hours. If you have less time, skip the museum and schoolhouse, and max out on ogling the magnificent building itself, inside and out.

# A Dream Made Real

For over 130 years, Barcelona has labored to bring Antoni Gaudí's vision to reality. Local craftsmen often cap off their careers by spending a couple of years on this exciting construction site. The present architect has been at it since 1985. The work is funded exclusively by private donations and entry fees, which is another reason its completion has taken so long. Your admission helps pay for the ongoing construction.

Like Gothic churches of medieval times, the design has evolved over the decades. At heart, it's Gothic, a style much admired by Gaudí. He added his own Art Nouveau/Modernisme touches, guided by nature and engineering innovations. Today the site bristles with cranking cranes, rusty forests of rebar, and scaffolding. Sagrada Família offers a fun look at a living, growing bigger-than-life building.

## Sagrada Família Timeline

**1882:** The church is begun in Gothic-revival style (by architect Francisco de Paula del Villar).

**1883:** Paula del Villar quits, and Antoni Gaudí is hired—and proceeds to completely re-envision the church's design.

**1892:** Gaudí begins the Nativity Facade.

**1914:** Gaudí turns his attention exclusively to the Sagrada Família.

**1925:** The first bell tower is completed.

**1926:** Gaudí dies with the project about 20 percent complete.

**1936-1939:** The Spanish Civil War halts all work; the crypt is burned, along with many of Gaudí's plans.

**1950s:** Building resumes in earnest with the start of the Passion Facade.

**1976:** The four Passion spires are finished, bringing the total of completed spires to eight (out of 18 planned).

**1980s:** Computer technology is introduced, greatly accelerating the pace of construction.

**2000:** The nave roof is completed.

**2005:** Passion statues are completed.

**2010:** Crossing vaults are finished (enclosing the roof), and Pope Benedict XVI dedicates the church as a basilica.

**2026?** The church could be finished by the 100th anniversary of Gaudí's death. Make a date to attend the dedication with your kids...to teach them a lesson in delayed gratification.

**Nearby:** Inviting parks flank the building, facing the two completed facades.

## BACKGROUND

Gaudí labored on the Sagrada Família for 43 years, from 1883 until his death in 1926 (see sidebar). Since then, construction has moved forward in fits and starts, though much progress was made in recent decades, thanks to Barcelona's 1992 Olympics renaissance, the ensuing rediscovery of the genius of Gaudí, and advances in technology. In 2010, the main nave was finished enough to host a consecration Mass by the pope (as a Catholic church, it is used for services, though irregularly). As I stepped inside on my last visit, the brilliance of Gaudí's vision for the interior was apparent.

The main challenges today: Ensure that construction can withstand the vibrations caused by the speedy AVE trains rumbling underfoot, construct the tallest church spire ever built, and find a way to buy out the people who own the condos in front of the planned Glory Facade so that Gaudí's vision of a grand esplanade approaching the church can be realized. The goal to finish the church by the 100th anniversary of Gaudí's death, in 2026, may seem overly optimistic. But, with money from millions of visitors pouring in each year, this goal appears more obtainable as time goes by.

# The Tour Begins

• *Start outside the Nativity Facade (where the entry lines for individuals are located), on the eastern side of the church. Before heading to the entrance, take in the...*

## ❶ View of the Exterior

Stand and imagine how grand this church will be when completed. The four 330-foot spires topped with crosses are just a fraction of this mega-church. When finished, the church will have 18 spires. Four will stand at each of the three entrances. Rising above those will be four taller towers, dedicated to the four Evangelists. A tower dedicated to Mary will rise still higher—400 feet. And in the very center of the complex will stand the grand 560-foot Jesus tower, topped with a cross that will shine like a spiritual lighthouse, visible even from out at sea.

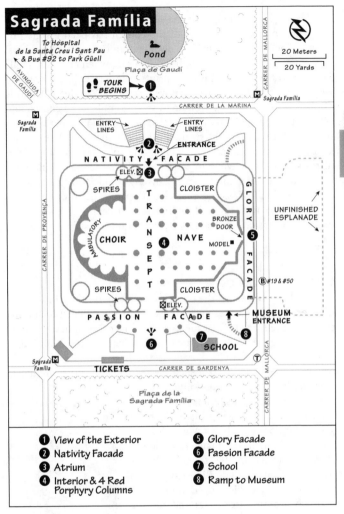

**Sagrada Família**

To Hospital
de la Santa Creu i Sant Pau
& Bus #92 to Park Güell

Pond

Plaça de Gaudí

AVINGUDA DE GAUDÍ

TOUR BEGINS ❶

Ⓜ Sagrada Família

CARRER DE LA MARINA

Ⓜ Sagrada Família

ENTRY LINES    ENTRY LINES

❷  ENTRANCE

N A T I V I T Y   F A C A D E

ELEV. ⊠ ❸

SPIRES          CLOISTER

T R A N S E P T

CHOIR   AMBULATORY   NAVE

BRONZE DOOR

MODEL ■

❹          ❺

SPIRES          CLOISTER

⊠ELEV.

P A S S I O N   F A C A D E

CARRER DE PROVENÇA

G L O R Y   F A C A D E

UNFINISHED ESPLANADE

Ⓑ #19 & #50

MUSEUM ENTRANCE

❼          ❽

❻      SCHOOL

Ⓜ Sagrada Família

TICKETS    CARRER DE SARDENYA    Ⓣ

CARRER DE MALLORCA

Plaça de la Sagrada Família

20 Meters
20 Yards

❶ View of the Exterior
❷ Nativity Facade
❸ Atrium
❹ Interior & 4 Red Porphyry Columns
❺ Glory Facade
❻ Passion Facade
❼ School
❽ Ramp to Museum

The Nativity Facade—where tourists enter today—is only a side entrance to the church. The grand main entrance will be around to the left. A nine-story apartment building will eventually have to be torn down to accommodate the church's entrance esplanade. The three facades—Nativity, Passion, and Glory—will chronicle Christ's life from birth to death to resurrection. Inside and out, a goal of the church is to bring the lessons of the Bible to the world. Despite his boldly modern architectural vision, Gaudí was fundamentally traditional and deeply religious. He designed the Sagrada Família to be a bastion of solid Christian values in the midst of what was a humble workers' colony in a fast-changing city.

When Gaudí died, only one section (on the Nativity Facade) had been completed. The rest of the church has been inspired by Gaudí's long-range vision, but designed and executed by others. This artistic freedom was amplified in 1936, when civil war shelling burned many of Gaudí's blueprints. Supporters of the ongoing work insist that Gaudí, who enjoyed saying, "My client [God] is not in a hurry," knew he wouldn't live to complete the church and recognized that later architects and artists would rely on their own muses for inspiration. Detractors maintain that the church's design is a uniquely, intensely personal one and that it's folly (if not disrespectful) for anyone to try to guess what Gaudí would have intended. Studying the various plans and models in the museum below the church, it's clear that Gaudí's plan evolved dramatically the longer he worked. Is it appropriate to keep implementing a century-old vision that can no longer be modified by its creator? Discuss.

• *Now approach the...*

## ❷ Nativity Facade

This is the only part of the church essentially finished in Gaudí's lifetime. The four spires decorated with his unmistakably nonlinear sculpture mark this facade as part of his original design. Mixing Gothic-style symbolism, images from nature, and Modernista asymmetry, the Nativity Facade is the best example of Gaudí's original vision, and it established the template for future architects who would work on the building.

The theme of this facade, which faces the rising sun, is Christ's birth. A statue above the doorway shows Mary, Joseph, and Baby Jesus in the manger, while curious cows peek in. It's the Holy Family—or "Sagrada Família"—to whom this church is dedicated. Flanking the doorway are the three Magi and adoring shepherds. Other statues show Jesus as a young carpenter and angels playing musical instruments. Higher up on the facade, in the arched niche, Jesus crowns Mary triumphantly.

The facade is all about birth and new life, from the dove-covered Tree of Life on top to the turtles at the base of the columns flanking the entrance. At the bottom of the Tree of Life is a white pelican. Because it was believed that this noble bird would kill itself to feed its young, it was often used in the Middle Ages as a symbol for the self-sacrifice of Jesus. The chameleon gargoyles at the outer corners of the facade (just above door level) represent the changeability of life. It's as playful as the Passion Facade is grim. Gaudí's

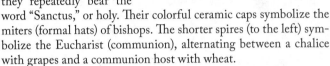

plans were for this facade to be painted. Cleverly, this attractive facade was built and finished first to bring in financial support for the project.

The four **spires** are dedicated to apostles, and they repeatedly bear the word "Sanctus," or holy. Their colorful ceramic caps symbolize the miters (formal hats) of bishops. The shorter spires (to the left) symbolize the Eucharist (communion), alternating between a chalice with grapes and a communion host with wheat.

The doors in the middle of the facade were designed by the Sagrada Família's head sculptor, Etsuro Sotoo. Born in Japan, Sotoo visited Barcelona for the first time in 1978 and fell in love with the project. He worked hard to become a part of it, and even converted to Catholicism. Go up to the doors and find the small colorful bugs and leaves, which have not been painted, but treated with chemicals to produce the colors you see.

• *Enter the church. As you pass through Sotoo's doors into the* ❸ *atrium, look right to see one of the* **elevators** *up to the towers. For now, continue into the...*

## ❹ Interior

Typical of even the most traditional Catalan and Spanish churches, the floor plan is in the shape of a Latin cross, 300 feet long and 200 feet wide. Ultimately, the church will encompass 48,000 square feet, accommodating 8,000 worshippers. The nave's roof is 150 feet high. The crisscross arches of the ceiling (the vaults) show off Gaudí's distinctive engineering. Throughout the interior, video screens and diagrams explain elements

of this engineering feat. The church's roof and flooring were only completed in 2010—just in time for Pope Benedict XVI to arrive and consecrate the church.

Part of Gaudí's religious vision was a love for nature. He said, "Nothing is invented; it's written in nature." Like the trunks of trees, these **columns** (56 in all) blossom with life, complete with branches, leaves, and knot-like capitals. The columns are a variety of colors—brown clay, gray granite, dark-gray basalt. The taller columns are 72 feet tall; the shorter ones are exactly half that.

The angled columns form many **arches.** You'll see both parabolas (U-shaped) and hyperbolas (flatter, elliptical shapes). Gaudí's starting point was the Gothic pointed arch used in medieval churches. But he tweaked it after meticulous study of which arches are best at bearing weight.

**Windows** let light filter in like the canopy of a rainforest, giving both privacy and an intimate connection with God. The clear glass is temporary and is gradually being replaced by stained glass. Notice how splashes of color breathe even more life into this amazing space. The morning light shines in through blues, greens, and other cool colors, whereas the evening light shines through reds, oranges, and warm tones. Gaudí envisioned an awe-inspiring canopy with a symphony of colored light to encourage a contemplative mood.

High up at the back half of the church, the U-shaped **choir**—suspended above the nave—can seat 1,000. The singers will eventually be backed by four organs (there's one now).

Work your way up the grand nave, walking through this forest of massive columns. At the center of the church stand four **red porphyry columns,** each marked with an Evangelist's symbol and name in Catalan: angel (Mateu), lion (Marc), bull (Luc), and eagle (Joan). These columns support a ceiling vault that's 200 feet high—and eventually will also support the central steeple, the 560-foot Jesus tower with the shining cross. The steeple will be further supported by four underground pylons, each consisting of 8,000 tons of cement. It will be the tallest church steeple in the world, though still a few feet shorter than the city's highest point at the summit of Montjuïc hill, as Gaudí believed that a creation of man should not attempt to eclipse the creation of God.

Stroll behind the altar through one side of the **ambulatory** to see a short video about the architect and his work. A wall cuts off the space, so to reach a small chapel set aside for prayer and meditation on the other side, you must go through the nave to the opposite side of the main aisle of chairs. Before the entrance to the chapel you can look through windows down at the **crypt** (which holds the tomb of Gaudí). Peering down into that surprisingly traditional space, imagine how the church was started as a fairly conventional, 19th-century Neo-Gothic building until Gaudí was given the responsibility to finish it.

• *Head to the far end of the church, to what will eventually be the main entrance. Just inside the door, find the **bronze model** of the floor plan for the completed church. Facing the doors, look high up to see Josep Maria Subirachs' statue of one of Barcelona's patron saints, **George (Jordi).** While you can't see it, imagine what outside these doors will someday be the...*

## ❺ Glory Facade

Study the life-size image of the **bronze door,** emblazoned with the Lord's Prayer in Catalan, surrounded by "Give us this day our daily bread" in 50 lan-

guages. If you were able to walk through the actual door, you'd be face-to-face with...drab, doomed apartment blocks. In the 1950s, the mayor of Barcelona, figuring this day would never really come, sold the land destined for the church project. Now the city must buy back these buildings in order to complete Gaudí's vision: that of a grand esplanade leading to this main entry. Four towers will rise. The facade's sculpture will represent how the soul passes through death, faces the Last Judgment, avoids the pitfalls of hell, and finds its way to eternal glory with God. Gaudí purposely left the facade's design open for later architects—stay tuned.

• *Head back up the nave, and exit through the left transept. Before passing through the doors, look down at the fine porphyry floor with scenes of Jesus' entry into Jerusalem. To the left, notice the second **elevator** up to the towers. Once outside, back up to take in the...*

## ❻ Passion Facade

Judge for yourself how well Gaudí's original vision has been carried out by later artists. The Passion Facade's four spires were designed by Gaudí and completed (quite faithfully) in 1976. But the lower part was only inspired by Gaudí's designs. The stark sculptures were interpreted freely (and controversially) by Josep Maria Subi-

rachs (1927-2014), who completed the work in 2005.

Subirachs tells the story of Christ's torture and execution. The various scenes—Last Supper, betrayal, whipping, and so on—zigzag up from bottom to top, culminating in Christ's crucifixion over the doorway. The style is severe and unadorned, quite different from Gaudí's signature playfulness. But the bone-like archways are closely based on Gaudí's original designs. And Gaudí had made it clear that this facade should be grim and terrifying.

The facade is full of symbolism. A

stylized Alpha and Omega is over the door (which faces the setting sun). Jesus, hanging on the cross, has hair made of an open book, symbolizing the word of God. To the left of the door is a grid of numbers, always adding up to 33—Jesus' age at the time of his death. The distinct face of the man below and left of Christ is a memorial to Gaudí. Now look high above: The two-ton figure suspended between the towers is the soul of Jesus, ascending to heaven.

• *Now head into the small building outside the Passion Facade. This is the...*

## ❼ School

Gaudí erected this school for the children of the workers building the church. Today, it displays a classroom and a replica of Gaudí's desk as it was the day he died.

• *Back outside, head down the ramp, where you'll find WCs and the entrance to the...*

## ❽ Museum

Housed in what will someday be the church's crypt, the museum displays Gaudí's original **models and drawings,** and chronicles the

progress of construction over the past 130-plus years.

Upon entering, you'll see **photos** (including one of the master himself) and a **timeline** illustrating how construction work has progressed from Gaudí's day to now. Before turning into the main hall, find **three different visions** for this church. Notice how the arches evolved as Gaudí tinkered—from the original, pointy Neo-Gothic arches, to parabolic ones, to the hyperbolic style he eventually settled on. Also in this hall are replicas of the **pulpit** and **confessional** that Gaudí designed.

As you wander, notice how the **plaster models,** used for the church's construction, don't always match the finished product—these are ideas, not blueprints set in stone. The Passion Facade model, at the other end of the museum near the exit, shows Gaudí's original vision, with which Subirachs tinkered very freely (see "Passion Facade," earlier). All of the models make clear the influence of nature. The columns seem light, with branches springing forth and capitals that look like palm trees.

Go up the main hallway walking under a huge **model of the nave,** and past some Gaudí-designed iron works (on the left).

On the right is a small exhibit commemorating **Pope Benedict XVI**'s 2010 visit to consecrate the church. On the left is the intriguing **"Hanging Model"** for Gaudí's unfinished Church of Colònia Güell (in a suburb of Barcelona), featuring a design similar to the Sagrada Família. The model illustrates how the architect used gravity to calculate the arches that support the church. Wires dangle like suspended chains, forming perfect hyperbolic arches. Attached to these are bags, representing the weight the arches must support. Flip these arches over, and they can bear the heavy weight of the roof. The mirror below the model shows how the right-side-up church is derived from this.

Farther along, a small hallway on the left leads to some original Gaudí architectural **sketches** in a dimly lit room and a worthwhile 20-minute **movie** (continuously shown in Catalan with subtitles).

From the end of this hall, you have another opportunity to look down into the crypt and at **Gaudí's tomb.** Gaudí lived on the site for more than a decade and is buried in the Neo-Gothic 19th-century crypt (also viewable from the ambulatory). There's a move afoot to make Gaudí a saint. Gaudí prayer cards provide words of devotion to his beatification. Perhaps someday his tomb will be a place of pilgrimage.

On the right, you can peek into a busy **workshop** still used for making the same kinds of plaster models Gaudí used to envision the final product in three dimensions.

From here, you can either exit the museum to a gift shop, or backtrack through the museum and exit the church through the Passion Facade. Outside, look back and pause for a moment to pay homage to the man who made all this possible. Gaudí—a faithful Catholic whose medieval-style mysticism belied his career as a Modernista architect—was certainly driven to greatness by his passion for God.

• Our tour is over. From here, you have several options.

**Return to Central Barcelona:** You can either hop on the Metro or take one of two handy buses (both stop on Carrer de Mallorca, directly in front of the Glory Facade). Bus #19 takes you back to the **Old City** in 15 minutes, stopping near the cathedral and in the El Born district (with the ◫ Picasso Museum and ◫ El Born Walk). Bus #50 goes to the heart of the **Eixample** (corner of Gran Via de les Corts Catalanes and Passeig de Gràcia—near the start of the ◫ Eixample Walk), then continues on to Plaça Espanya where you can hop off for the **Montjuïc** sites (see "Getting to Montjuïc" on page 61).

*Visit **Park Güell**: The park (described next) sits nearly two (uphill) miles to the northwest. By far the easiest way to get there is to spring for a taxi (around €12).*

*But if you prefer public transportation and don't mind a little walking, here's a scenic way to get there that also takes you past another, often overlooked Modernista masterpiece: the striking **Hospital de la Santa Creu i Sant Pau** (see listing on page 58). With the Nativity Facade at your back, walk to the near-left corner of the park across the street. Then cross the street to reach the diagonal Avinguda de Gaudí (between the Repsol gas station and the KFC). Follow the funky lamp-posts four blocks gradually uphill (about 10 minutes) along Avinguda de Gaudí, a pleasantly shaded, café-lined pedestrian street, to reach the hospital.*

*After your visit, facing the main entrance, go right to catch bus #92 on Carrer de Sant Antoni Maria Claret, which will take you to the side entrance of Park Güell.*

# PARK GÜELL TOUR

Tucked in the foothills at the edge of Barcelona, this fanciful park—designed by Antoni Gaudí—combines playful design, inviting spaces, and a terrace offering sweeping views over the rooftops of the city.

When the entire park was free to enter, it became so popular that it was nearly trampled by tourists, obscuring the very sights they'd come to see. To control crowds, the part of the park with the most popular sights was declared the Monumental Zone, which requires an admission fee and a timed entry to visit. This fairly compact zone contains a pair of gingerbread-style houses, a grand staircase monitored by a colorful dragon, a forest of columns supporting a spectacular view terrace, and an undulating balcony slathered in tile shards.

Outside the zone, the rest of the park contains the Gaudí House Museum, Calvary viewpoint, picnic area, and a pleasant network of nature trails—all of which (except the museum) are free.

No matter where you visit—inside the zone or out—what you're sure to see is Barcelonans and tourists alike enjoying a day at the park.

## Orientation

**Cost and Hours:** Much of the park is free, but you'll need a timed-entry ticket to get close to the iconic Gaudí features—the trademark dragon, tiled stairway, wavy benches, view terrace, and more—in the **Monumental Zone** (€8 at the gate or €7 online, www.parkguell.cat). The number of visitors admitted to the Monumental Zone at any one time is strictly limited, so it's smart to **reserve ahead online** as much as three months in advance. Once inside, you can stay in the Monumental Zone as long as you want, but when you leave the zone, you can't return. The Monumental Zone is open daily 8:00-21:30, Nov-March 8:30-18:00.

The **Gaudí House Museum,** outside the Monumental Zone, costs €5.50 (€31 combo-ticket includes Sagrada Família church and its audioguide; cheaper online), and is open daily 10:00-20:00, Oct-March until 18:00, www.casamuseugaudi. org.

**Length of this Tour:** An hour is plenty to take this tour, but the park is a pleasant place to linger longer.

**Getting There:** Park Güell is about 2.5 miles from Plaça de Catalunya, beyond the Gràcia neighborhood in Barcelona's foothills. If asking for directions, be aware that Catalans pronounce it "Park Gway" (sounds like "parkway").

To reach the historical front entrance (described below), it's easiest to take a **taxi** from downtown (about €12). You can also take the blue **Tourist Bus** from Plaça de Catalunya (stops about two blocks downhill from entrance), or a **Metro-plus-bus combination** (ride Metro to Joanic stop, look for Carrer de l'Escorial exit, walk up Carrer de l'Escorial to bus stop in front of #20, and hop on bus #116 to park entrance).

There's also a side entrance to the park (described below). It's accessible by **public bus** #24 (which you can catch from Plaça de Catalunya) or #92 (from near the Sagrada Família; for directions on connecting these two sights, see page 164).

**Getting In:** The Monumental Zone has four entrances for ticket holders—two of which also sell tickets. If you arrive at the park's historical front entrance (with two small buildings and an iron gate—currently exit only), attendants will direct you to the entrances, ticket booths, and ticket machines at the far-left or far-right corners of the Monumental Zone.

If you arrive at the park's side entrance, you'll find a ticket office, information desk, and WCs near the bus stop. Follow the Rosary Pathway (to the left of the building) to one of two view-terrace entrances.

Hang on to your ticket; you'll need to show it at the exit when you leave.

**Eating:** Options are limited. The park has a **snack bar** with tables offering simple sandwiches and beverages by the historical front entrance. There are a few basic cafés on the streets leading to the historical entrance. If you've packed a **picnic** (a good idea), head anywhere outside the Monumental Zone—eating is not allowed inside the ticketed area.

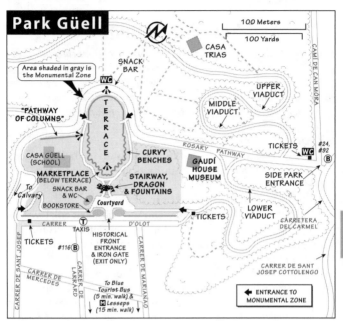

## OVERVIEW

Funded by his frequent benefactor Eusebi Güell, Gaudí intended this 30-acre garden to be a 60-residence housing project—a kind of gated community. Work began in 1900, but progress stalled in 1914 with the outbreak of World War I, and the project never resumed. Only two houses were built, neither designed by Gaudí— the structures are now home to the Gaudí House Museum and Casa Trias (not open to the public). As a high-income housing development, it flopped; but as a park, it's a delight, offering another peek into Gaudí's eccentric genius in a setting that's more natural than man-made—appropriate considering the naturalism that pervades Gaudí's work.

Many sculptures and surfaces in the park are covered with colorful *trencadís* mosaics—broken ceramic bits rearranged into new patterns. This Modernista invention, made of discarded tile, dishes, and even china dolls from local factories, was an easy, cheap, and aesthetically pleasing way to cover curvy surfaces like benches and columns. Although Gaudí promoted the technique, most of what you see was executed by his collaborator, Josep Maria Jujol.

# The Tour Begins

• *This tour assumes you're arriving at the historical front entrance. If you arrive at the side of the park and already have your Monumental Zone ticket, walk past the building (ticket office) and along the path to the view-terrace entrance. Enter and walk down to the stairway, picking up this tour on the inside of the historical front entrance.*

## Historical Front Entrance

Before entering the park, notice the **mosaic medallions** along the outside wall that say "park" in English—a reminder that Park Güell was modeled on the British "garden city" concept of integrating urban communities with green space.

Enjoy Gaudí's historical front entrance (now exit only) with its palm-frond **gate** and gas lamps (1900-1914) on either side, made of wrought iron. Gaudí's dad was a blacksmith, and he always enjoyed this medium.

Two Hansel-and-Gretel gingerbread lodges flank this former entrance, signaling to visitors that the park is a magical space. To

get inside, you need to go to one of two entries located at the far corners of the Monumental Zone. Once you're in, make your way back to the historical front entrance for a closer look at the lodges. One of the buildings houses a bookshop; the other is home to the skippable **La Casa del Guarda,** a branch of the Barcelona History Museum (MUHBA). The sparse exhibit inside features video slideshows about Gaudí's building methods and works, old black-and-white movies of the age, and no real artifacts. True Gaudí fans might want to take a close look at the

structure, though, as it's one of the few built examples of his ideas for simple housing. (The Gaudí House Museum, described later, is more interesting to me.)

• *Now face the grand...*

## Stairway

The **cave-like enclosures** flanking the stairs were functional: One was a garage for Eusebi Güell's newfangled automobiles, while the other was a cart shelter.

Three **fountains** are stacked in the middle of the stairway. The first, at the base of the steps, is rocky and leafy, typical of Gaudí's naturalism. Next is a red-and-gold-striped Catalan shield with the head of a serpent poking out. The third is a very famous dragon—an icon of the park (and of Barcelona). While the dragon—slain by Barcelona's patron saint, George (Jordi)—is a symbol of Catalan pride, this creature also evokes the crocodile mascot of Nîmes, France, where Eusebi Güell spent much of his youth. As for the ornamental brown tripod at the top of the stairs: Is it the Oracle of Delphi? The tail of the serpent whose head pokes out down below? Or something else entirely? Gaudí lets the viewer decide.

• *At the top, dip into the...*

## Marketplace (Hall of 100 Columns)

This space was designed to house a **produce market** for the neighborhood's 60 mansions. The Doric columns—each lined at the base

with white ceramic shards—add to the market's vitality (despite the hall's name, there are only 86 columns). White ceramic pieces also cover the multiple domes of the ceiling, which is interrupted by colorful mosaic rosettes. Look up to find four giant sun-like decorations representing the four seasons. Notice the hook in the middle of each one, where a lantern could be hung. Arranged around these are smaller rosettes, meant to suggest the lunar

cycle. Street performers and musicians like the acoustics here.

• *Continue up the left-hand staircase, looking left, down the playful...*

## "Pathway of Columns"

Gaudí drew his inspiration from nature, and this arcade is like a

surfer's perfect tube. This is one of many clever double-decker **viaducts** that Gaudí designed for the grounds: vehicles up top, pedestrians in the portico down below. Gaudí intended these walkways to remind visitors of the pilgrim routes that crisscross Spain (such as the famous Camino de

Santiago). Eusebi Güell lived in the pink house (now a school) next to the terrace. This house predates the park project and was not designed by Gaudí.

*• At the top of the stairway, you pop out on the...*

## Terrace

Sit on a colorful bench and enjoy one of Barcelona's best views. (Find Gaudí's Sagrada Família church in the distance.) The 360-foot-

long bench is designed to fit your body ergonomically. Supposedly, Gaudí enlisted a construction worker as his guinea pig to figure out exactly where to place the lumbar support (back in a time when "ergonomics" and "lumbar support" hadn't even been invented). To Gaudí, this terrace evoked ancient Greek theaters that burrowed scenically into the sides of hills—but its primary purpose was that of the ancient Greek agora, a wide-open meeting place. Gaudí engineered a water-catchment system by which rain hitting this plaza would flow through natural filters, then through the columns of the market below to a 300,000-gallon underground cistern. The water was bottled and sold as a health cure (this location—far away from polluting city factories—had a healthy cachet); excess water powers the park's fountains. Notice the lion's-head gargoyles and the big stone droplets that cling to the outside edge of the terrace, which hint at this hidden functional purpose.

*• From here, with the city at your back, the **Gaudí House Museum** is to your right, and the **Calvary** is high up on your left, almost hidden behind trees (both described next). These sights are outside the Monumental Zone; remember that once you leave the zone, you can't return.*

## Gaudí House Museum

This pink house with a steeple, standing in the middle of the park (near one of the side entrances), was Gaudí's home for 20 years. Designed not by Gaudí but by a fellow architect, it was originally built as a model home to attract prospective residents. Gaudí lived here from 1906 until 1925. His humble artifacts are mostly gone, but the house is now a museum with some quirky Gaudí furniture. Though small, it offers a good taste of what could have been if the envisioned housing development had prospered.

The main drag connecting this house to the terrace, called the **Rosary Pathway,** is lined with giant stone balls that represent the beads of a rosary. During the years he lived here, the reverent Gaudí would pray the rosary while walking this path.

## The Calvary

High on a wooded hill beyond the pink school building is a stubby stone tower topped with three crosses, representative of the Hill of Calvary where Jesus was crucified. Gaudí envisioned the topography of Park Güell as a metaphor for the soul's progress: starting at the low end and toiling uphill to reach spiritual enlightenment (a chapel was originally intended to occupy this spot). And indeed, the park's higher paths seem to converge to lead pilgrims to this summit. The tower rewards those who huff up here with grand views over Barcelona and its bay.

## The Rest of the Park

Like any park, this one is made for aimless rambling. As you wander, imagine living here a century ago—if this gated community had succeeded and was filled with Barcelona's wealthy. When considering the failure of Park Güell as a community development, also consider that it was an idea a hundred years ahead of its time. Back then, high-society ladies didn't want to live so far from the cultural action. Today, the surrounding neighborhoods are some of the wealthiest in town, and a gated community here could be a big hit.

• *To return to the city center after your visit, take a taxi (you'll find some waiting outside the historical front entrance) or the Metro. To reach the Metro station, hop on bus #116 to Plaça de Lesseps (confirm direction with driver) or walk 15 minutes downhill from the park's main entrance to the Lesseps Metro stop (walk straight ahead down Carrer de Larrard, turn right on busy Travessera de Dalt, and walk for several blocks to reach the Metro entrance). You can also catch bus #24 from the side of the park back to Plaça de Catalunya.*

**PARK GÜELL**

# SLEEPING IN BARCELONA

Choosing the right neighborhood in Barcelona is as important as choosing the right hotel. All of my recommended accommodations are in safe areas convenient to sightseeing. The area around Plaça de Catalunya, Barcelona's central square, is filled with business-class hotels. Near the Ramblas—the city's pedestrian boulevard—you'll find cheaper, less-refined places with more character. For Old World charm, stay in Barcelona's Old City. For an uptown feel, sleep in the Eixample.

Book your accommodations well in advance, especially if you'll be traveling during peak season or if your trip coincides with a major holiday or festival (see page 314). Note, though, that Barcelona can be busy any time of year.

Despite being Spain's most expensive city, Barcelona has reasonably priced rooms. Cheap places are more crowded in summer; fancier business-class hotels fill up in winter and may offer discounts on weekends and in summer. When considering relative hotel values, in summer and on weekends you can often get modern comfort in centrally located business-class hotels for about the same price (€100) as you'll pay for ramshackle charm. Any special prices, discounts, and offers of breakfast included are valid only when you book directly with the hotel. For more information and tips on pricing, getting deals, making reservations, seasonal differences, and other accommodation options—including apartments and other short-term rentals—see page 272.

# Sleep Code

Hotels are classified based on the average price of a standard double room without breakfast in high season.

| | |
|---|---|
| **$$$$** | **Splurge:** Most rooms over €170 |
| **$$$** | **Pricier:** €130-170 |
| **$$** | **Moderate:** €90-130 |
| **$** | **Budget:** €50-90 |
| **¢** | **Backpacker:** Under €50 |
| **RS%** | **Rick Steves discount** |

Unless otherwise noted, credit cards are accepted, hotel staff speak basic English, and free Wi-Fi is available. Comparison-shop by checking prices at several hotels (on each hotel's own website, on a booking site, or by email). For the best deal, *book directly with the hotel*. Ask for a discount if paying in cash; if the listing includes **RS%,** request a Rick Steves discount.

## NEAR PLAÇA DE CATALUNYA

These hotels have sliding-glass doors leading to shiny reception areas, air-conditioning, and modern bedrooms. Most are on big streets within two blocks of Barcelona's exuberant central square, where the Old City meets the Eixample. As business-class hotels, they have hard-to-pin-down prices that fluctuate with demand. In summer and on weekends, supply often far exceeds the demand, and many of these places cut prices to around €100. Most of these are located between two Metro stops: Catalunya and Universitat; if arriving by Aerobus, note that the bus also stops at both places. Some of my recommended hotels are on Carrer Pelai, a busy street; for these, request a quieter room in back.

**$$$$ Hotel Catalonia Plaça Catalunya** has four stars, an elegant old entryway with a modern reception area, splashy public spaces, slick marble and hardwood floors, 140 comfortable rooms, and a garden courtyard with a pool a world away from the big-city noise. It's a bit pricey for the quality of the rooms—you're paying for the posh lobby (air-con, elevator, a half-block off Plaça de Catalunya at Carrer de Bergara 11, Metro: Catalunya, tel. 933-015-151, www.hoteles-catalonia.com, catalunya@hoteles-catalonia.es).

**$$$$ Hotel Midmost** (owned by the same people as Hotel Denit, listed later) is a little west of Plaça de Catalunya. It has 60 rooms; a more upscale, four-star style; a rooftop terrace; and a mini swimming pool (family rooms, air-con, elevator, Carrer de Pelai 14, Metro: Universitat, tel. 935-051-100, www.hotelmidmost.com, info@hotelmidmost.com).

**$$$ Hotel Reding Croma,** on a quiet street a 10-minute walk west of the Ramblas and the Plaça de Catalunya action, is a slick and sleek place renting 44 mod, color-themed rooms at a reason-

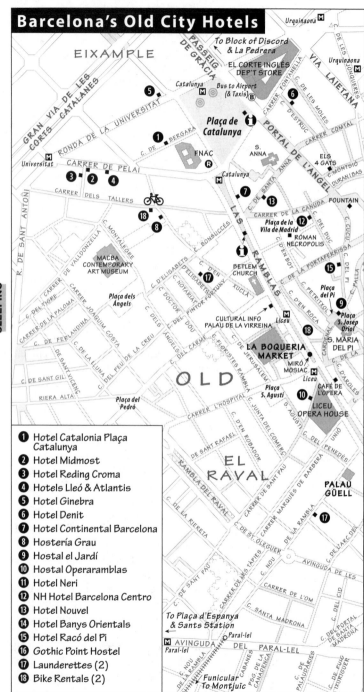

# Barcelona's Old City Hotels

1. Hotel Catalonia Plaça Catalunya
2. Hotel Midmost
3. Hotel Reding Croma
4. Hotels Lleó & Atlantis
5. Hotel Ginebra
6. Hotel Denit
7. Hotel Continental Barcelona
8. Hostería Grau
9. Hostal el Jardí
10. Hostal Operaramblas
11. Hotel Neri
12. NH Hotel Barcelona Centro
13. Hotel Nouvel
14. Hotel Banys Orientals
15. Hotel Racó del Pi
16. Gothic Point Hostel
17. Launderettes (2)
18. Bike Rentals (2)

SLEEPING

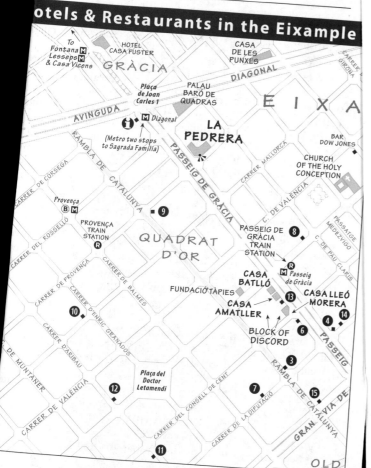

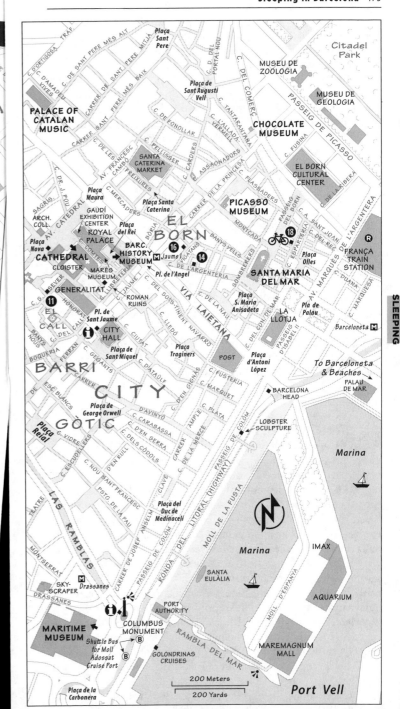

stful rooms are located in the El Born district on a pedestrian-
ed street between the cathedral and Church of Santa Maria del
Iar (air-con, elevator, Carrer de l'Argenteria 37, 50 yards from
Ietro: Jaume I, tel. 932-688-460, www.hotelbanysorientals.com,
servas@hotelbanysorientals.com).

$$$ **Hotel Racó del Pi,** part of the H10 hotel chain, is a qual-
y, professional place with generous public spaces and 37 modern,
right, quiet rooms. It's located on a wonderful pedestrian street
nmersed in the Barri Gòtic (air-con, around the corner from
aça del Pi at Carrer del Pi 7, 3-minute walk from Metro: Liceu,
l. 933-426-190, www.h10hotels.com, h10.raco.delpi@h10hotels.
m).

able price (RS%, air-con, elevator, Carrer de Gravina 5, Metro: Universitat, tel. 934-121-097, www.hotelreding.com, recepcion@ hotelreding.com).

**$$$ Hotel Lleó** (YAH-oh) is well-run, with 92 big, bright, and comfortable rooms; a great breakfast room; and a generous lounge (air-con, elevator, small rooftop pool, Carrer de Pelai 22, midway between Metros: Universitat and Catalunya, tel. 933-181-312, www.hotel-lleo.com, info@hotel-lleo.com).

**$$$ Hotel Ginebra** is a modern and fresh version of the old-school *pension* in a classic, well-located building at the corner of Plaça de Catalunya (RS%—use code "HGinebra-RickSteves" and print voucher, family rooms, breakfast available, laundry, air-con, elevator, Rambla de Catalunya 1, Metro: Catalunya, tel. 932-502-017, www.ginebrahotel.es, info@barcelonahotelginebra.com, Brits Alfred and Ivon).

**$$ Hotel Denit** is a small, stylish, 36-room hotel on a pedestrian street two blocks off Plaça de Catalunya. It's chic, minimalist, and fun: Guidebook tips decorate the halls, and the rooms are sized like T-shirts, from small to extra large (includes breakfast, air-con, elevator, Carrer d'Estruc 24, Metro: Catalunya, tel. 935-454-000, www.denit.com, info@denit.com).

**$$ Hotel Atlantis** is solid, with 50 big, nondescript, modern rooms and fair prices for the location (includes breakfast, air-con, elevator, Carrer de Pelai 20, midway between Metros: Universitat and Catalunya, tel. 933-189-012, www.hotelatlantis-bcn.com, inf@hotelatlantis-bcn.com).

## ON OR NEAR THE RAMBLAS:
## AFFORDABLE HOTELS WITH "PERSONALITY"

These places are generally family-run, with ad-lib furnishings, more character, and lower prices.

**$$$ Hotel Continental Barcelona,** in a building overlooking the top of the Ramblas, offers classic, tiny view-balcony opportunities if you don't mind the noise. Its 40 rooms come with clashing carpets and wallpaper, and perhaps one too many clever ideas, but most are comfortable. Choose between your own little Ramblas-view balcony (where you can eat your breakfast) or a quieter back room. J. M.'s (José María's) free breakfast and all-day snack-and-drink bar are a plus (some rooms with balconies, air-con, elevator, quiet terrace, Ramblas 138, Metro: Catalunya, tel. 933-012-570, www.hotelcontinental.com, barcelona@hotelcontinental.com).

**$$ Hostería Grau** is a homey, family-run, and renovated extremely eco-conscious hotel. It has 24 cheery rooms a few blocks off the Ramblas in the colorful university district—but double-glazed windows keep it quiet (some rooms with balconies, family rooms, strict cancellation policy, air-con, elevator, 200 yards up Carrer dels

Tallers from the Ramblas at Ramelleres 27, Metro: C 933-018-135, www.hostalgrau.com, bookgreen@hos Monica).

**$ Hostal el Jardí** offers 40 clean, remodeled room square in the Barri Gòtic. Many of the tight, plain, c come with petite balconies (for an extra charge) and enjo Parisian ambience. It's a good deal only if you value square-with-Barri-Gòtic ambience—you're definitely the location. Book well in advance, as this family-ru an avid following (air-con, elevator, some stairs, halfw Ramblas and cathedral at Plaça Sant Josep Oriol 1, Mo tel. 933-015-900, www.eljardi-barcelona.com,    res eljardi-barcelona.com).

**$ Hostal Operaramblas,** with 68 simple rooms 2 the Ramblas, is clean, institutional, modern, and a great street can feel a bit seedy at night, but it's safe, and the h secure (RS%—use code "operaramblas," air-con in sum tor, Carrer de Sant Pau 20, Metro: Liceu, tel. 933-188-operaramblas.com, info@operaramblas.com).

## OLD CITY

These accommodations are buried in Barcelona's Old Ci in the Barri Gòtic. The Catalunya, Liceu, and Jaume I M flank this tight tangle of lanes; I've noted which stop(s) a each.

**$$$$ Hotel Neri** is posh, pretentious, and soph with 22 rooms spliced into the ancient stones of the Bar overlooking an overlooked square (Plaça Sant Felip Ner from the cathedral. It has pricey modern art on the bedro dressed-up people in its gourmet restaurant, and high-cla (air-con, elevator, rooftop tanning deck, Carrer de Sant Metro: Liceu or Jaume I, tel. 933-040-655, www.hotel info@hotelneri.com).

**$$$ NH Hotel Barcelona Centro,** with 156 rooms a ful chain-hotel predictability, is professional yet friendly, l the Barri Gòtic just three blocks off the Ramblas (air-con, Carrer del Duc 15, Metro: Catalunya or Liceu, tel. 932-www.nh-hotels.com, nhbarcelonacentro@nh-hotels.com).

**$$$ Hotel Nouvel,** in an elegant, Victorian-style bui a handy pedestrian street, is less business oriented and off character than the others listed here. It boasts royal lounge comfy rooms (includes breakfast, air-con, elevator, Carrer Anna 20, Metro: Catalunya, tel. 933-018-274, www.hote com, info@hotelnouvel.com).

**$$$ Hotel Banys Orientals,** a modern, boutique-typ has a people-to-people ethic and refreshingly straight price

1. Hotel Granvía
2. Hotel Yurbban Trafalgar
3. Hotel Continental Palacete
4. Hostal Oliva
5. BCN Fashion House B&B
6. Centric Point Hostel
7. Somnio Hostel & Mon Vinic Wine Bar
8. La Rita Restaurant
9. La Bodegueta
10. Restaurante la Palmera
11. La Flauta
12. Cinc Sentits
13. Restaurant Tenorio
14. Tapas 24
15. Ciutat Comtal Cerveceria

## EIXAMPLE

For an uptown, boulevard-like neighborhood, sleep in the Eixample, a 10-minute walk from the Ramblas action. Most of these places use the Passeig de Gràcia or Catalunya Metro stops. Because these stations are so huge—especially Passeig de Gràcia, which sprawls underground for a few blocks—study the maps posted in the station to establish which exit you want before surfacing.

**$$$$ Hotel Granvía,** filling a palatial, brightly renovated 1870s mansion, offers a large, peaceful sun patio, several comfortable common areas, and 58 spacious modern rooms (family rooms, air-con, elevator, Gran Via de les Corts Catalanes 642, Metro: Passeig de Gràcia, tel. 933-181-900, www.hotelgranvia.com, hgranvia@nnhotels.com).

**$$$$ Hotel Yurbban Trafalgar** is a small, classy boutique hotel with 56 rooms and a masculine-minimalist decor. Their roof-top bar, tiny pool, and views alone are worth the price of your stay (air-con, free self-service laundry, gym, near the Palace of Catalan Music at Carrer de Trafalgar 30, a long block from Metro: Urquinaona, tel. 932-680-727, www.yurbban.com, trafalgar@yurbban.com).

**$$$ Hotel Continental Palacete,** with 22 small rooms, fills a 100-year-old chandeliered mansion. With flowery wallpaper and ornately gilded stucco, it's gaudy in the city of Gaudí, but it's also friendly, quiet, and well located. Guests have unlimited access to the outdoor terrace and the "cruise-inspired" fruit, veggie, and drink buffet (RS%, includes breakfast, air-con, 2 blocks northwest of Plaça de Catalunya at corner of Rambla de Catalunya and Carrer de la Diputació, Rambla de Catalunya 30, Metro: Passeig de Gràcia, tel. 934-457-657, www.hotelcontinental.com, palacete@hotelcontinental.com).

**$$ Hostal Oliva,** family-run with care, is a spartan, old-school place with 15 basic, bright, high-ceilinged rooms. It's on the fourth floor of a classic old Eixample building—with a beautiful mahogany elevator—in a perfect location, just a couple of blocks above Plaça de Catalunya (cheaper rooms with shared bath, corner of Passeig de Gràcia and Carrer de la Diputació, Passeig de Gràcia 32, Metro: Passeig de Gràcia, tel. 934-880-162, www.hostaloliva.com, info@hostaloliva.com).

**$$ BCN Fashion House B&B** is a meditative place with 10 basic rooms, a peaceful lounge, and a leafy backyard terrace on the first floor of a nondescript old building (cheaper rooms with shared bath, some rooms with veranda, 2-night minimum stay, includes breakfast, between Carrer d'Ausiàs Marc and Ronda de Sant Pere at Carrer del Bruc 13, just steps from Metro: Urquinaona, mobile 637-904-044, www.bcnfashionhouse.com, info@bcnfashionhouse.com).

## OTHER ACCOMMODATIONS
### Hostels
¢ **Equity Point Hostels:** Barcelona has a terrific chain of well-run and centrally located hostels (tel. 932-312-045, www.equity-point.com), offering plenty of opportunities to meet other backpackers. They're open 24 hours but aren't party hostels, so they enforce quiet after 23:00. There are three locations to choose from: the Eixample, Barri Gòtic, or near the beach. **Centric Point Hostel** is a huge place renting 400 cheap beds at what must be the best address in Barcelona (bar, kitchen, Passeig de Gràcia 33—see map on page 178, Metro: Passeig de Gràcia, tel. 932-151-796, www.centricpointhostel.com). **Gothic Point Hostel** rents 130 beds a

block from the Picasso Museum (roof terrace, Carrer Vigatans 5—see map on page 174, Metro: Jaume I, reception tel. 932-687-808, www.gothicpoint.com). **Sea Point Hostel** has 70 beds on the beach nearby, but it's closed roughly November through February (Plaça del Mar 4—see map on page 75, Metro: Barceloneta, reception tel. 932-247-075, www.equity-point.com/our-hostels).

¢ **Somnio Hostel,** an innovative smaller place, has nine simple, clean rooms (RS%, cheaper rooms with shared bath, private rooms available; air-con, Carrer de la Diputació 251, second floor, Metro: Passeig de Gràcia, tel. 932-725-308, www.somniohostels.com, info@somniohostels.com). They have a second location that's five blocks farther out.

## Apartments

Consider this option if you're traveling as a family, in a group, or staying five days or longer. Websites such as Airbnb and VRBO let you correspond directly with property owners or managers, or consider one of the sites listed below. Some specialize in Barcelona, while others also cover other European cities. For more information on renting apartments, see page 278 in the Practicalities chapter.

Friendly Rentals (www.friendlyrentals.com) has a number of listings in Barcelona (and other European cities), or you can try a local agency, such as Top Barcelona Apartments (http://top-barcelona-apartments.com) or MH Apartments (www.mhapartments.com). I've had good luck with Cross-Pollinate, a reputable booking agency representing B&Bs and apartments in a handful of European cities, including Barcelona (US tel. 800-270-1190, www.cross-pollinate.com, info@cross-pollinate.com).

Some Barcelona residents see turn-key vacation rentals as damaging to the fabric of traditionally residential neighborhoods, especially when they're rented to rowdy bachelor/bachelorette parties. I like to counterbalance this trend by treating my temporary Barcelona home—and neighbors—with a little extra courtesy.

# EATING IN BARCELONA

Barcelona, the capital of Catalan cuisine, offers a tremendous variety of colorful places to eat, ranging from workaday eateries to
homey Catalan bistros *(cans),* crowded tapas bars, and avant-garde
restaurants. In general, restaurants in Barcelona rise to a higher
level than elsewhere in Spain, propelled by talented chefs who
aren't afraid to experiment, the relative affluence, and the availabil-
ity of good, fresh ingredients—especially fish and seafood.

In my recommendations, I've distinguished tapas places
(which serve small plates throughout the afternoon and evening)
from more formal restaurants (with generous portions, no tapas,
and service that starts much later than the American norm). Most
of my recommended eateries—grouped by neighborhood and
handy to the sights—are practical, characteristic, affordable, and
lively, with a busy tapas scene at the bar, along with restaurant tables where larger plates can be enjoyed family-style. To avoid bad,
touristy restaurants, a good rule of thumb is not to eat (or drink) on
the Ramblas or Passeig de Gràcia.

Catalan tapas menus most often include seafood (cod, hake,
tuna, squid, and anchovies), delicious local olives, and a traditional
sausage called *butifarra.* In restaurants, you'll see Catalan favorites
such as *fideuà,* a thin, flavor-infused noodle served with seafood—a
kind of Catalan paella—and *arròs negre,* black rice cooked in squid
ink. *Pa amb tomàquet* is the classic Catalan way to eat bread—toasted white bread with olive oil, tomato, and a pinch of salt. It's often

served with tapas and used to make sandwiches. While the famous cured *jamón* (ham) is more Spanish than it is Catalan, you'll still find lots of it in Catalunya (see the "Sampling *Jamón*" sidebar on page 283). All this food is accompanied by local beers, wines, and, of course, the beloved sweet vermouth.

## EATING TIPS

For general advice on eating in Barcelona, including details on ordering, dining (at restaurants and in tapas bars), and tipping, along with information on typical cuisine and beverages, see page 279. For help deciphering menus, see the "Tapas Menu Decoder" on page 288. Thanks to Joe Littenberg of the recommended Barcelona Taste food tour (see page 34), who helped make this information on eating in Barcelona appropriately Catalan—as opposed to just Spanish with a Barcelona accent.

**Hours:** As in the rest of Spain, the people of Catalunya eat late—lunch around 14:00 (and as late as 16:00), and dinner after 21:00. The earliest you can go to a restaurant for dinner is about 20:30, when the place is empty or filled with tourists. Going after 21:00 is better, but if you wait until 22:00, it can be hard to get into popular restaurants. Note that many restaurants close in August (or July), when the owners take a vacation.

Although tapas are served throughout the day, the real action begins late—21:00 or after. For less competition at the bar, go early or on Monday and Tuesday (but check to see if the place is open, as many close on Sunday or Monday).

For advice on adapting to the Spanish eating schedule, see page 279.

**Bread and Water:** Most places don't automatically give you bread with your meal. If you ask for it, you'll usually receive *pa amb tomàquet* (bread with tomato spread), and you will be charged. Barcelona's tap water is safe to drink and free, but some bar owners are rather insistent on not serving it to their clientele, as it doesn't taste particularly good. For details on how to ask for water, see page 290.

**Local-Style Tapas:** Catalans have an affinity for Basque culture, so you'll find a lot of Basque-style tapas places here, where they lay out bite-size tapas (called *pintxos*, or *pinchos*) on the countertop. These places are user-friendly, as you are free to take what you want, and you don't have to look at a menu or wait to be served; just grab what looks good, order a drink, and save your toothpicks (they'll count them up at the end to tally your bill). I've listed several of these bars (including Taverna Basca Irati and Sagardi Euskal Taberna), but there are many others. Look for signs reading *basca* or *euskal taberna* (*euskal* means "Basque")—or just keep an eye out for places with lots of toothpicks. You'll also find traditional Catalan

## Restaurant Price Code

I've assigned each eatery a price category, based on the average cost of a typical main course (or 2-3 tapas). Drinks, desserts, and splurge items (steak and seafood) can raise the price considerably.

|  |  |
|---|---|
| **$$$$** | **Splurge:** Most main courses over €20 |
| **$$$** | **Pricier:** €15-20 |
| **$$** | **Moderate:** €10-15 |
| **$** | **Budget:** Under €10 |

In Spain, takeout food is **$**; a basic tapas bar or no-frills sit-down eatery is **$$**; a casual but more upscale tapas bar or restaurant is **$$$**; and a swanky splurge is **$$$$**.

tapas bars and *bodegas* (originally a name denoting wine cellars but preserved as many *bodegas* evolved into restaurants).

**Catalan in Restaurants:** Catalan and Spanish (in that order) are the official languages of Barcelona. While menus are usually in both languages, and many times English as well, these days—with the feisty spirit of independence stoked—you may find some menus in just Catalan, or Catalan and English without Spanish. Throughout this book, I've given most food terms in Spanish and added Catalan where helpful. For terms in Spanish and Catalan, consult the "Tapas Menu Decoder" on page 288 and the list of drink terms on page 287.

In any Catalan bar or restaurant, an occasional *"si us plau"* (please) or *"moltes gràcies"* (thank you very much) will go a long way with the locals. An *"adéu"* (good-bye), *"que vagi bé!"* (have a good one!), or, in the evening, *"bona nit"* (good evening/night) on your way out the door will certainly earn you a smile. And, as they say in Catalan, *"Bon profit!"* (Bon appétit)!

## NEAR THE RAMBLAS

The entire length of the Ramblas itself is a tourist trap. Simply put: Do not eat or drink on the Ramblas (to make the rip-off prices even worse, when it comes time to pay, you may find that your bag has been stolen). But within a few steps of the Ramblas, you'll find handy lunch places, an inviting market hall, and some good vegetarian options. For locations, see the map on page 186.

## Lunching Simply yet Memorably near the Ramblas

Although these places are enjoyable for a lunch break during your Ramblas sightseeing, many are also open for dinner.

**$$ Taverna Basca Irati** serves 40 kinds of hot and cold Basque *pintxos* for €2 each. These are small open-faced sandwiches—like sushi on bread. Muscle in through the hungry local crowd, get an empty plate from the waiter, and then help yourself. Every few minutes, waiters circulate with platters of new, still-warm munchies. Grab one as they pass by...it's addictive (you'll be charged by the number of toothpicks left on your plate when you're done). For drink options, look for the printed menu on the wall in the back. Wash down your food with Rioja (full-bodied red wine), Txakolí (sprightly Basque white wine), or *sidra* (apple wine) poured from on high to add oxygen and bring out the flavor (daily 11:00-24:00, a block off the Ramblas, behind arcade at Carrer del Cardenal Casanyes 17, Metro: Liceu, tel. 933-023-084).

**$$ Restaurant Elisabets** is a rough little neighborhood eatery packed with antique radios. It's popular with young locals and tourists alike for its €12 "home-cooked" three-course lunch special; even cheaper *menú rapid* options are available (13:00-16:00 only). Stop by for lunch, survey what those around you are enjoying, and order what looks best. Apparently, locals put up with the service for the tasty food (cash only, Mon-Sat 7:30-23:00, closed Sun and Aug, 2 blocks west of Ramblas on far corner of Plaça del Bonsuccés at Carrer d'Elisabets 2, Metro: Catalunya, tel. 933-175-826).

**$$ Café Granja Viader** is a quaint time capsule, family-run since 1870. They boast about being the first dairy business to bottle and distribute milk in Spain. This feminine-feeling place—specializing in baked and dairy treats, toasted sandwiches, and light meals—is ideal for a traditional breakfast. Or indulge your sweet tooth: Try a glass of *orxata* (or *horchata*—*chufa*-nut milk, summer only), *llet mallorquina* (Majorca-style milk with cinnamon, lemon, and sugar), *crema catalana* (crème brûlée, their specialty), or *suis* ("Swiss"—hot chocolate with a snowcap of whipped cream). *Mel i mató* is fresh cheese with honey...very Catalan (Mon-Sat 9:00-13:00 & 17:00-21:00, closed Sun, a block off the Ramblas behind Betlem Church at Xuclà 4, Metro: Liceu, tel. 933-183-486).

**Cafeteria:** For a quick, affordable lunch with a view, the ninth-floor cafeteria at **$$ El Corte Inglés** can't be beat (salads and sandwiches; also has a café with cheap coffee and a pricier sit-down restaurant, Mon-Sat 9:30-21:30, closed Sun, Plaça de Catalunya, Metro: Catalunya, tel. 933-063-800).

**Picnics:** Shoestring tourists buy groceries at **El Corte Inglés** (described above, supermarket in basement), **Carrefour Market** (Mon-Sat 10:00-22:00, closed Sun; Ramblas 113, Metro: Liceu), and **La Boqueria** market (closed Sun, described next).

**EATING**

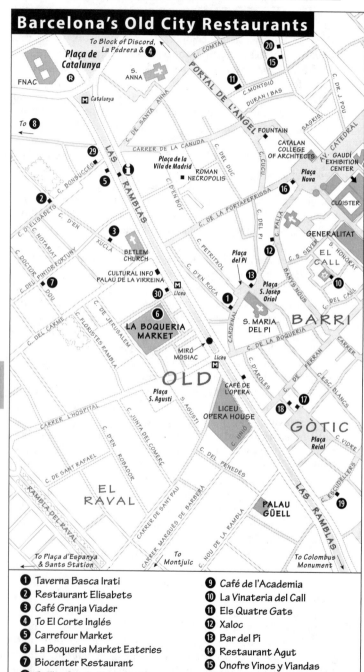

# Barcelona's Old City Restaurants

1. Taverna Basca Irati
2. Restaurant Elisabets
3. Café Granja Viader
4. To El Corte Inglés
5. Carrefour Market
6. La Boqueria Market Eateries
7. Biocenter Restaurant
8. To Flax & Kale Restaurant, Teresa Carles & Mucci's Pizza
9. Café de l'Academia
10. La Vinateria del Call
11. Els Quatre Gats
12. Xaloc
13. Bar del Pi
14. Restaurant Agut
15. Onofre Vinos y Viandas
16. Bilbao Berria Pintxos & Tapas

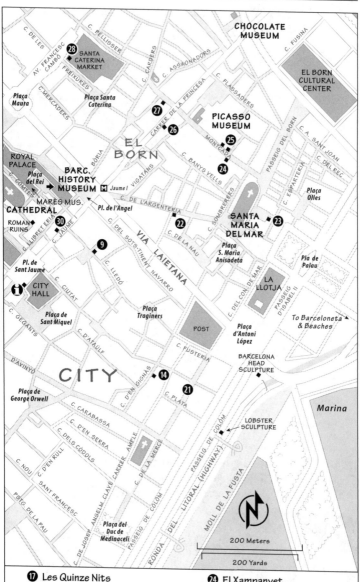

**EATING**

17 Les Quinze Nits
18 La Crema Canela
19 La Fonda
20 La Dolça Herminia
21 Carrer de la Mercè Tapas Bars
22 Sagardi Euskal Taberna
23 Vegetalia Vegetarian Restaurant
24 El Xampanyet
25 Tapeo
26 Bar Brutal
27 Bar del Pla
28 Santa Caterina Cuines
29 Mucci's Pizza
30 Wok to Walk (2)

## Budget Meals Around Town

Bright, clean, and inexpensive **sandwich shops** proudly hold the cultural line against the fast-food invasion that has hamburgerized the rest of Europe. Catalan sandwiches are made to order with the classic tomato-spread bread, *pa amb tomàquet*. You'll see two big local chains (Bocatta and Pans & Company) everywhere, but these serve mass-produced McBaguettes ordered from a multilingual menu. I've had better luck with hole-in-the-wall sandwich shops—virtually as numerous as the chains—where you can see exactly what you're getting. While Pans & Co. is low-end, places like Conesa Entrepans (with a handy branch on Plaça de Sant Jaume) offer better quality.

Kebab places are also a good, super-cheap standby; you'll see them all over town. Another popular budget option is the empanada—a pastry turnover filled with seasoned meat and vegetables. In basic restaurants and bars, you'll often find daily lunch specials *(menú del día)* for about €12. And you can always graze cheaply in bars offering an array of affordable tapas and individual bites called *pintxos* (or *pinchos*).

For other options, try **$ Mucci's Pizza,** with good, fresh pizza slices and empanadas (two locations just off the Ramblas, at Bonsuccés 10 and Tallers 75). **$ Wok to Walk** makes tasty food on the run, serving up noodles and rice in takeaway containers with your choice of meat and/or veggies and finished with a savory sauce (convenient branches near Plaça de Sant Jaume and Liceu Metro station).

## In and near La Boqueria Market

Try eating at one of Barcelona's covered market halls (La Boqueria or Santa Caterina) at least once. (For more on Santa Caterina Market, see page 119).

Like most farmers markets in Europe, La Boqueria Market is ringed by colorful, good-value eateries. Lots of stalls sell fun takeaway food—especially fruit salads and fresh-squeezed juices—ideal for picnickers. There are several good bars—many with enticing plates of seafood—around the market, busy with shoppers munching at the counter (breakfast, tapas all day, coffee). The market, and most of the eateries listed here (unless noted), are open Monday through Saturday from 8:00 until 20:00 (though things get very quiet after about 16:00) and closed on Sunday (nearest Metro: Liceu). For a more complete description of the market itself, see page 85 of my Ramblas Ramble chapter.

**$$$ Pinotxo Bar** is just to the right as you enter the market. It's a fun—if touristy—spot for coffee, breakfast (spinach *tortillas,* or whatever's cooking, with toast), or tapas. Fun-loving Juan and his family are La Boqueria fixtures. Grab a stool across the way to sip your drink with people-watching views. Be careful—this place can get expensive (Mercat de la Boqueria 466, tel. 933-171-731, www.pinotxobar.com).

**$$$ Casa Guinart** might seem a bit spendy for a market eatery, but it's worth the price for the quality of the ingredients. One of the few old-time places surviving around La Boqueria, today it's bohemian-chic with an elegant and inviting scene both inside and out; the tables are seemingly designed to help you enjoy the market action. Look for it in the far-right corner as you enter the market (daily 10:00-23:30, Ramblas 95, tel. 933-178-887, www.casaguinart.com).

**Other Diners Under the La Boqueria Roof:** Several busy counters immersed in the commotion of the market crank out enticing seafood plates (be careful of the price) and simpler traditional dishes and drinks. **$$ Kiosko Universal** (to the left as you enter) is appreciated for its seafood. The eateries toward the back are more accessible and affordable.

## Vegetarian Eateries near the Ramblas

**$$ Biocenter,** a Catalan soup-and-salad restaurant busy with local vegetarians, takes its cooking very seriously and feels a bit more like a real restaurant than most (weekday lunch specials include soup or salad and plate of the day, Mon-Sat 13:00-23:00, Sun until 16:00, 2 blocks off the Ramblas at Carrer del Pintor Fortuny 25, Metro: Liceu, tel. 933-014-583).

**$$ Flax & Kale** is a top-end vegetarian place, and the nearby campus gives it a university vibe. As its name suggests, this place serves seriously healthy dishes and juices in a delightful, spacious indoor setting (daily, 5-minute walk from the top of the Ramblas at Carrer Tallers 74, tel. 933-175-664). Its sister location, named for the founder, **Teresa Carles,** is also good but has a standard and more forgettable setting (closer to the Ramblas, just off Carrer Tallers at Carrer Jovellanos 2, Metro: Universitat or Catalunya, tel. 933-171-829).

**EATING**

## BARRI GÒTIC

These eateries populate Barcelona's atmospheric Gothic Quarter, near the cathedral. Choose between a sit-down meal at a restaurant or a string of tapas bars. For locations, see the map on page 186.

### Restaurants

**$$$ Café de l'Academia** is a delightful place on a pretty square tucked away in the heart of the Barri Gòtic—but patronized mainly by the neighbors. They serve refined cuisine with Catalan roots, using what's fresh from the market. The candlelit, air-conditioned interior is rustic yet elegant, with soft jazz, flowers, and modern art. And if you want to eat outdoors on a convivial, mellow square...this is the place. Reservations can be smart (lunch specials, open Mon-Fri 13:00-15:30 & 20:00-23:00, closed Sat-Sun, near the City Hall square, off Carrer de Jaume I up Carrer de la Dagueria at Carrer dels Lledó 1, Metro: Jaume I, tel. 933-198-253).

**$$$ La Vinateria del Call,** buried deep in the Jewish Quarter, is one of the oldest wine bars in town. It offers a romantic restaurant-style meal of tapas with fine local wines. You can eat at the bar, but I'd settle in at a candlelit table. They have more than 100 well-priced wines, including a decent selection of Catalan wines at €2.50 a glass. Three or four plates of their classic tapas will fill two people (daily 19:30-24:00; with back to church, leave Plaça de Sant Felip Neri and walk two short blocks to Sant Domènec del Call 9; Metro: Jaume I, tel. 933-026-092).

**$$$ Els Quatre Gats** ("The Four Cats") was once the haunt of the Modernista greats—including a teenaged Picasso, who first publicly displayed his art here, and architect Josep Puig i Cadafalch, who designed the building. Inspired by Paris' famous Le Chat Noir café/cabaret, Els Quatre Gats celebrated all that was modern at the turn of the 20th century (for more on the illustrious history of the place, see page 98 in the Barri Gòtic Walk). You can snack or drink at the bar, or go into the back for a sit-down meal after 19:00. While touristy (less so later), the food and service are good, and the prices aren't as high as you might guess (weekday lunch specials, daily 10:00-24:00, just steps off Avinguda del Portal de l'Angel at Carrer de Montsió 3, Metro: Catalunya, tel. 933-024-140).

**$$$ Xaloc** is a fine place in the old center for nicely presented gourmet tapas. It has a woody, modern, relaxed, and spacious dining room with a fun energy, good service, and reasonable prices. The walls are covered with *Ibérica* hamhocks and wine bottles. They focus on home-style Catalan classics—and though the food here doesn't impress locals, tourists find the place classy and comfortable. A gazpacho, plank of ham, *pa amb tomàquet*, and nice glass of wine make a fine light meal (daily, drinks and cold tapas 11:00-23:00, kitchen open 13:00-17:00 & 19:00-23:00, a block toward the cathedral from Plaça de Sant Josep Oriol at Carrer de la Palla 13, Metro: Catalunya, tel. 933-011-990).

**$$ Bar del Pi** is a simple, hardworking bar serving salads, sandwiches, and tapas. It has just a handful of tables on the most inviting little square in the Barri Gòtic (daily 9:00-23:00 except closed Tue in winter, Plaça de Sant Josep Oriol 1, Metro: Liceu, tel. 933-022-123).

**$$$$ Restaurant Agut,** around since 1924, features a comfortable, wood-paneled dining room that's modern and sophisticated, but still retains a slight bohemian air. The pictures lining the walls are by Catalan artists who are said to have exchanged their canvases for a meal. The menu includes very tasty traditional Catalan food, with some seasonal specialties (weekday lunch specials, Tue-Sat 13:30-16:00 & 20:30-23:30, Sun 13:30-16:00, closed Mon, just up from Carrer de la Mercè and the harbor at Carrer d'En Gignàs 16, Metro: Jaume I, tel. 933-151-709, www.restaurantagut.com).

**$$ Onofre Vinos y Viandas,** owned and run by Marisol and Angel, is a tiny wine bar (20 wines by the glass) with a few simple tables behind walls of wine bottles. Foodie but without pretense, and no tourists, it has a fun, creative, accessible menu—be adventurous and try the brandy foie shavings (daily 10:00-16:30 & 19:30-24:00, near the Palace of Catalan Music, Carrer de les Magdalenes 19, tel. 933-176-937).

**$$ Bilbao Berria Pintxos and Tapas** is a hardworking tapas bar, like its Basque sisters around town. It faces the cathedral, with tables outside on the square, and sells little open-faced sandwiches and fun bites for €2 per toothpick. The food is a notch above other tapas chains (Plaça Nova 3, tel. 933-170-124).

**$$ Andilana** is a chain offering the impression of fine dining at a budget price. Its six restaurants are wildly popular for their artfully presented Spanish and Mediterranean cuisine; crisp, modern ambience; and unbeatable prices (three-course €10 lunches and €16-21 dinners—both with wine). These places are a hit with tourists on a tight budget—be warned that they are notoriously busy. **Les Quinze Nits** has great seating right on atmospheric Plaça Reial (daily 12:30-23:30, at #6—you'll see the line form around 20:30, right before they open their large upstairs dining room, tel. 933-173-075). Two others are within a block: **La Crema Canela,** a few steps above Plaça Reial, feels cozier than the others and is the only one that takes reservations (Mon-Thu 13:00-23:00, Fri-Sun until 23:30, Passatge de Madoz 6, tel. 933-182-744). **La Fonda** is a block below Plaça Reial (daily 13:00-23:30, Carrer dels Escudellers 10, tel. 933-017-515). Another location, **La Dolça Herminia,** is near the Palace of Catalan Music in El Born (daily 13:00-15:45 & 20:30-23:30, 2 blocks toward the Ramblas from Palace of Catalan

**EATING**

Music at Carrer de les Magdalenes 27, Metro: Jaume I, tel. 933-170-676). Another restaurant in the chain, **La Rita,** is described on page 195.

## Tapas on Carrer de la Mercè in the Barri Gòtic

This area lets you experience a rare, unvarnished bit of old Barcelona with great *tascas*—colorful local tapas bars. Get small plates (for

maximum sampling) by asking for "tapas," not the bigger "*raciones.*" Glasses of *vino tinto* go for about €1. And though trendy uptown restaurants are safer, better-lit, and come with English menus and less grease, these places will stain your journal. The neighborhood's dark, the regulars are

rough-edged, and you'll get a glimpse of a crusty Barcelona from before the affluence hit. Try Galician *pimientos de Padrón*—Russian roulette with little green peppers that are lightly fried in oil and salted...only a few are jalapeño-spicy. At the cider bars, it's traditional to order *queso de cabrales* (a very moldy blue cheese) and spicy chorizo (sausage), ideally prepared *al diablo* ("devil-style")—soaked in wine, then flambéed at your table. Several places serve *leche de pantera* (panther milk)—liquor mixed with milk.

From the bottom of the Ramblas (near the Columbus Monument, Metro: Drassanes), hike east along Carrer de Josep Anselm Clavé. When you reach Plaça de la Mercè, follow the small street (Carrer de la Mercè) that runs along the right side of the square's church. For a montage of edible memories, wander the next three or four blocks and consider these spots, stopping wherever looks most inviting. If you want more refined bar-hopping possibilities, skip over to Carrer Ample and Carrer d'En Gignàs, inland streets parallel to Carrer de la Mercè.

All of these places are moderately priced, and most close down around 23:00. **$$ Bar Celta** (marked *la pulpería,* at #9, eases you into the scene with fried fish, octopus, and *patatas bravas,* all with Galician Ribeiro wine. Farther down at the corner (#28), **$$ La Plata** keeps things wonderfully simple, serving extremely cheap plates of sardines (€3), little salads, and small glasses of keg wine (€1). **$$ Tasca el Corral** (#17) serves mountain favorites from northern Spain by the half-*ración* (see their list), such as *queso de cabrales,* chorizo *al diablo,* and *cecina* (cured meat, like *jamón* but made from beef)—drink them with *sidra* (hard cider sold by the bottle-€6). **$$ Sidrería Tasca La Socarrena** (#21) offers hard cider from Asturias in €6.50 bottles with *queso de cabrales* and chorizo.

At the end of Carrer de la Mercè, **$$ Cerveceria Vendimia** is a dive that slings tasty clams and mussels. You can sit at the bar and point to what looks good. Their *pulpo* (octopus) is more expensive than other choices but is the house specialty.

## EL BORN

El Born (a.k.a. La Ribera), the hottest neighborhood in town, sparkles with eclectic and trendy as well as subdued and classy little restaurants hidden in the small lanes surrounding the Church of Santa Maria del Mar. While I've listed a few well-established tapas bars that are great for light meals, to really dine, simply wander around for 15 minutes and pick the place that tickles your gastronomic fancy. I think those who say they know what's best in this area are kidding themselves—it's changing too fast and the choices are too personal. One thing's for sure: There are a lot of talented and hardworking restaurateurs with plenty to offer. Consider starting off your evening with a glass of fine wine at one of the *enotecas* on the square facing the Church of Santa Maria del Mar (such as La Vinya del Senyor). Sit back and admire the pure Catalan Gothic architecture. Most of my listings are nearby. Many restaurants and shops in this area are, like the Picasso Museum, closed on Mondays.

For all of these eateries, use Metro: Jaume I. For locations, see the map on page 186.

### Near the Church of Santa Maria del Mar

**$$ Sagardi Euskal Taberna** offers a wonderful array of Basque goodies—tempting *pintxos* and *montaditos* (small open-faced sandwiches) at €2 each—along its

huge bar. Ask for a plate and graze (just take whatever looks good). You can sit on the square with your plunder for about 20 percent extra. Wash it down with Txakolí, a Basque white wine poured from the spout of a huge wooden barrel into a glass as you watch. When you're done, they'll count your toothpicks to tally your bill. Study the two price lists—bar and terrace—posted at the bar (daily 12:00-24:00, Carrer de l'Argenteria 62, tel. 933-199-993). Note that Sagardi serves the same *pintxos* as Taverna Basca Irati, described earlier.

**$$ Vegetalia Vegetarian Restaurant,** facing the Monument of Catalan Independence and the Church of Santa Maria del Mar, is a basic vegetarian diner with a cheery, healthy-feeling interior and a few dainty tables for two outside facing the church (good three-course lunch special, daily from 11:00, tel. 930-177-256).

## Near the Picasso Museum

**$$$ El Xampanyet** ("The Little Champagne Bar"), a colorful family-run bar with a fun-loving staff (Juan Carlos, his mom, and the man who may be his father), specializes in tapas and anchovies—and their cheap homemade *cava* (Spanish champagne) goes straight to your head. Don't be put off by the seafood from a tin: Catalans like it this way. A *sortido* (assorted plate) of *carne* (meat) or *pescado* (fish) with *pa amb tomàquet* makes for a fun meal. This place is filled with tourists during the sightseeing day, but it's a local favorite after dark. The scene is great, but—especially during busy times—it's tough without Spanish skills. When I asked about the price, Juan Carlos said, "Who cares? The ATM is just across the street" (same price at bar or table, Tue-Sun 12:00-15:30 & 19:00-23:00, closed Sun evening and Mon, a half-block beyond the Picasso Museum at Carrer de Montcada 22, tel. 933-197-003).

**$$ Tapeo** is a mod, classy alternative to the funky Xampanyet across the street. It has a long bar and tiny tables with stools and serves near-gourmet tapas (Tue-Sun 12:00-16:00 & 19:00-24:00, closed Mon, Carrer de Montcada 29, tel. 933-101-607).

**$$$ Bar Brutal** is a creative, fun-loving, and edgy bohemian-chic place with a young local following. It serves a mix of Spanish and Italian dishes with an emphasis on wines—especially natural wines, with plenty available by the glass (Mon-Sat 13:00-24:00, closed Sun, Carrer de Princesa 14, tel. 932-954-797).

**$$$ Bar del Pla** is a local favorite—near the Picasso Museum but far enough away from the tourist crowds. This brightly lit, classic diner/bar—overlooking a tiny crossroads next to Barcelona's oldest church—serves traditional Catalan dishes, *raciones,* and tapas. Their *croquetas,* tripe, and crispy beef with foie gras (€6) are highlights. They also have a local IPA on tap for a change of pace from regular Spanish beer. Prices listed on the fun and accessible menu are the same at the bar or at a table. Eating at the bar puts you in the middle of a great scene (Mon-Sat 12:00-23:00, closed Sun; with your back to the Picasso Museum, head right two blocks past Carrer de la Princesa to Carrer de Montcada 2; tel. 932-683-003, www.bardelpla.cat).

**At Santa Caterina Market: $$ Santa Caterina Cuines** is a bright and modern restaurant with shared tables under the open rafters of a modern market hall. There's also a handy tapas bar and fine outdoor seating on the square. Their menu—with vegetarian, international, and Mediterranean dishes, all made from market-fresh and seasonal ingredients—cross-references everything on an innovative grid (outside tables OK for both restaurant and tapas bar, daily 13:00-16:00 & 18:30-23:30, Avinguda de Francesc Cambo 16, tel. 932-689-918, no reservations).

## EIXAMPLE

The people-packed boulevards of the Eixample are lined with appetizing eateries featuring breezy outdoor seating. Choose between a real restaurant or an upscale tapas bar (for the best variety, I prefer Rambla de Catalunya). For locations, see the map on page 178.

## Restaurants

**$$ La Rita** is a fresh and dressy little restaurant serving Catalan and Mediterranean cuisine near the Block of Discord. Their €11 lunch and €16 dinner specials are a great value. Like most of its sister Andilana restaurants—described on page 190—its prices attract a loyal following, so arrive early...or wait (daily 13:00-15:45 plus Sun-Thu 20:00-23:00 and Fri-Sat 21:00-23:00, near corner of Carrer de Pau Claris and Carrer d'Aragó at d'Aragó 279, a block from Metro: Passeig de Gràcia, tel. 934-872-376).

**$$ La Bodegueta** is an atmospheric below-street-level bodega serving hearty wines, homemade vermouth, *anchoas* (anchovies), tapas, and *flautas*—sandwiches made with flute-thin baguettes. On a nice day, it's great to eat outside, sitting in the median of the boulevard under shady trees. Its three-course lunch special with wine is a deal (Mon-Fri only, 13:00-16:00). A long block from Gaudí's La Pedrera, this makes a fine sightseeing break (Mon-Sat 7:00-24:00, Sun 18:30-24:00, at intersection with Carrer de Provença, Rambla de Catalunya 100, Metro: Provença, tel. 932-154-894).

**$$$ Restaurante la Palmera** serves a mix of Catalan, Mediterranean, and French cuisine in an elegant room with bottle-lined walls. This untouristy place offers great food, service, and value— for me, a very special meal in Barcelona. They have three zones: the classic main room, a more forgettable adjacent room, and a few outdoor tables. I like the classic room. Reservations are smart (creative €24 six-plate *degustation* lunch—also available at dinner Mon-Wed, open Mon-Sat 13:00-15:45 & 20:00-23:30, closed Sun, Carrer d'Enric Granados 57, at the corner with Carrer Mallorca, Metro: Provença, tel. 934-532-338, www.lapalmera.cat).

**$$ La Flauta** fills two floors with enthusiastic eaters (I prefer the ground floor). It's fresh and modern, with a fun, no-stress menu featuring small plates, creative *flauta* sandwiches, and a three-course lunch deal. Consider the list of *tapas del día*. Good wines by the glass are listed on the blackboard (Mon-Sat 7:00-24:00, closed Sun, upbeat and helpful staff, no reservations, just off Carrer de la Diputació at Carrer d'Aribau 23, Metro: Universitat, tel. 933-237-038).

**$$$$ Cinc Sentits** ("Five Senses"), with only about 30 seats, is my gourmet recommendation. At this chic, minimalist, slightly snooty place, all the attention goes to the fine service and beautifully presented dishes. The €55 *formula* lunch *menú* and the *quatre plats* (€100) and *sis plats* (€120) dinner *menús* are unforgettable extravaganzas. Each comes with a wine-pairing option. Expect *menús* only—no à la carte. It's run by Catalans who lived in Canada (so there's absolutely no language barrier) and serve avant-garde cuisine inspired by Catalan traditions and ingredients. Reservations are essential (Tue-Sat 13:30-15:00 & 20:30-22:00, closed Sun-Mon, near Carrer d'Aragó at Carrer d'Aribau 58, between Metros: Universitat and Provença, tel. 933-239-490, www.cincsentits.com, maître d' Eric).

**$$ Restaurant Tenorio** hides between the famous buildings and clamoring tourists in the Block of Discord. It's an actual restaurant with a tapas bar in front. This modern and spacious place is good for large groups and serves a mix of international and Catalan dishes, concocted in the bustling open kitchen at the back (daily, Passeig de Gràcia 37, Metro: Passeig de Gràcia, tel. 932-720-592).

**$$$$ Mon Vinic ("World of Wine")**—a sleek, trendy wine bar that's evangelical about local wine culture—offers an amazing eating experience, with an open kitchen, a passion for fine food, and little pretense. Considered one of the top wine bar/restaurants in town, their renowned chef creates Catalan and Mediterranean dishes for enjoying with the wine. Diners are provided an iPad; use it to read descriptions of the 50 or so open bottles, virtually "visit" each winery, and "meet" the vintner. The faces of farmers—considered the unsung heroes of the food industry—are projected on the wall. They don't turn the tables, and hope you'll spend the evening, so reserve in advance. For a more casual visit, they have a tapas bar (no reservations) in front where you'll also be empowered by an iPad and wine (closed Sun, starters designed to share, creative tapas, lunch specials, Diputació 249, Metro: Passeig de Gràcia, tel. 932-726-187, www.monvinic.com). Isabelle Brunet, who cofounded Mon Vinic in 2008, is the head sommelier.

## Tapas Bars in the Eixample

Many trendy and touristic tapas bars in the Eixample offer a cheery welcome and slam out the appetizers. These two are particularly handy to Plaça de Catalunya and the Passeig de Gràcia artery (closest Metro stops: Catalunya and Passeig de Gràcia).

**$$$ Tapas 24** makes eating fun. This local favorite, with a few street tables, fills a spot a few steps below street level with happy energy, friendly service, funky decor (white counters and mirrors), and good yet pricey tapas. Along with daily specials and fine breakfasts, the menu has all the typical standbys and quirky inventions. The *tapas del dio* list is particularly good. The owner, Carles Abellan, is one of Barcelona's hot chefs; although his famous fare is pricey, you can enjoy it without going broke. Same prices whether you dine at the bar, a table, or outside. Come early or wait; no reservations are taken (daily 9:00-24:00, just off Passeig de Gràcia at Carrer de la Diputació 269, tel. 934-880-977).

**$$ Ciutat Comtal Cerveceria** is an Eixample favorite, full of tourists, with an elegant bar and tables plus good seating out on the Rambla de Catalunya for all that people-watching action. It's packed after 21:00, when you'll likely need to put your name on a list and wait. While it has no restaurant-type menu, the list of tapas and *montaditos* is easy, fun, and comes with a great variety (including daily specials, daily 8:00-24:00, facing the intersection of Gran Via de les Corts Catalanes and Rambla de Catalunya at Rambla de Catalunya 18, tel. 933-181-997).

## BARCELONETA AND THE BEACH

The nearest Metro stop to this former sailors' quarter is Barceloneta; the bus will get you closer—the best ones are #V15 (catch it at Plaça de Catalunya or along Via Laietana), #59 (from the top of the Ramblas), or #D20 (from the Columbus Monument). For the locations of these eateries, see the map on page 75.

### On or near the Main Square

The main square in the middle of Barceloneta (Plaça del Poeta Boscà) is homey, with a 19th-century iron-and-glass market, families at play in the park, and lots of hole-in-the-wall eateries and bars.

**$$ El Guindilla Taverna del Mercat**, in the market and spilling onto the square, is a good value for a basic local meal in a neighborhood family setting (great outdoor tables, daily, Plaça del Poeta Boscà 2, tel. 932-215-458).

**$ Baluard,** one of Barcelona's most highly regarded artisan bakeries, faces one side of the big market hall. Line up with the locals to get a loaf of heavenly bread, a pastry, or a slice of pizza (Mon-Sat 8:00-21:00, closed Sun, Carrer del Baluard 38, tel. 932-211-208).

**$$$$ Restaurante Can Solé,** serving seafood since 1903, is a splurge. Hiding on a nondescript lane between the square and the marina, this venerable yet homey restaurant draws a celebrity crowd, judging by the autographed pictures of the famous and not-so-famous that line the walls (Tue-Sat 13:30-16:00 & 20:30-23:00, closed Sun-Mon, Carrer de Sant Carles 4, one block off the harborfront promenade, tel. 932-215-012, www.restaurantcansole.com).

### On the Waterfront

The main drag—Passeig de Joan de Borbó—faces the city and is lined with many interchangeable seafood restaurants and cafés. Consider **$$$$ La Mar Salada,** a traditional seafood restaurant with a slightly modern twist (weekday lunch *menú*, Wed-Mon 13:00-16:00 & 20:00-23:00, closed Tue, indoor and outdoor seating, Passeig de Joan de Borbó 59, tel. 932-212-127).

## On the Beach

The *chiringuito* tradition of funky eateries lining Barcelona's beach now has serious competition from trendy bars and restaurants. A piece of modern art in the sand—a bunch of cubical shacks piled high—stands like a memorial to these beloved-but-seasonal beach joints. Now the spendy places have moved in, and all along the beach you have restaurants offering both indoor and terrace tables with a sea view. My favorites are at the far south end near the towering Hotel W.

**$$$$ Pez Vela** is the top-end option with a fashionable local crowd and its own disc jockey (Passeig del Mare Nostrum 19, tel. 932-216-317). Cheaper—and with far less pretense—is the next-door **$$$ Ristorante Mamarosa,** a family-friendly Italian place (Passeig del Mare Nostrum 21, tel. 933-123-586).

EATING

# BARCELONA WITH CHILDREN

Barcelona is a great place to travel with kids; it's bubbling with inexpensive, quirky sights and an infectious human spirit. Sure, there's an amusement park, a zoo, and a science museum, but your kids will have an adventure simply wandering down the city's tangled streets. And when it's time for a break, Barcelona has one of Europe's best urban beach scenes.

## Trip Tips

### PLAN AHEAD
Get your trip off to a good start with careful kid-oriented planning.
- Choose hotels in an area with wide, strollable streets, small parks, and a family-friendly feel—try Eixample or Barceloneta. If you're staying a week or more, or if your kids love playing in the sand, consider renting an apartment (see page 181) near one of Barcelona's many beaches.
- If traveling with infants, plan on bringing or buying a light stroller for neighborhood walks, and a child backpack for riding the Metro.
- If traveling with older kids, readily available Wi-Fi makes bringing a mobile device worthwhile. Most parents find it worth the peace of mind to buy a supplemental messaging plan for the whole family: Adults can stay connected to teenagers while allowing them maximum independence (see page 291).

### EATING
Your kids may be surprised to find out that Catalan food is nothing like Mexican food back home. Picky eaters may have a hard time

with *jamón*, deep-fried dishes, and strange seafood. Try these tips to keep your kids content throughout the day.

- Start the day with a good breakfast (at hotels, kids sometimes eat free).

- Seek out commonly available, kid-friendly food choices such as a *tortilla de patatas* (potato-egg omelette), *bikinis* or *sandwich mixto* (grilled ham-and-cheese sandwich), *empanada de atún-pollo, carne picada,* or *jamón y queso* (savory pastry filled with tuna, chicken, ground beef, or ham and cheese), or *bocadillo* (French-bread sandwich usually filled with meat, cheese, or egg). For breakfast, try *una tosatada con mantequilla y merme-lada* (toast with butter and jam) or a croissant, along with *zumo natural* (fresh squeezed orange juice). Fruit, cereal, and yogurt are available at the supermarket.

- Sweet treats popular with little travelers include *curros con chocolate* (fried dough strips with chocolate sauce for dipping), *ensaimada* (a Mallorca-style croissant with powdered sugar), *crema catalane* (like a crème brûlée), and *torró/turrón* (a nougat confection).

- Picnic lunches or dinners work well. Try large grocery stores such as Carrefour Market, El Corte Inglés, or Bonpreu. Or drop by a *panadería* (bakery), which will likely have baguette sandwiches, pizza by the slice, and *empanadas* (meat pies). Near the beach? Head to the market—El Mercat de la Barce-loneta—near the Barceloneta Metro stop (Mon-Thu and Sat 7:00-15:00, Fri 7:00-20:00, closed Sun; Plaça de la Font 1, tel. 932-216-471). Having snacks on hand can avoid meltdowns (and can help your kids avoid them, too).

- Choose easy eateries. A good, safe (though not exotic) bet is the cafeteria/restaurant at the **$ El Corte Inglés** department store on Plaça de Catalunya (service all day, €7 kids menu). Quick chain restaurants such as Bocatta or Pans & Company serve reasonably priced *bocadillos* (sandwiches) and fries—and grownups can order a beer. For a sweet break for both you and the kids, try the **$ Pudding** café. You can snack or have a light meal sitting next to a giant mushroom or in the kids' play area (books and board games). It's near the Plaça de Cata-lunya; look for it around the corner from the Gran Vía about two blocks from the Passeig de Gràcia (cupcakes, sandwiches/quiche, daily 11:00-21:00, Carrer de Pau Claris 90, tel. 936-678-748, www.puddingbarcelona.com).

- Catalans eat late—usually about 21:00 or 22:00—and dinner can take two hours. If you're eating late with your kids at a res-taurant, bring something to occupy them and seek out places on squares where kids can run free while you dine. Catalan

## Barcelona Books for Kids

Get your kids into the spirit of Barcelona with these books about the city and some of its most influential former residents. (Also see "Recommended Books and Films," which includes some good choices for teenagers, on page 315.)

*A Stroll with Mr. Gaudí* (Pau Estrada, 2013). In this fun introduction to Barcelona's architecture, Antoni Gaudí takes a walk through the city, visiting famous landmarks.

*Building with Nature: The Life of Antoni Gaudí* (Rachel Rodriguez and Julie Paschkis, 2009). Beautiful, folksy illustrations enliven the biography of Barcelona's most famous architect.

*Let's Visit Barcelona!: Adventures of Bella & Harry* (Lisa Manzione and Kristine Lucco, 2012). Two Chihuahuas visit Barcelona with their family, learning basic Spanish phrases and visiting famous landmarks.

*Mission Barcelona: A Scavenger Hunt Adventure* (Catherine Aragon, 2014). This interactive scavenger hunt will keep your youngsters engaged throughout your trip.

*Molly and the Magic Suitcase: Molly Goes to Barcelona* (Chris Oler and Amy Houston Oler, 2013). With the help of a magic suitcase, Molly and her brother trek to Barcelona in search of adventure.

*Pablo Picasso: Meet the Artist* (Patricia Geis, 2014). Young readers will enjoy this look at Picasso's art, and may just be inspired to create some of their own.

*Picasso and Minou* (P.I. Maltbie and Pau Estrada, 2005). This beautifully illustrated book tells the story of Picasso and his work through the eyes of his cat, Minou.

children go out and stay out late, so don't worry about your kids disturbing others as they gambol around the plaza.

## SIGHTSEEING

The key to a successful Barcelona family vacation is to slow down. Tackle one or two key sights each day, mix in a healthy dose of pure fun at a park or beach, and take extended breaks when needed.

- Buy your child a trip journal, and encourage him or her to write down observations, thoughts, and favorite sights and memories. This journal could end up being your child's favorite souvenir.

- Incorporate your child's interests into each day's plans. Let your kids make some decisions: choosing lunch spots or deciding which stores to visit. Turn your kid into your personal tour guide and navigator of the Metro system. Deputize your child to lead you on my self-guided walks and museum tours.

- Since a trip is a splurge for parents, the kids should enjoy a larger allowance, too. Provide ample money and ask your kids to buy their own treats, postcards, and trinkets within that daily budget.

- Follow this book's crowd-beating tips to the letter. Kids despise long lines even more than you do.

- Seek out kid-friendly museums, such as CosmoCaixa or the Maritime Museum. And limit museum visits to 45 minutes—period! Kids will tolerate a little culture if it's short and focused, with plenty of breaks. Museum audioguides are great for older children. If you're visiting art museums with younger children, hit the gift shop first so you can buy postcards; then hold a scavenger hunt to find the pictured artwork. When boredom sets in, try "I spy" games.

- If you allow kids to explore a museum or neighborhood on their own, be sure to establish a clear meeting time and place.

- It's good to have a "what if" procedure in place in case something goes wrong. Give your kids your hotel's business card, your phone number (if you brought a mobile phone), and emergency taxi fare. Let them know to ask to use the phone at a hotel if they are lost. And if they have their own mobile phones, show them how to make calls in Spain (see page 294).

## Sights and Activities

### KID-CENTRIC ATTRACTIONS
#### Tibidabo

This 100-year-old amusement park (the city's oldest) sits atop the Tibidabo foothills above town; visiting it could easily fill an entire day. The fun starts even before you arrive—you can take an underground train to a trolley (€5.50, Fri-Sat only), then ride up a funicular right to the park entrance (€7.70, €4.10 with park admission). At the top are Disneyland-like rides and some vintage attractions appealing to younger children, teens, and adults alike. Many enjoy the maze of mirrors—you have to wear gloves so the mirrors stay fingerprint-free. Older kids might like modern attractions such as a 4-D cinema show and the Tibidabo Express roller-coaster. Those on a budget can enjoy a handful of rides for €2 each without buying the full entrance ticket, including an old-fashioned carousel and a Ferris wheel that gives you breathtaking views of Barcelona.

**Cost and Hours:** Free for kids under 3 feet tall, €10.30 for kids between 3 and 4 feet, €28.50 for those over 4 feet; for more info, opening hours, and directions, see page 60.

## CosmoCaixa

One of Europe's most advanced science museums, CosmoCaixa features hands-on exhibits, many of which are specifically geared toward small children. Youngsters will love *¡Toca toca!* (Touch touch!), an exhibit exploring the natural world, while the newly renovated 3-D planetarium (€4 extra) may entice older kids and teens. Other kid-focused highlights include a jungle greenhouse and a treasure hunt.

**Cost and Hours:** €4, free for kids under 16 and on first Sun of the month; Tue-Sun 10:00-20:00, closed Mon; Metro: Tibidabo, then hop on bus #196 for one stop or walk about 15 minutes to the museum, Carrer d'Isaac Newton 26; tel. 932-126-050, www.obrasocial.lacaixa.es.

## Barcelona Zoo (Zoo de Barcelona)

This enormous zoo, which gained fame in the 1960s as the home of the only known albino gorilla in the world, *Copito de Nieve* (Snowflake), is inside Citadel Park (see page 76). The zoo features all the kid-recognizable animals such as tigers, hippos, and zebras as well as oddities like Komodo dragons. Daily shows with the dolphins and sea lions in "Aquamara," the small SeaWorld-like marina arena, may impress the young and old.

**Cost and Hours:** €12 for kids 3-12, free for kids 2 and under, €20 for teens and adults, cheaper online; hours vary by season, summer hours daily 10:00-20:00; Metro: Barceloneta, Ciutadella-Vila Olímpica, Marina, or Arc de Triomf; tel. 902-457-545, www.zoobarcelona.cat.

## Barcelona Aquarium at Port Vell
## (L'Aquàrium de Barcelona Port Vell)

Located on the waterfront not far from the Columbus Monument, the aquarium is home to more than 11,000 animals. Its star attraction is the "Oceanarium," a 262-foot underwater glass tunnel that lets you walk beneath schools of deep-sea creatures such as sharks and stingrays. The IMAX Theater next door shows movies in Spanish or Catalan, sometimes with English subtitles. The Port Vell area is an inviting mix of towering sailboats and a steady flow of people on the boardwalk in the midst of daily life; the green space offers room for a picnic or quick rest from sightseeing.

**Cost and Hours:** €15 for kids 5-10, €7 for kids 3-4, free for kids 2 and under, €20 for visitors 11 and over, cheaper online; daily 9:30-21:00, July-Aug until 23:00; Metro: Drassanes or Barceloneta, Moll d'Espanya del Port Vell, tel. 932-217-474, www.aquariumbcn.com.

## Magic Fountains (Font Màgica)

This popular, free spectacle uses classic and modern tunes—including film scores—as the soundtrack for a fanciful water show. Built for the 1929 World's Fair and renovated before the 1992 Olympics, it's part of a web of ponds and waterfalls on Avinguda Maria Cristina in Montjuïc.

**Cost and Hours:** Free 20-minute shows start on the half-hour; almost always May-Sept Thu-Sun 21:00-23:00, no shows Mon-Wed; Oct-April Fri-Sat 19:00-20:30, no shows Sun-Thu; Metro: Espanya; see page 72.

# MUSEUMS AND EXHIBITS

## Art Museums

A short visit to some of Barcelona's modern and contemporary art museums could dazzle your kids. All of the following offer educational programs aimed at children and their families.

**Museu d'Art Contemporani** (MACBA) houses a vast collection of artwork from the past 50 years and offers lectures, video screenings, and special exhibits covering contemporary culture and art. The museum's square is also a roller-skaters' hangout; it's fun to watch the tricks before going inside (€10, free for kids 13 and under; Mon and Wed-Fri 11:00-19:30, Sat 10:00-21:00, Sun 10:00-15:00, closed Tue, Metro: Universitat or Catalunya, Plaça dels Àngels 1, tel. 934-120-810, www.macba.cat).

The **Picasso Museum** gives kids a chance to marvel at the artist's early works (see page 48).

If you feel like venturing outside of the city for a surreal experience, a two-hour drive or train ride will take you to the **Salvador Dalí Theater-Museum** in the town of Figueres (see page 242).

## Chocolate Museum (Museu de la Xocolata)

Satisfy everyone's sweet tooth while learning the history of traditional Catalan confectionery through a range of kid-friendly exhibits. You'll see chocolate statues of just about anything and everything—including Barcelona soccer players. Family activities may even include painting with chocolate.

**Cost and Hours:** €5, free for kids 6 and under; Mon-Sat 10:00-19:00, summer until 20:00, Sun 10:00-15:00 year-round; Carrer del Comerç 36, Metro: Jaume I, tel. 932-687-878, www.museuxocolata.cat; see page 52.

## Maritime Museum (Museu Marítim de Barcelona)

While some of its permanent exhibits are not on display, the museum still illuminates the history of Catalunya's rich maritime past from the 13th to the 21st century. Boat aficionados and sailors-to-be enjoy the collection of model boats and seafaring gadgets, as well as the sprawling marina.

**Cost and Hours:** Museum—€7, free for kids 16 and under, daily 10:00-20:00; *Santa Eulàlia*—€3, included with museum admission, Tue-Sun 10:00-20:30 except Sat when it opens at 14:00, Nov-March until 17:30, closed Mon year-round; Avinguda de la Drassanes, Metro: Drassanes, tel. 933-429-920, www. mmb.cat; see page 41.

**Nearby:** The museum also includes the *Santa Eulàlia* (docked on the Moll de la Fusta quay), a historic three-masted schooner from 1918 that was meticulously restored to its original state. It's especially fun to visit on Saturday mornings, when the schooner sails around the harbor—reserve well in advance (Sat 10:00-13:00, €6 for kids 6-14, €12 for adults, tel. 933-429-920, reserves. mmaritim@diba.cat).

## Natural Science Blue Museum (Museu Blau de Ciencies Naturals)

A good choice for any kid interested in nature, this natural history museum—home to more than three million specimens—celebrates the diversity in flora, fauna, and geology in Catalunya and beyond. Its main exhibit, Planet Earth, follows the birth of our planet and the evolution of life. A special space, the "Science Nest," has activities designed for preschoolers, but you'll need to reserve your visit in advance (closed Aug, though museum is open).

**Cost and Hours:** €6, free for kids 15 and under, free on Sun after 15:00, €7 combo ticket with Botanical Gardens (see below); Tue-Sat 10:00-19:00, Sun 10:00-20:00; closed Mon; Metro: El Maresme-Fòrum, Plaza Leonardo da Vinci 4-5, tel. 932-566-002, www.museuciencies.cat.

## Botanical Gardens

Montjuïc is the home of the natural history museum's Botanical Gardens and its Botanical Institute, as well as the recently reopened Historical Botanical Garden. A network of paths follows the natural terrain, taking visitors past 87 outdoor exhibits known as "phytoepisodes."

**Cost and Hours:** €3.50, free for kids under 16, €7 combo-ticket with Natural Science Blue Museum; daily June-Aug 10:00-20:00, closes earlier off-season; take bus #193 from Plaça d'Espanya or the Montjuïc funicular from Paral-lel, main entrance between Olympic Stadium and castle—see map on page 62, Carrer Dr. Font i Quer 2; tel. 932-564-160, www.museuciencies.cat.

## Olympic and Sports Museum
## (Museu Olímpic i de l'Esport)

Barcelona hosted the Olympics in 1992 and has never been the same since. Sports-crazed kids might enjoy this museum, as well

as exploring what is left of the adjacent, anticlimactic 1992 Olympic Stadium. The mod-yet-tacky museum offers up several kid-friendly multimedia installations, such as a virtual race against an Olympic athlete, but it ultimately appeals only to Olympics fanatics.

**Cost and Hours:** €5.10, free for kids 14 and under; Tue-Sat 10:00-20:00 (Oct-March until 18:00), Sun 10:00-14:30, closed Mon; Avinguda de l'Estadi 60, Metro: Espanya, tel. 932-925-379, www.museuolimpicbcn.cat; see page 68.

### Camp Nou Soccer Stadium

"Barça" is to Barcelona what the Cowboys are to Dallas; the city lives and breathes for this top-ranked soccer team, as evidenced by their motto, "More Than a Club." The team's pricey visitors center has an interactive museum, features memorabilia from past seasons of glory, and includes a behind-the-scenes visit onto the soccer field. An English audioguide helps explain the exhibits—and the city's soccer obsession. The crowded, energetic FC Barcelona superstore *(La FC Botiga)* is a cool spot for kids and teens as well (pick up a scarlet-and-blue jersey or scarf as a souvenir).

**Cost and Hours:** €1 for kids 6-13, free for kids 5 and under, €23 for teens and adults, audioguide included; mid-April-early Oct Mon-Sat 10:00-20:00 (off-season closes at 18:30), Sun 10:00-14:30; shorter hours on game days, Metro: Maria Cristina or Collblanc, Carrer d'Arístides Mallol 12, toll tel. 902-189-900, www.fcbarcelona.com/camp-nou.

## PARKS AND BEACHES
### Citadel Park (Parc de la Ciutadella)

Barcelona's most central park sprawls its grassy fields and large avenues across the grounds of an old fortress, and offers plenty for curious kids to discover. Attractions include a giant mammoth statue, a small lake with rental rowboats and duck feeding, a large Baroque fountain *(La Cascada)*, and several outdoor events held throughout the year. The Barcelona Zoo is also accessible from the park. Bikes can be rented from the bike-rental shop opposite the entrance to the park on Passeig de Picasso and Avinguda del Marquès de l'Argentera (park open daily 10:00 until dusk; north of França train station, Metro: Arc de Triomf, Barceloneta, or Ciutadella/Vila Olímpica; see page 76).

### Horta Labyrinth Park (Parc del Laberint d'Horta)

Away from the city center in an unassuming location lies the most tranquil green space in town. With barely a tourist in sight, the park holds a handful of Neoclassical and Romantic gardens, highlighted by a small central maze that was used in the filming of Guillermo del Toro's hit, *Pan's Labyrinth* (2006) and Tom Tykwer's *Perfume* (2006). There are more than 20 water features—pools, fountains, reservoirs, canals, and an artificial waterfall—and the tricky labyrinth should provide ample entertainment as youngsters and teens attempt to figure out the puzzle.

**Cost and Hours:** About €1.50 for kids 5-14, free for kids 4 and under, about €2.25 for adults, free on Wed and Sun; daily May-Sept 10:00-21:00, closes earlier off-season, last entry one hour before closing; Metro: Mundet, then a 15-minute walk, the park is behind a velodrome.

### Sant Sebastià, Barceloneta, and Nova Icària Beaches

These are the closest, longest, and busiest beaches (with Sant Sebastià preferred by locals). Both are near the city center, making them a good stop before or after sightseeing. A long boardwalk with food, drink, and ice-cream options lines Sant Sebastià and Barceloneta; on the sand, you'll come upon children's play areas (including one with a cool climbing frame). Expect beach sports such as Ping Pong, beach volleyball,

and the Basque handball game, *pelota*. Look out on the waves, and you'll also spot a surfer or two.

If you don't care for crowds, head instead for the nearby Nova Icària beach; this more tranquil beach is frequented by families. Nova Icària is within walking distance of the 1992 Olympic Marina, a popular place for sailing and boating. All of these beaches are accessible from the Old City area by bus or Metro; see page 74 for directions.

CHILDREN

## OTHER EXPERIENCES

### *Sardana* Dance

The easy-to-do *sardana* is a beloved traditional symbol of Catalan unity and pride. Kids might enjoy this spectacle of local culture (see page 45 for location and time).

### Cable Car (El Transbordador Aeri del Port)

This is a fun and scenic ride between the Barcelona waterfront and Montjuïc, providing spectacular views of the city. Note that the car is often crowded and very slow-moving; if there's a long line, it may not be worth the wait (see page 64 for details).

CHILDREN

# SHOPPING IN BARCELONA

Barcelona is a fantastic shopping destination, whatever your taste or budget. The streets of the Barri Gòtic and El Born are bursting with characteristic hole-in-the-wall shops, while the Eixample is the upscale "uptown" shopping district. The area around Avinguda del Portal de l'Angel (at the northern edge of the Barri Gòtic) has a number of department and chain stores.

Most shops are open Monday through Friday from about 9:00 or 10:00 until lunchtime (around 13:00 or 14:00). After the siesta, they reopen in the evening, around 16:30 or 17:00, and stay open until 20:00 or 21:00. Large stores and some smaller shops in touristy zones may remain open through the afternoon—but don't count on it. On Saturdays, many shops are open in the morning only. On Sundays, most shops are closed (though the Maremagnum complex on the harborfront is open).

Consider these tips for shopping in Barcelona:

- If you need souvenirs, find a souvenir shop or consult your neighborhood supermarket for that saffron or *torró*—perfect for tucking into your suitcase at the last minute.

- For more elaborate purchases, large department stores provide painless one-stop shopping.

- Barcelona—particularly its Old City—is studded with hundreds of delightful neighborhood boutiques, the best of which specialize in a unique item and do it well. If you're a collector of anything in particular, do some homework to find the perfect shop.

- For information on VAT refunds and customs regulations, see page 269. For clothing size comparisons between the US and Europe, see page 318 of the appendix.

# What to Buy

## HOME AND DESIGN GOODS

Consider picking up prints, books, posters, decorative items, or other keepsakes featuring works by your favorite artist (Picasso, Dalí, Miró, Gaudí, etc.). Gift shops at major museums are open to the public (such as the Picasso Museum and Gaudí's La Pedrera) and are a bonanza for art and design lovers. Model-ship builders will be fascinated by the offerings at the Maritime Museum shop.

In this design-oriented city, home decor shops are abundant and fun to browse, offering a variety of Euro-housewares unavailable back home. For something more classic, look for glassware or other items with a dash of Modernista style.

Decorative tile and pottery can be a good keepsake. Eixample sidewalks are paved with distinctively patterned tiles, which are sold in local shops.

## FOODIE ITEMS

Foodies might enjoy shopping for olive oil, wine, spices (such as saffron or sea salts), high-quality canned foods and preserves, dried beans, and other Spanish food items. Remember, these must be sealed to make it back through US customs (see page 270). Cooks can look for European-style gadgets at kitchen-supply stores.

*Torró* (or *turrón* in Spanish) is the beloved nougat treat that's traditionally eaten around Christmastime, but has become popular anytime.

## CLOTHING, JEWELRY, AND ACCESSORIES

Department and chain stores can be fun to explore for clothing—including fashions you won't find back home.

An *espardenya* (or *alpargata* in Spanish) is a soft-canvas, rope-soled shoe (known in the US as an espadrille). It originated as humble peasant footwear in the 14th century in the Pyrenean region (including Catalunya, Occitania, and the Basque Country), but has become popular in modern times for its lightweight comfort in hot weather. A few shops in Barcelona (including La Manual Alpargatera, described later) still make these the traditional way.

Jewelry shops are popular here. While the city doesn't have a strictly local style, finding a piece with a Modernista flourish gives it a Barcelona vibe.

Accessories crafted from discarded materials into stylish, useful products (such as handbags) sell well in "green" Barcelona.

## CATALAN PRIDE

If you're intrigued by Catalunya's culture, consider a Catalan flag (gold and red stripes). And if you're a fan of Catalunyan independence, pick up one with the blue triangle and star.

Sports fans love jerseys, scarves, and other gear associated with the wildly popular Barça soccer team. As you wander, you'll likely see official football team shops.

# Shopping Spots

## THE OLD CITY

The Barri Gòtic bursts with shopping opportunities, from international chain stores to creative artisan shops (I'll point out a few on my Barri Gòtic Shopping Walk, below). Neighboring El Born may be the most appealing place in Barcelona for boutique-hopping. My 🕮 **El Born Walk** chapter, designed partly as a framework for shoppers, suggests a route through the heart of this district and points you to streets worth exploring.

### Barri Gòtic Shopping Walk
### (from the Cathedral to the Ramblas)

Most visitors going between the cathedral and the Ramblas follow the straight shot along the wide Carrer de la Portaferrissa.

This drag is lined with mostly international clothing stores catering to teens and young adults (H&M, Mango, etc.). For a more characteristic route—leading you through far more interesting streets lined with little local shops—plunge into some lanes just to the south. This brief, U-shaped walk is designed to lead you through some of the Barri Gòtic's most enjoyable shopping streets. Keep in mind that many shops are closed during the midafternoon siesta and on Sundays. For shop locations, see the "Barri Gòtic Walk" map on page 96.

• Begin on **Plaça Nova,** *the long square in front of the cathedral. At the west end of that square, stand facing the old Roman towers and the big BARCINO letters. Turn 90 degrees to the right, and just to the left of the restaurant (Bilbao Berria "BB"—good for a quick tapas bite with fine seating facing the cathedral), head up the tight lane called...*

**Carrer de la Palla:** This is ideal for antiques, with a half-dozen ancient-feeling shops crammed with mothballed treasures. (You'll also find, on the left, a fenced-in area with fragments of the old Roman walls, which functions today as a schoolyard soccer field at recess time.) Mixed in are a few contemporary art galleries, offbeat shops (such as **Librería Angel Batlle** at #23, selling books and vintage posters), and a motorcycle museum. Stay on this street until you reach the fork, marked by the building with **Caelum**—a casual but classy-feeling café that sells a wide range of nun-made pastries from convents around Spain. Peruse the boxes of sisterly goodies, and consider sticking around for a coffee—either on the charming main floor or down in the cellar (open long hours daily, Carrer de la Palla 8).

The big news in this area is the recent lifting of rent controls. This change has brought a sudden, massive increase in rents, driving many venerable shops out of business and threatening the character of this delightful neighborhood.

From here, detour left and head down **Carrer dels Banys Nous,** which curves gracefully south as it follows the route of the original Roman wall; while you'll have to backtrack a bit, it's another great shopping street with antiques, designer "transformer dresses" (at #17), and a bridal shop. About 100 yards down this street, on the left at #10, the sprawling **Oliver** shop (selling home decor, women's clothing, and accessories) has the remains of an old Arabic bath in the back. Directly across the lane, **Artesania Catalunya,** a large market-space run by the city, features handmade items from Catalan artisans. You can typically find ceramics, jewelry, leather goods, and accessories, but the artisans and merchandise change every few months (Mon-Sat 10:00-20:00, Sun until 14:00, Carrer dels Banys Nous 11).

Backtrack to Caelum, and take a hard left down Carrer de la Palla to another fine shop, **Oro Líquido** ("Liquid Gold"), which sells a wide range of high-quality olive oils from around Spain (Mon-Sat 10:00-20:30, shorter hours Sun, Carrer de la Palla 8).

• *After another block, you'll pop out on the charming, café-lined Plaça de Sant Josep Oriol, facing the Church of Santa Maria del Pi (a popular venue for guitar concerts). Skirt around the right side of the church to find...*

**Plaça del Pi:** While small, this square—named for its *pi* (or pine) tree—has some worthwhile shops. Gentlemen enjoy checking out the genteel **Josep Roca,** a *ganiveteria* (cutlery shop) selling knives, shaving gear, and other manly items (Mon-Sat 10:00-20:00 but closes midday, closed Sun, Plaça del Pi 3). Nearby, at Plaça del Pi 2, is a small outlet branch of the colorful Barcelona clothing designer, **Custo** (for the full Custo experience, visit their shop on the Ramblas, at #120). On many days, local food and crafts markets set up on this square.

• *Head up the street immediately left of Josep Roca...*

**Carrer de Petritxol:** This fun, narrow, characteristic lane (pronounced peht-ree-CHUHL) is decorated with historic tiles. It's a fun combination of art galleries (such as **Sala Parés**, at #5, where Picasso had his first professional exhibition in town—step in and enjoy the latest in 150 years of art exhibits), fancy jewelry shops, and simple local places for hot chocolate and churros or other treats.

For a great *churros con chocolate* break, stop into **Granja La Pallaresa,** near the end of the street on the left (at #11). Elegant, older ladies gather here for the Spanish equivalent of teatime. For a more local treat, try an *ensaimada* (Mallorca-style croissant with powdered sugar) or the *crema catalane* (like a crème brûlée). Three doors further down (at #15) is **Vicens,** a fancy sweets shop specializing in *torró.* They offer generous plates of samples, lots of varieties on sale in small quantities, and a warm welcome.

And if you're looking for handmade ballet flats, you'll find them in a rainbow of colors at the family-run **Kokua** (at #18); they also sell bags, with a bigger selection of colors and sizes at their nearby shop at Carrer de la Boquería 30.

• *You'll dead-end onto touristy Carrer de la Portaferrissa. Head one block left to get to the Ramblas, or five blocks right to return to the cathedral. Or retrace your steps, this time poking into side streets to discover more shops.*

## More Shops in the Barri Gòtic

The streets described in the above walk are just the beginning. While exploring the many other characteristic lanes of the Barri Gòtic, keep an eye out for these shops.

**Sabater Hermanos** (abbreviated "Hnos." on the sign) continues a family tradition of making and selling handmade, natural, colorful soaps. The simple but fragrant shop feels like an artisanal Lush. To buy soap and call it a culturally redeemable souvenir, look for the bars shaped like characteristic Barcelona sidewalk tiles (daily 10:30-21:00, cash only, Plaça Sant Felip Neri 1—see map on page 96).

**Papirum** is an inviting, classic, artisan shop selling craft paper, stationery, and hand-bound blank books (Mon-Sat 10:00-20:30 except closed Sat 14:00-17:00, closed Sun, Baixada de la Llibreteria 2—see map on page 96, run by Dolores Crespo and family).

**Som Naturals** sells earthy baby and toddler clothing, designed and handmade by locals Dora Garriga and Jordi Cugat. They use 100-percent natural burlap and cotton. Their wares also regularly appear in artisan markets around town (Mon-Fri 16:00-19:00, Sat 10:00-15:00 & 16:00-21:00, closed Sun, Carrer Santa Anna 37—see map on page 96).

The street called **Carrer de Sant Domènec del Call,** which runs through the old Jewish Quarter (and is described on my Barri Gòtic Walk), is lined with some fun cafés, plus a guitar shop and a few other interesting stores.

**La Manual Alpargatera,** dating from the 1940s, is an *espardenya* store famous for making and selling these affordable, comfy shoes (Mon-Sat 9:30-20:00, closes at midday, closed Sun, 7 Carrer d'Avinyó, just off Carrer de Ferran between the Ramblas and Plaça Sant Jaume).

**Herbolari Ferran,** on Plaça Reial (to the right as you enter the square from the Ramblas), is a fine and aromatic shop of herbs, with fun souvenirs such as top-quality saffron, or *safra* (also a pleasant little café inside, Mon-Fri 9:30-14:00 & 16:30-20:00, closed Sat-Sun, downstairs at Plaça Reial 18, see map on page 80).

**Carrer Ample,** the street one block up from the tapas-loaded Carrer de la Mercè (in the lower part of Barri Gòtic—just above the waterfront), feels local but with little bursts of trendy energy. For example, **Papabubble** is a candy shop where you can watch treats being made the old-fashioned way (daily 10:00-14:00 & 15:00-19:30, Carrer Ample 28).

Other Barri Gòtic streets are loaded with fun shopping opportunities. On the other side of the Ramblas (two blocks below Plaça de Catalunya), stroll down skinny **Carrer de Bonsuccés** (it turns into **Carrer d'Elisabets**) and poke into the little boutiques along the way (such as the tiny, fashionable clothing store, **Passé Composé,** at #12).

## THE EIXAMPLE

This ritzy "uptown" district is home to some of the city's top-end shops. In general, you'll find a lot of big international names along **Passeig de Gràcia,** the main boulevard that runs from Plaça de Catalunya to the Gaudí sights—an area fittingly called the "Golden Quarter" (Quadrat d'Or). Appropriately enough, the "upper end" of Passeig de Gràcia has the fancier shops—Gucci, Luis Vuitton, Escada, Chanel, and so on—while the southern part of the street is relatively "low-end" (Zara, Mango, Camper). One block to the west, **Rambla de Catalunya** holds more local (but still expensive) options: fashion, home decor, jewelry, perfume, and so on. The streets that connect Rambla de Catalunya to Passeig da Gràcia are also home to some fine shops.

**Cubiñá,** three blocks east and a block south, is a highly regarded furniture and home-decor shop—worth a peek for its upscale-mod collection, as well as for the Domènech i Montaner building that houses it (Mon-Sat 10:00-14:00 & 16:30-20:30, closed Sun, Carrer Mallorca 291).

Farther south, the street called **Consell de Cent** has a variety of art galleries (close to Plaça de Catalunya, roughly between Passeig de Gràcia and Carrer d'Enric Granados). And much farther to the west, the broad main boulevard **Diagonal** is another popular shopping zone—especially the stretch between Plaça de Francesc

Macià and where it crosses Gran Via de Carles III (at the Maria Cristina Metro stop).

This neighborhood is also home to some fun kitchen stores: Try **Gadgets & Cuina** (Carrer d'Aragó 249) or **The Kitchen Company** (Carrer de Provença 246).

## AVINGUDA DEL PORTAL DE L'ANGEL

Barcelona natives do most of their shopping at big department stores. While most chains have several locations scattered around the city, you'll find the highest concentration on one convenient street, Avinguda del Portal de l'Angel, which connects Plaça de Catalunya with the cathedral. On this street, and throughout town, you'll find all of the following: El Corte Inglés is "Macy's-plus," the Spanish answer to one-stop shopping—everything from clothes, housewares, and furniture to electronics, bonsai trees, a travel agency, haircuts, and cheap souvenirs (get the complete list by picking up an English directory at their info desk). The chain **Zara** is focused on clothes. (Shops like Zara can vary from store to store—for example, the one in Barri Gòtic has more casual clothes, while the one along the ritzy Diagonal street emphasizes business attire.) Zara also owns several smaller clothing stores, including **Massimo Dutti** (upscale business attire, like Banana Republic), **Bershka** (teens), and **Pull and Bear** (young adults—sort of the Spanish Gap). The Barcelona-based **Mango** is another popular clothing chain, along with **Desigual** (with boldly colorful designs), the teen-oriented French chain **Pimkie,** and the more sophisticated **Podivm** and **Blanco.** Big international clothing chains include **H&M, Esprit,** and **Benetton. Camper,** which started in Mallorca, sells stylish but comfy shoes. **Yamamay** and **Women's Secret** are the Spanish answer to Victoria's Secret. **Intimissimi,** along with its parent company, **Calzedonia,** are Italian lingerie and swimwear stores. For Spanish fashion, simply walk down the street and dip into any of these that appeal.

At the top of Avinguda del Portal de l'Angel, Plaça de Catalunya has some large shops—including a gigantic **El Corte Inglés**

(with a supermarket in the basement and a ninth-floor view café, Mon-Sat 10:00-22:00, closed Sun) and, across the square, **FNAC**—a French department store that sells electronics, music, books, and tickets for major concerts and events (Mon-Sat 10:00-22:00, closed Sun).

## LAS ARENAS MALL

While the shops inside it are nothing special, the Las Arenas shopping mall itself is—since it fills Barcelona's repurposed bullring. After Catalunya outlawed bullfighting in 2010, the former *plaça de toros* was converted into a modern mall with chain stores, a food court, a view terrace on top, and an escalator that trundles all the way up through its wide-open atrium (daily 10:00-22:00, small fee if you take exterior elevator, Gran Via de les Corts Catalanes 373-385). Located on Plaça d'Espanya, it's convenient to combine with a visit to the Montjuïc sights (see page 74).

# NIGHTLIFE IN BARCELONA

Like all of Spain, Barcelona is extremely lively after hours. People head out for dinner at 22:00, then bar-hop or simply wander the streets until well after midnight. Some days it seems that more people are out and about at 2:00 in the morning (party time) than at 2:00 in the afternoon (siesta time). The most "local" thing you can do here after sunset is to explore neighborhood watering holes and find your favorite place to nurse a cocktail. I've described several parts of town ideally suited to doing just that. For a musical event, consider taking in a serious performance at a fancy venue (such as the Palace of Catalan Music or the Liceu Opera House), or opt for a jazz, flamenco, or classical guitar show.

**Information:** The TI hands out a free, monthly, user-friendly *Time Out BCN Guide* (in English, with descriptions of each day's main events and websites for getting tickets). The TI's culture website is also helpful: http://barcelonacultura.bcn.cat. The weekly *Guía del Ocio,* sold at newsstands for €1.20 (or free in some hotel lobbies), is a Spanish-language entertainment listing (with guidelines for English speakers inside the back cover; also available online at www.guiadelocio.com). Although it's in Catalan only, the *Butxaca* monthly cultural agenda includes a detailed schedule that's easy to figure out (available free around town and at Palau de la Virreina—described next, www.butxaca.com). Other resources are the monthly *Barcelona Planning.com* (www.barcelonaplanning.com), quarterly *See Barcelona* (www.seebarcelona.com), and monthly *Barcelona Metropolitan* (www.barcelona-metropolitan.com); all are available for free from the TI.

**Palau de la Virreina,** an arts-and-culture information office, provides details on Barcelona cultural events—music, opera, and theater (daily 10:00-20:30, Ramblas 99—see map on page 80, tel. 933-161-000, www.lavirreina.bcn.cat). A ticket desk is next door.

**Getting Tickets:** Most venues sell tickets through their websites, or you can book through www.ticketmaster.es or www.telentrada.com for most events. You can also get tickets through the box offices in the main El Corte Inglés department store or the giant FNAC electronics store (both on Plaça de Catalunya, extra booking fee), or at the ticket desk in Palau de la Virreina (listed earlier).

# Music and Dance

## CONCERTS

Several classy venues host high-end performances.

The **Palace of Catalan Music** (Palau de la Música Catalana), with one of the finest Modernista interiors in town (see listing on page 49), offers a full slate of performances, ranging from symphonic to Catalan folk songs to chamber music to flamenco (€20-50 tickets, purchase online or in person, box office open Mon-Sat 9:30-21:00, Sun 10:00-15:00, Carrer Palau de la Música 4, Metro: Urquinaona, box office tel. 902-442-882).

The **Liceu Opera House** (Gran Teatre del Liceu), right in the heart of the Ramblas, is a pre-Modernista, sumptuous venue for opera, dance, children's theater, and concerts (tickets from €10, buy tickets online up to 1.5 hours before show or in person, Ramblas 51, box office just around the corner at Carrer Sant Pau 1, Metro: Liceu, box office tel. 934-859-913, www.liceubarcelona.cat).

Another, much less architecturally interesting venue for classical music is **L'Auditori,** the home of the city's orchestra (boxy modern building northeast of Old City at Lepant 150; Metro: Glòries, Marina, or Monumental; tel. 932-479-300, www.auditori.cat).

Some of Barcelona's top sights host good-quality concerts. Try **La Pedrera** (described later under "Jazz"), **Fundació Joan Miró** (www.fundaciomiro-bcn.org), and **CaixaForum** (http://obrasociallacaixa.org—choose "CaixaForum Barcelona" from the "Centros Obra Social" drop-down menu).

## TOURISTY PERFORMANCES
## OF SPANISH CLICHÉS

Two famously Spanish types of music—flamenco and Spanish guitar—have little to do with Barcelona or Catalunya, but are performed to keep visitors happy. If you're headed for other parts of Spain where these musical forms are more typical (such as Andalucía for flamenco), you might as well wait until you can experience the real deal. But if this is your only stop in Spain, here are some options.

# Sights Open Late

Many of Barcelona's major sights are open well into the evening (and the hop-on, hop-off **Tourist Bus** runs until 20:00 daily in summer). If you'd like to extend your sightseeing day, here's where to do it:

## Near the Ramblas

**Maritime Museum:** Daily until 20:00 (*Santa Eulàlia* Schooner: April-Oct Tue-Sun until 20:30)

**Palau Güell:** April-Oct Tue-Sun until 20:00

**La Boqueria Market:** Mon-Sat until 20:00, though quiet after about 16:00

## Barri Gòtic and El Born

**Cathedral of Barcelona:** Mon-Fri until 19:30, Sat-Sun until 20:00

**Gaudí Exhibition Center:** Daily until 20:00 in summer

**Frederic Marès Museum:** Sun until 20:00

**Barcelona History Museum:** Sun until 20:00

**Picasso Museum:** Thu until 21:30

**Santa Caterina Market:** Tue and Thu-Fri until 20:30

**Church of Santa Maria del Mar:** Daily until 20:30

## Eixample and Beyond

**Sagrada Família:** April-Sept daily until 20:00

**La Pedrera (Casa Milà):** March-Oct daily until 20:00; also hosts nighttime visits

**Casa Batlló:** Daily until 21:00

**Park Güell:** April-Oct daily until 21:30 (Gaudí House Museum: April-Sept daily until 20:00)

## Montjuïc and Vicinity

**Fundació Joan Miró:** Thu until 21:00 year-round, also April-Oct Tue-Wed and Fri-Sat until 20:00

**Catalan Art Museum:** May-Sept Tue-Sat until 20:00

**Magic Fountains:** May-Sept Thu-Sun 21:00-23:00, Oct-April Fri-Sat 19:00-20:30

**CaixaForum:** Daily until 20:00

**Las Arenas (Bullring Mall):** Shops daily until 22:00, terrace restaurants until 24:00

**Flamenco:** While flamenco is foreign to Catalunya (locals say that it's like going to see country music in Boston), there are some good places to view this unique Spanish artform. Head to **Palau Dalmases,** in an atmospheric old palace courtyard in the heart of El Born, for the highest-quality performances I've found (€25 includes a drink, daily at 19:30 and 21:30, also hosts opera and jazz, Carrer de Montcada 20, tel. 933-100-673, www.palaudalmases. com).

**Tarantos,** on Plaça Reial in the heart of the Barri Gòtic, puts on cheap, brief (30 minutes), riveting flamenco performances several times nightly—an easy and inexpensieve way to see it. Performances are in a touristy little bar/theater with about 50 seats (€15; nightly at 20:30, 21:30, and 22:30; Plaça Reial 17, tel. 933-191-789, www.masimas.com/en/tarantos).

Another option is the pricey (and relatively high-quality) **Tablao Cordobés** on the Ramblas (€45 includes a drink, €79.50 includes mediocre buffet dinner and better seats, 2-3 performances/day, Ramblas 35, tel. 933-175-711, www.tablaocordobes.com).

For flamenco in a concert-hall setting, try one of the Palace of Catalan Music's regular performances (see listing earlier, under "Concerts").

**Spanish Guitar:** "Masters of Guitar" concerts are offered nearly nightly at 21:00 in the Barri Gòtic's Church of Santa Maria del Pi (€23 at the door, €4 less if you buy at least 3 hours ahead—look for ticket-sellers in front of church and scattered around town, Plaça del Pi 7; sometimes in Sant Jaume Church instead, at Carrer de Ferran 28; tel. 647-514-513, www.maestrosdelaguitarra.com). The same company also does occasional concerts in the Palace of Catalan Music (€30-35). Similar guitar concerts are performed at the Church of Santa Anna (see page 95).

## JAZZ

On summer weekends, a particularly classy option is the **"Summer Nights at La Pedrera"** concerts at Gaudí's Modernista masterpiece in the Eixample. This evening rooftop concert series generally features live jazz and also gives you the chance to see the La Pedrera (Casa Milà) rooftop illuminated (€27, late June-early Sept Thu-Sat at 22:30, book advance tickets online or by phone, tel. 902-101-212, www.lapedrera.com).

**Hotel Casa Fuster,** a Modernista landmark designed by Lluís Domènech i Montaner, is a luxury hotel that hosts a Woody Allen-inspired jazz night each Thursday (in the basement of Café Vienés, 21:00-23:00, €19, reservations recommended, across Avinguda Diagonal from the Eixample at Passeig de Gràcia 132, tel. 932-553-006, http://cafevienesjazzclub.blogspot.com).

**Jamboree** jazz and dance club, right on Plaça Reial, features two jazz sets nightly, at 20:00 and 22:00, in a cellar under brick vaults (€12-25 in advance, a euro or two more at the door, check schedule online or stop by to pick one up, Plaça Reial 17, Metro: Liceu, tel. 933-191-789, www.masimas.com/en/jamboree).

Also consider the divey **Harlem Jazz Club** (€6-10, a couple of blocks off Plaça Reial at Comtessa de Sobradiel 8, tel. 933-100-755, www.harlemjazzclub.es).

# After-Hours Hangout Neighborhoods

Most Barcelonans' idea of "nightlife" is hopping from bar to bar with a circle of friends, while nibbling tapas and enjoying a vari-

ety of drinks (see "Spanish Drinks," page 287). The streets are jammed with people. In general, the weekend progression (Thu-Sat) goes like this: dinner at around 22:00; a music club for cocktails and DJ music from midnight; then, at about 2:00 or 3:00 in the morning, hit the discos until dawn. The following neighborhoods let you join this social ritual.

## EL BORN

Passeig del Born, a broad park-like strip stretching from the Church of Santa Maria del Mar up to the old market hall, is lined with inviting bars and nightspots. The side streets also teem with options. Wander to find a place that appeals to you.

Right on Passeig del Born is **Miramelindo**, a local favorite—mellow yet convivial, with two floors of woody ambience and a minty aura from all those mojitos the bartenders are mashing up (Passeig del Born 15). **Palau Dalmases,** in the atmospheric courtyard of an old palace, slings cocktails when it's not hosting flamenco shows (described earlier). **La Vinya del Senyor** is a fine place for a good glass of wine out on the square in front of the Church of Santa Maria del Mar.

The **Aire de Barcelona** Arab-style thermal baths, across from Citadel Park, are open late. Recently renovated with great style, these are ideal for recovering from a busy day of sightseeing (€33/person for 1.5 hours, massage also possible; reserve ahead—a week ahead for weeknights, a month ahead for weekends; Passeig Picasso 22, tel. 902-555-789, www.airedebarcelona.com).

## PLAÇA REIAL AND NEARBY

This elegant-feeling square, just off the Ramblas in the Barri Gòtic, has a trendy charm. It bustles with popular bars and restaurants offering inflated prices at pleasant outdoor tables. While not a great place to eat (the only one worth seriously considering for a meal is the recommended **Les Quinze Nits**), this is a great place to sip a before- or after-dinner drink. **Ocaña Bar,** at #13, has a dilapidated-mod interior, a see-through industrial kitchen that serves up tapas, rickety-chic secondhand tables out on the square, and another cocktail bar downstairs (open nightly). Or there's always the student option: Buy a cheap €1 beer from a convenience store (you'll find several just off the square, including a few along Carrer dels Escudellers, just south of Plaça Reial), then grab a free spot on the square, either sitting on one of the few fixed chairs, perched along the rim of the fountain, or simply leaning up against a palm tree.

Plaça Reial is also home to the **Tarantos** flamenco bar and **Jamboree** jazz club (both described earlier). You'll find a variety of nightclubs here, including the hip **Sidecar Factory Club** (at #7, often live music, www.sidecarfactoryclub.com) and the hidden, mellow, pipe-happy **Barcelona Pipa Club** (at #3—find and ring the doorbell to get inside, this member's club opens to the public around 22:00, www.bpipaclub.com).

Wandering the streets near the square leads to other nightlife options. **Carrer de Escudellers** is a significantly rougher scene—a few trendy options are mixed in with several sketchy dives. Much closer to the harbor, **Carrer de la Mercè** (described on page 192 of the Eating in Barcelona chapter) has its share of salty sailors' pubs and more youthful bars. The next street up, **Carrer Ample,** has a similar scene.

## BARCELONETA

A broad beach stretches for miles from the former fishermen's quarter at Barceloneta to the Fòrum. Every 100 yards or so is a *chiringuito*—a shack selling drinks and light snacks. Originally these sold seafood, but now they keep locals and tourists well-lubricated. It's a very fun, lively scene on a balmy summer evening and a nice way to escape the claustrophobic confines of the city to enjoy some sea air and the day's final sun rays.

Barceloneta itself has a broad promenade facing the harbor, lined with interchangeable seafood restaurants. But the best beach experience is beyond the tip of Barceloneta. From here, a double-decker boardwalk runs the length of the beach, with a cool walkway up above and a series of fine seafood restaurants with romantic candlelit beachfront seating tucked down below. Pricey but well-regarded places featuring high-quality Catalan cuisine are **Agua, Cala Nuri,** and **Arenal.** Farther along, **Carpe Diem Lounge Club** (a.k.a. CDLC) is a fun Turkish-themed chill-out bar with cozy lounging sofas—ideal for a post-dinner drink; later, it becomes an edgier disco.

**Nightclubs:** Around Frank Gehry's glittering fish sculpture (at the former Olympic village) are several popular discos, crowded with partying twentysomethings. These get going extremely late—the kind of place where you have to be on the list, look good, and pay upwards of €10 for a drink. One of the most famous—and exclusive—is **Opium Mar,** a haunt of Barça footballers and other celebrities (www.opiummar.com). Beyond the beach, at the Olympic port, you'll find more bars with chill-out music (which later turn into livelier discos).

## MONTJUÏC

With a little hustle, in summer it's possible to string together a fun evening of memorable views from the Montjuïc hilltop. Start with sweeping city vistas as you ride the Aeri del Port cable car (catch it at the tip of the Barceloneta peninsula; see page 64) up to the park's Miramar viewpoint. From there, head up to Montjuïc Castle on foot for more breathtaking views. Finally, wind your way around the hilltop to the Catalan Art Museum and reward yourself with a drink at its terrace café—a prime spot for taking in the Magic Fountains show, which makes a dramatic splash every half-hour (Thu-Sun nights in summer; see page 72). For a splurge, consider dinner at the museum's **Òleum Restaurant** (open until 23:30), which also overlooks the fountains and the entire 1929 Expo site.

## THE EIXAMPLE

Barcelona's upscale uptown isn't quite as lively or funky as some other neighborhoods, but a few streets have some fine watering holes. Walk along the inviting, park-like **Rambla de Catalunya,** or a couple of blocks over, along **Carrer d'Enric Granados** and **Carrer d'Aribau** (near the epicenter of the Eixample's gay community); all of these streets are speckled with cocktail bars offering breezy outdoor seating. In the opposite direction (east of Passeig de Gràcia), **Bar Dow Jones**—popular with the American expat student crowd—has a clever gimmick: Drink prices rise and fall like the stock market (Carrer del Bruc 97).

## GRÀCIA

A bit farther flung, and more local-feeling because of it, the Gràcia neighborhood sits between the Eixample and Park Güell. Known for its design schools and its international art-house cinema (the Cines Verdi, www.cines-verdi.com/barcelona), it's the unpretentious but intellectual corner of town. Though it lacks the twisty-Gothic-lanes ambience of the Old City, Gràcia feels more like a small town (which it was, before it was swallowed up by an expanding Barcelona). It's popular with students—both local and international—and can be a bit rowdy. The district is even more vibrant in

August, when it hosts the Festa Major de Gràcia, with street music everywhere (see page 26).

The most interesting stretch of Gràcia is squeezed between two Metro stops: Fontana, on the L3 (green) line; and Joanic, on the L4 (yellow) line. Here's a handy bar-crawl route: From the Fontana stop, exit and turn left, heading down the shop-lined Carrer d'Astúries. After crossing the busy Carrer del Torrent de l'Olla, keep going straight two short blocks to **Carrer de Verdi.** You'll find several nightspots up and down this street, and a block over, at **Plaça de la Virreina** (where several places fill the square in front of the church with outdoor tables). From there you can head down Carrer de Torrijos, with more options—including **Café Salambo,** with an Art Deco vibe (at #51, www.cafesalambo.com). A right turn at Carrer de Ramón y Cajal leads you (in three blocks) to your grand finale, **Plaça del Sol,** the epicenter of Gràcia nightlife.

## TIBIDABO

Many people enjoy heading up to Tibidabo for drinks with a great view—ideal for watching the sunset. At the top of the Tramvía Blau (blue trolley)—which is also the bottom of the Tibidabo funicular—you'll find two places: **Mirabé** (nightly from 19:00, Manuel Arnús 2) and **Mirablau** (Plaça Dr. Andreu). While this probably isn't worth the long trip from downtown (unless you're a panorama seeker), it's handy to combine with a visit to Tibidabo or Park Güell.

Come here for a pricey drink with a view—not for dinner. And remember that transportation back downtown after 22:00 is limited to taxis. (The trolley only runs Sat-Sun until 19:30, and bus #196 stops running at about 22:00 daily.)

# BARCELONA CONNECTIONS

This chapter covers Barcelona's airports, main train station, cruise port, and main bus station.

I don't advise driving in Barcelona—thanks to its excellent public transportation and taxis, you won't need a car here, and the parking fees are outrageously expensive (for example, the lot behind La Boqueria Market charges upwards of €25/day).

## By Plane

Most flights use Barcelona's **El Prat de Llobregat Airport;** a few budget flights use a smaller airstrip 60 miles away, called **Girona–Costa Brava Airport.** Information on both airports can be found on the official Spanish airport website, www.aena-aeropuertos.es.

### EL PRAT DE LLOBREGAT AIRPORT
Barcelona's primary airport is eight miles southwest of town (airport code: BCN, info tel. 913-211-000). It has two large terminals, linked by shuttle buses. Terminal 1 serves Air France, Air Europa, American, British Airways, Delta, Iberia, Lufthansa, United, US Airways, Vueling, and others. EasyJet, Ryanair, and minor airlines use the older Terminal 2, which is divided into sections A, B, and C.

Terminal 1 and the bigger sections of Terminal 2 (A and B) each have a post office, a pharmacy, a left-luggage office, plenty of good cafeterias in the gate areas, and ATMs (use the bank-affiliated ATMs in the arrivals hall).

### Getting Between the Airport and Downtown
To get downtown cheaply and quickly, take the bus or train (about 30 minutes on either).

**By Bus:** The Aerobus (#A1 and #A2, corresponding with Terminals 1 and 2) stops immediately outside the arrivals lobby of both terminals (and in each section of Terminal 2). In about 30 minutes, it takes you downtown, where it makes several stops, including at Plaça d'Espanya and Plaça de Catalunya—near many of my recommended hotels (departs every 5 minutes, from airport 6:00-1:00 in the morning, from downtown 5:30-24:30; €5.90 one-way, €10.20 round-trip, buy ticket from machine, from driver, or on their website; tel. 934-156-020, www.aerobusbcn.com).

**By Train:** The RENFE train (on the "R2 Sud" Rodalies line) leaves from Terminal 2 and involves more walking. Head down the long orange-roofed overpass between sections A and B to reach the station (2/hour at about :08 and :38 past the hour, 20 minutes to Sants station, 25 minutes to Passeig de Gràcia station—near Plaça de Catalunya and many recommended hotels, 30 minutes to França station; €4.10 or covered by T10 Card—described on page 28—which you can purchase from machines at the airport train station). If you are arriving or departing from Terminal 1, you will have to use the airport shuttle bus to connect with the train station, so leave extra time.

Long-term plans call for the RENFE train and eventually the AVE to be extended to Terminal 1. Stay tuned.

**By Metro:** Take Metro's L9 Sud (orange) line from either Terminal 1 or 2, to Zona Universitária, then transfer to the L3 (green) line and ride to a downtown stop (Passeig de Gràcia, Plaça de Catalunya, or Liceu). To reach the airport from downtown via Metro, take line L3 to Zona Universitária, and transfer to line L9 in the direction of Aeroport T1 (8/hour, 20-30 minutes, runs daily 5:00 until late, including all night Sat; use €4.50 *Billet Aeroport* or any "Hola BCN!" travel card—the T10 and single-ride Metro tickets do not work for this ride).

**By Taxi:** A taxi between the airport and downtown costs about €35 (including €3.10 airport supplement). For good service, you can round up to the next euro on the fare—but keep in mind that the Spanish don't tip cabbies. To get to the cruise port, ask for *"tarifa cuatro"*—a €39 flat rate between the airport and the cruise port, all fees included.

## GIRONA–COSTA BRAVA AIRPORT

Some budget airlines use this airport, located 60 miles north of Barcelona near Girona (airport code: GRO, tel. 972-186-600, www.aena-aeropuertos.es). If you're arriving on a Ryanair flight, you can take a **bus** (#604), run by Ryanair and operated by Sagalés, to the Barcelona Nord bus station (departs airport about 20-25 minutes after each arriving flight, 1.25 hours, €16, tel. 902-361-550, www.sagales.com). You can also take a Sagalés bus (#607 or #601, hourly,

25 minutes, €2.75) or a taxi (€25) to the town of Girona, then catch a train to Barcelona (at least hourly, 1.5 hours, €15-20). A taxi between the Girona airport and Barcelona costs at least €130.

## CHEAP FLIGHTS

Check the reasonable flights from Barcelona to Sevilla or Madrid. **Vueling** is Iberia's most popular discount airline; for example, Barcelona-Madrid flights cost as little as €40 if booked well in advance (tel. 902-333-933, www.vueling.com). These two airlines typically offer €80 flights to Madrid: **Iberia** (tel. 902-400-500, www.iberia. com) and **Air Europa** (tel. 902-401-501 or 932-983-907, www. aireuropa.com). For more information on flights within Europe, see page 309.

# By Train

Virtually all trains end up at Barcelona's **Sants train station,** west of the Old City (described next). AVE trains from Madrid go only

to Sants station. But many other trains also pass through other stations en route, such as **França station** (between the El Born and Barceloneta neighborhoods), or the downtown **Passeig de Gràcia** or **Plaça de Catalunya** stations (which are also Metro stops—and very close to most of my recommended hotels). Figure out which stations your train stops at (ask the conductor), and get off at the one most convenient to your hotel.

## SANTS TRAIN STATION

Barcelona's main train station is vast and sprawling, but manageable. In the large lobby area under the upper tracks, you'll find a TI, ATMs, a world of handy shops and eateries, car-rental kiosks, and, in the side concourse, a classy, quiet Sala Club lounge for travelers with first-class reservations (TV, free drinks, study tables, and coffee bar). Sants is the only Barcelona station with luggage storage (€3.50-5/day, daily 5:30-23:00, follow signs to *consigna*, at far end of hallway from tracks 13-14).

In the vast main hall is a very long wall of ticket windows. Figure out which one you need before you wait in line (all are labeled in English). Generally, windows 1-7 (on the left) are for local commuter and *media distancia* trains, such as to Sitges; windows 8-21 handle advance tickets for long-distance *(larga distancia)* trains beyond Catalunya; the information windows are 22-26—go here first if you're not sure which window you want; and windows

27-31 sell tickets for long-distance trains leaving today. These window assignments can shift in off-season. The information booths by windows 1 and 21 can help you find the right line and can provide some train schedules.

Scattered nearby are train-ticket vending machines. The red-and-gray machines sell tickets for local and *media distancia* trains within Catalunya. The purple machines are for national RENFE trains (be aware that you may have difficulty using a US credit card); these machines can also print out prereserved tickets if you have a confirmation code. And the orange machines sell local *Rodalies* train tickets. There are usually attendants around the machines to help you.

An easier option for English-speaking travelers staying in Barcelona is to buy your tickets at the travel agencies inside El Corte Inglés department stores. See page 302 for more info.

**Getting Downtown:** To reach the center of Barcelona, take a train or the Metro. To ride the subway, follow signs for the Metro (red *M*), and hop on the L3 (green) or L5 (blue) line, both of which link to a number of useful points in town. Purchase tickets for the Metro at touch-screen machines near the tracks (where you can also buy the cost-saving T10 Card, explained on page 28).

To zip downtown even faster (just five minutes), you can take any Rodalies de Catalunya suburban train from track 8 (R1, R3, or R4) to Plaça de Catalunya (departs at least every 10 minutes). Your long-distance RENFE train ticket comes with a complimentary ride on Rodalies, as long as you use it within three hours before or after your travels. Look for a code on your ticket labeled *Combinat Rodalies* or *Combinado Cercanías*. Go to the orange commuter ticket machines, touch *Combinat Rodalies*, type in your code, and the machine will print your ticket. There is usually an attendant around to help you.

## TRAIN CONNECTIONS

Unless otherwise noted, all of these trains depart from Sants station; however, remember that some trains also stop at other stations more convenient to the downtown tourist zone: França station, Passeig de Gràcia, or Plaça de Catalunya. Figure out if your train stops at these stations (and board there) to save yourself the trip to Sants.

If departing from the downtown Passeig de Gràcia station, where three Metro lines converge with the rail line, you might find the underground tunnels confusing. You can't access the RENFE station directly from some of the entrances. Use the northern entrances to this station (rather than the southern "Consell de Cent" entrance, which is closest to Plaça de Catalunya).

Train info: tel. 902-320-320, www.renfe.com.

**From Barcelona by Train to Madrid:** The AVE train to Madrid is faster than flying (when you consider that you're zipping from downtown to downtown). The train departs at least hourly. The nonstop train is a little more expensive but faster (€130, 2.5 hours) than the train that makes a few stops (€110, 3 hours). Regular reserved AVE tickets can be prepurchased (often with a discount) at www.renfe.com and picked up at the station. If you have a rail pass, see page 300 for info on booking AVE seats. For a cheaper, non-AVE option, there's a slow overnight train to Madrid (9 hours, €45, add *litera* or *couchette* for €13).

**From Barcelona by Train to: Sitges** (departs from both Passeig de Gràcia and Sants, 4/hour, 40 minutes), **Montserrat** (departs from Plaça d'Espanya—*not* from Sants, hourly, 1 hour, €21 round-trip, includes cable car or rack train to monastery—see details on page 233), **Figueres** (hourly, 1 hour via AVE or Alvia to Figueres-Vilafant; hourly, 2 hours via local trains to Figueres station), **Sevilla** (2/day direct, more with transfer in Madrid, 5.5 hours), **Granada** (1/day, 8 hours via AVE and regional bus, transfer in Antequera), **Salamanca** (8/day, 7 hours, change in Madrid from Atocha station to Chamartín station via Metro or *cercanías* train; also 1/day with a change in Valladolid, 8.5 hours), **San Sebastián** (2/day, 6 hours), **Málaga** (8/day via AVE, 6.5 hours; some with transfer), **Lisbon** (no direct trains, head to Madrid and then catch night train to Lisbon, 17 hours—or fly).

**From Barcelona by Train to France:** Direct high-speed trains run to **Paris** (2-4/day, 6.5 hours), **Lyon** (1/day, 5 hours), and **Toulouse** (1/day, 3 hours), and there are more connections with transfers.

## By Bus

Most buses depart from the Nord bus station at Metro: Arc de Triomf, but confirm when researching schedules (www.barcelonanord. com). Destinations served by Alsa buses (tel. 902-422-242, www. alsa.es) include **Madrid** and **Madrid's Barajas Airport** (nearly hourly, 8 hours), and **Salamanca** (2/day, 11 hours). Sarfa buses (tel. 902-302-025, www.sarfa.com) serve many **coastal resorts,** including **Cadaqués** (1-2/day, 3 hours).

The Mon-Bus leaves from the university and Plaça d'Espanya in downtown Barcelona to **Sitges** (2/hour, 1 hour, www.monbus. cat). One bus departs daily for the **Montserrat** monastery, leaving from Carrer de Viriat near Sants station (1.5 hours, see page 235).

# By Cruise Ship

Cruise ships arrive in Barcelona at one of three ports, all just south-west of the Old City, beneath Montjuïc). If your trip includes cruis-ing beyond Barcelona, consider my guidebook, *Rick Steves Mediter-ranean Cruise Ports.*

Most cruise ships arrive in Barcelona at the **Moll Adossat/Muelle Adosado** port, about two miles from the bottom of the Ramblas. This port has four modern, airport-like terminals (lettered A through D); most have a café, shops, and TI kiosk; some have Internet ac-cess and other services. Two other terminals are far less commonly used: the **World Trade Center,** just off the southern end of the Ramblas (a 10-minute walk from the Columbus Monument), and **Moll de la Costa,** tucked just beneath Montjuïc (ride the free, private shuttle bus to World Trade Center; from there, it's a short walk or taxi ride to the Columbus Monument).

**Getting Downtown:** From any of the cruise terminals, it's easy to reach the Ramblas. **Taxis** meet each arriving ship and are waiting as you exit any of the terminal buildings. The short trip into town runs about €15-20, as much as €10 more when traffic is heavy (the €3.10 cruise-port surcharge is legit). To get to the air-port, ask for *"tarifa cuatro"*—a €39 flat rate between the airport and the cruise port, all fees included. Taxis on this rate must use the most direct route or face fines.

You can also take a **shuttle bus** from Moll Adossat/Muelle Adosado to the bottom of the Ramblas, then walk or hop on public transportation to various sights. The #T3 shuttle (Portbús) departs from the parking lot in front of each of the port's four terminals and drops you right on the waterfront near the Columbus Monu-ment (€3.50 round-trip, €2.50 one-way, 2-3/hour, timed to cruise ship arrival, 5-15 minutes, tel. 932-986-000). The return bus back to the port leaves roughly from where you were dropped off (look for a covered bus stop bench and blue-and-white sign reading *Bus Port Cruises*—don't wait at the stop with no bench marked *Bus Port Cruises Final*). If you're confused, there is usually someone standing by the bus stop to help.

# DAY TRIPS FROM BARCELONA

*Montserrat • Figueres • Cadaqués • Sitges*

Four fine sights are day-trip temptations from Barcelona. Pilgrims with hiking boots head 1.5 hours into the mountains for the most sacred spot in Catalunya: Montserrat. Fans of Surrealism can enjoy a fantasy in Dalí-land by combining a stop at the Dalí Theater-Museum in Figueres (one to two hours from Barcelona) with a day or two in the classy and often sleepy port-town getaway of Cadaqués (pictured above, an hour from Figueres; note that the Salvador Dalí House in Cadaqués requires reservations to visit). Or for a quick escape from the city, head 40 minutes south to the charming and free-spirited beach town of Sitges.

# Montserrat

Montserrat—the "serrated mountain"—rockets dramatically up from the valley floor northwest of Barcelona. With its unique rock

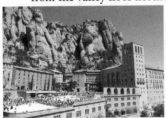

formations, a dramatic mountaintop monastery (also called Montserrat), and spiritual connection with the Catalan people and their struggles, it's a popular day trip. This has been Catalunya's most important pilgrimage site for a thousand years. Hymns explain how the mountain was carved by little angels with golden saws. Geologists blame nature at work.

Once upon a time, there was no mountain. A river flowed here, laying down silt that solidified into sedimentary layers of hard rock. Ten million years ago, the continents shifted, and the land around the rock massif sank, exposing this series of peaks that

DAY TRIPS

reach upward to 4,000 feet. Over time, erosion pocked the face with caves and cut vertical grooves near the top, creating the famous serrated look.

The monastery is nestled in the jagged peaks at 2,400 feet, but it seems higher because of the way the rocky massif rises out of nowhere. The air is certainly fresher than in Barcelona. In a quick day trip, you can view the mountain from its base, ride a funicular up to the top of the world, tour the basilica and museum, touch a Black Virgin's orb, hike down to a sacred cave, and listen to Gregorian chants by the world's oldest boys' choir.

Montserrat's monastery is Benedictine, and its 30 monks carry on its spiritual tradition. Since 1025, the slogan *"ora et labora"* ("prayer and work") has pretty much summed up life for a monk here.

The Benedictines welcome visitors—both pilgrims and tourists—and offer this travel tip: Please remember that the most important part of your Montserrat visit is not enjoying the architecture, but rather discovering the religious, cultural, historical, social, and environmental values that together symbolically express the life of the Catalan people.

## GETTING TO MONTSERRAT

Barcelona is connected to the valley below Montserrat by a convenient train; from there, a cable car or rack railway (your choice) takes you up to the mountaintop. You have to decide whether to take the cable car or the rack railway when you buy your ticket in Barcelona—see the "Tickets to Montserrat" sidebar. Both options are similar in cost and take about the same amount of time. (It's about 1.5 hours each way from downtown Barcelona to the monastery.)

Driving or taking the bus round out your options.

### By Train Plus Cable Car or Rack Railway

Trains leave hourly from Barcelona's Plaça d'Espanya to Montserrat. Take the Metro to Espanya, then follow signs for Montserrat (showing a graphic of a train and the *FGC* symbol—for Ferrocarrils de la Generalitat de Catalunya) through the tunnels to the FGC station. Once there, check the overhead screens or ask for help (staff are usually at the ticket machines) to find the track for train line R5 (direction: Manresa, departures at :36 past each hour; additional departures Mon-Fri at 11:56 and 12:56).

Hang onto your train ticket; you'll need it to exit the FGC station when you return to Plaça d'Espanya. You'll ride about an hour on the train. As you reach the base of the mountain, get out at the Montserrat-Aeri station for the cable car, or continue another few minutes to the next station—Monistrol de Montserrat (or simply "Monistrol de M.")—for the rack railway.

**Cable Car or Rack Train?** For the sake of scenery and fun, I enjoy the little German-built cable car more than the rack railway.

way. Departures are more frequent (4/hour rather than hourly on the railway), but because the cable car is small, you may wait a while to get on (up to an hour when crowded). If you're afraid of heights, take the rack train. Paying extra (about €5) to ride both isn't worthwhile.

**Cable Car, from Montserrat-Aeri Station:** Departing the train, follow signs to the cable-car station (covered by your train or combo-ticket; 4/hour, 5-minute trip, daily 10:00-19:00, www.aeridemontserrat.com). Don't linger on the platform: Make your way to the cable car quickly, or you may have to wait to go up.

# Tickets to Montserrat

Various combo-tickets cover your journey to Montserrat, as well as some of the sights you'll visit there. All begin with the train from Barcelona's Plaça d'Espanya, and include either the cable car or rack railway—you'll have to specify one or the other when you buy the ticket (same price for either option). You can't go one way and come back the other unless you pay extra (about €5) for the leg that's not included in your ticket.

The basic option is to buy a **train ticket** to Montserrat (€21 round-trip, includes cable car or rack railway to monastery, Eurail pass not valid, tel. 932-051-515, www.fgc.es). Note that if you buy this ticket in Barcelona, then decide at Montserrat that you want to use the funiculars to go higher up the mountain or to the Sacred Cave, you can buy a €13 ticket covering both funiculars at the TI or at either funicular.

If you plan to do some sightseeing once at Montserrat, it makes sense to spend a little more on one of two combo-tickets offered by the train company: The €29.50 **Trans Montserrat** ticket includes your round-trip Metro ride in Barcelona to and from the train station, the train trip, the cable car or rack railway, unlimited trips on the two funiculars at Montserrat, and entry to the disappointing audiovisual presentation. The €47 **Tot Montserrat** ticket includes all of this, plus the good Museum of Montserrat and a self-service lunch (served daily 12:00-16:00). If you expect to do it all, you'll save at least €5 with either of these combo-tickets. But during the off-season, ask the TI whether one of the funiculars or the cable car is closed for maintenance; if so, the combo-ticket may not be worth it (or available).

You can get advice about your ticket choice and return schedules at the Montserrat Cremallera (rack railway) or cable-car information booths at Plaça d'Espanya station (daily 8:00-14:00). Then purchase any of these options from the ticket machines—if you need help, ask one of the TI officials standing by in the morning. To use your included round-trip Metro ride to get *to* the station, buy the ticket in advance at the Plaça de Catalunya TI. If you buy your ticket online (www.montserratvisita.com), you must take your purchase voucher to the Cremallera rack-railway information booth during open hours (daily 8:00-14:00) to receive an actual ticket. Combo-tickets may be available at the Barcelona TI's online shop (www.bcnshop.barcelonaturisme.com).

On the way back down, cable cars depart from the monastery every 15 minutes; make sure to give yourself enough time to catch a Barcelona-bound train (these leave at :05 and :45 past the hour Mon-Fri, only at :45 Sat-Sun).

**Rack Railway (Cremallera), from Monistrol de Montserrat Station:** From this station you can catch the Cremallera rack railway up to the monastery (covered by your train or combo-ticket; cheaper off-season, hourly, 20-minute trip, www.cremalleredemontserrat.com). On the return trip, this train departs the monastery at :15 past the hour, allowing you to catch the Barcelona-bound train leaving Monistrol de Montserrat at :45 past the hour. The last convenient connection leaves the monastery at 18:15 (Sat-Sun at 20:15). Confirm the schedule when you arrive, as specific times can change year to year. Note that there is one intermediate stop on this line (Monistrol-Vila, at a large parking garage), but—either coming or going—you want to stay on until the end of the line.

## By Car

Once drivers get out of Barcelona (Road A-2, then C-55), it's a short 30-minute drive to the base of the mountain, then a 10-minute series of switchbacks to the actual site (where you can find parking for €5/day). It may be easier to park your car down below and ride the cable car or rack railway up; there is plenty of free parking at the Monistrol-Vila rack-railway station (cable car—€6.60 one-way, €10 round-trip; rack railway—€6.50 one-way, €10.30 round-trip, €14 version also includes Museum of Montserrat).

## By Bus

One bus per day connects downtown Barcelona directly to the monastery at Montserrat (departs from Carrer de Viriat near Barcelona's Sants station daily at 9:15, returns from the monastery to Barcelona at 18:00 June-Sept, at 17:00 Oct-May, €5 each way, 1.5 hours, operated by Autocares Julià, www.autocaresjulia.es). You can also take a four-hour **bus tour** offered by the Barcelona Guide Bureau (€49, leaves Mon-Sat at 15:00 from Plaça de Catalunya; see page 32). However, since the other options are scenic, fun, and relatively easy, the only reason to take a bus is to avoid transfers.

# Orientation to Montserrat

When you arrive at the base of the mountain, look up the rock face to find the cable-car line, the monastery near the top, and the tiny building midway up (marking the Sacred Cave).

However you make your way up to the Montserrat monastery, it's easy to get oriented once you arrive at the top. Everything is within a few minutes' walk of your entry point. All of the transit options—including the rack railway and cable car—converge at the big train station. Above those are both funicular stations: one up to the ridge top, the other down to the Sacred Cave trail. Across the street is the TI, and above that (either straight up the stairs or up the ramp around the left side) is the main square. To the right

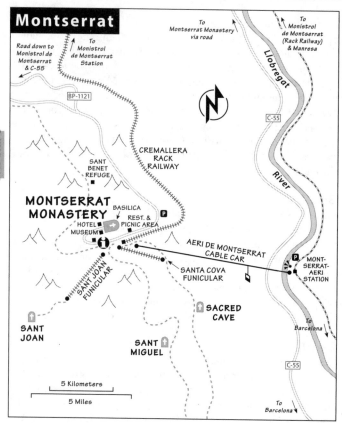

of the station, a long road leads along the cliff to the parking lot; a humble farmers market along here sells *mel y mató*, a characteristic Catalan cheese with honey.

**Crowd-Beating Tips:** Arrive early or late, as tour groups mob the place midday. Crowds are less likely on weekdays and worst on Sundays.

## TOURIST INFORMATION

The square below the basilica houses a helpful TI, right across from the rack-railway station (daily from 9:00, closes just after last train heads down—roughly 18:45, or 20:15 on weekdays in July-Aug, tel. 938-777-701, www.montserratvisita.com). A good audioguide, available only at the TI, describes the general site and basilica (€6.50 includes book; €14 includes entrance to museum, bland audiovisual presentation, and book). If you're a hiker, ask for the handout outlining hiking options here. Trails offer spectacular

**DAY TRIPS**

# The History of Montserrat

The first hermit monks built huts at Montserrat around A.D. 900. By 1025, a monastery was founded. The Montserrat Escolania, or Choir School, soon followed, and is considered to be the oldest music school in Europe (they still perform—see "Choir Concert" on page 241).

Legend has it that in medieval times, some shepherd children saw lights and heard songs coming from the mountain. They traced the sounds to a cave (now called the Sacred Cave, or Santa Cova), where they found the Black Virgin statue (La Moreneta), making the monastery a pilgrim magnet.

In 1811 Napoleon's invading French troops destroyed Montserrat's buildings, though the Black Virgin, hidden away by monks, survived. Then, in the 1830s, the Spanish royalty—tired of dealing with pesky religious orders—dissolved the monasteries and convents.

But in the 1850s, the monks returned as part of Catalunya's (and Europe's) renewed Romantic appreciation for all things medieval and nationalistic. (Montserrat's revival coincided with other traditions born out of rejuvenated Catalan pride: the much-loved FC Barcelona soccer team; Barcelona's Palace of Catalan Music; and even the birth of local sparkling wine, *cava*.) Montserrat's basilica and monastery were reconstructed and became, once more, the strongly beating spiritual and cultural heart of the Catalan people.

Then came Francisco Franco, the dictatorial leader who wanted a monolithic Spain. To him Montserrat represented Catalan rebelliousness. During Franco's long rule, from 1939 to 1975, the *sardana* dance was still illegally performed here (but with a different name), and literature was published in the outlawed Catalan language. In 1970, 300 intellectuals demonstrating for more respect for human rights in Spain were locked up in the monastery for several days by Franco's police.

But now Franco is history. The 1990s brought another phase of rebuilding (after a forest fire and rain damage), and the Montserrat community is thriving once again, unafraid to display its pride for the Catalan people, culture, and faith.

views (on clear days) to the Mediterranean and even (on clearer days) to the Pyrenees.

The audiovisual center (upstairs from the TI) provides some cultural and historical perspective—and an entrance to their big gift shop. The lame interactive exhibit—nowhere near as exciting as the mountains and basilica outside—includes touch screens and a seven-minute video (available in English when there is enough demand). Learn about the mountain's history, and get a glimpse into the daily lives of the monastery's resident monks (€5, covered by Trans Montserrat and Tot Montserrat combo-tickets, same hours as TI).

# Sights in Montserrat

### Self-Guided Montserrat Spin Tour

From the main square in front of the basilica complex, face the main facade and take this spin tour. Like a good pilgrim, face Mary, the high-up centerpiece of the facade. Below her to the left is St. Benedict, the sixth-century monk who established the rules that came to govern Montserrat's monastery. St. George, the symbol of Catalunya, is on the right (amid victims of Spain's Civil War).

Five arches line the base of the facade. The one on the far right leads pilgrims to the high point of any visit, the Black Virgin (a.k.a. La Moreneta). The center arch leads into the basilica's courtyard, and the arch second from left directs you to a small votive chapel filled with articles representing prayer requests or thanks.

Now look left of the basilica, where delicate arches mark the 15th-century monks' cloister. The monks have planted four trees here, hoping to harvest only their symbolism (palm = martyrdom, cypress = eternal life, olive = peace, and laurel = victory). Next to the trees are a public library and a peaceful reading room. The big archway is the private entrance to the monastery. Still turning to your left, then comes the modern hotel and, below that, the glass-fronted museum. Other buildings provide cells for pilgrims. The Sant Joan funicular lifts hikers up to the trailhead (you can see the tiny building at the top). From there you can take a number of fine hikes (described later). Another funicular station descends to the Sacred Cave. And, finally, five arches separate statues of founders of the great religious orders. Step over to the arches for a commanding view (on a clear day) of the Llobregat River, meandering all the way to the Mediterranean.

### ▲▲Basilica

Although there's been a church here since the 11th century, the present structure was built in the 1850s, and the facade only dates from 1968. The decor is Neo-Romanesque, so popular with the Romantic artists of the late 19th century. The basilica itself is ringed with interesting chapels, but the focus is on the Black Virgin (La Moreneta) sitting high above the main altar.

**Cost and Hours:** Free; La Moreneta viewable Mon-Sat 8:00-10:30 & 12:00-18:30, Sun 19:30-20:15; church itself has longer hours and daily services (Mass at 11:00 at the main altar, at 12:00 or 13:00 and 19:30 in side chapels, vespers at 18:45); www.abadiamontserrat.net.

**Visiting the Basilica:** Montserrat's top attraction is **La Moreneta**, the small wood statue of the Black Virgin, discovered in the

Sacred Cave in the 12th century. Legend says she was carved by St. Luke (the gospel writer and supposed artist), brought to Spain by St. Peter, hidden away in the cave during the Moorish invasions, and miraculously discovered by shepherd children. (Carbon dating says she's 800 years old.) While George is the patron saint of Catalunya, La Moreneta is its patroness, having been crowned as such by the pope in 1881. "Moreneta" is usually translated as "black" in English, but the Spanish name actually means "tanned." The statue was originally lighter, but it darkened over the centuries from candle smoke, humidity, and the natural aging of its original varnish. Pilgrims shuffle down a long, ornate passage leading alongside the church for their few moments alone with the Virgin (keep an eye on the time if you want to see the statue; there are no visits Mon-Sat 10:30-12:00, or before 19:30 on Sun).

Join the line of pilgrims (along the right side of the church). Though Mary is behind a protective glass case, the royal orb she

cradles in her hands is exposed. Pilgrims touch Mary's orb with one hand and hold their other hand up to show that they accept Jesus. Newlyweds in particular seek Mary's blessing.

Immediately after La Moreneta, to the right, is the delightful Neo-Romanesque prayer **chapel,** where worshippers can sit behind the Virgin and pray. The ceiling, painted in the Modernista style in 1898 by Joan Llimona, shows Jesus and Mary high in heaven. The trail connecting Catalunya with heaven seems to lead through these serrated mountains. The lower figures symbolize Catalan history and culture.

You'll leave by walking along the **Ave Maria Path** (along the outside of the church), which thoughtfully integrates nature and the basilica. Thousands of colorful votive candles are all busy helping the devout with their prayers. Before you leave the inner courtyard and head out into the main square, pop in to the humble little room with the many votive offerings. This is where people leave personal belongings (wedding dresses, baby's baptism outfits, wax replicas of body parts in need of healing, and so on) as part of a prayer request or as a thanks for divine intercession.

### Museum of Montserrat

This bright, shiny, and cool collection of paintings and artifacts was mostly donated by devout Catalan Catholics. While it's nothing really earth-shaking, you'll enjoy an air-conditioned wander past lots of antiquities and fine artwork. Head upstairs first to see some lesser-known works by the likes of Picasso, Caravaggio, Monet, Renoir, Pissarro, Degas, and local Modernista artists (Ramón Casas, Santiago Rusiñol, Isidro Nonell, and Joaquim Mir). One gallery shows how artists have depicted the Black Virgin of Montserrat over the centuries in many different styles. Down on the main floor, you'll see ecclesiastical gear, a good icon collection, and more paintings, including—at the very end—works by Dalí and a few Picasso sketches and prints.

**Cost and Hours:** €7, covered by Tot Montserrat combo-ticket, daily 10:00-17:45, July-Aug until 18:45, tel. 938-777-745.

### ▲Sant Joan Funicular and Hikes

This funicular climbs 820 feet above the monastery in five minutes. At the top of the funicular, you are at the starting point of a 20-minute walk that takes you to the Sant Joan Chapel (follow sign for *Ermita de St. Joan*). Other hikes also begin at the trailhead by the funicular (get details from TI before you ascend; basic map with suggested hikes posted by upper funicular station). For a quick and easy chance to get out into nature and away from

the crowds, simply ride up and follow the most popular hike—a 45-minute, mostly downhill loop through mountain scenery back to the monastery. To take this route, go left from the funicular station; the trail—marked *Monestir de Montserrat*—will first go up to a rocky crest before heading downhill.

**Cost and Hours:** Funicular—€6.80 one-way, €10.50 round-trip, covered by Trans Montserrat and Tot Montserrat combo-tickets, goes every 20 minutes, more often with demand.

### Sacred Cave (Santa Cova)

The Moreneta was originally discovered in the Sacred Cave (or Sacred Grotto), a 40-minute hike down from the monastery (then another 50 minutes back up). The path (c. 1900) was designed by devoted and patriotic Modernista architects, including Gaudí and Josep Puig i Cadafalch. It's lined with Modernista statues depicting scenes corresponding to the Mysteries of the Rosary. While the original Black Virgin statue is now in the basilica, a replica sits in the cave. A three-minute funicular ride cuts 20 minutes off the hike. (The funicular may be closed for repairs.) If you're here late in the afternoon, check the schedule before you head into the Sacred Cave to make sure you don't miss the final ride back down the mountain. Missing the last funicular could mean catching a train back to Barcelona later than you had planned.

**Cost and Hours:** Funicular—€2.60 one-way, €4 round-trip,

covered by Trans Montserrat and Tot Montserrat combo-tickets, goes every 20 minutes, more often with demand.

### Choir Concert

Montserrat's Escolania, or Choir School, has been training voices for centuries. Fifty young boys, who live and study in the monastery itself, make up the choir, which performs daily except Saturday. The boys sing for only 10 minutes, the basilica is jam-packed, and it's likely you'll see almost nothing. Also note that if you attend the evening performance, you'll miss the last train or cable-car ride down the mountain.

**Cost and Hours:** Free, generally Mon-Fri at 13:00, Sun at 12:00, and Sun-Thu at 18:45, choir on vacation late June-late Aug, check schedule at www.montserratvisita.com.

## Sleeping and Eating in Montserrat

**($$$$ = Splurge, $$$ = Pricier, $$ = Moderate, $ = Budget)**
An overnight here gets you monastic peace and a total break from the modern crowds. There are ample rustic cells for pilgrim visitors, but tourists might prefer **$$ Hotel Abat Cisneros.** A three-star hotel with 82 rooms and all the comforts, is low-key and appropriate for a sanctuary (half- and full-board available, elevator, tel. 938-777-701, www.montserratvisita.com, reserves@larsa-montserrat.com).

Montserrat is designed to feed hordes of pilgrims and tourists. You'll find a cafeteria along the main street (across from the train station) and a grocery store and bar with simple sandwiches where the road curves on its way up to the hotel. In the other direction, follow the covered walkway below the basilica to reach the Mirador dels Apòstols, with a bar, cafeteria, restaurant, and picnic area. The Hotel Abat Cisneros also has a restaurant, and the Montserrat-Aeri train station has a ramshackle but charming family-run bar with outdoor tables, simple food, and views of the mountain and the cable cars. The best option is to pack a picnic from Barcelona, especially if you plan to hike.

# Figueres

The town of Figueres (feeg-YEHR-ehs)—conveniently connected by train to Barcelona—is of sightseeing interest only for its Salvador Dalí Theater-Museum. In fact, the entire town seems Dalí-dominated. But don't be surprised if you also find French shoppers bargain-hunting. Some of the cheapest shops in Spain—called *ventas*—are here to lure French visitors.

## GETTING TO FIGUERES

Figueres is an easy day trip from Barcelona, or a handy stopover en route to France. It has two train stations on opposite sides of town: **Figueres-Vilafant** (served by the high-speed train from Barcelona's Sants station, hourly, 1 hour) and **Figueres** (served by the less expensive but less convenient regional train; departs from Barcelona's Sants station or from the RENFE station at Metro: Passeig de Gràcia; hourly, 2 hours; slightly more expensive *media distancia* trains are 20 minutes faster than *regional* trains). If you're visiting Figueres on your way to Paris, it's possible to take the high-speed train in the morning, visit the Dalí Theater-Museum, and catch the late afternoon TGV to Paris. Note that neither train station has baggage storage, but the bus station (across from Figueres station) and the Dalí Theater-Museum do. For bus connections to Cadaqués, see page 247.

**Arrival in Figueres:** From Figueres-Vilafant station, take the bus marked *Estació AVE-Figueres* (€1.70), and get off on Carrer Empordá—ask the driver for the Dalí museum. From here, it's a 5- to 7-minute walk to the museum—go up Carrer Empordá to the TI on the corner, take a left up Avinguda Salvador Dalí, a right on Pep Ventura, then your first left up Pujada Castell, where you will see the museum.

From Figueres station, simply follow *Museu Dalí* signs (and the crowds) for the 15-minute walk to the museum.

# Sights in Figueres

### ▲▲▲Dalí Theater-Museum (Teatre-Museu Dalí)

This is *the* essential Dalí sight—and, if you like Dalí, one of Eu-

rope's most enjoyable museums, period. Inaugurated in 1974, the museum is a work of art in itself. Ever the entertainer and promoter, Dalí personally conceptualized, designed, decorated, and painted it to showcase his life's work. The museum fills a former theater and is the artist's mausoleum (his tomb is in the crypt below center stage). It's also a kind of mausoleum to Dalí's creative spirit.

Dalí had his first public art showing at age 14 here in this building when it was a theater, and he was baptized in the church just across the street. The place was sentimental to him. After the theater was destroyed in the Spanish Civil War, Dalí struck a deal with the mayor: Dalí would rebuild the theater as a museum to his works, Figueres would be put on the sightseeing map...and the money's been flowing in ever since.

Even the building's exterior—painted pink, studded with golden loaves of bread, and topped with monumental eggs and a geodesic dome—exudes Dalí's outrageous public persona.

**Cost and Hours:** €14; timed-entry tickets can be purchased on the website in advance, if you miss your time, you don't lose your ticket—just wait in the ticket line to change it; July-Sept daily 9:00-20:00; Oct-June Tue-Sun 9:30-18:00—except from 10:30 Nov-Feb, closed Mon; last entry 45 minutes before closing, tel. 972-677-500, www.salvador-dali.org. No flash photography. The free and required bag check (you can check everything from backpacks to small suitcases) has your belongings waiting for you at the exit.

**Coin-op Tip:** Much of Dalí's art is movable and coin-operated—bring a few €0.20 and €1 coins, and keep an eye out for the machines where you insert them. It's fun to gather other museum-goers in a group to experience these animated works together.

**Visiting the Museum:** The museum has two parts—the theater-mausoleum and the "Dalí's Jewels" exhibit in an adjacent building. There's no logical order for a visit (that would be un-Surrealistic), and the museum can be mobbed at times. Naturally, there's no audioguide. Dalí said there are two kinds of visitors: those who don't need a description, and those who aren't worth a description. At the risk of offending Dalí, I've written this loose commentary to attach some meaning to your visit.

Stepping through or around the courtyard, go into the **theater** (with its audience of statues) and face the stage. You know how you can never get a cab when it's raining? Pop a coin into Dalí's personal 1941 Cadillac and it rains inside the car. Look above, atop the tire tower: That's the boat Dalí enjoyed with his soul mate, Gala—his emotional life preserver, who kept him from going overboard. When she died, so did he (for his last seven years). Blue tears made of condoms drip below the boat.

To the left of the **stage,** squint at the big digital Abraham Lincoln, and president #16 comes into focus. Approach the painting to find that Abe's facial cheeks are Gala's butt cheeks—or use the coin-operated telescope (at the far end of the room) or your phone's camera to focus on his face. Under the painting, a door leads to the **Treasures Room,** with the greatest collection of original Dalí oil paintings in the museum. (Many of the artworks on the walls are prints.) You'll see Cubist visions of Cadaqués and dreamy portraits of Gala. Crutches—a recurring Dalí theme—represent Gala, who kept him supported whenever a meltdown threatened.

Make your way downstairs to the ground floor, below the stage, and pay respect at the artist's **crypt,** within dimly lit rooms

## Salvador Dalí (1904-1989)

When Salvador Dalí was asked, "Are you on drugs?" he replied, "I am the drug...take me."

Labeled by various critics as sick, greedy, paranoid, arrogant, and a clown, Dalí produced some of the most thought-provoking and trailblazing art of the 20th century. His erotic, violent, disjointed imagery continues to disturb and intrigue today.

Born in Figueres to a well-off family, Dalí showed talent early. He was expelled from Madrid's prestigious art school—twice—but formed longtime friendships with playwright and poet Federico García Lorca and filmmaker Luis Buñuel.

After a breakthrough art exhibit in Barcelona in 1925, Dalí moved to Paris. He hobnobbed with fellow Spaniards Pablo Picasso and Joan Miró, along with a group of artists exploring Sigmund Freud's theory that we all have a hidden part of our mind, the unconscious "id," which surfaces when we dream. Dalí became the best-known spokesman for this group of Surrealists, channeling his id to create photo-realistic dream images (melting watches, burning giraffes) set in bizarre dreamscapes.

His life changed forever in 1929, when he met an older, married Russian woman named Gala who would become his wife, muse, model, manager, and emotional compass. Dalí's popularity

filled with golden sculptures. Back upstairs, continue to the famous **Homage to Mae West room,** a tribute to the sultry seductress. Dalí loved her attitude. Saying things like, "Why marry and make one man unhappy, when you can stay single and make so many so happy?" Mae West was to conventional morality what Dalí was to conventional art. Climb to the vantage point where the sofa lips, fireplace nostrils, painting eyes, and drapery hair come together to make the face of Mae West.

Dalí's art can be playful, but also disturbing. He was passionate about the dark side of things, but with Gala for balance, he managed never to go off the deep end. Unlike Pablo Casals (the Catalan cellist) and Pablo Picasso (another local artist), Dalí didn't

spread to the US, where he (and Gala) weathered the WWII years.

In the prime of his career, Dalí's work became less Surrealist and more classical, influenced by past masters of painted realism (Velázquez, Raphael, Ingres) and by his own study of history, science, and religion. He produced large-scale paintings of historical events (e.g., Columbus discovering America, the Last Supper) that were collages of realistic scenes floating in a surrealistic landscape, peppered with thought-provoking symbols.

Dalí—an extremely capable technician—mastered many media, including film. *An Andalusian Dog* (*Un Chien Andalou*, 1929, with Luis Buñuel) was a cutting-edge montage of disturbing, eyeball-slicing images. He designed Alfred Hitchcock's big-eye backdrop for the dream sequence of *Spellbound* (1945). He made jewels for the rich and clothes for Coco Chanel, wrote a novel and an autobiography, and pioneered what would come to be called "installations." He also helped develop "performance art" by showing up at an opening in a diver's suit or by playing the role he projected to the media—a super-confident, waxed-mustached artistic genius.

In later years, Dalí's over-the-top public image contrasted with his ever-growing illness, depression, and isolation. He endured the scandal of a dealer overselling "limited editions" of his work. When Gala died in 1982, Dalí retreated to his hometown, living his last days in the Torre Galatea of the Theater-Museum complex, where he died of heart failure.

Dalí's legacy as an artist includes his self-marketing persona, his exceptional ability to draw, his provocative pairing of symbols, and his sheer creative drive.

go into exile under Franco's dictatorship. Pragmatically, he accepted both Franco and the Church, and was supported by the dictator. Apart from the occasional *sardana* dance (see sidebar on page 45), you won't find a hint of politics in Dalí's art.

Wander around. You can spend hours here, wondering is it real or not real? Am I crazy, or is it you? Beethoven is painted with squid ink applied by a shoe on a stormy night. Jesus is made with candle smoke and an eraser. It's fun to see the Dalí-ization of art classics. Dalí, like so many modern artists, was inspired by the masters—especially Velázquez.

The former theater's **smoking lounge** is a highlight, displaying portraits of Gala and Dalí (with a big eye, big ear, and a dark side) bookending a Roman candle of creativity. The fascinating ceiling painting shows the feet of Gala and Dalí as they bridge the earth and the heavens. Dalí's drawers are wide open and empty, indicating that he gave everything to his art.

Leaving the theater, keep your ticket and pop into the adjacent **"Dalí's Jewels"** exhibit. It shows sketches and paintings of jewelry Dalí designed, and the actual pieces jewelers made from those surreal visions: a mouth full of pearly whites, a golden finger corset, a fountain of diamonds, and the breathing heart. Explore the ambiguous perception worked into the big painting titled *Apotheosis of the Dollar.*

# Cadaqués

Since the late 1800s, Cadaqués (kah-dah-KEHS) has served as a haven for intellectuals and artists alike. The fishing village's craggy coastline, sun-drenched colors, and laid-back lifestyle inspired Fauvists such as Henri Matisse and Surrealists such as René Magritte, Marcel Duchamp, and Federico García Lorca. Even Picasso, drawn to this enchanting coastal haunt, painted some of his Cubist works here.

Salvador Dalí, raised in nearby Figueres, brought international fame to this sleepy Catalan port in the 1920s. As a kid Dalí spent summers here in the family cabin, where he was inspired by the rocky landscape that would later be the backdrop for many Surrealist canvases. In 1929, he met his future wife, Gala, in Cadaqués. Together they converted a fisherman's home in nearby Port Lligat into their semipermanent residence, dividing their time between New York, Paris, and Cadaqués. And it was here that Dalí did his best work.

In spite of its fame, Cadaqués is mellow and feels off the beaten path. If you want a peaceful beach-town escape near Barcelona, this is a good place. From the moment you descend into the town, taking in whitewashed buildings and deep blue waters, you'll be struck by the port's tranquility and beauty. Join the locals playing chess or cards at the cavernous Casino Coffee House (harborfront, with games and pay Wi-Fi). Have a glass of *vino tinto* or *cremat* (a traditional rum-and-coffee drink served flambé-style) at one of the seaside cafés. Savor the lapping waves, brilliant sun, and gentle breeze. And, for sightseeing, the reason to come to Cadaqués is the Salvador Dalí House, a 20-minute walk from the town center at Port Lligat.

## GETTING TO CADAQUÉS

Reaching Cadaqués is very tough without a car. There are no trains and only a few buses a day. A taxi from Figueres is another option.

**By Car:** It's a twisty drive from Figueres (figure 45-60 minutes). In Cadaqués, drivers should park in the big lot just above the

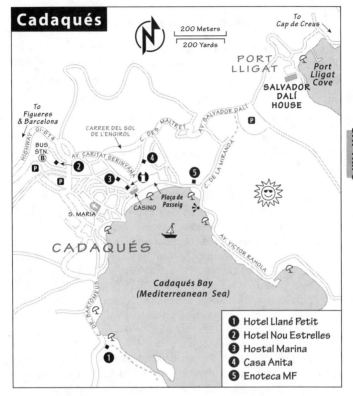

**Cadaqués**

To Cap de Creus

200 Meters
200 Yards

PORT LLIGAT

Port Lligat Cove

SALVADOR DALÍ HOUSE

To Figueres & Barcelona

CARRER DEL SOL DE L'ENGIROL

AV. SALVADOR DALÍ

C. DES MALTRET

C. DE LA MIRANDA

BUS STN.

AV. CARITAT BERINYANA

Plaça de Passeig

CASINO

S. MARIA

CADAQUÉS

AV. VICTOR RAHOLA

C. DE SANT BARTOMEU

Cadaqués Bay
(Mediterreanean Sea)

❶ Hotel Llané Petit
❷ Hotel Nou Estrelles
❸ Hostal Marina
❹ Casa Anita
❺ Enoteca MF

**DAY TRIPS**

city—don't try to park near the harborfront. To reach the Salvador Dalí House, follow signs near Cadaqués to Port Lligat (easy parking). As only one small road goes in and out of town, you may run into traffic during the summer months.

**By Bus:** Sarfa buses serve Cadaqués from **Figueres** (3/day, 1 hour) and from **Barcelona** (1-2/day, 3 hours). You can buy bus tickets to Cadaqués at Barcelona TIs on Plaça de Catalunya, Plaça Sant Jaume, and at the Columbus Monument. Bus info: Barcelona toll tel. 902-302-025, Cadaqués tel. 972-258-713, Figueres tel. 972-674-298, www.sarfa.com.

**By Taxi:** A taxi from Figueres is about the same price (€60-70) for a round-trip—including the drive to Port Lligat and a couple of hours' wait—as it is to be dropped off. You can arrange a ride over the phone in advance (tel. 972-505-043; good Spanish skills help—or ask your hotelier), or in person at the taxi stand on the Rambla in Figueres (from the Dalí Theater-Museum, walk down Carrer Sant Pere to the Rambla). Driver Josep María has an official taxi-and-van service and offers the same rates (mobile 696-906-476).

# Orientation to Cadaqués

## TOURIST INFORMATION

The TI is at Carrer Cotxe 2 (July-Sept Mon-Sat 9:00-21:00, Sun 10:00-13:00 & 17:00-20:00, shorter hours off-season plus closed for lunch, tel. 972-258-315, www.visitcadaques.org).

## HELPFUL HINTS

**Exchange Rate:** €1 = about $1.20

**Country Calling Code:** 34 (see page 294 for dialing instructions)

**Golf Carts:** EcoCar has a handful of electric golf carts that can take you around Cadaqués, including to Port Lligat, the bus station, and out to Cap de Creus—with spectacular cliff-top views (short rides-€4, Cap de Creus-€8, cash only, tel. 618-883-656, www.ecocarcadaques.com, Diego).

**Local Guide: Merce Donat** is a creative guide who organizes tours in and around Cadaqués, including a 1.5-hour walk through the old town (€6/person), a full-day "Get Surreal" Dalí-themed tour by bike and on foot (€55/person, includes Dalí house entry, bike, and a surreal snack), and family tours (reserve in advance, per-person prices increase if group is smaller than 10, mobile 686-492-369, www.rutes-cadaques.info, rutescadaques@gmail.com).

**Tourist Train:** The **Es Trenet de Cadaqués** tourist train goes around town and to Port Lligat and back, with a few photo stops—this is not a way to get to the Dalí house (€9, departs at 11:00 and on the hour 15:00-18:00, 1 hour). It also does a loop to Cap de Creus, where you can get off for about 20 minutes to enjoy the views before returning to Cadaqués (€16, departs at 12:00, 2 hours; for either tour, purchase tickets at the booth in the square just below the casino, tel. 653-829-442, www.estrenetdecadaques.cat).

# Sights near Cadaqués

### ▲▲▲Salvador Dalí House
### (Casa Museu Salvador Dalí)

Once Dalí's home, this house in Port Lligat (a 20-minute walk from town) gives fans a chance to explore his labyrinthine compound. This is the best artist's house I've toured in Europe. It shows how a home can really reflect the creative spirit of an artistic genius and his muse. The ambience, both inside and out, is perfect for a Surrealist hanging out with his

creative playmate. The bay is ringed by sleepy islands. Fishing boats are jumbled on the beach. After the fishermen painted their boats, Dalí asked them to clean their brushes on his door—creating an abstract work of art he adored (which you'll see as you line up to get your ticket).

**Cost and Hours:** €11 (€5 to tour only the garden); mid-June-mid-Sept daily 9:30-21:00; mid-Feb-mid-June and mid-Sept-early Jan Tue-Sun 10:30-18:00, closed Mon; closed early Jan-mid-Feb. Last tour departs 50 minutes before closing. No bags are allowed in the house; the baggage check is free.

**Reservations:** You must reserve in advance to visit the house—call or use the website (tel. 972-251-015, www.salvador-dali.org). In summer, book a week in advance. You must arrive 30 minutes early to pick up your ticket, or they'll sell it. If you can't get a reservation to see the house, you can reserve or buy on-site a ticket to visit the surrounding olive garden.

**Getting There:** Parking is free nearby. There are no buses, but you can arrange a ride to and from in an **EcoCar** (see "Helpful Hints," earlier). Alternatively, the house is a 20-minute, one-mile walk over the hill from Cadaqués to Port Lligat. (The path, which cuts across the isthmus, is much shorter than the road.)

**Visiting the House:** Only 8-10 people are allowed in (no large groups) every 10 minutes. Inside, there are five sections, each with a guard who gives you a brief explanation in English and then turns you loose for a few minutes. The entire visit takes 50 minutes. Before your tour, enjoy the 15-minute video that plays in the waiting lounge (with walls covered in Dalí media coverage) just across the lane from the house.

The house's interior is left almost precisely as it was in 1982, when Gala died and Dalí moved out. You'll see Dalí's studio (the clever easel cranks up and down to allow the artist to paint while seated, as he did eight hours a day); the bohemian-yet-divine living room (complete with a mirror to reflect the sunrise onto their bed each morning); the phallic-shaped swimming pool, which was the scene of orgiastic parties; and the painter's study (with his favorite mustaches all lined up). Like Dalí's art, his home is offbeat, provocative, and fun.

Surrounding the house is the olive garden. Wander here to find a Dalí sculpture and see the house's exterior up close. There's also a small building where you can view short films about Dalí's time in Port Lligat.

## Sleeping in Cadaqués

($$$$ = Splurge, $$$ = Pricier, $$ = Moderate, $ = Budget)

If you stay overnight in Cadaqués, you can return to Figueres by pre-arranging for a Figueres taxi to pick you up, by contacting a Cadaqués taxi (ask at the TI), or by bus (see "Getting to Cadaqués," earlier).

**$$ Hotel Llané Petit,** with 32 spacious rooms (half with view balconies), is a small resort-like hotel with its own little beach, a 10-minute walk south of the town center (RS%, some view rooms, air-con, elevator, pay parking, Dr. Bartomeus 37, tel. 972-251-020, www.llanepetit.com, info@llanepetit.com).

**$ Hotel Nou Estrelles** is a big, concrete exercise in efficient, economic comfort. Facing the bus stop a few blocks in from the waterfront, this family-run hotel offers 15 rooms at a great value (air-con, elevator, Carrer Sant Vicens, tel. 972-259-100, www.hotelnouestrelles.com, reservas@hotelnouestrelles.com, Emma).

**$ Hostal Marina** is run by a local family with care and enthusiasm and has 27 fresh rooms at a great location a block from the harborfront main square (some rooms with balcony, family rooms, no elevator, Riera 3, tel. 972-159-091, www.hostalmarinacadaques.com, info@hostalmarinacadaques.com, Pau and Isabel).

## Eating in Cadaqués

There are plenty of eateries along the beach, and the lane called Carrer Miguel Rosset (across from Hotel La Residencia) has several places worth considering. The Martín Faixó family has eateries all over town, including the traditional **$$ Casa Anita,** where you'll sit with others around a big table and enjoy house specialties of fresh local fish and homemade *helado* (ice cream). Finish your meal with a glass of sweet Muscatel (Calle Miquel Rosset 16, tel. 972-258-471, Joan and family).

For something more modern, try **$$$ Enoteca MF** for their creative tapas and *raciones,* prepared with local ingredients that they mostly produce or catch themselves (Riba des Poal, closed Wed and Sun evenings and Nov-Jan, mobile 682-107-142).

# Sitges

Sitges (SEE-juhz) is one of Catalunya's most popular resort towns. Because the town beautifully mingles sea and light, it's long been an artists' colony. Here you can still feel the soul of the Modernistas...in the architecture, the museums, the salty sea breeze, and the relaxed rhythm of life. Today's Sitges is a world-renowned vacation destination among the gay community. Despite its jet-set status, the Old Town has managed to retain its charm. With a much slower pulse than Barcelona, Sitges is an enjoyable break from the big city.

If you visit during one of Sitges' two big **festivals** (St. Bartholomew on Aug 24 and St. Tecla on Sept 23), you may see teams of *castellers* competing to build human pyramids.

To reach Sitges, you can take the train or bus. Southbound **trains** depart Barcelona from the Sants and Passeig de Gràcia stations (take frequent Rodalies train on the dark-green line R2 toward Sant Vincenç de Calders, 40 minutes). The **TI** is a couple of blocks northwest of the train station (Morera 1, tel. 938-944-251, www.sitgestur.cat). The Mon-Bus Company runs an easy and frequent **bus** from downtown Barcelona (with stops near the university and Plaça d'Espanya) that stops at Barcelona's airport en route to Sitges (1 hour, www.monbus.cat).

**Visiting Sitges:** Sitges basically has two attractions—its tight-and-tiny Old Town (with a few good museums) and its long, luxurious beaches. To head into the heart of town, exit the train station straight ahead (past a TI kiosk—open in summer) and walk down Carrer Francesc Gumà. When it dead-ends, continue right onto Carrer de Jesús, which takes you to the town's tiny main square, Plaça del Cap de la Villa. (Keep an eye out for directional signs.) From here, turn left down Carrer Major ("Main Street"), which leads you past the old market hall (now an art gallery) and the town hall to a beautiful terrace next to the main church.

Take time to explore the **Old Town**'s narrow streets. They're crammed with cafés, boutiques, and all the resort staples. The focal point, on the waterfront, is the 17th-century Baroque-style **Sant Bartomeu i Santa Tecla Church.** The terrace in front of the church will help you get the lay of the land. Poke into the Old Town or take the grand staircase down to the beach promenade.

As an art town, Sitges has seen its share of creative people—some of whom have left their mark in the form of appealing museums. Walking along the water behind the church, you'll find two of the town's three museums (www.museusdesitges.com). The **Museu Maricel** displays the eclectic artwork of a local collector, including some Modernista works, pieces by

Sitges artists, and a collection of maritime-themed works. The **Museu Cau Ferrat** bills itself as a "temple of art," as collected by local intellectual Santiago Rusiñol. In addition to paintings and drawings, it has ironwork, glass, and ceramics. Also on this square, you'll see **Palau Maricel**—a sumptuous old mansion that's sometimes open to the public for concerts in the summer (ask at TI). The third museum is the **Museu Romàntic.** Offering a look at 19th-century bourgeois lifestyles (and a collection of 400 antique dolls) in an elegant mansion, it's a few blocks up (one block west of main square—head out of the square on the main pedestrian street, then take the first right turn, to Sant Gaudenci 1).

Nine **beaches,** separated by breakwaters, extend about a mile southward from town. Stroll down the seaside promenade, which stretches from the town to the end of the beaches. Anyone can enjoy the sun, sea, and sand, or you can rent a beach chair to relax like a pro. The crowds thin out about halfway down, and the last three beaches are more intimate and cove-like. Along the way, restaurants and *chiringuitos* (beach bars) serve tapas, paella, and drinks. If you walk all the way to the  end, you can continue inland to enjoy the nicely landscaped **Terramar Gardens** (Jardins de Terramar).

**Sleeping in Sitges:** Hotel values are not much better in this swanky beach resort than in Barcelona. As this is a party town, expect some noise after hours (request a quiet room). Consider **$$ Hotel Celimar** (small but modern rooms in a classic Modernista building facing the beach, Paseo de la Ribera 20, tel. 938-110-170, www.hotelcelimar.com) or the larger, family-run **$$ Hotel Romàntic** (an old-fashioned-elegant, quirky place in an old villa a few blocks from the beach, Sant Isidre 33, tel. 938-948-375, www.hotelromantic.com).

# BARCELONA: PAST & PRESENT

Barcelona has thrived for 2,500 years. Its location is ideal: on a gently sloping plain facing the Mediterranean, where east-west sea trade meets the natural north-south highway to northern Europe. In its day, Barcelona has been a Roman retirement colony, a maritime power, a dynamo of the Industrial Age, and a cradle for all things modern. Today it cobbles together all these elements into a one-of-a-kind culture.

Keep in mind that Catalunya's history is quite distinct from that of the rest of Spain. Catalans pride themselves on their different language and independent traditions. When the rest of Spain was riding high, Catalunya was often in the doldrums, and vice versa.

The painter Joan Miró said, "We Catalans believe that you must plant your feet firmly on the ground in order to jump high in the air." This optimistic Catalan spirit—earthy but creative—has blossomed again and again through their history. Free spirits like Picasso, Dalí, Miró, Gaudí—and even Wilfred the Hairy—have all come from this small corner of Europe.

## PREHISTORY AND ROMAN ORIGINS
### (C. 500 B.C.-A.D. 500)

The original Iberian inhabitants settled atop Barcelona's hills overlooking the harbor, creating settlements on Montjuïc and around today's Plaça de Sant Jaume. They called their town "Barkeno." The name may (or may not) derive from the famous family of Hannibal Barca—the Carthaginian gen-

eral who passed through the area with his war elephants en route to attacking Rome, in 218 B.C.

In 19 B.C., the (future) Roman Emperor Augustus conquered Iberia. The Romans made "Hispania" their agricultural breadbasket to feed the vast Empire. In Catalunya, they planted grapes on large farming estates and shipped the wine abroad from Barcelona's busy port. Roman "Barcino"—a pleasant, sun-bathed valley with Mediterranean breezes—became a retirement colony for soldiers.

Like most Roman cities, Barcino had a forum in the center of town (today's Plaça de Sant Jaume) and a grid pattern of streets. It was a tight, 30-acre town of some 4,000 inhabitants contained within a wall (the area around today's cathedral). More broadly, the Romans brought Barcelona the Latin language (which became modern Catalan) and a connection to the wider world.

## Sights

- Barcelona History Museum (with Roman ruins in basement)
- Temple of Augustus
- Big, sculpted BARCINO letters on Plaça Nova
- Remnants of the Roman wall (especially the towers on Plaça Nova, near the cathedral)
- Roman necropolis near the Ramblas

## MEDIEVAL (500-1000)

As the Roman Empire crumbled, Barcelona made a peaceful transition, coming under the protection of Christian Visigoths from

Germany who had strong Roman ties. Christianity had entered Barcelona during Rome's last years (when martyrs such as Santa Eulàlia were persecuted). The feisty Christians built their cathedral—the core of today's cathedral—atop the Roman Temple of Jupiter.

In 711, the Moors (Muslim invaders from North Africa) swept through Spain, and Barcelona surrendered without a fight. While Moorish culture went on to dominate much of Spain for the next 700 years, its impact on Catalunya was minimal. In 801, Barcelona was liberated by Charlemagne's son, who made it part of the Frankish empire under the rule of Frankish "Counts." When Count Wilfred the Hairy (so called because he was; ruled 878-898) declared himself independent of the Franks, he launched a Golden Age in Barcelona.

## Sights
- Cathedral (with its original fourth-century font)
- Santa Eulàlia's tomb and silver statue in the cathedral

## THE KINGDOM OF ARAGON (1000-1500)
Wilfred the Hairy's heirs sprouted and grew into powerful sea-traders who connected Catalunya to the world. When Count

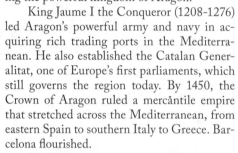

Ramon of Barcelona married Petronila of Aragon in 1137, it united their two realms, creating the powerful kingdom of Aragon.

King Jaume I the Conqueror (1208-1276) led Aragon's powerful army and navy in acquiring rich trading ports in the Mediterranean. He also established the Catalan Generalitat, one of Europe's first parliaments, which still governs the region today. By 1450, the Crown of Aragon ruled a mercàntile empire that stretched across the Mediterranean, from eastern Spain to southern Italy to Greece. Barcelona flourished.

In 1469 came another powerful marriage: King Ferdinand II of Aragon married Isabel of Castile. This power couple—the so-called Catholic Monarchs—united the peninsula's two largest kingdoms. They drove the last Moors out of Granada, expelled the Jews, and created a unified nation-state. They sent Christopher Columbus to explore new lands under the Spanish flag. And where did Columbus come first to debrief the Catholic Monarchs upon his return? To Barcelona.

## Sights
- The medieval legacy lives on in lots of Neo-Gothic and medieval motifs in Modernisme (especially the city symbol of St. George slaying the dragon)
- The El Born neighborhood, which flourished during this time
- Catalan Art Museum (excellent Romanesque collection)
- Columbus Monument
- Plaça del Rei and the Royal Palace, where Columbus met Ferdinand and Isabel
- The coffin of Count Ramon in the cathedral
- Generalitat building and statue of Jaume I on Plaça de Sant Jaume
- The churches of Santa Maria del Mar, Santa Maria del Pi, and the Chapel of St. Agatha (at the Royal Palace), plus the *extra muro* ("outside the walls") Church of Santa Anna

# Church Architecture

History comes to life when you visit a centuries-old church. Even if you don't know your apse from a hole in the ground, learning a few simple terms will enrich your experience. Note that not every church will have every feature, and a "cathedral" isn't a type of architecture, but rather a designation for a church that's a governing center for a local bishop.

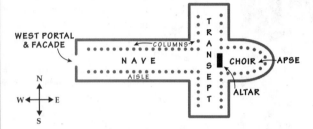

**Aisles:** The long, generally low-ceilinged arcades that flank the nave.

**Altar:** The raised area with a ceremonial table (often adorned with candles or a crucifix), where the priest prepares and serves the bread and wine for Communion.

**Apse:** The space beyond the altar, generally bordered with small chapels.

**Barrel Vault:** A continuous round-arched ceiling that resembles an extended upside-down U.

**Choir:** A cozy area, often screened off, located within the church nave and near the high altar, where services are sung in a more intimate setting, often blocking the common people from viewing the altar.

**Cloister:** Covered hallways bordering a square or rectangular open-air courtyard, traditionally where monks and nuns got fresh air.

**Facade:** The exterior surface of the church's main (west) entrance, generally highly decorated.

**Groin Vault:** An arched ceiling formed where two equal barrel vaults meet at right angles. Less common usage: term for a medieval jock strap.

**Narthex:** The area (portico or foyer) between the main entry and the nave.

**Nave:** The long, central section of the church (running west to east, from the entrance to the altar) where the congregation sits or stands during the service.

**Transept:** In a traditional cross-shaped floor plan, the transept is one of the two parts forming the "arms" of the cross. The transepts run north-south, perpendicularly crossing the east-west nave.

**West Portal:** The main entry to the church (on the west end, opposite the main altar).

- Montserrat monastery, dating from medieval times

## DECLINE (1500-1800)

Ironically, the glorious age of Ferdinand and Isabel also sowed the seeds of Barcelona's decline. Columbus' discoveries opened new Atlantic trade routes that made Barcelona's Mediterranean trade routes obsolete. Meanwhile, the center of royal power slowly shifted from Barcelona to the region midway between Aragon and Castile—the growing city of Madrid. While the rest of Spain enjoyed an unprecedented Golden Age of fabulous New World wealth and influence (producing artists such as El Greco, Velázquez, Goya, and Murillo), Barcelona became a poor and forgotten backwater.

On September 11, 1714—a date that is still marked by Catalunya's most sobering holiday—Catalan independence ended. Barcelona found itself on the losing end in the War of Spanish Succession (1701-1714), having sided against the eventual winner, the French-backed King Philip V. On September 11, Philip's forces overran the city walls and massacred those who had stood against him.

For more than a century, the Spanish crown centered in Madrid would punish the rebellious Catalans. They suppressed the Catalan language, culture, and institutions. The Generalitat was disbanded. Trade with the Americas was forbidden. For surveillance and control, the Castilians built an imposing citadel on one side of town and a fortress atop Montjuïc on the other, and ordered that nothing could be built beyond the reach of the fort's cannons. Barcelona spiraled down into a dirty, cramped city contained within its medieval wall.

## Sights

- Monument to Catalan Independence in El Born (honoring the victims of September 11, 1714)
- Castle of Montjuïc
- Citadel Park (previously the site of the citadel)
- Barceloneta fishermen's quarter (built to house those displaced by Citadel construction)
- Betlem Church on the Ramblas (rare example of Baroque)

## INDUSTRIAL REVIVAL AND CULTURAL RENAISSANCE (1800-1900)

In the 1800s, another revolution was brewing—the Industrial Revolution. Blessed with soft coal and rushing rivers from the Pyrenees, Barcelona harnessed the power to stoke textile mills. Having finally been given permission to trade with the Americas (1788), they imported cotton and shipped the finished cloth abroad from their busy harbor. Workers flocked in from the countryside, drawn by good-paying jobs. Barcelona's population doubled, reaching a million, and it created a thriving middle class.

By 1850—while the rest of Spain stagnated as a fading colonial power—Catalunya was humming. In 1854, Queen Isabella II finally loosened Madrid's death-grip, allowing the growing city to tear down the medieval wall and expand northward, creating the Eixample neighborhood of modern boulevards. They used new technology to make life better for everyday citizens, bringing in modern plumbing, streetlights, and the first rail line in Spain. The city hosted a World's Fair in 1888 that renovated the city (and gave us the Columbus Monument and other urban improvements).

There was a cultural renaissance of the Catalan language and the arts. Historians divide the movement (somewhat arbitrarily) into two parts. The Renaixença (roughly 1840-1880) was a rediscovery of Catalunya's historic roots and national identity, similar to the Romantic movements sweeping all of Europe. Suddenly, people were embracing the language and traditions of their forebears. Writers wrote in Catalan, and artists revived the medieval motifs of Barcelona's 14th-century glory days. This energy flowed naturally into Modernisme (roughly 1890-1910), which continued the love affair with Catalunya's traditions while championing all things modern—things like streetcars and electric lights. The new technology was also meant to be beautiful, and Modernisme is Barcelona's version of the curvy, wistful Art Nouveau style found elsewhere in Europe. As the old city walls came down, Modernista architects like Antoni Gaudí remade the city with fanciful buildings—made of a modern concrete-and-iron substructure but decorated with colorful, playful, medieval motifs.

### Sights

- The Eixample neighborhood, with the Block of Discord, La Pedrera, and other buildings
- Sagrada Família

- Other Gaudí and Modernista sights (see sidebar on page 146)

## TURBULENT 20th CENTURY

By the turn of the 20th century, Barcelona was seething with change. Industrialization had made factory owners rich, but the working class was still poor, living in dirty slums and working in unsafe factories. Barcelona's Socialists fought for the right to bathroom breaks, while anarchists bombed the Liceu Opera House. The unrest culminated in the bloody riots of "Tragic Week" (1909), during which dozens of churches were vandalized and demonstrators were shot in the streets.

Barcelona developed a reputation across Spain as a breeding ground for liberals, troublemakers, and nonconformists. In the art world, young Pablo Picasso captured the plight of society's disenfranchised (in his Blue Period), then moved to Paris and—with fellow artist Georges Braque—broke all the rules of art by pioneering Cubism. Joan Miró perplexed the masses with his childlike doodles, and Salvador Dalí shocked and astonished with his Surrealistic dreamscapes.

When Spain splintered into its bitter civil war (1936-1939)—pitting democratic Republicans against fascist Nationalists—left-leaning Barcelona became the natural capital of the Republican side. The fascists, under General Francisco Franco (1892-1975), invited Mussolini's Italian air force to bomb Barcelona, killing a thousand citizens. When Barcelona finally fell in 1939, the war was effectively over. For the next  four decades, Franco would rule Spain with an iron fist.

Catalunya was punished. The Generalitat was abolished after having been restored just a few years earlier, and the Catalan president was executed by firing squad. Franco began a program of Castilianization to assimilate the region into greater Spain. The Catalan language and traditions were suppressed. You couldn't buy a newspaper in Catalan or hear the people's language spoken on TV. You couldn't dance the *sardana*. Simultaneously, the region was flooded with poor, Castilian-speaking farmers from the rest of Spain, looking for work. The city expanded way too fast, throwing up dusty gray concrete buildings amid suburban sprawl.

But Catalunya kept the flame alive with underground newspapers and a president-in-exile living in France. Finally, Franco

## Catalans You May Know

Catalans invented the submarine, assassinated Leon Trotsky, and founded San Diego. Here are a few names you may be familiar with.

**Pablo Picasso** (1881-1973): Though he was born in Andalucía (to Spanish, not Catalan, parents) and spent his adult life in France, Picasso's formative teenage years were spent in Barcelona's Barri Gòtic.

**Salvador Dalí** (1904-1989): The master Surrealist was born in Figueres, spent holidays in Cadaqués, and passed his formative years in Barcelona, where he exhibited his early works and soaked up Gaudí's dreamlike architecture.

**Joan Miró** (1893-1983): Raised in the Barri Gòtic, he divided his adulthood living between Barcelona and Paris. His whimsical sculptures and ceramics adorn Barcelona.

**Antoni Gaudí** (1852-1926): Resident of the Barri Gòtic (in his youth), the Eixample (in young adulthood), and Park Güell (in his twilight years). Gaudí's buildings are the iconic symbols of Barcelona's Modernista revival.

**Pau (Pablo) Casals** (1876-1973): A world-class cellist who's often described as one of the best musicians ever to pick up the instrument, he retired to French Catalunya in protest against Franco.

**Bacardi Rum Family:** The world-famous rum company was founded in Cuba in 1814 by a man from Sitges; it's now run by his great-great-grandson.

**Juan Antonio Samaranch** (1920-2010): The longtime president of the International Olympic Committee (r. 1980-2001) was born and raised in Barcelona.

**Ferran Adrià** (b. 1962): This celebrity chef revolutionized cuisine with his innovations in molecular gastronomy at the (now-closed) Costa Brava restaurant El Bulli.

**Antoni Tàpies** (1923-2012): Spain's best-known postwar artist is most famous for his distinctive mud-caked canvases.

**Pau Gasol** (b. 1980) and **Marc Gasol** (b. 1985): Basketball-playing brothers who gained fame in the NBA.

**Rafael Nadal** (b. 1986): The "King of Clay," a world-ranked tennis player and winner of multiple Grand Slams, is from the Catalan-speaking island of Mallorca.

died in 1975, and—on September 11, 1977—millions of Catalan patriots flooded the streets to demand they get their culture back.

It ushered in a third Golden Age for Catalunya. The Generalitat and Catalan president returned. Catalan became the sole official language in schools. Barcelona reinvented itself, spiffing up old quarters with new buildings and expanding the Metro system. The Sagrada Família, after nearly a century of false starts, made dramatic progress. In 1992, a revived Barcelona hosted the Summer Olympic Games—for which they rebuilt Montjuïc and the waterfront—and put on a modern face for the world.

## Sights

- Picasso Museum
- Fundació Joan Miró, plus Liceu mosaic in the Ramblas, *Woman and Bird* sculpture, and other public works by Miró
- Figueres, hometown of Salvador Dalí
- Cadaqués, a mecca for modern artists
- 1929 World Expo Fairgrounds, including Magic Fountains (at the base of Montjuïc, near Plaça d'Espanya)
- Fresh-looking Montjuïc (with Olympic Stadium) and the rejuvenated waterfront
- *Barcelona Head* sculpture by Roy Lichtenstein, on the waterfront

## CATALUNYA TODAY: FEISTY AND PROUD

Today Catalunya speeds into the future on a course that may diverge from the rest of Spain. With each visit, I seem to hear more Catalan and less Spanish spoken in the streets. With a population of 1.6 million, Barcelona is Spain's second city.

Along with the rest of Spain, Catalunya has suffered from the global economic downturn that began in 2008. Spain's real-estate bubble burst, banks stopped lending, and unemployment soared. So many young Spaniards are out of work that a new name was coined to describe them: *"generación ni-ni"* (the neither-nor generation). Under pressure from the European Union, Spain is working to dig itself out of debt.

Barcelona continues its legacy of spirited independence. Regular massive demonstrations fill Plaça de Catalunya, as the people fight to regain their cultural heritage. As if to underscore their cultural distance from greater Spain, in 2010 Barcelona outlawed the widely popular Spanish pastime of bullfighting. The Las Arenas bullring is now a shopping mall.

In 2014—300 years after the massacre that ended its independence—Catalunya held a referendum on leaving Spain. Eighty percent of those who voted backed independence (though polls indicate that residents are fairly evenly split on the matter). The national government called the vote illegal under the Spanish constitution.

But the secessionist movement was only warming up; upon winning a majority in 2015 regional elections, Catalan nationalist parties passed a motion to begin the secession process. Their 18-month "roadmap" toward statehood calls for designing a Catalan constitution and starting to build an army, a central bank, and a judicial system by early 2017. The Spanish government, unsurprisingly, proclaimed the plans unconstitutional.

In January 2016, the Catalan parliament elected separatist Charles Puigdemont as president of the regional government. His determination to "chase the invaders out of Catalonia" enlivened the secessionist movement after months of political deadlock. While the outcome remains unclear, it's certain that the proud Catalan people will continue to push for more autonomy.

## Sights

- *Sardana* dances in front of the cathedral
- The red-and-gold flag of Catalunya flapping in the breeze

For more on history, consider *Europe 101: History and Art for the Traveler*, written by Rick Steves and Gene Openshaw (available at www.ricksteves.com).

# PRACTICALITIES

This chapter covers the practical skills of European travel: how to get tourist information, pay for things, sightsee efficiently, find good-value accommodations, eat affordably but well, use technology wisely, and get between destinations smoothly. To study ahead and round out your knowledge and skills, check out "Resources from Rick Steves."

## Tourist Information

Spain's national tourist office **in the US** will fill brochure requests and answer your general travel questions by email (newyork. information@tourspain.es). Scan their website (www.spain.info) for practical information and sightseeing ideas; you can download many brochures free of charge. Also see www.barcelonaturisme. cat.

**In Barcelona,** a good first stop is generally at any of its tourist information offices (abbreviated TI in this book; see page 21 for locations). Be aware that TIs are in business to help you enjoy spending money in their town. (Once upon a time, they were actually information services, but today some have become ad agencies masquerading as TIs.) While this corrupts much of their advice—and you can get plenty of information online—I still make a point to swing by the local TI to confirm sightseeing plans, pick up a city map, and get information on public transit (including bus and train schedules), walking tours, special events, and nightlife. Prepare a list of questions and a proposed plan to double-check.

**Websites for Barcelona:** In addition to the TI websites listed earlier, try www.barcelonaplanning.com, www.guiadelocio.com/barcelona, and www.butxaca.com. The latter two sites focus on events.

## Travel Tips

**Emergency and Medical Help:** In **Spain,** dial 091 for police help and 112 in any emergency (medical or otherwise). In **Barcelona,** dial 092 for the local police. If you get sick, do as the locals do and go to a pharmacist for advice. Or ask at your hotel for help—they'll know the nearest medical and emergency services.

**Theft or Loss:** To replace a passport, you'll need to go in person to an embassy or consulate office (see page 313). If your credit and debit cards disappear, cancel and replace them (see "Damage Control for Lost Cards" on page 268). File a police report, either on the spot or within a day or two; you'll need it to submit an insurance claim for lost or stolen rail passes or travel gear, and it can help with replacing your passport or credit and debit cards. For more information, see www.ricksteves.com/help.

**Avoiding Theft and Scams:** Like anywhere in Europe, thieves target tourists, especially in Barcelona. They break into cars, snatch purses, and pick pockets. Thieves have been known to zip by on motorbikes to grab handbags from pedestrians or even from cars in traffic. A fight or commotion is often created to enable pickpockets to work unnoticed. Someone in a small group pushing you as you enter or exit a crowded subway car may have one hand in your pocket.

Be on guard, use a money belt, and treat any disturbance around you as a smoke screen for theft. Don't believe any "police officers" looking for counterfeit bills.

**Time Zones:** Spain, like most of continental Europe, is generally six/nine hours ahead of the East/West coasts of the US. The exceptions are the beginning and end of Daylight Saving Time: Europe "springs forward" the last Sunday in March (two weeks after most of North America), and "falls back" the last Sunday in October (one week before North America). For a handy online time converter, try www.timeanddate.com/worldclock.

**Business Hours:** For visitors, Spain is a land of strange and frustrating schedules. Many businesses respect the afternoon si-esta. When it's 100 degrees in the shade, you'll understand why. The biggest museums stay open all day. Smaller ones often close for a siesta. Shops are generally open from about 9:00 to 13:00 and from 16:00 to 20:00, longer in touristy places. Small shops are often open on Saturday only in the morning, and closed all day Sunday. Banking hours are generally Monday through Friday from 9:00 to 14:00.

Saturdays typically have earlier closing hours. Sundays have the same pros and cons as they do for travelers in the US: Sight-seeing attractions are generally open, while shops and banks are closed, public transportation options are fewer (for example, no bus service to or from smaller towns), and there's no rush hour. Friday and Saturday evenings are lively; Sunday evenings are quiet.

**Watt's Up?** Europe's electrical system is 220 volts, instead of North America's 110 volts. Most newer electronics (such as lap-tops, battery chargers, and hair dryers) convert automatically, so you won't need a converter plug, but you will need an adapter plug with two round prongs, sold inexpensively at travel stores in the US. Avoid bringing older appliances that don't automatically con-vert voltage; instead, buy a cheap replacement in Europe.

**Discounts:** Discounts are not listed in this book. However, many sights offer discounts for youths (up to age 18), students (with proper identification cards, www.isic.org), families, seniors (loosely defined as retirees or those willing to call themselves seniors), and groups of 10 or more. Always ask. Some discounts are available only for citizens of the European Union (EU).

**Online Translation Tips:** Google's Chrome browser instant-ly translates websites. You can also paste text or the URL of a for-eign website into the translation window at http://translate.google. com. The Google Translate app converts spoken English into most European languages (and vice versa) and can also translate text it "reads" with your mobile device's camera.

# Money

This section offers advice on how to pay for purchases on your trip (including getting cash from ATMs and paying with plastic), deal-ing with lost or stolen cards, VAT (sales tax) refunds, and tipping.

## WHAT TO BRING

Bring both a credit card and a debit card. You'll use the debit card at cash machines (ATMs) to withdraw local cash for most pur-chases, and the credit card to pay for larger items. Some travelers carry a third card, in case one gets demagnetized or eaten by a temperamental machine.

PRACTICALITIES

---

## Exchange Rate

### 1 euro (€) = about $1.20

To convert prices in euros to dollars, add about 20 percent: €20 = about $24, €50 = about $60. (Check www.oanda.com for the latest exchange rates.) Just like the dollar, one euro (€) is broken down into 100 cents. Coins range from €0.01 to €2, and bills range from €5 to €500 (bills over €50 are rarely used).

---

For an emergency stash, bring $100-200 in hard cash. Although banks in some countries don't exchange dollars, in a pinch you can always find exchange desks at major train stations or airports—convenient but with crummy rates.

## CASH

Although credit cards are widely accepted in Europe, day-to-day spending is generally more cash-based. I find cash is the easiest— and sometimes only—way to pay for cheap food, bus fare, taxis, and local guides. Some vendors will charge you extra for using a credit card, some won't accept foreign credit cards, and some won't take any credit cards at all. Having cash on hand can help you avoid a stressful predicament if you find yourself in a place that won't accept your card.

Throughout Europe, ATMs are the easiest and smartest way for travelers to get cash. They work just like they do at home. To withdraw money from an ATM (called a *cajero automático* in Spanish and *caixer automàtic* in Catalan), you'll need a debit card (ideally with a Visa or MasterCard logo), plus a PIN code (numeric and four digits). For increased security, shield the keypad when entering your PIN code, and don't use an ATM if anything on the front of the machine looks loose or damaged (a sign that someone may have attached a "skimming" device to capture account information). Try to withdraw large sums of money to reduce the number of per-transaction bank fees you'll pay.

When possible, use ATMs located outside banks—a thief is less likely to target a cash machine near surveillance cameras, and if your card is munched by a machine during banking hours, you can go inside for help. Stay away from "independent" ATMs such as Travelex, Euronet, YourCash, Cardpoint, and Cashzone, which charge huge commissions, have terrible exchange rates, and may try to trick users with "dynamic currency conversion" (described later). Although you can use a credit card to withdraw cash at an ATM, this comes with high bank fees and only makes sense in an emergency.

While traveling, if you want to access your accounts online, be sure to use a secure connection (see page 296).

Pickpockets target tourists. To safeguard your cash, wear a money belt—a pouch with a strap that you buckle around your waist like a belt and tuck under your clothes. Keep your cash, credit cards, and passport secure in your money belt, and carry only a day's spending money in your front pocket or wallet.

## CREDIT AND DEBIT CARDS

For purchases, Visa and MasterCard are more commonly accepted than American Express. Just like at home, credit or debit cards

work easily at larger hotels, restaurants, and shops. I typically use my debit card to withdraw cash to pay for most purchases. I use my credit card sparingly: to book hotel reservations, to buy advance tickets for events or sights, to cover major expenses (such as car rentals or plane tickets), and to pay for things online or near the end of my trip (to avoid another visit to the ATM). While you could instead use a debit card for these purchases, a credit card offers a greater degree of fraud protection.

**Ask Your Credit- or Debit-Card Company:** Before your trip, contact the company that issued your debit or credit cards.

Confirm that your **card will work overseas,** and alert them that you'll be using it in Europe; otherwise, they may deny transactions if they perceive unusual spending patterns.

Ask for the specifics on transaction **fees.** When you use your credit or debit card—either for purchases or ATM withdrawals— you'll typically be charged additional "international transaction" fees of up to 3 percent (1 percent is normal). If your card's fees seem high, consider getting a different card just for your trip: Capital One (www.capitalone.com) and most credit unions have low-to-no international fees.

Verify your daily ATM **withdrawal limit,** and if necessary, ask your bank to adjust it. I prefer a high limit that allows me to take out more cash at each ATM stop and save on bank fees; some travelers prefer to set a lower limit in case their card is stolen. Note that foreign banks also set maximum withdrawal amounts for their ATMs.

Get your bank's emergency **phone number** in the US (but not its 800 number, which isn't accessible from overseas) to call collect if you have a problem.

Ask for your credit card's **PIN** in case you need to make an emergency cash withdrawal or encounter payment machines using the chip-and-PIN system; the bank won't tell you your PIN over the phone, so allow time for it to be mailed to you.

**Chip and PIN:** While much of Europe is shifting to a chip-and-PIN security system for credit cards, Spain still uses the old magnetic-stripe technology. (European chip-and-PIN cards are embedded with an electronic security chip, and require a four-digit PIN to make a purchase.) If you happen to encounter chip and PIN, it will probably be at payment machines, such as those at toll roads or unattended gas pumps. On the outside chance that a machine won't take your card, find a cashier who can make your card work (they can print a receipt for you to sign), or find a machine that takes cash. Most American travelers don't run into problems. Still, it pays to carry euros; remember, you can always use an ATM to withdraw cash with your magnetic-stripe debit card.

If you're concerned, ask if your bank offers a chip-and-PIN card. Andrews Federal Credit Union (www.andrewsfcu.org) and the State Department Federal Credit Union (www.sdfcu.org) offer these cards and are open to all US residents.

**Dynamic Currency Conversion:** If merchants or hoteliers offer to convert your purchase price into dollars (called dynamic currency conversion, or DCC), refuse this "service." You'll pay extra for the expensive convenience of seeing your charge in dollars. Some ATMs and retailers try to confuse customers by presenting DCC in misleading terms. If an ATM offers to "lock in" or "guarantee" your conversion rate, choose "proceed without conversion." Other prompts might state, "You can be charged in dollars: Press YES for dollars, NO for euros." Always choose the local currency.

## DAMAGE CONTROL FOR LOST CARDS

If you lose your credit or debit card, you can stop people from using your card by reporting the loss immediately to the respective global customer-assistance centers. Call these 24-hour US numbers collect: Visa (tel. 303/967-1096, toll-free number in Spain is 900-991-124), MasterCard (tel. 636/722-7111), and American Express (tel. 336/393-1111). In Spain, to make a collect call to the US, dial 900-990-011. Press zero or stay on the line for an English-speaking operator. European toll-free numbers (listed by country) can be found at the websites for Visa and MasterCard.

If you are the secondary cardholder, you'll need to provide the primary cardholder's identification-verification details (such as birth date, mother's maiden name, or Social Security number). You can generally receive a temporary card within two or three business days in Europe (see www.ricksteves.com/help for more).

If you report your loss within two days, you typically won't be responsible for any unauthorized transactions on your account, although many banks charge a liability fee of $50.

## TIPPING

Tipping in Spain isn't as automatic and generous as it is in the US. For special service, tips are appreciated, but not expected. As in the US, the proper amount depends on your resources, tipping philosophy, and the circumstances, but some general guidelines apply.

**Restaurants:** If eating at the counter of a tapas bar, there's no need to tip, though it's fine to round up the bill with a few small coins. At restaurants with table service, if a service charge is included in the bill, add about 5 percent; if it's not, leave 10 percent. For more details on tipping in restaurants and tapas bars, see pages 284 and 286.

**Taxis:** For a typical ride, just round up your fare a bit (for instance, if the fare is €4.85, pay €5). If the cabbie hauls your bags and zips you to the airport to help you catch your flight, you might want to toss in a little more. But if you feel like you're being driven in circles or otherwise ripped off, skip the tip.

**Services:** In general, if someone in the tourism or service industry does a super job for you, a small tip of a euro or two is appropriate...but not required. If you're not sure whether (or how much) to tip, ask a local for advice.

## GETTING A VAT REFUND

Wrapped into the purchase price of your Spanish souvenirs is a Value-Added Tax (VAT) of 21 percent (in Spain, it's called IVA—*Impuesto sobre el Valor Añadido*). You're entitled to get most of that tax back if you purchase more than €90.15 (about $100) worth of goods at a store that participates in the VAT-refund scheme. Typically, you must ring up the minimum at a single retailer—you can't add up your purchases from various shops to reach the required amount.

Getting your refund is usually straightforward and, if you buy a substantial amount of souvenirs, well worth the hassle. If you're lucky, the merchant will subtract the tax when you make your purchase. (This is more likely to occur if the store ships the goods to your home.) Otherwise, you'll need to:

**Get the paperwork.** Have the merchant completely fill out the necessary refund document. You'll have to present your passport. Get the paperwork done before you leave the store to ensure you'll have everything you need (including your original sales receipt).

**Get your stamp at the border or airport.** Process your VAT document at your last stop in the European Union (such as the airport) with the customs agent who deals with VAT refunds. Arrive an additional hour early before you need to check in for your flight to allow time to find the local customs office—and to stand in line. It's best to keep your purchases in your carry-on. If they're too large or dangerous to carry on (such as knives), pack them in your checked bags and alert the check-in agent. You'll be sent (with your tagged bag) to a customs desk outside security; someone will examine your bag, stamp your paperwork, and put your bag on the belt. You're not supposed to use your purchased goods before you leave. If you show up at customs wearing your new flamenco outfit, officials might look the other way—or deny you a refund.

**Collect your refund.** You'll need to return your stamped document to the retailer or its representative. Many merchants work with services, such as Global Blue or Premier Tax Free, that have offices at major airports, ports, or border crossings (either before or after security, probably strategically located near a duty-free shop). These services, which extract a 4 percent fee, can refund your money immediately in cash or credit your card (within two billing cycles). Other refund services may require you to mail the documents from home, or more quickly, from your point of departure (using an envelope you've prepared in advance or one that's been provided by the merchant). You'll then have to wait—it can take months.

## CUSTOMS FOR AMERICAN SHOPPERS

You are allowed to take home $800 worth of items per person duty-free, once every 31 days. You can take home many processed and packaged foods: vacuum-packed cheeses, dried herbs, jams, baked goods, candy, chocolate, oil, vinegar, mustard, and honey. Fresh fruits and vegetables and most meats are not allowed, with exceptions for some canned items. As for alcohol, you can bring in one liter duty-free (it can be packed securely in your checked luggage, along with any other liquid-containing items).

To bring alcohol (or liquid-packed foods) in your carry-on bag on your flight home, buy it at a duty-free shop at the airport. You'll increase your odds of getting it onto a connecting flight if it's packaged in a "STEB"—a secure, tamper-evident bag. But stay away from liquids in opaque, ceramic, or metallic containers, which usually cannot be successfully screened (STEB or no STEB).

For details on allowable goods, customs rules, and duty rates, visit http://help.cbp.gov.

# Sightseeing

Sightseeing can be hard work. Use these tips to make your visits to sights meaningful, fun, efficient, and painless.

## MAPS AND NAVIGATION TOOLS

A good map is essential for efficient navigation while sightseeing. The black-and-white maps in this book are concise and simple, designed to help you locate recommended destinations, sights, and local TIs, where you can pick up more in-depth maps. Maps with even more detail are sold at newsstands and bookstores.

You can also use a mapping app on your mobile device. Be aware that pulling up maps or looking up turn-by-turn walking directions on the fly requires an Internet connection: To use this feature, it's smart to get an international data plan (see page 292) or only connect using Wi-Fi. With Google Maps or Apple Maps, it's possible to download a map while online, then go offline and navigate without incurring data-roaming charges, though you can't search for an address or get real-time walking directions. A handful of other apps—including City Maps 2Go, OffMaps, and Navfree—also allow you to use maps offline.

## PLAN AHEAD

Set up an itinerary that allows you to fit in all your must-see sights. For a one-stop look at opening hours, see "Barcelona at a Glance" (page 38; also see the "Daily Reminder" on page 20). Most sights keep stable hours, but you can easily confirm the latest by checking with the TI or visiting museum websites.

Don't put off visiting a must-see sight—you never know when a place will close unexpectedly for a holiday, strike, or restoration. Many museums are closed or have reduced hours at least a few days a year, especially on holidays such as Christmas, New Year's, and Labor Day (May 1). A list of holidays is on page 314; check online for possible museum closures during your trip. In summer, some sights may stay open late. Off-season, many museums have shorter hours.

Going at the right time helps avoid crowds. This book offers tips on the best times to see specific sights. Try visiting popular sights very early or very late. Evening visits are usually peaceful, with fewer crowds. For Barcelona, see the "Sights Open Late" sidebar on page 219).

Study up. To get the most out of the sight descriptions in this book, read them before you visit. Gaudí seems less gaudy if you understand his artistic vision.

## AT SIGHTS

Here's what you can typically expect:

**Entering:** Be warned that you may not be allowed to enter if you arrive less than 30 to 60 minutes before closing time. And guards start ushering people out well before the actual closing time, so don't save the best for last.

Some important sights have a security check, where you must open your bag or send it through a metal detector. Some sights require you to check daypacks and coats. (If you'd rather not check

PRACTICALITIES

your daypack, try carrying it tucked under your arm like a purse as you enter.)

At churches—which often offer interesting art (usually free) and a cool, welcome seat—a modest dress code (no bare shoulders or shorts) is encouraged though rarely enforced.

**Photography:** If the museum's photo policy isn't clearly posted, ask a guard. Generally, taking photos without a flash or tripod is allowed. Some sights ban photos altogether; others ban selfie sticks.

**Temporary Exhibits:** Museums may show special exhibits in addition to their permanent collection. Some exhibits are included in the entry price, while others come at an extra cost (which you may have to pay even if you don't want to see the exhibit).

**Expect Changes:** Artwork can be on tour, on loan, out sick, or shifted at the whim of the curator. Pick up a floor plan as you enter, and ask the museum staff if you can't find a particular item. Say the title or artist's name, or point to the photograph in this book, and ask, *"¿Dónde está?"* (DOHN-day eh-STAH; meaning, "Where is?").

**Audioguides and Apps:** Many sights rent audioguides, which generally offer dry-but-useful recorded descriptions in English (about €3-4). If you bring your own headphones, you can enjoy better sound and avoid holding the device to your ear. To save money, bring a Y-jack and share one audioguide with your travel partner. Increasingly, museums and sights offer apps—often free—that you can download to your mobile device (check their websites). And, I've produced a free, downloadable audio tour covering parts of the Ramblas, Barri Gòtic, and El Born neighborhoods; look for the ∩ in this book. For more on my audio tours, see page 8.

**Services:** Important sights may have an on-site café or cafeteria (usually a handy place to rejuvenate during a long visit). The WCs at sights are free and generally clean.

**Before Leaving:** At the gift shop, scan the postcard rack or thumb through a guidebook to be sure that you haven't overlooked something that you'd like to see.

Every sight or museum offers more than what is covered in this book. Use the information in this book as an introduction—not the final word.

# Sleeping

I favor hotels and restaurants that are handy to your sightseeing activities. Rather than list hotels scattered throughout a city, I choose hotels in my favorite neighborhoods. My recommendations run the gamut, from dorm beds to fancy rooms with all the comforts.

A major feature of this book is its extensive and opinionated listing of good-value rooms. I like places that are clean, central, relatively quiet at night, reasonably priced, friendly, small enough to have a hands-on owner and stable staff, and run with a respect for Spanish traditions. I'm more impressed by a convenient location and a fun-loving philosophy than flat-screen TVs and a fancy gym.

In Spain, high season *(temporada alta)* is from July to September; shoulder season *(temporada media)* is roughly April through June and October; and low season *(temporada baja)* runs from November through March. But Barcelona can be busy any time of year. Book your accommodations well in advance, especially if you want to stay at one of my top listings or if you'll be traveling during peak times or during any holidays or festivals. See page 314 for a list of major holidays and festivals; for tips on making reservations, see page 277. In Barcelona, trade fairs crop up throughout the year and can send rates soaring (search for trade fair dates at www. firabarcelona.com/en/home).

## RATES AND DEALS

I've categorized my recommended accommodations based on price, indicated with a dollar-sign rating (see sidebar). The price ranges suggest an estimated cost for a one-night stay in a standard double room with a private toilet and shower in high season, don't include breakfast, and assume you're booking directly with the hotel (not through a booking site, which extracts a commission and logically closes the door on special deals).

Room prices can fluctuate significantly with demand and amenities (size, views, room class, and so on), but these relative price categories remain constant. Hoteliers are encouraged to quote prices with the IVA tax included. If you have any doubts, ask. Additionally, the city of Barcelona levies a tourist tax (ranging from €0.65-2.25/person per night).

Room rates are especially volatile at larger hotels that use "dynamic pricing" to predict demand. Rates can skyrocket during festivals and conventions, while business hotels can have deep discounts on weekends when demand plummets. For this reason, of the many hotels I recommend, it's difficult to say which will be the best value on a given day—until you do your homework.

Once your dates are set, check the specific price for your preferred stay at several hotels. You can do this either by comparing prices online on the hotels' own websites, or by emailing several hotels directly and asking for their best rate. Even if you start your search on a booking site such as TripAdvisor or Booking.com, you'll usually find the lowest rates through a hotel's own website.

Many hotels offer a discount to those who pay cash or stay longer than three nights. To cut costs further, try asking for a cheap-

**PRACTICALITIES**

PRACTICALITIES

## Sleep Code

Hotels are classified based on the average price of a standard double room without breakfast in high season.

| | |
|---:|:---|
| **$$$$** | **Splurge:** Most rooms over €170 |
| **$$$** | **Pricier:** €130-170 |
| **$$** | **Moderate**: €90-130 |
| **$** | **Budget**: €50-90 |
| **¢** | **Backpacker:** Under €50 |
| **RS%** | **Rick Steves discount** |

Unless otherwise noted, credit cards are accepted, hotel staff speak basic English, and free Wi-Fi is available. Comparison-shop by checking prices at several hotels (on each hotel's own website, on a booking site, or by email). For the best deal, *book directly with the hotel*. Ask for a discount if paying in cash; if the listing includes **RS%**, request a Rick Steves discount.

er room (for example, with a shared bathroom or no window). If breakfast is included, offer to skip it.

Additionally, some accommodations offer a special discount for Rick Steves readers, indicated in this guidebook by the abbreviation "RS%." Discounts vary: Ask for details when you book. Generally, to qualify you must book direct (that is, not through a booking site), mention this book when you reserve, show the book upon arrival, and sometimes pay cash or stay a certain number of nights. In some cases, you may need to enter a discount code (which I've provided in the listing) in the booking form on the hotel's website. Rick Steves discounts apply to readers with ebooks as well as printed books. Understandably, discounts do not apply to promotional rates.

## TYPES OF ACCOMMODATIONS
### Hotels
Spain offers some of the best accommodations values in Western Europe. In this book, the price for a double room ranges from about $60 (very simple, toilet and shower down the hall) to $400 (maximum plumbing and more), with most clustering at about $150.

In addition to double rooms, most hotels offer single rooms, and some offer larger rooms for four or more people (I call these "family rooms" in the listings). Some hotels can add an extra bed to a double room to make a triple for a small charge.

Spain has stringent restrictions on smoking in public places. Smoking is not permitted in common areas, but hotels can designate 10 percent of their rooms for smokers.

Street noise in Spain is high (Spaniards are notorious night owls), and walls and doors tend to be very thin—earplugs are a

## Keep Cool

If you're visiting Spain in the summer, the extra expense of an air-conditioned room can be money well spent. Most hotel rooms with air-conditioners come with a control stick (like a TV remote; sometimes the hotel requires a deposit) that generally has similar symbols and features: fan icon (click to toggle through wind power, from light to gale); louver icon (choose steady airflow or waves); snowflake and sunshine icons (cold air or heat, depending on season); clock ("O" setting: run X hours before turning off; "I" setting: wait X hours to start); and the temperature control (21 or 22 degrees Celsius is comfortable; also see the thermometer diagram on page 319). When you leave your room for the day, turning off the air-conditioning is good form. Be aware that some hotels have centrally controlled air-conditioning—and the manager may choose the temperature (with an eye on his bottom line).

**PRACTICALITIES**

necessity. Always ask to see your room first. If you suspect night noise will be a problem, request a quiet *(tranquilo)* room in the back or on an upper floor *(piso alto)*. In most cases, view rooms *(con vista)* come with street noise. You'll often sleep better and for less money in a room without a view.

Hotels can sometimes occupy one floor of a building with a finicky vintage elevator or slightly dingy entryway. The hotelier doesn't control the common areas of the building, so try not to let the entryway atmosphere color your opinion of the hotel. Hotel elevators are often very small—pack light. You may need to send your bags up one at a time.

Some hotels don't use central heat before November 1 and after April 1 (unless it's unusually cold); prepare for cool evenings if you travel in spring and fall. Summer can be extremely hot. Consider air-conditioning, fans, and noise (since you'll want your window open). Many rooms come with mini refrigerators.

If you're arriving in the morning, your room probably won't be ready. Check your bag safely at the hotel and dive right into sightseeing. To guard against theft in your room, keep valuables out of sight. Some rooms come with a safe, and other hotels have safes at the front desk. I've never bothered using one.

Hoteliers can be a great help and source of advice. Most know their city well, and can assist you with everything from public transit and airport connections to finding a good restaurant, the nearest launderette, or a late-night pharmacy.

Even at the best places, mechanical breakdowns occur: Sinks leak, hot water turns cold, toilets may gurgle or smell, the Wi-Fi goes out, or the air-conditioning dies when you need it most. Report your concerns clearly and calmly at the front desk. For more

## The Good and Bad of Online Reviews

User-generated review sites and apps such as Yelp, Booking. com, and TripAdvisor are changing the travel industry. These sites can give you a consensus of opinions about everything from hotels and restaurants to sights and nightlife. If you scan reviews of a hotel and see several complaints about noise or a rotten location, it tells you something important that you'd never learn from the hotel's own website.

But review sites are only as good as the judgment of their reviewers. And while these sites work hard to weed out bogus users, my hunch is that a significant percentage of user reviews are posted by friends or enemies of the business being reviewed.

As a guidebook writer, my sense is that there is a big difference between this uncurated information and a guidebook. A user-generated review is based on the experience of one person, who likely stayed at one hotel and ate at a few restaurants, and doesn't have much of a basis for comparison. A guidebook is the work of a trained researcher who visited many alternatives to assess their relative value. I recently checked out some top-rated user-reviewed hotel and restaurant listings in various towns; when stacked up against their competitors, some were gems, while just as many were duds.

Both types of information have their place, and in many ways, they're complementary. If something is well-reviewed in a guidebook, and also gets good ratings on one of these sites, it's likely a winner.

complicated problems, don't expect instant results. Any legitimate place is legally required to have a complaint book *(libro de reclamaciones)*. A request for this book will generally prompt the hotelier to solve your problem to keep you from writing a complaint.

While it's customary to pay for your room upon departure, it can be a good idea to settle your bill the day before, when you're not in a hurry and while the manager's in. That way you'll have time to discuss and address any points of contention.

Above all, keep a positive attitude. Remember, you're on vacation. If your hotel is a disappointment, spend more time out enjoying the place you came to see.

### *Hostales* and *Pensiones*

Budget hotels—called *hostales* and *pensiones*—are easy to find, inexpensive, and, when chosen properly, a fun part of the Spanish cultural experience. These places are often family-owned, and may or may not have amenities like private bathrooms and air-conditioning. Don't confuse a *hostal* with a hostel—a Spanish *hostal* is an inexpensive hotel, not a hostel with bunks in dorms.

# Making Hotel Reservations

Reserve your rooms several weeks or even months in advance—
or as soon as you've pinned down your travel dates. Note that
some national holidays (and, in Barcelona, trade fairs) merit your
making reservations far in advance (see page 314).

**Requesting a Reservation:** It's easiest to book your room
through the hotel's website. (For the best rates, use the hotel's
official site and not a booking agency's site.) If there's no reservation form, or for complicated requests, send an email (see
sample). Most recommended hotels take reservations in English.

The hotelier wants to know:
- the size of your party and type of rooms you need
- your arrival and departure dates, written European-style—
  day followed by month and year (for example, 18/06/17 or
  18 June 2017); include the total number of nights
- special requests (such as en suite bathroom vs. down the
  hall, cheapest room, twin beds vs. double bed, quiet room)
- applicable discounts (such as a Rick Steves reader discount, cash discount, or promotional rate)

**Confirming a Reservation:** Most places will request a credit-
card number to hold your room. If they don't have a secure online
reservation form—look for the *https*—you can email it (I do), but
it's safer to share that confidential info via a phone call or fax.

**Canceling a Reservation:** If you must cancel, it's courteous—
and smart—to do so with as much notice as possible, especially for
smaller family-run places. Cancellation policies can be strict; read
the fine print or ask about these before you book. Many discount
deals require prepayment, with no refunds for cancellations.

**Reconfirming a Reservation:** Always call or email to reconfirm your room reservation a few days in advance. For B&Bs or
very small hotels, I call again on my day of arrival to tell my host
what time I expect to get there (especially important if arriving
late—after 17:00).

**Phoning:** For tips on how to call hotels overseas, see page
294.

PRACTICALITIES

| From: | rick@ricksteves.com |
|---|---|
| Sent: | Today |
| To: | info@hotelcentral.com |
| Subject: | Reservation request for 19-22 July |

Dear Hotel Central,
I would like to stay at your hotel. Please let me know if you have a
room available and the price for:
- 2 people
- Double bed and en suite bathroom in a quiet room
- Arriving 19 July, departing 22 July (3 nights)

Thank you!
Rick Steves

## Short-Term Rentals

A short-term rental—whether an apartment, house, or room in a local's home—is an increasingly popular alternative to a guesthouse or hotel, especially if you plan to settle in one location for several nights. For stays longer than a few days, you can usually find a rental that's comparable to—or even cheaper than—a hotel room with similar amenities. Plus, you'll get a behind-the-scenes peek into how locals live.

The rental route isn't for everyone. Many places require a minimum night stay, and compared to hotels, rentals usually have less-flexible cancellation policies. Also you're generally on your own: There's no hotel reception desk, breakfast, or daily cleaning service.

**Finding Accommodations:** Websites such as www.airbnb.com, www.roomorama.com, and www.vrbo.com let you browse properties and correspond directly with European property owners or managers. Or, for more guidance, consider using a rental agency such as www.interhomeusa.com or www.rentavilla.com. Agency-represented apartments may cost more, but this route often offers more help and safeguards than booking direct. For a list of agencies specializing in Barcelona apartment rentals, see page 181.

Before you commit to a rental, be clear on the details, location, and amenities. I like to virtually "explore" the neighborhood using the Street View feature on Google Maps. Also consider the proximity to public transportation, and how well-connected it is with the rest of the city. Ask about amenities that are important to you (elevator, laundry, coffee maker, Wi-Fi, parking, etc.). Reading reviews from previous guests can help identify trouble spots that are glossed over in the official description.

**Apartments:** If you're staying somewhere for four nights or longer, it's worth considering an apartment (anything less than that isn't worth the extra effort involved, such as arranging key pickup, buying groceries, etc.). Apartment rentals can be especially cost-effective for groups and families. European apartments, like hotel rooms, tend to be small by US standards. But they often come with laundry machines and small, equipped kitchens, making it easier and cheaper to dine in. If you make good use of the kitchen (and Europe's great produce markets), you'll save on your meal budget.

**Private and Shared Rooms:** Renting a room in someone's home is a good option for those traveling alone, as you're more likely to find true single rooms—with just one single bed, and a price to match. Beds range from air-mattress-in-living-room basic to plush-B&B-suite posh. Some places allow you to book for a single night; if staying for several nights, you can buy groceries just as you would in a rental house. While you can't expect your host to also be your tour guide—or even to provide you with much info—

some may be interested in getting to know the travelers who come through their home.

**Other Options:** Swapping homes with a local works for people with an appealing place to offer, and who can live with the idea of having strangers in their home (don't assume where you live is not interesting to Europeans). A good place to start is HomeExchange (www.homeexchange.com).

To sleep for free, Couchsurfing.com is a vagabond's alternative to Airbnb. It lists millions of outgoing members, who host fellow "surfers" in their homes.

## Hostels

A hostel *(albergue juvenil)* provides cheap beds in dorms where you sleep alongside strangers for about €20-30 per night. Travelers of any age are welcome if they don't mind dorm-style accommodations and meeting other travelers. Most hostels offer kitchen facilities, guest computers, Wi-Fi, and a self-service laundry. Hostels almost always provide bedding, but the towel's up to you (though you can usually rent one for a small fee). Family and private rooms are often available.

**Independent hostels** tend to be easygoing, colorful, and informal (no membership required; www.hostelworld.com). You may pay slightly less by booking direct with the hostel. **Official hostels** are part of Hostelling International (HI) and share an online booking site (www.hihostels.com). HI hostels typically require that you be a member or pay extra per night.

# Eating

Spanish cuisine is hearty, and meals are served in big, inexpensive portions. You can eat well in restaurants for about €15-20—or even more cheaply and more varied if you graze on appetizer-sized tapas in bars.

The Spanish eating schedule—lunch from 13:00 to 16:00, dinner after 21:00—frustrates many visitors. Most Spaniards eat one major meal of the day—lunch *(comida)*—around 14:00, when stores close, schools let out, and people gather with their friends and family for the siesta. Because most Spaniards work until 19:30, supper *(cena)* is usually served at about 21:00 or 22:00. And, since few people want a heavy meal that late, many Spaniards eat a light tapas dinner.

Generally, no self-respecting *casa de*

*comidas* ("house of eating"—when you see this label, you can bet it's a good, traditional eatery) serves meals at American hours. If you're looking for the "nontouristy restaurant," remember that a popular spot is often filled with tourists at 20:00; then at 22:00 the scene is entirely different—and more authentic.

**Survival Tips for Spanish Eating Schedules:** To bridge the gap between their coffee-and-roll breakfast and late lunch, many Spaniards eat a light meal at about 11:00 *(almuerzo)*. This can be a light lunch at a bar or a *bocadillo* (baguette sandwich)—hence the popularity of fast-food *bocadillo* chains such as Pans & Company. Besides *bocadillos,* bars often have slices of *tortilla española* (potato omelet) and fresh-squeezed orange juice. For your main meal of the day, you can either eat a late lunch at a restaurant at around 15:00, then have a light tapas snack for dinner; or reverse it, having a tapas meal in the afternoon, followed by a late restaurant dinner. Either way, tapas bars are the key.

## RESTAURANT PRICING

I've categorized my recommended eateries based on price, indicated with a dollar-sign rating (see sidebar). The price ranges suggest the average price of a typical main course—but not necessarily a complete meal. Obviously, expensive items (steak, seafood, truffles), fine wine, appetizers, and dessert can significantly increase your final bill.

The dollar-sign categories also indicate the overall personality and "feel" of a place:

**$ Budget** eateries include street food, takeaway, order-at-the-counter shops, basic cafeterias, bakeries selling sandwiches, and so on.

**$$ Moderate** eateries are typically nice (but not fancy) sit-down restaurants, ideal for a straightforward, fill-the-tank meal. Most of my listings fall in this category—great for getting a good taste of the local cuisine on a budget.

**$$$ Pricier** eateries are a notch up, with more attention paid to the setting, service, and cuisine. These are ideal for a memorable meal that's still relatively casual and doesn't break the bank. This category often includes affordable "destination" or "foodie" restaurants.

**$$$$ Splurge** eateries are dress-up-for-a-special-occasion-swanky—Michelin star-type restaurants, typically with an elegant setting, polished service, pricey and intricate cuisine, and an expansive (and expensive) wine list.

I haven't categorized places where you might assemble a picnic, snack, or graze: supermarkets, delis, ice-cream stands, cafés or bars specializing in drinks, chocolate shops, and so on.

---

## Restaurant Price Code

I've assigned each eatery a price category, based on the average cost of a typical main course (or 2-3 tapas). Drinks, desserts, and splurge items (steak and seafood) can raise the price considerably.

| | |
|---|---|
| **$$$$** | **Splurge:** Most main courses over €20 |
| **$$$** | **Pricier:** €15-20 |
| **$$** | **Moderate:** €10-15 |
| **$** | **Budget:** Under €10 |

In Spain, takeout food is **$**; a basic tapas bar or no-frills sit-down eatery is **$$**; a casual but more upscale tapas bar or restaurant is **$$$**; and a swanky splurge is **$$$$**.

## BREAKFAST

Hotel breakfasts are generally handy, optional, and pricey (about €6 and up). Start your day instead with a Spanish flair at a corner bar or at a colorful café near a market hall (and pay just €2-3). Ask for the *desayunos* (breakfast special, usually only available until noon), which can include coffee, a roll (or sandwich), and juice for one price—much cheaper than ordering them separately. Sandwiches can either be on white bread (called "sandwich") or on a baguette *(bocadillo)*.

A basic and standard savory breakfast item is the *tostada (torrada* in Catalan)—toasted white bread with olive oil and cured ham, *fuet* (a typical Catalan cured sausage), or cheese. Other options include the *bikini* (grilled ham-and-cheese sandwich) or a slice of *tortilla española* (potato omelet), which is often accompanied by *pa amb tomàquet* (toasted white bread with olive oil, tomato, and salt).

Those with a sweet tooth will find various sweet rolls *(bollos* or *bollería)*. If you like a doughnut and coffee in American greasy-spoon joints, try the Spanish equivalent: *churros* (or the thicker *porras*) that you dip in warm chocolate pudding or your *café con leche*.

I've listed some key words for breakfast (in some cases, I've also provided the Catalan translation in parentheses). For coffee and other beverages, see page 290.

*Bamba de nata:* Cream puff

*Bikini:* Grilled ham-and-cheese sandwich, named after a local Barcelona bar, Sala Bikini

*Bocadillo (bocata) con jamón/queso/mixto:* Baguette sandwich with ham/cheese/both

*Bocadillo (bocata) mixto con huevo:* Baguette sandwich with ham and cheese and an over-easy egg on top

*Bollos/bollería (pastisseria):* Sweet pastry

*Caracola:* "Snail"-shaped pastry, similar to a cinnamon roll

*Churros (xurros):* Fried dough pastry that you dip in warm chocolate pudding or *café con leche* (*porras* is the thicker version)

*Croissant a la plancha:* Croissant grilled and slathered with butter

*Napolitana:* Rolled pastry, filled with chocolate (similar to French *pain au chocolat*) or *crema* (cream)

*Palmera:* Palm-shaped pastry, like a French *palmier* or "elephant ear"

*Pan (pa) de molde/de barra:* Bread (sandwich bread/baguette)

*Rosquilla:* Hard doughnut

*Sandwich, tostado:* White bread sandwich, toasted

*Tortilla española (truita de patata):* Potato omelet

*Tostada (torrada) con aceite y tomate:* Toasted bread with olive oil and tomato

## SPANISH RESTAURANTS

While Spain's tapas bars offer small plates throughout the afternoon and evening, formal restaurants have a standard à la carte menu, serve generous portions (no tapas), and start their service much later than the American norm. But many eateries blur the distinction between a bar and a restaurant, boasting both a bar and some sit-down tables in the back or outside on the *terraza*. These more-casual places are likely to serve *raciones* (described later) rather than bite-size tapas or restaurant entrées.

When restaurant-hunting, choose a spot filled with locals, not the place with the big neon signs boasting, "We Speak English and Accept Credit Cards." And avoid any restaurant that posts big photographs of its food. Venturing even a block or two off the main drag leads to higher-quality food for less than half the price of the tourist-oriented places. Locals eat better at lower-rent locales.

Don't expect "My name is Carlos and I'll be your waiter tonight" cheery service. Service is often *serio*—it's not friendly or unfriendly...just white-shirt-and-bow-tie proficient.

Whether you go to a restaurant or bar, you won't be bothered by indoor smoke. Smoking is banned in closed public spaces.

**Ordering:** While menus at formal restaurants are generally broken down by courses or categories, more casual eateries (and tapas bars) may feature dishes served in portions called *raciones* (*racions* in Catalan), or the smaller half-servings, *media-raciones* (*mitja racions* in Catalan). Smaller tapas plates are more commonly served at bars than at sit-down restaurants.

# Sampling *Jamón*

*The* staple of Spanish cuisine, *jamón* (hah-MOHN) is prosciut-

to-like ham that's dry-cured and aged. It's generally sliced thin (right off the hock) and served at room temperature. *Jamón* can be eaten straight, served in a *bocadillo* (baguette sandwich), or mixed into a wide variety of dishes. Bars proudly hang ham hocks from the rafters as part of the decor. *Jamón* is more than a food. It's a way of life. Spaniards treasure memories of Grandpa thinly carving a *jamón,* supported in a *jamonero* (ham-hock holder), during Christmas, just as we savor the turkey carving at Thanksgiving.

Like connoisseurs of fine wine, Spaniards debate the merits of different breeds of pigs, the pig's diet, and the quality of the curing. The two major types of ham are *jamón serrano,* from white pigs whose meat is cured in the *sierras* (mountains) of Spain, and the higher-quality *jamón ibérico,* made with the back legs of black-hooved pigs (a.k.a. *pata negra,* "black foot"). Originating in Spain, these "Iberian" black pigs are said to be fatter and happier (slaughtered much later than other pigs), thereby producing particularly fine ham. Another indication of quality is *de bellota,* which means the pig was raised on acorns *(bellotas). Jamón ibérico de bellota* is, to Spanish connoisseurs, as good as it gets. (Ham labeled *Jamón ibérico de recebo* or *de cebo* is still good, but comes from pigs that are partly or entirely grain-fed rather than acorn-fed.) Additionally, there are regional variations of *jamón* indicating high quality, some of them officially controlled by EU authorities.

To sample this delicacy without the high price tag you'll find in bars and restaurants, go to the local market. Ask for 100 grams of top-quality ham (*cien gramos de jamón ibérico extra;* about €70/kilo, so your portion will run about €7), and enjoy it as a picnic with red wine and a baguette. To round out the perfect picnic, also pick up 100 grams of *salchichón* (salami), 100 grams of *chorizo* (spicy sausage), 100 grams of characteristic *manchego* or *cabrales* cheese, and some olives and pickles.

Typically, couples or small groups can share a few *raciones*, making this an economical way to eat and a great way to explore the regional cuisine. Ordering *media-raciones* may cost a bit more per ounce, but you'll broaden your tasting experience. Two people can fill up on four *media-raciones*.

For a budget meal in a restaurant, try a *plato combinado* (combination plate), which usually includes portions of one or two main dishes, a vegetable, and bread for a reasonable price; or the *menú del día* (menu of the day), a substantial three- to four-course meal that usually comes with a carafe of house wine.

Menus in Barcelona feature lots of seafood, along with local favorites such as *fideuà* (a kind of Catalan paella made with seafood and a thin, flavor-infused noodle), and *arròs negre*—black rice cooked in squid ink. Spanish cooks love garlic and olive oil—many dishes are soaked in both. You'll see plenty of *jamón* (ham) on menus, though it is more typically Spanish than Catalan (for more on *jamón*, see the sidebar on page 283). The cheapest meal is a simple *bocadillo de jamón* (ham sandwich on a baguette), sold virtually everywhere.

Spanish cuisine can be a bit heavy for Americans more accustomed to salads, fruits, and grains. Good vegetarian and lighter options exist, but you'll have to seek them out. The secret to getting your veggies at restaurants is to order two courses. For your first course, resist the cheese-and-ham appetizers and instead choose the creamed vegetable soup, *parrillada de verduras* (sautéed vegetables), *ensalada mixta*, or other green option. (Spaniards rarely eat only a salad, so salads tend to be small and simple—just lettuce, tomatoes, and maybe olives and tuna.) Main courses such as meats or fish are usually served with only a garnish, not a side of vegetables.

**Tipping:** At restaurants with table service, a service charge is generally included in the bill (*servicio incluido; servei inclós* in Catalan). Most Spaniards tip nothing or next to nothing on top of that, but if you like to tip for good service, give up to 5 percent extra. If service is not included (*servicio no incluido; servei no inclós* in Catalan), you could tip up to 10 percent. At most places, you can leave the tip on the table. But if you're eating at an outdoor café, hand the tip to your server to avoid having it swiped by a passerby. It's best to tip in cash even if you pay with credit card. Otherwise the tip may never reach your server.

## TAPAS BARS

Tapas are small portions of seafood, salads, meat-filled pastries, deep-fried tasties, and other delicious bites, typically costing €3-5 a plate. You can eat well any time of day in tapas bars. Some are sit-down, while others are more stand-up.

Chasing down a particular bar for tapas nearly defeats the

purpose and spirit of tapas— they are impromptu. Just drop in at any lively place. There is nothing wrong with ordering a tapa or two to start before deciding whether to stay at the same bar or move on. Part of the joy of eating at tapas bars is turning it into a mobile feast, visiting two or three bars during a single meal.

I'll be blunt: The authentic tapas experience can be intimidating. It generally involves elbowing up to a bar crowded with pushy locals, squinting at a hand-scrawled monolingual chalkboard menu, and trying to order from the brusque bartender.

Basque-style bars, which have an array of tapas platters already laid out, are popular in Barcelona and can be less daunting, as you simply point to or grab what you want (see page 183). These tapas are called *pintxos* (or *pinchos*). Note that Barcelona's tapas bars generally don't provide a free, small tapa with the purchase of a drink as may be found elsewhere in Spain.

**Where to Sit:** Locate the price list (often posted in fine type on a wall somewhere) to see the menu options and price tiers. Eating and drinking at a bar is usually cheapest if you sit or stand at the counter *(barra)*. You may pay a little more to sit at a table (*mesa* or *salón*) and still more for an outdoor table *(terraza)*. Traditionally, tapas are served at the bar, and *raciones* (and *media-raciones*) are served at tables, where food can be shared "family style." You may be "obligated" to order *raciones* if sitting at a table.

It's bad form to order food at the bar, then take it to a table. If you're standing and a table opens up, it's OK to move as long as you signal to the waiter; anything else you order will be charged at the higher *mesa/salón* price. In the right place, a quiet snack and drink on a terrace on a town square is well worth the extra charge. But the cheapest seats sometimes get the best show. Sit at the bar and study your bartender—he's an artist.

Bars can be extremely crowded with locals, and non-native speakers can find it hard to get in an order—or even find a place to sit. You'll have more room, and get better service, by showing up before the local crowd. Try to be there by 13:30 for lunch, and 20:30-21:00 for dinner. For less competition at the bar, go on Monday and Tuesday (but check first to make sure they're open).

**Ordering:** To figure out what you want, read the posted or printed menu. Use the "Tapas Menu Decoder" on page 288 to sort through your options. You can also look around to see what appeals on other patrons' plates. Sometimes a few selections are displayed under glass at the counter. Handwritten signs that start out *"Hay"* mean "Today we have," as in *"Hay caracoles"* ("Today we have snails").

When you're ready to order, be assertive or you'll never be served. Your bartender isn't a "waiter," in any sense. He's not there to patiently help you sort through your options—he wants to take your order, period. Hang back and observe before ordering. To grab his attention, say *"por favor"* (please; *"si us plau"* in Catalan); you can also say *"perdone"* (excuse me; *"perdó"* in Catalan). Then quickly rattle off what you'd like (pointing to other people's food if necessary). To ask for the price of a dish, say *"¿Cuánto cuesta una tapa?"* (*"Quant costa una tapa?"* in Catalan).

Some bars push *raciones* (dinner plate-sized) portions rather than smaller tapas (saucer-sized). Ask for the smaller tapas portions or a *media-ración* (listed as ½ ración on a menu), though some bars simply don't serve anything smaller than a *ración*.

If you're undecided about what to order, it's fun to try an inexpensive sampler plate. Ask for *una tabla de canapés variados* to get a plate of various little open-faced sandwiches. Or ask for a *surtido de* (an assortment of) *charcutería* (a mixed plate of meat) or *queso* (cheese). *Un surtido de jamón y queso* means a plate of different hams and cheeses. Order bread and two glasses of red wine on the right square, and you've got a romantic (and €10) dinner for two.

**Paying and Tipping:** Don't worry about paying until you're ready to leave (they're keeping track of your tab). To get the bill, ask: *"¿La cuenta?"* (*"El compte?"* in Catalan). If you order a meal at a counter—as you often will when sampling tapas at a bar—there's no need to tip (though if you buy a few tapas, you can round up the bill a few small coins).

## TYPICAL DESSERTS

In Spain, desserts are often an afterthought. Fruit is considered a dessert (and generally not served for breakfast or as a snack—except to kids). Dessert menus usually have a fruit option. Here are a few items you may see on Spanish menus:

***Arroz con leche:*** Rice pudding

***Brazo de Gitano:*** Sponge cake filled with butter cream; literally "Gypsy's arm"

***Crema catalana:*** Catalan take on crème brûlée (Barcelona)

***Flan de huevo:*** Flan (crème caramel)

*Fruta de la estación/fruta de temporada:* Fruit in season
*Helados, variados:* Ice cream, various flavors
*Queso:* Cheese
*Mel i mató:* Light Catalan cheese with honey (Barcelona)
*Músic de fruits secs:* Selection of nuts and dried fruits (Barcelona)
*Torrijas:* Sweet fritters, like French toast, available during Lent
    and Easter

## SPANISH DRINKS
### Alcoholic Beverages

If visiting several different tapas bars in a night (as you should),
ordering a drink at each can add up (both for your head and your
wallet). To avoid getting drunk too quickly, consider ordering a
*caña* (small beer), a shandy type drink called a *clara* (beer mixed
with lemon soda, or with a Sprite-style soda), or a *tinto de verano*
(red wine with lemon soda), which Spaniards generally prefer to
sangria (a punch of red wine mixed with fruit slices). For more
phrases, see the lists, below.

**Wine and Spirits:** Spain is one of the world's leading pro-
ducers of grapes, and that means lots of excellent wine: both red
*(tinto)* and white *(blanco)*. Major wine regions include Valdepeñas
(both red and white wines made in Don Quixote country south of
Toledo); Penedès (cabernet-style wines from near Barcelona); Rioja
(spicy, lighter reds from the tempranillo grape, from the high plains
of northern Spain); and Ribera del Duero (reds from northwest of
Madrid).

For a basic glass of red wine, you can order *un tinto.* But for
quality wine, ask for *un crianza* (old), *un reserva* (older), or *un gran
reserva* (oldest). For good, economical wine, I always ask for *un
crianza*—for little or no extra money than a basic *tinto,* you'll get
a quality, aged wine. *Cava* is Spain's answer to champagne. For
nondrinkers, *mosto* is excellent Spanish grape juice that hasn't been
fermented into its alcoholic cousin.

Here are some common terms (the phrases in parentheses are
Catalan):
*Afrutado (afruitat):* Fruity
*Amontillado, fino, manzanilla:* Rich, dry sherries
*Cava:* Sparkling wine (Spanish champagne)
*Chato (gotet):* Small glass of house wine
*Dulce (dolç):* Sweet
*Jerez (Xerès):* Sherry (fortified wine from Jerez)
*Mosto (most):* Nonalcoholic grape juice—red or white
*Mucho cuerpo (molt cos):* Full-bodied
*¡Salud! (Salut!):* Cheers!
*Seco (sec):* Dry

**PRACTICALITIES**

# Tapas Menu Decoder

You can often just point to what you want on the menu or in the display case, say *por favor* or *si us plau* (Catalan), and get your food, but these words will help. Since many of Barcelona's tapas bars use Catalan terms, I've given both Spanish and Catalan (in parentheses), when applicable.

| | |
|---|---|
| *a la parrilla (a la graella)* | barbecued |
| *a la plancha (a la planxa)* | grilled (on a flat-top griddle) |
| *aceitunas (olives)* | olives |
| *al ajillo* | with garlic |
| *albóndigas (mandonguilles)* | spiced meatballs with sauce |
| *almejas (cloïsses), a la marinera* | clams, in paprika sauce |
| *almendras (ametlles)* | almonds (usually fried) |
| *anchoas (anxoves)* | cured anchovies (salted or in oil) |
| *atún (tonyina)* | tuna |
| *bacalao (bacallà)* | cod |
| *bocadillo (entrepà/bocata)* | baguette sandwich, cheap and basic |
| *bombas (bombes)* | fried meat-and-potato ball |
| *boquerones (seitons), en vinagre* | fresh anchovies, marinated in olive oil, vinegar, and garlic |
| *brocheta (broqueta)* | shish kebab (on a stick) |
| *calamares fritos (calamars fregits)* | fried squid rings |
| *canapé* | tiny open-faced sandwich |
| *caracoles (cargols)* | tree snails (May-Sept) |
| *champiñones (xampinyons)* | mushrooms |
| *charcutería (xarcuteria)* | cured meats |
| *chorizo (xoriço)* | spicy sausage |
| *croquetas (croquetes)* | croquettes—breaded and fried béchamel with fillings such as ham |
| *empanadillas (crestes)* | pastries stuffed with meat or seafood |
| *ensaladilla rusa (ensalada russa)* | potato salad with lots of mayo, peas, and carrots |
| *espinacas, con garbanzos (espinacs, amb cigrons)* | spinach, with garbanzo beans |
| *flauta* | sandwich made with flute-thin baguette |
| *frito (fregit)* | fried |
| *fuet* | Catalan salami-like sausage |
| *gambas, con cáscara (gambes, amb closca)* | shrimp, with shell |
| *gazpacho* | cold tomato soup |
| *guiso (estofat)* | stew |

| | |
|---|---|
| *jamón (pernil)* | cured ham (like prosciutto) |
| *judías verdes (mongetes tendres)* | green beans |
| *lomo (llom)* | pork tenderloin |
| *mejillones (musclos)* | mussels |
| *merluza (lluç)* | hake (whitefish) |
| *montadito* | tapa "mounted" on bread |
| *morcilla (botifarró)* | blood sausage |
| *morro* | pig snout |
| *paella* | saffron rice dish with seafood and meat |
| *pan (pa)* | bread |
| *patatas bravas (patates braves)* | fried potatoes with spicy tomato sauce |
| *pescaditos fritos (peixet fregit)* | assortment of fried little fish |
| *pimiento, relleno (pebrot, farcit)* | pepper, stuffed |
| *pimientos de Padrón (pebrots de Padró)* | lightly fried small green peppers, only a few of which are jalapeño-hot |
| *pinchos morunos (pintxos morunos)* | skewer of spicy lamb or pork |
| *pisto (samfaina)* | mixed sautéed vegetables |
| *pollo, alioli (pollastre, all i oli)* | chicken, with garlic and olive oil sauce |
| *pulga, pulguita, or pepito (entrepà petit)* | a small, closed baguette sandwich |
| *pulpo (pop)* | octopus |
| *queso (formatge)* | cheese |
| *queso manchego (formatge manxec)* | classic Spanish sheep-milk cheese |
| *rabas (rabes)* | squid rings |
| *rabo de toro (cua de bou)* | bull's-tail stew (fatty and oh so tender) |
| *revuelto, de setas (remenat, de bolets)* | scrambled eggs, with wild mushrooms |
| *salchichón (llonganissa)* | salami-like sausage |
| *sandwich (sandvitx)* | American-style sandwich on square bread |
| *sardinas (sardines)* | sardines |
| *surtido de (assortit)* | assortment of |
| *tabla serrana (assortit d'embotits i formatges)* | hearty plate of meat and cheese |
| *tortilla española (truita de patata)* | potato omelet |
| *tortilla de jamón/queso (truita de pernil/formatge)* | potato omelet with ham/cheese |
| *variado de fritos (peixet fregits)* | mix of various fried fish |

*Tinto de verano:* Red wine, usually with lemon soda and often a slice of lemon (similar to sangria)

*Un blanco (un vi blanc):* Small glass of house white wine

*Un crianza (un criança):* Glass of nicely aged, quality wine

*Un reserva/gran reserva:* Much higher-quality (and more expensive) wine

*Un tinto (un vi negre):* Small glass of house red wine

*Vermú (vermut):* Vermouth (sweet, generally)

*Vino blanco (vi blanc):* White wine

*Vino rojo (vi negre):* Red wine

**Beer:** Spaniards rarely ask for a "*cerveza.*" Instead, they usually specify a size or type when ordering, such as a *caña* (small beer; see the list of words below for other sizes).

Most places just have the standard local beer—a light lager—on tap. In Barcelona, local options include Estrella Damm, the trendier Moritz, and various craft beers. One of the most appreciated Spanish lagers is Estrella Galicia (no relation to Estrella Damm; comes from Galicia region).

*Caña (canya):* Small glass of draft beer (around 200ml, or a little less than a half pint)

*Cerveza (cervesa):* Beer

*Clara con limón/con casera:* Shandy—small beer with lemonade/with soda

*Doble:* Typically double a *caña,* but size can vary

*Mediana:* Bottle of beer (330ml, or nearly three-quarters of a pint)

*Quinto:* Small bottle of beer (200ml, or less than half a pint)

*Sidra:* Dry cider that's a bit more alcoholic than beer

*Tubo:* Tall, thin glass of beer (about 300ml, or over half a pint)

*Una cerveza sin (una cervesa sense):* Nonalcoholic beer

## Water, Coffee, and Other Nonalcoholic Drinks

If ordering mineral water in a restaurant, request a *botella de agua grande* (big bottle), as they like to push the more profitable small bottles. For a glass of tap water, specify *un vaso de agua del grifo.* If you insist on *del grifo,* not *embotellada* (bottled), you'll usually get it. Note that tap water in Barcelona does not taste particularly good, and some places would rather not serve it to their customers (though it is safe to drink).

Spain's bars often serve fresh-squeezed orange juice. For something completely different, try the sweet and milky *horchata,* traditionally made from chufa (a.k.a. tigernuts or earth almonds).

Here are some common beverage phrases (where applicable, I've provided the Catalan translation in parentheses):

*Agua con/sin gas (aigua amb/sin gas):* Water with/without bubbles

*Botella de agua grande:* Big bottle of water

*Café con leche (café amb llet):* Espresso with hot milk

*Café solo:* Shot of espresso, sometimes with hot water added

*Cortado (tallat):* Espresso with a little milk

*Horchata (orxata):* Cold, sweet, creamy drink, similar to rice or almond milk

*Leche:* Milk

*Jarra de agua:* Pitcher of tap water

*Refresco (Refresc):* Soft drink (common brands are Coca-Cola, Fanta—*limón* or *naranja,* and Schweppes—*limón* or *tónica*)

*Té/infusion:* Tea

*Vaso de agua del grifo (got d'aigua de l'aixeta):* Glass of tap water

*Zumo:* Juice

*Zumo de naranja, natural:* Orange juice, freshly squeezed

# Staying Connected

One of the most common questions I hear from travelers is, "How can I stay connected in Europe?" The short answer is: more easily and cheaply than you might think.

The simplest solution is to bring your own device—mobile phone, smartphone, tablet, or laptop—and use it just as you would at home (following the tips below, such as connecting to free Wi-Fi whenever possible). Another option is to buy a European SIM card for your mobile phone—either your US phone or one you buy in Europe. Or you can travel without a mobile device and use European landlines and computers to connect. Each of these options is described below, and you'll find even more details at www.ricksteves.com/phoning. For a very practical one-hour lecture covering tech issues for travelers, see www.ricksteves.com/travel-talks.

## USING YOUR OWN MOBILE DEVICE IN EUROPE

Without an international plan, typical rates from major service providers (AT&T, Verizon, etc.) for using your device abroad are about $1.70/minute for voice calls, 50 cents to send text messages, 5 cents to receive them, and $10 to download one megabyte of data. But at these rates, costs can add up quickly. Here are some budget tips and options.

**Use free Wi-Fi whenever possible.** Unless you have an unlimited-data plan, you're best off saving most of your online tasks for Wi-Fi (pronounced *wee-fee* in Spanish). You can access the Internet, send texts, and make voice calls over Wi-Fi. Most accommodations in Europe and many Spanish airports offer free Wi-Fi.

## Hurdling the Language Barrier

Imported from the Old World throughout the New, Spanish is the most widely spoken Romance language in the world. With its straightforward pronunciation, Spanish is also one of the simplest languages to learn. However, Barcelona adds its own twist: About 75 percent of Barcelonans speak Catalan, the language unique to the Catalunya region. Though all Barcelonans speak Spanish, many locals insist on speaking Catalan first.

Many Barcelonans—especially those in the tourist trade—speak English. Still, many people don't. Locals visibly brighten when you know and use some key Catalan or Spanish words (see "Catalan Survival Phrases" on page 323 and "Spanish Survival Phrases" on page 321). Learn the key phrases. Travel with a phrase book, particularly if you want to interact with the Spanish people. You'll find that doors open more quickly and with more smiles when you can speak a few words of the language.

Many cafés (including Starbucks and McDonald's) have free hotspots for customers; look for signs offering it and ask for their Wi-Fi password when you buy something. You'll also often find Wi-Fi at TIs, city squares, major museums, public-transit hubs, airports, and aboard trains and buses.

**Sign up for an international plan.** Most providers offer a global calling plan that cuts the per-minute cost of phone calls and texts, and a flat-fee data plan. Your normal plan may already include international coverage (T-Mobile's does).

Before your trip, call your provider or check online to confirm that your phone will work in Europe, and research your provider's international rates. Activate the plan a day or two before you leave, then remember to cancel it when your trip's over.

**Minimize the use of your cellular network.** When you can't find Wi-Fi, you can use your cellular network to connect to the Internet, text, or make voice calls. When you're done, avoid further charges by manually switching off "data roaming" or "cellular data" (in your device's Settings menu; for help, ask your service provider or Google it). Another way to make sure you're not accidentally using data roaming is to put your device in "airplane" or "flight" mode (which also disables phone calls and texts), and then turn on Wi-Fi as needed.

Don't use your cellular network for bandwidth-gobbling tasks, such as Skyping, downloading apps, and watching YouTube: Save these for when you're on Wi-Fi. Using a navigation app such as Google Maps over a cellular network takes lots of data, so do this sparingly or use it offline.

**Limit automatic updates.** By default, your device constantly checks for a data connection and updates apps. It's smart to disable these features so your apps will only update when you're on Wi-Fi, and to change your device's email settings from "auto-retrieve" to "manual" (or from "push" to "fetch").

It's also a good idea to keep track of your data usage. On your device's menu, look for "cellular data usage" or "mobile data" and reset the counter at the start of your trip.

**Use Skype or other calling/messaging apps for cheaper calls and texts.** Certain apps let you make voice or video calls or send texts over the Internet for free or cheap. If you're bringing a tablet or laptop, you can also use them for voice calls and texts. All you have to do is log on to a Wi-Fi network, then contact any of your friends or family members who are also online and signed into the same service. You can make voice and video calls using Skype, Viber, FaceTime, and Google+ Hangouts. If the connection is bad, try making an audio-only call. You can also make voice calls from your device to telephones worldwide for just a few cents per minute using Skype, Viber, or Hangouts if you buy credit first.

To text for free over Wi-Fi, try apps like Google+ Hangouts, WhatsApp, Viber, and Facebook Messenger. Apple's iMessage connects with other Apple users, but make sure you're on Wi-Fi to avoid data charges.

## USING A EUROPEAN SIM CARD IN A MOBILE PHONE

This option works well for those who want to make a lot of voice calls at cheap local rates, and those who need faster connection speeds than their US carrier provides overseas. Either buy a basic cell phone in Europe (as little as $40 from mobile-phone shops anywhere), or bring an "unlocked" US phone (check with your carrier about unlocking it). With an unlocked phone, you can replace the original SIM card (the microchip that stores info about the phone) with one that will work with a European provider.

In Europe, buy a SIM card. Inserted into your phone, this card gives you a European phone number—and European rates. SIM cards are sold at mobile-phone shops, department-store electronics counters, newsstands, and vending machines. Costing about $5-10, they usually include about that much prepaid calling credit, with no contract and no commitment. A SIM card that also includes data costs (including roaming) will cost $20-40 more for one month of data within the country you bought it. This can be faster than data roaming through your home provider. To get the best rates, buy a new SIM card whenever you arrive in a new country.

I like to buy SIM cards at a mobile-phone shop where there's a clerk to help explain the options and brands. Certain brands—including Lebara and Lycamobile, both of which operate in multiple

# How to Dial

## International Calls

Whether phoning from a US landline or mobile phone, or from a number in another European country, here's how to make an international call. I've used one of my recommended Madrid hotels as an example (tel. 915-212-900).

**Initial Zero:** Drop the initial zero from international phone numbers—except when calling Italy.

**Mobile Tip:** If using a mobile phone, the "+" sign can replace the international access code (for a "+" sign, press and hold "0").

### US/Canada to Europe

Dial 011 (US/Canada international access code), country code (34 for Spain), and phone number.

▶ To call the Madrid hotel from home, dial 011-34-915-212-900.

### Country to Country Within Europe

Dial 00 (Europe international access code), country code, and phone number.

▶ To call the Madrid hotel from Germany, dial 00-34-915-212-900.

### Europe to the US/Canada

Dial 00, country code (1 for US/Canada), and phone number.

▶ To call from Europe to my office in Edmonds, Washington, dial 00-1-425-771-8303.

## Domestic Calls

To call within Spain (from one Spanish landline or mobile phone to another), simply dial the phone number.

▶ To call the Madrid hotel from Barcelona, dial 915-212-900.

## More Dialing Tips

**Spanish Phone Prefixes:** Spain uses a direct-dial nine-digit system. Land lines start with 9, and mobile lines start with 6

European countries—are reliable and economical. Ask the clerk to help you insert your SIM card, set it up, and show you how to use it. In some countries—including Spain—you'll be required to register the SIM card with your passport as an antiterrorism measure (which may mean you can't use the phone for the first hour or two).

Find out how to check your credit balance. When you run out of credit, you can top it up at newsstands, tobacco shops, mobile-phone stores, or many other businesses (look for your SIM card's logo in the window), or online.

or 7. Note that calls to a European mobile phone are substantially more expensive than calls to a fixed line.

**Toll and Toll-Free Calls:** Spain's toll-free numbers start with 900; numbers that start with 901 and 902 have per-minute fees. International rates apply to US toll-free numbers dialed from Spain—they're not free.

**More Phoning Help:** See www.howtocallabroad.com.

| European Country Codes | | | |
|---|---|---|---|
| Austria | 43 | Italy | 39 |
| Belgium | 32 | Latvia | 371 |
| Bosnia-Herzegovina | 387 | Montenegro | 382 |
| Croatia | 385 | Morocco | 212 |
| Czech Republic | 420 | Netherlands | 31 |
| Denmark | 45 | Norway | 47 |
| Estonia | 372 | Poland | 48 |
| Finland | 358 | Portugal | 351 |
| France | 33 | Russia | 7 |
| Germany | 49 | Slovakia | 421 |
| Gibraltar | 350 | Slovenia | 386 |
| Great Britain | 44 | Spain | 34 |
| Greece | 30 | Sweden | 46 |
| Hungary | 36 | Switzerland | 41 |
| Ireland & N. Ireland | 353 / 44 | Turkey | 90 |

**PRACTICALITIES**

## UNTETHERED TRAVEL: PUBLIC PHONES AND COMPUTERS

It's possible to travel in Europe without a mobile device. You can check email or browse websites using public computers and Internet cafés, and make calls from your hotel room and/or public phones.

Phones in your **hotel room** generally have a fee for placing local and "toll-free" calls, as well as long-distance or international calls—ask for the rates before you dial. Since you're never charged for receiving calls, it's better to have someone from the US call you in your room.

If these fees are low, hotel phones can be used inexpensively for calls made with cheap international phone cards (*tarjetas tele-*

## Tips on Internet Security

Using the Internet while traveling brings added security risks, whether you're accessing the Internet with your own device or at a public terminal using a shared network. Here are some tips for securing your data:

First, make sure that your device is running the latest version of its operating system and security software, and that your apps are up-to-date. Next, ensure that your device is password- or passcode-protected so thieves can't access it if your device is stolen. For extra security, set passwords on apps that access key info (such as email or Facebook).

On the road, use only legitimate Wi-Fi hotspots. Ask the hotel or café staff for the specific name of their Wi-Fi network, and make sure you log on to that exact one. Hackers sometimes create a bogus hotspot with a similar or vague name (such as "Hotel Europa Free Wi-Fi"). The best Wi-Fi networks require a password. If you're not actively using a hotspot, turn off your device's Wi-Fi connection so it's not visible to others.

Be especially cautious when accessing financial information online. Experts say it's best to use a banking app rather than sign in to your bank's website via a browser (the app is less likely to get hacked). Refrain from logging in to any personal finance sites on a public computer. Even if you're using your own mobile device at a password-protected hotspot, there's a remote chance that a hacker who's logged on to the same network could see what you're doing.

Never share your credit-card number (or any other sensitive information) online unless you know that the site is secure. A secure site displays a little padlock icon, and the URL begins with *https* (instead of the usual *http*).

*fónicas con códigos;* sold at many post offices, newsstands, street kiosks, tobacco shops, and train stations). You'll either get a prepaid card with a toll-free number and a scratch-to-reveal PIN code, or a code printed on a receipt.

You'll see **public pay phones** in post offices and train stations. The phones generally come with multilingual instructions, and most work with insertable phone cards (*tarjetas telefónicas;* sold at post offices, newsstands, etc.). Each European country has its own insertable phone card—so your Spanish card won't work in an Italian phone.

**Public computers** are easy to find. Many hotels have one in their lobby for guests to use; otherwise you can find them at Internet cafés, *locutorios* (call centers), or public libraries (ask your hotelier or the TI for the nearest location). If typing on a European keyboard, use the "Alt Gr" key to the right of the space bar to insert the extra symbol that appears on some keys. If you can't locate a special character (such as @), simply copy it from a web page and paste it into your email message.

## MAIL

You can mail one package per day to yourself worth up to $200 duty-free from Europe to the US (mark it "personal purchases"). If you're sending a gift to someone, mark it "unsolicited gift." For details, visit www.cbp.gov, select "Travel," and search for "Know Before You Go." The Spanish postal service works fine, but for quick transatlantic delivery (in either direction), consider services such as DHL (www.dhl.com).

# Transportation

If your trip will cover more of Spain than just Barcelona, you may need to take a long-distance train or bus, rent a car, or fly. Consider these factors: Cars are best for three or more traveling together (especially families with small kids), those packing heavy, and those delving into the countryside. Trains and buses are best for solo travelers, blitz tourists, city-to-city travelers, and those who don't want to drive in Europe. Intra-European flights are an increasingly inexpensive option. While a car gives you more freedom, trains and buses zip you effortlessly and scenically from city to city, usually dropping you in the center, often near a TI.

Cars are an expensive headache in places like Barcelona. For more detailed information on transportation throughout Europe, including trains, flying, buses, renting a car, and driving, see www.ricksteves.com/transportation.

## TRAINS

**RENFE** (the acronym for the Spanish national train system) used to mean "Really Exasperating, and Not For Everyone," but it has moved into the 21st century. For information and reservations, visit www.renfe.com or dial RENFE's national number (toll tel. 902-320-320) from anywhere in Spain. You'll find tips on buying tickets later in this section.

### Types of Trains

Spain categorizes trains this way:

The high-speed train called the **AVE** (AH-vay, stands for *Alta Velocidad Española*) whisks travelers between Madrid and Barcelona in less than three hours, and Barcelona and Sevilla in six hours. For decades, Spain's trains didn't fit on

# Public Transportation Routes in Iberia

Europe's tracks, but AVE trains run on standard European-gauge rails. AVE trains can be priced differently according to their time of departure. Peak hours *(punta)* are most expensive, followed by *llano* and *valle* (quietest and cheapest times). Tickets for these trains typically go on sale two months in advance. AVE trains are almost entirely covered by the Eurail pass (but book ahead). Tickets generally go on sale 60-62 days in advance.

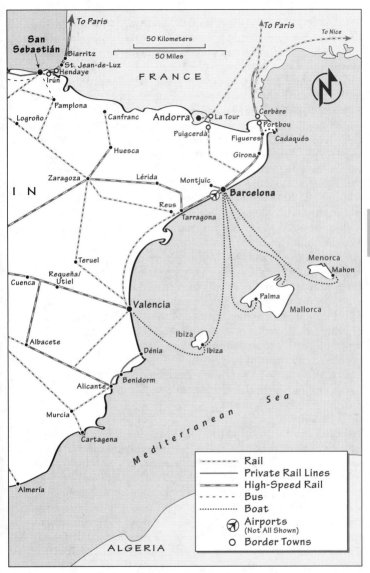

A related high-speed train, the **Alvia,** runs on AVE lines but can switch to Iberian track without stopping.

**Avant** trains are also high-speed—typically about as fast as AVE—but designed for shorter distances. They also tend to be cheaper than AVE, even on the same route. If you're on a tight budget, compare your options before buying.

The **Talgo** is fast, air-conditioned, and expensive, and runs on AVE rails. **Intercity** and **Electro** trains fall just behind Talgo in speed, comfort, and expense. **Rápido, Tranvía, Semidirecto,** and **Expreso** trains are generally slower. **Cercanías** and **Rodalies** are commuter trains for big-city workers and small-town tourists. **Regional** and **Correo** trains are slow, small-town milk runs. Trains get more expensive as they pick up speed, but all are cheaper per mile than their northern European counterparts. Spain loves to name trains, so you may encounter types of trains not listed here. The names Euromed and Altaria also indicate faster trains that require reservations. These can cost significantly less than AVE on some routes. Ask about the travel time for each option when buying your tickets.

*Salidas* means "departures," and *llegadas* is "arrivals." On train schedules, "LMXJVSD" stands for the days of the week in Spanish, starting with Monday. A train that runs "LMXJV-D" doesn't run on Saturdays. *Laborables* can mean Monday through Friday or Monday through Saturday.

**Overnight Trains:** For long trips, I go overnight on the train or I fly (see "Flights" on page 309). Overnight trains (and buses) are usually less expensive and slower than the daytime rides, not counting any sleeper fees. Most overnight trains have berths and beds that you can rent (not included in the cost of your train ticket or rail pass). A sleeping berth *(litera)* costs extra, with the price depending on the route and type of compartment. Night trains are popular, so it's smart to reserve in advance, even from home. Travelers with first-class reservations are entitled to use comfortable "Intercity" lounges in train stations in Spain's major cities.

## Rail Passes

You can buy a Eurail Spain "flexi" rail pass that allows train travel for a given number of days over a longer period of time, but you'll pay separately ($12) for seat reservations on nearly all trains. (Passholders can't reserve online through RENFE but can make a more expensive reservation at www.raileurope.com for delivery before leaving the US.) Buying individual train tickets in advance or as you go in Spain can be less expensive, and gives you better access to seat reservations (which are limited for rail-pass holders). Individual ticket prices already include seat reservations when required (for instance, for fast trains and longer distances). RENFE also offers their own, eticketed "Renfe Spain Pass" that works entirely differently. It counts trips instead of calendar days, requires reservations to be made in chronological order, and is only sold on their website.

If your trip extends beyond Spain, consider the Eurail Select rail pass for two to four neighboring countries. Two-country options are France-Spain, Portugal-Spain, or Italy-Spain (see chart). These passes are sold only outside Europe. Even if you have a rail pass, use buses when they're more convenient and direct than the

# Rail Passes

Prices listed are for 2016 and are subject to change. For the latest prices, details, and train schedules (and easy online ordering), see www.ricksteves.com/rail.

"Saver" prices are per person for two or more people traveling together. "Youth" means under age 26. Up to two kids age 4-11 travel free with each adult on any Eurail-brand pass. Additional kids pay the youth rate. Kids under age 4 travel free.

**Map key:**

Approximate point-to-point one-way second-class rail fares in US dollars. First class costs 50 percent more. Advance purchase ticket discounts also available. Add up fares for your itinerary to see whether a rail pass will save you money. Dashed lines are buses and ferries (not covered by passes).

PRACTICALITIES

## SPAIN PASS

|  | 1st Class Indiv. | 1st Class Saver | 1st Class Youth | 2nd Class Indiv. | 2nd Class Saver | 2nd Class Youth |
|---|---|---|---|---|---|---|
| 3 days in 1 month | $263 | $224 | $211 | $211 | $180 | $173 |
| 4 days in 1 month | 312 | 266 | 251 | 251 | 214 | 205 |
| 5 days in 1 month | 353 | 301 | 284 | 284 | 242 | 231 |
| 8 days in 1 month | 463 | 394 | 372 | 372 | 317 | 303 |

Select Pass prices now vary depending on which countries they cover. Since the Portugal-Spain two-country Select Pass is in the upper price category, many travelers will find the three-country, medium-priced Select Pass to be cheaper for Portugal, Spain, and either France or Italy. This works if you want first class or qualify for youth discounts. Italy-Spain is also a two-country option, but does not cover trains through France. See website www.ricksteves.com for 4-country option and more details.

## EURAIL SELECT PASS–UPPER PRICE RANGE PASS

| 3 Countries | 1st Class Indiv. | 1st Class Saver | 1st Class Youth | 2nd Class Youth |
|---|---|---|---|---|
| 5 days in 2 months | $440 | $375 | $354 | $289 |
| 6 days in 2 months | 485 | 413 | 389 | 318 |
| 8 days in 2 months | 567 | 483 | 455 | 372 |
| 10 days in 2 months | 638 | 543 | 512 | 417 |

| 2 Countries | 1st Class Indiv. | 1st Class Saver | 1st Class Youth | 2nd Class Indiv. | 2nd Class Saver | 2nd Class Youth |
|---|---|---|---|---|---|---|
| 4 days in 1 month | $362 | $308 | $291 | $291 | $248 | $238 |
| 5 days in 1 month | 408 | 348 | 328 | 328 | 280 | 268 |
| 6 days in 1 month | 451 | 384 | 362 | 362 | 309 | 296 |
| 8 days in 1 month | 525 | 447 | 421 | 421 | 359 | 344 |
| 10 days in 1 month | 591 | 504 | 474 | 474 | 404 | 387 |

trains. Remember to reserve ahead for the fast AVE trains and overnight journeys.

For more detailed advice on figuring out the smartest rail-pass options for your train trip, visit www.ricksteves.com/rail.

## Buying Train Tickets

Trains can sell out, so it's smart to buy your tickets a day in advance, even for short rides. You have four options for buying train tickets: at the station, at a travel agency, online, or by phone. Since station ticket offices can get very crowded, most travelers will find it easiest to go to a travel agency, most of which charge only a nominal service fee.

**At the Station:** You will likely have to wait in a line to buy your ticket. First find the correct line—at bigger stations, there might be separate windows for short-distance, long-distance, advance, and "today" *(para hoy)* tickets. To avoid wasting time in the wrong line, read the signs carefully, and ask a local (or a clerk at an information window) which line you need. You might have to take a number—watch others and follow their lead. While clerks accept regular US credit cards, most RENFE ticket machines only take chip-and-PIN credit cards.

As another option, you could buy tickets or reservations at the RENFE offices located in more than 100 city centers. These are more central and multilingual—also less crowded and confusing— than the train station.

**Travel Agency:** The best choice for most travelers is to buy tickets at an English-speaking travel agency. The El Corte Inglés department stores (with locations in most Spanish cities) often have handy travel agencies inside. Look for a train sticker in agency windows.

**Online:** Although the website www.renfe.com is useful for confirming schedules and prices, you cannot dependably buy tickets online unless you use PayPal or have a European credit card. (The website rejects nearly every attempt to use a US card.) But with patience and enough Spanish language skill, you may nab an online discount of up to 60 percent (available 2 weeks to 2 months ahead of travel). Online vendors based in the US include www.raileurope.com (may not offer advance discounts) and www. petrabax.com (expect a small fee).

**By Phone:** You can purchase your ticket by phone (toll tel. 902-240-202), then pick it up at the station by punching your confirmation code *(localizador)* into one of the machines. Discounts up to 40 percent off are offered a week or more ahead by phone (and at stations).

You can also reserve tickets by phone, then buy them at the station, which you must do a few days before departure (at a ticket window, usually signed *"venta anticipada"*). You can't pay for reserved tickets at the station on your day of travel.

**The Fine Print:** First-class tickets cost 50 percent more than second class—often as much as a domestic flight. Discounted tickets come with restrictions, such as being nonrefundable and nonchangeable. Be sure to read all the details carefully at time of purchase.

## BUSES

Spain's bus system is confusing (www.movelia.es is a good place to begin researching schedules and carriers). There are a number of different bus companies (though usually clustered within one building), sometimes running buses to the same destinations and using the same transfer points. If you have to transfer, make sure to look for a bus with the same name/logo as the company you bought the ticket from. Larger stations have a consolidated information desk with all schedules. In smaller stations, check the destinations and schedules posted on each office window. (If your connection requires a transfer to another company's bus in a different city, don't count on getting help from the originating clerk to figure out the onward connection.) Bus service on holidays, Saturdays, and especially Sundays can be less frequent.

If you arrive in a city by bus and plan to leave by bus, spend some time at the station upon arrival to check your departure options and buy a ticket in advance if necessary (and possible). If you're downtown, need a ticket, and the bus station isn't central, save time by asking at the TI about travel agencies that sell bus tickets.

You can (and most likely will be required to) stow your luggage under the bus. Your ticket comes with an assigned seat; if the bus is full, you should take that seat, but if it's uncrowded, most people just sit where they like. For longer rides, give some thought to which side of the bus will get the most sun, and sit on the opposite side, even if the bus is air-conditioned and has curtains. Your ride likely will come with a soundtrack: recorded Spanish pop music, radio, or sometimes videos. If you prefer your own soundtrack, bring a mobile device and headphones. Buses are nonsmoking.

Drivers and station personnel rarely speak English. Buses generally lack WCs, but they stop every two hours or so for a break (usually 15 minutes, but can be up to 30). Drivers announce how long the stop will be, but if in doubt, ask the driver, "How many minutes here?" *("¿Cuántos minutos aquí?")*. Listen for the bus horn as a final call before departure. Bus stations have WCs (rarely with toilet paper) and cafés that offer quick but overpriced food.

## TAXIS

Most taxis are reliable and cheap. Drivers generally respond kindly to the request, "How much is it to _____, more or less?"

*("¿Cuánto cuesta a _____, más o menos?").* Spanish taxis have extra supplements (for luggage, nighttime, Sundays, train/bus-station or airport pickup, and so on). Locals usually don't tip cabbies, but you could round up the fare (maximum of 10 percent) if you'd like. City rides cost about €8. Keep a map in your hand so the cabbie knows (or thinks) you know where you're going. Big cities have plenty of taxis. In many cases, couples travel by cab for little more than the cost of two bus or subway tickets.

## RENTING A CAR

If you're renting a car in Spain, bring your driver's license. You're also technically required to have an International Driving Permit—an official translation of your driver's license (sold at your local AAA office for $15 plus the cost of two passport-type photos; see www.aaa.com). While that's the letter of the law, I generally rent cars without having this permit. How this is enforced varies from country to country: Get advice from your rental company.

Rental companies require you to be at least 21 years old and to have held your license for one year. Drivers under the age of 25 may incur a young-driver surcharge, and some rental companies do not rent to anyone 75 or older. If you're considered too young or old, look into leasing (covered later), which has less stringent age restrictions.

Research car rentals before you go. It's cheaper to arrange most car rentals from the US. Consider several companies to compare rates.

Most of the major US rental agencies (including Avis, Budget, Enterprise, Hertz, and Thrifty) have offices throughout Europe. Also consider the two major Europe-based agencies, Europcar and Sixt. It can be cheaper to use a consolidator, such as Auto Europe/Kemwel (www.autoeurope.com—or the often cheaper www.autoeurope.eu) or Europe by Car (www.europebycar.com), which compares rates at several companies to get you the best deal—but because you're working with a middleman, it's especially important to ask in advance about add-on fees and restrictions.

Always read the fine print carefully for add-on charges—such as one-way drop-off fees, airport surcharges, or mandatory insur-

**Spain by Car**

FRANCE

Santiago de Compostela — 285M · 6H — Comillas — Santillana del Mar — 80M · 1.5H — Bilbao — St-Jean-de-Luz — 20M · .75H — San Sebastián

200M · 2.5H — 95M 2.5H — 10M · .25H — Potes — 50M · 1.5H — 125M 2.5H — 60M 1.25H — 55M · 1.5H

270M · 5.5H — León — 120M · 2H — 135M · 2.5H — 125M · 2.5H (VIA VITORIA) — Pamplona

140M · 2.5H — 210M · 3.5H — Burgos — 115M 2H

Porto — 220M · 4H — Salamanca — 150M · 3H — 60M 1.5H — 150M · 3.5H — Segovia — Zaragoza — 115M · 3H — Barcelona

75M · 1.25H — Coimbra — 185M · 4H — Ávila — 55M 1H — 60M 1.25H — Madrid — 205M 3.5H — 220M · 3.5H

Lisbon — 125M · 2H — 520M · 9H — 70M · 1.5H — 45M 1H — 225M · 3.5H — Valencia

Évora — 315M · 5.5H — Toledo — **S P A I N**

85M 1.5H — 200M · 3.5H — 220M 4H — 330M · 5.5H

79M · 3.5H — Córdoba — 90M · 2H — 225M 3.5H — 225M

Salema — 180M · 3H — Sevilla — 155M · 3H — 100M · 3H — Ronda — Granada

55M · 1.5H — Arcos — 50M · 2H — 120M · 2H — 65M · 1.25H

70M · 2H — 70M · 1.5H — Nerja

50M · 1.25H — Tarifa — 60M · 1.75H

.5H FERRY — Tangier — Gibraltar

Barcelona to Cerbère (French border) 110m · 2h

m = miles
h = hours
···· = ferry

NOTE: YOUR TIMES MAY VARY BASED ON TRAFFIC, CONSTRUCTION & ROAD CONDITIONS.

PRACTICALITIES

---

ance policies—that aren't included in the "total price." You may need to query rental agents pointedly to find out your actual cost.

For the best deal, rent by the week with unlimited mileage. To save money on fuel, you can request a diesel car. I normally rent the smallest, least-expensive model with a stick shift (generally cheaper than an automatic). Almost all rentals are manual by default, so if you need an automatic, request one in advance; be aware that these cars are usually larger models and not as maneuverable on narrow, winding roads.

Figure on paying roughly $230 for a one-week rental. Allow extra for supplemental insurance, fuel, tolls, and parking. For trips of three weeks or more, look into leasing (described later); you'll save money on insurance and taxes.

**Picking Up Your Car:** Big companies have offices in most cities, but small local rental companies can be cheaper.

Compare pickup costs (downtown can be less expensive than the airport) and explore drop-off options. Always check the hours of the location you choose: Many rental offices close from midday Saturday until Monday morning and, in smaller towns, at lunchtime.

When selecting a location, don't trust the agency's description of "downtown" or "city center." In some cases, a "downtown" branch can be on the outskirts of the city—a long, costly taxi ride from the center. Before choosing, plug the addresses into a mapping website. You may find that the "train station" location is handier. But returning a car at a big-city train station or downtown agency can be tricky; get precise details on the drop-off location and hours, and allow ample time to find it.

When you pick up the rental car, check it thoroughly and make sure any damage is noted on your rental agreement. Rental agencies in Europe are very strict when it comes to charging for even minor damage, so be sure to mark everything. Before driving off, find out how your car's gearshift, lights, turn signals, wipers, radio, and fuel cap function, and know what kind of fuel the car takes (diesel vs. unleaded). When you return the car, make sure the agent verifies its condition with you. Some drivers take pictures of the returned vehicle as proof of its condition.

## Car Insurance Options

When you rent a car, you are liable for a very high deductible, sometimes equal to the entire value of the car. Limit your financial risk with one of these three options: Buy Collision Damage Waiver (CDW) coverage with a low or zero deductible from the car-rental company, get coverage through your credit card (free, if your card automatically includes zero-deductible coverage), or get collision insurance as part of a larger travel-insurance policy.

Basic **CDW** includes a very high deductible (typically $1,000-1,500), costs $10-30 a day (figure roughly 30 percent extra), and reduces your liability, but does not eliminate it. When you reserve or pick up the car, you'll be offered the chance to "buy down" the basic deductible to zero (for an additional $10-30/day; this is sometimes called "super CDW" or "zero-deductible coverage").

If you opt for **credit-card coverage,** you'll technically have to decline all coverage offered by the car-rental company, which means they can place a hold on your card (which can be up to the full value of the car). In case of damage, it can be time-consuming to resolve the charges with your credit-card company. Before you decide on this option, quiz your credit-card company about how it works.

If you're already purchasing a **travel-insurance policy** for your trip, adding collision coverage can be an economical option. For example, Travel Guard (www.travelguard.com) sells affordable renter's collision insurance as an add-on to its other policies; it's valid everywhere in Europe except the Republic of Ireland, and some Italian car-rental companies refuse to honor it, as it doesn't cover you in case of theft.

For more on car-rental insurance, see www.ricksteves.com/cdw.

## Leasing

For trips of three weeks or more, consider leasing (which automatically includes zero-deductible collision and theft insurance). By technically buying and then selling back the car, you save lots of money on tax and insurance. Leasing provides you a brand-new car with unlimited mileage and a 24-hour emergency assistance program. You can lease for as few as 21 days to as long as five and a half months. Car leases must be arranged from the US. One of many companies offering affordable lease packages is Europe by Car (www.europebycar.com/lease).

## Navigation Options

If you'll be navigating using your phone or a GPS unit from home, remember to bring a car charger and device mount.

**Your Mobile Device:** The mapping app on your mobile phone works fine for navigation in Europe, but for real-time turn-by-turn directions and traffic updates, you'll generally need access to a cellular network. A helpful exception is Google Maps, which provides turn-by-turn driving directions and recalibrates even when it's offline.

To use Google Maps offline, you must have a Google account and download your map while you have a data connection. Later—even when offline—you can call up that map, enter your destination, and get directions. View maps in standard view (not satellite view) to limit data demands.

**GPS Devices:** If you prefer the convenience of a dedicated GPS unit, consider renting one with your car ($10-30/day). These units offer real-time turn-by-turn directions and traffic conditions without the data requirements of an app. Note that the unit may only come loaded with maps for its home country; if you need additional maps, ask. Also make sure your device's language is set to English before you drive off.

A less-expensive option is to bring a GPS device from home. Be aware that you'll need to buy and download European maps before your trip.

**Maps and Atlases:** Even when navigating primarily with a mobile app or GPS, I always make it a point to have a paper map. The free maps you get from your car-rental company usually don't have enough detail. It's smart to buy a better map before you go, or pick one up at European gas stations, bookshops, newsstands, and tourist shops.

## DRIVING

Driving in rural Spain is great—traffic is sparse and roads are generally good. But a car is a pain in big cities. Drive defensively. If you're involved in an accident, you will be in for a monumental headache. Spaniards love to tailgate. Don't take it personally; let impatient drivers pass you and enjoy the drive. In smaller towns, following signs to *Centro Ciudad* will get you to the heart of things.

**Freeways and Tolls:** Spain's freeways come with tolls, but save huge amounts of time. Each toll road *(autopista de peaje)* has its own pricing structure, so tolls vary. Near some major cities, you must prepay for each stretch of road you drive; on other routes, you take a ticket where you enter the freeway, and pay when you exit. Payment can be made in cash or by credit or debit card (credit-card-only lanes are labeled *"vias automáticas"*; cash lanes are *"vias manuales"*).

Because road numbers can be puzzling and inconsistent, be ready to navigate by city and town names. Memorize some key road words: *salida* (exit), *de sentido único* (one way), *despacio* (slow), *adelantamiento prohibido* (no passing). Mileage signs are in kilometers (see page 317 for a conversion formula into miles).

**Road Rules:** Seatbelts are required by law. Children under 12 must ride in the back seat, and children up to age 3 must have a child seat. You must put on a reflective safety vest any time you get out of your car on the side of a highway or unlit road (most rental-car companies provide one—check when you pick up the car). Those who use eyeglasses are required by law to have a spare pair in the car.

Be aware of typical European road rules; for example, many countries require headlights to be turned on at all times, and nearly all forbid talking on a mobile phone without a hands-free headset. In Europe, you're not allowed to turn right on a red light, unless there is a sign or

## STOP AND LEARN THESE ROAD SIGNS

| | | | |
|---|---|---|---|
| **50** Speed Limit (km/hr) | Yield | No Passing | End of No Passing Zone |
| DIRECCIÓN ÚNICA One Way | Intersection | Main Road | Expressway |
| Danger | No Entry | Cars Prohibited | All Vehicles Prohibited |
| No Through Road | Restrictions No Longer Apply | Yield to Oncoming Traffic | No Stopping |
| Parking | No Parking | ADUANA DOUANE Customs | Peace |

signal specifically authorizing it, and on expressways it's illegal to pass drivers on the right. Ask your car-rental company about these rules, or check the US State Department website (www.travel. state.gov, search for your country in the "Learn about your destination" box, then click on "Travel and Transportation").

**Traffic Cops:** Watch for traffic radars and expect to be stopped for a routine check by the police (be sure your car-insurance form is up-to-date). Small towns come with speed traps and corruption. Tickets, especially for foreigners, are issued and paid for on the spot. Insist on a receipt *(recibo)*, so the money is less likely to end up in the cop's pocket.

**Fuel:** Gas and diesel prices are controlled and the same everywhere—about $6.50 a gallon for gas, and about $6 a gallon for diesel (gas is priced by the liter in Spain). Unleaded gas *(gasolina sin plomo)* is either *normal* or *super*. Note that diesel is called *diesel* or *gasóleo*—pay attention when filling your tank.

**Theft:** Choose parking places carefully. Stow valuables in the trunk during the day and leave nothing worth stealing in the car overnight. While you should avoid parking lots with twinkly asphalt, thieves break car windows anywhere, even at stoplights. If your car's a hatchback, take the trunk cover off at night so thieves can look in without breaking in. Try to make your car look locally owned by hiding the "tourist-owned" rental-company decals and putting a local newspaper in your front or back window. Parking attendants all over Spain holler, *"Nada en el coche"* ("Nothing in the car"). And they mean it. Ask your hotelier for advice on parking. In cities you can park safely but expensively in guarded lots.

## FLIGHTS

The best comparison search engine for both international and intra-European flights is www.kayak.com. For inexpensive flights within Europe, try www.skyscanner.com.

**Flying to Europe:** Start looking for international flights four to six months before your trip, especially for peak-season travel. Off-season tickets can usually be purchased a month or so in advance. Depending on your itinerary, it can be efficient to fly into one city and out of another. If your flight requires a connection in Europe, see our hints on navigating Europe's top hub airports at www.ricksteves.com/hub-airports.

**Flying Within Europe:** If you're considering a train ride that's more than five hours long, a flight may save you both time and money. When comparing your options, factor in the time it takes to get to the airport and how early you'll need to arrive to check in.

Well-known cheapo airlines include easyJet (www.easyjet. com) and Ryanair (www.ryanair.com). But be aware of the potential drawbacks of flying with a discount airline: nonrefundable and

PRACTICALITIES

nonchangeable tickets, minimal or nonexistent customer service, pricey and time-consuming treks to secondary airports, and stingy baggage allowances with steep overage fees. If you're traveling with lots of luggage, a cheap flight can quickly become a bad deal. To avoid unpleasant surprises, read the small print before you book. These days you can also fly within Europe on major airlines affordably—and without all the aggressive restrictions—for around $100 a flight.

**Flying to the US and Canada:** Because security is extra tight for flights to the US, be sure to give yourself plenty of time at the airport. It's also important to charge your electronic devices before you board because security checks may require you to turn them on (see www.tsa.gov for latest rules).

## Resources from Rick Steves

**Begin your trip at www.ricksteves.com:** My mobile-friendly **website** is *the* place to explore Europe. You'll find thousands of fun articles, videos, photos, and radio interviews organized by country; a wealth of money-saving tips for planning your dream trip; monthly travel news dispatches; a collection of over 30 hours of practical travel talks; my travel blog; my latest guidebook updates (www.ricksteves.com/update); and my free Rick Steves Audio Europe app. You can also follow me on Facebook and Twitter.

Our **Travel Forum** is an immense, yet well-groomed collection of message boards, where our travel-savvy community answers questions and shares their personal travel experiences—and our well-traveled staff chimes in when they can be helpful (www.ricksteves.com/forums).

Our **online Travel Store** offers travel bags and accessories that I've designed specifically to help you travel smarter and lighter. These include my popular carry-on bags (which I live out of four months a year), money belts, totes, toiletries kits, adapters, other accessories, and a wide selection of guidebooks and planning maps (www.ricksteves.com/shop).

Choosing the right **rail pass** for your trip—amid hundreds of options—can drive you nutty. Our website will help you find the perfect fit for your itinerary and your budget: We offer easy, one-stop shopping for rail passes, seat reservations, and point-to-point tickets.

**Tours:** Want to travel with greater efficiency and less stress? We organize tours with more than three dozen itineraries and more than 800 departures reaching the best destinations in this book... and beyond. Our Spain tours include Best of Barcelona & Madrid in 8 days, Best of Basque Country of Spain & France in 9 days, My Way Spain in 11 days, and Best of Spain in 14 days.

You'll enjoy great guides, a fun bunch of travel partners (with small groups of 24 to 28 travelers), and plenty of room to spread out in a big, comfy bus when touring between towns. You'll find European adventures to fit every vacation length. For all the details, and to get our Tour Catalog visit www.ricksteves.com/tours or call us at 425/608-4217.

**Books:** *Rick Steves Barcelona* is one of many books in my series on European travel, which includes country guidebooks, city guidebooks (Rome, Florence, Paris, London, etc.), Snapshot guidebooks (excerpted chapters from my country guides), Pocket guidebooks (full-color little books on big cities, including Barcelona), "Best Of" guidebooks (condensed country guides in a full-color, easy-to-scan format), and my budget-travel skills handbook, *Rick Steves Europe Through the Back Door*. Most of my titles are available as ebooks.

My phrase books—for Spanish, Italian, French, German, and Portuguese—are practical and budget-oriented. My other books include *Europe 101* (a crash course on art and history designed for travelers), *Mediterranean Cruise Ports* and *Northern European Cruise Ports* (how to make the most of your time in port), and *Travel as a Political Act* (a travelogue sprinkled with tips for bringing home a global perspective). A more complete list of my titles appears near the end of this book.

**TV Shows:** My public television series, *Rick Steves' Europe*, covers Europe from top to bottom with over 100 half-hour episodes. To watch full episodes online for free, see www.ricksteves.com/tv.

**Travel Talks on Video:** You can raise your travel IQ with video versions of our popular classes (including talks on travel skills, packing smart, cruising, tech for travelers, European art for travelers, travel as a political act, and individual talks covering most European countries including Spain). See www.ricksteves.com/travel-talks.

**Audio:** My weekly public radio show, *Travel with Rick Steves*, features interviews with travel experts from around the world. A complete archive of 10 years of programs (over 400 in all) is available in the radio section of www.ricksteves.com/radio. Most of this audio content is available for free through my **Rick Steves Audio Europe** app (see page 8).

# APPENDIX

## Useful Contacts

### Emergency Needs
**Police:** Tel. 091 (nationwide), tel. 092 (local)
**Ambulance or Any Emergency:** Tel. 112

### Consulates
**US Consulate:** Tel. 932-802-227, after-hours emergency tel. 915-872-200, passport services Mon-Fri 9:00-13:00, closed Sat-Sun (Passeig Reina Elisenda de Montcada 23, http://barcelona.usconsulate.gov)
**Canadian Consulate:** Tel. 932-703-614, after-hours emergency tel. in Ottawa—call collect 613-996-8885 (Plaça de Catalunya 9, www.spain.gc.ca, click on "Contact Us," then "Consulate of Canada in Barcelona")

### Directory Assistance
In Spain, dial 11811 (€2.40/min) or 11818 (€0.55/call from private numbers).

# Holidays and Festivals

This list includes selected festivals in Barcelona, plus national holidays observed throughout Spain. Many sights and banks close on national holidays—keep this in mind when planning your itinerary. Before planning a trip around a festival, verify its dates by checking the festival's website or TI sites (www.spain.info). For more on Barcelona's festivals and feast days, see the "City of Festivals" sidebar on page 26.

Be prepared for big crowds during these holiday periods: Holy Week (Semana Santa) and Easter weekend, Labor Day, Ascension, Pentecost weekend, Assumption weekend, Spanish National Day, Constitution Day, followed closely by the Feast of the Immaculate Conception—both the previous and following weekends may be busy, and Christmas and New Year's. Look out for any local holiday that falls on a Tuesday or Thursday—the Spanish will often take Monday or Friday off as well to have a four-day weekend.

| | |
|---|---|
| **Jan 1** | New Year's Day |
| **Jan 6** | Epiphany (Día de los Reyes Magos) |
| **Mid-Feb** | Les Festes de Santa Eulàlia (parades, kid-friendly activities) |
| **March/April** | Holy Week: April 9-15, 2017; March 25-31, 2018 |
| **April** | Easter and Easter Monday: April 16-17, 2017; April 1-2, 2018 |
| **April 23** | St. George's Day |
| **May 1** | Labor Day (closures) |
| **May** | Ascension: May 25, 2017; May 10, 2018 |
| **May/June** | Pentecost and Whit Monday: June 3-4, 2017; May 19-20, 2018 |
| **May/June** | Corpus Christi: June 15, 2017; May 31, 2018 |
| **May-Sept (Saturdays)** | La Festa Catalana (local folk traditions) |
| **June 23** | Festival of St. John the Baptist (bonfires, fireworks) |
| **June-Aug** | Música als Parcs (jazz, classical music) |
| **July** | Grec Festival (music, arts) |
| **Mid-Aug** | Festes de Sant Roc (street festival) |

| Mid-Aug | Festa Major de Gràcia (music, dancing, food, and drink) |
| Aug 15 | Assumption of Mary (religious festival) |
| Late Aug | St. Bartholomew Festival, Sitges (carnival, traditional Catalan entertainments) |
| Sept 23 | St. Tecla Festival, Sitges (fireworks, castellers) |
| Late Sept | La Mercè Festival (fireworks, parades, music) |
| Oct 12 | Spanish National Day |
| Nov 1 | All Saints' Day |
| Dec 6 | Constitution Day |
| Dec 8 | Feast of the Immaculate Conception |
| Dec 13 | Feast of Santa Lucía |
| Dec 25 | Christmas |
| Dec 31 | New Year's Eve |

# Recommended Books and Films

To learn more about Barcelona's past and present, check out a few of these books and films.

## Nonfiction

*Barcelona* (Robert Hughes, 1992). This is an opinionated journey through the city's tumultuous history, with a focus on art and architecture. *Barcelona: The Great Enchantress* (2004) is a condensed version of Hughes' love song to his favorite city.

*Barcelona: A Thousand Years of the City's Past* (Felipe Fernandez-Armesto, 1992). A historical and artistic perspective on Barcelona, this book also details the tensions between the city and the rest of Spain.

*The Battle for Spain* (Antony Beevor, 2006). A prize-winning account of the disintegration of Spain in the 1930s, Beevor's work is the best overall history of the bloody civil war.

*Discovering Spain: An Uncommon Guide* (Penelope Casas, 1992). Casas, a well-known Spanish cookbook author, insightfully blends history, culture, and food in this personal guide.

*Homage to Barcelona* (Colm Tóibín, 1990). This rich history of Barcelona includes anecdotes from the author's time in the city.

*Homage to Catalonia* (George Orwell, 1938). Orwell writes a gripping account of his experiences in the Spanish Civil War fighting Franco's fascists.

*Hotel Florida: Truth, Love, and Death in the Spanish Civil War* (Amanda Vaill, 2014). In this popular history, Vaill reconstructs events of the Spanish Civil War through the letters, diaries, and photographs of the war correspondents who covered it.

*Iberia* (James Michener, 1968). Michener's tribute to Spain explores how the country's dark history created a contradictory and passionately beautiful land.

*The New Spaniards* (John Hooper, 2006). Hooper surveys all aspects of modern Spain, including its transition from dictatorship to democracy, its cultural traditions, and its changing society.

*Travelers' Tales: Spain* (Lucy McCauley, 1995). This collection of essays from numerous authors creates an appealing overview of Spain and its people.

## Fiction

*The Carpenter's Pencil* (Manuel Rivas, 2001). The psychological cost of Spain's Civil War is at the heart of this unsentimental tale of a revolutionary haunted by his past.

*Cathedral of the Sea* (Ildefonso Falcones, 2006). A humble medieval *bastaixo* who toils to build the Church of Santa Maria del Mar gradually climbs the social ladder of medieval Barcelona.

*The City of Marvels* (Eduardo Mendoza, 1986). A young man rises from poverty to wealth and power in 1890s Barcelona.

*For Whom the Bell Tolls* (Ernest Hemingway, 1940). After covering the Spanish Civil War from Madrid, Hemingway wrote his iconic novel about an American volunteer fighting Franco's fascist forces.

*Nada* (Carmen Laforet, 1943). This semiautobiographical novel details the experiences of an orphaned university student in post-civil-war Barcelona.

*The Queen's Vow* (C. W. Gortner, 2012). The life and times of Queen Isabel are vividly re-created in this historical novel.

*The Shadow of the Wind* (Carlos Ruiz Zafón, 2005). This best-selling thriller is set in 1950s Barcelona; sequels include *The Angel's Game* and *The Prisoner of Heaven*.

*Stories from Spain* (Genevieve Barlow and William Stivers, 1999). Readers follow nearly 1,000 years of Spanish history in brief short stories printed in Spanish and English.

## Films

*Barcelona* (1994). Two Americans try to navigate the Spanish singles scene and the ensuing culture clash.

*L'Auberge Espagnole* (2002). This comedy-drama chronicles the loves and lives of European students sharing an apartment in Barcelona.

*Manuale d'Amore* (2005). The four episodes of this film follow the love stories of four couples, with Barcelona and Rome as backdrops.

*The Mystery of Picasso* (1956). Picasso is filmed painting from behind a transparent canvas, allowing a unique look at his creative process.

*Salvador* (2006). Barcelona is the backdrop in this story about the life of Salvador Puig Antich, an anarchist and bank robber executed by Franco in the 1970s.

*Vicky Cristina Barcelona* (2008). In this Woody Allen film, a macho Spanish artist (Javier Bardem) tries to seduce two American women when his stormy ex-wife (Penélope Cruz) suddenly re-enters his life.

*Women on the Verge of a Nervous Breakdown* (1988). This film, about a woman's downward spiral after a breakup, is one of several piquant Pedro Almodóvar movies about relationships in the post-Franco era. Others include *All About My Mother* (1999), *Talk to Her* (2002), *Volver* (2006), and *Broken Embraces* (2009).

# Conversions and Climate

## NUMBERS AND STUMBLERS

- Europeans write a few of their numbers differently than we do. 1 = 1, 4 = 4, 7 = 7.
- In Europe, dates appear as day/month/year, so Christmas 2018 is 25/12/18.
- Commas are decimal points and decimals are commas. A dollar and a half is $1,50, one thousand is 1.000, and there are 5.280 feet in a mile.
- When counting with fingers, start with your thumb. If you hold up your first finger to request one item, you'll probably get two.
- What Americans call the second floor of a building is the first floor in Europe.
- On escalators and moving sidewalks, Europeans keep the left "lane" open for passing. Keep to the right.

## METRIC CONVERSIONS

A kilogram is 2.2 pounds, and 1 liter is about a quart, or almost four to a gallon. A kilometer is six-tenths of a mile. I figure kilometers to miles by cutting them in half and adding back 10 percent of the original (120 km: 60 + 12 = 72 miles, 300 km: 150 + 30 = 180 miles).

| | |
|---|---|
| 1 foot = 0.3 meter | 1 square yard = 0.8 square meter |
| 1 yard = 0.9 meter | 1 square mile = 2.6 square kilometers |
| 1 mile = 1.6 kilometers | 1 ounce = 28 grams |
| 1 centimeter = 0.4 inch | 1 quart = 0.95 liter |
| 1 meter = 39.4 inches | 1 kilogram = 2.2 pounds |
| 1 kilometer = 0.62 mile | 32°F = 0°C |

## CLOTHING SIZES

When shopping for clothing, use these US-to-European comparisons as general guidelines (but note that no conversion is perfect).

**Women:** For clothing or shoe sizes, add 30 (US shirt size 10 = European size 40; US shoe size 8 = European size 38-39).

**Men:** For shirts, multiply by 2 and add about 8 (US size 15 = European size 38). For jackets and suits, add 10. For shoes, add 32-34.

**Children:** For clothing, subtract 1-2 sizes for small children and subtract 4 for juniors. For shoes up to size 13, add 16-18, and for sizes 1 and up, add 30-32.

## BARCELONA'S CLIMATE

First line, average daily high; second line, average daily low; third line, average days without rain. For more detailed weather statistics for destinations in this book (as well as the rest of the world), check www.wunderground.com.

| J | F | M | A | M | J | J | A | S | O | N | D |
|---|---|---|---|---|---|---|---|---|---|---|---|
| 55° | 57° | 60° | 65° | 71° | 78° | 82° | 82° | 77° | 69° | 62° | 56° |
| 43° | 45° | 48° | 52° | 57° | 65° | 69° | 69° | 66° | 58° | 51° | 46° |
| 26 | 23 | 23 | 21 | 23 | 24 | 27 | 25 | 23 | 22 | 24 | 25 |

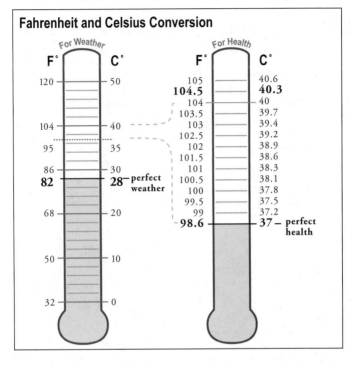

## Fahrenheit and Celsius Conversion

*Europe takes its temperature using the Celsius scale, while we opt for Fahrenheit. For a rough conversion from Celsius to Fahrenheit, double the number and add 30. For weather, remember that 28°C is 82°F—perfect. For health, 37°C is just right. At a launderette, 30°C is cold, 40°C is warm (usually the default setting), 60°C is hot, and 95°C is boiling. Your air-conditioner should be set at about 20°C.*

# Packing Checklist

Whether you're traveling for five days or five weeks, you won't need more than this. Pack light to enjoy the sweet freedom of true mobility.

## Clothing

- ❑ 5 shirts: long- & short-sleeve
- ❑ 2 pairs pants or skirt
- ❑ 1 pair shorts or capris
- ❑ 5 pairs underwear & socks
- ❑ 1 pair walking shoes
- ❑ Sweater or fleece top
- ❑ Rainproof jacket with hood
- ❑ Tie or scarf
- ❑ Swimsuit
- ❑ Sleepwear

## Money

- ❑ Debit card
- ❑ Credit card(s)
- ❑ Hard cash ($20 bills)
- ❑ Money belt or neck wallet

## Documents & Travel Info

- ❑ Passport
- ❑ Airline reservations
- ❑ Rail pass/train reservations
- ❑ Car-rental voucher
- ❑ Driver's license
- ❑ Student ID, hostel card, etc.
- ❑ Photocopies of all the above
- ❑ Hotel confirmations
- ❑ Insurance details
- ❑ Guidebooks & maps
- ❑ Notepad & pen
- ❑ Journal

## Toiletries Kit

- ❑ Toiletries
- ❑ Medicines & vitamins
- ❑ First-aid kit
- ❑ Glasses/contacts/sunglasses (with prescriptions)
- ❑ Earplugs
- ❑ Packet of tissues (for WC)

## Miscellaneous

- ❑ Daypack
- ❑ Sealable plastic baggies
- ❑ Laundry soap
- ❑ Spot remover
- ❑ Clothesline
- ❑ Sewing kit
- ❑ Travel alarm/watch

## Electronics

- ❑ Smartphone or mobile phone
- ❑ Camera & related gear
- ❑ Tablet/ereader/media player
- ❑ Laptop & flash drive
- ❑ Earbuds or headphones
- ❑ Chargers
- ❑ Plug adapters

## Optional Extras

- ❑ Flipflops or slippers
- ❑ Mini-umbrella or poncho
- ❑ Travel hairdryer
- ❑ Belt
- ❑ Hat (for sun or cold)
- ❑ Picnic supplies
- ❑ Water bottle
- ❑ Fold-up tote bag
- ❑ Small flashlight
- ❑ Small binoculars
- ❑ Insect repellent
- ❑ Small towel or washcloth
- ❑ Inflatable pillow
- ❑ Some duct tape (for repairs)
- ❑ Tiny lock
- ❑ Address list (to mail postcards)
- ❑ Postcards/photos from home
- ❑ Extra passport photos
- ❑ Good book

## Spanish Survival Phrases

Spanish has a guttural sound pronounced like the J in Baja California. In the phonetics, the symbol for this clearing-your-throat sound is the italicized *h*.

| English | Spanish | Pronunciation |
|---|---|---|
| Good day. | *Buenos días.* | **bweh**-nohs **dee**-ahs |
| Do you speak English? | *¿Habla Usted inglés?* | **ah**-blah oo-**stehd** een-**glays** |
| Yes. / No. | *Sí. / No.* | see / noh |
| I (don't) understand. | *(No) comprendo.* | (noh) kohm-**prehn**-doh |
| Please. | *Por favor.* | por fah-**bor** |
| Thank you. | *Gracias.* | **grah**-thee-ahs |
| I'm sorry. | *Lo siento.* | loh see-**ehn**-toh |
| Excuse me. | *Perdóne.* | pehr-**doh**-nay |
| (No) problem. | *(No) problema.* | (noh) proh-**bleh**-mah |
| Good. | *Bueno.* | **bweh**-noh |
| Goodbye. | *Adiós.* | ah-dee-**ohs** |
| OK. | *Vale.* | **bah**-lay |
| one / two | *uno / dos* | **oo**-noh / dohs |
| three / four | *tres / cuatro* | trehs / **kwah**-troh |
| five / six | *cinco / seis* | **theen**-koh / says |
| seven / eight | *siete / ocho* | see-**eh**-tay / **oh**-choh |
| nine / ten | *nueve / diez* | **nweh**-bay / dee-**ehth** |
| How much is it? | *¿Cuánto cuesta?* | **kwahn**-toh **kweh**-stah |
| Write it? | *¿Me lo escribe?* | may loh eh-**skree**-bay |
| Is it free? | *¿Es gratis?* | ehs **grah**-tees |
| Is it included? | *¿Está incluido?* | eh-**stah** een-kloo-**ee**-doh |
| Where can I buy / find...? | *¿Dónde puedo comprar / encontrar...?* | **dohn**-day **pweh**-doh kohm-**prar** / ehn-kohn-**trar** |
| I'd like / We'd like... | *Me gustaría / Nos gustaría...* | may goo-stah-**ree**-ah / nohs goo-stah-**ree**-ah |
| ...a room. | *...una habitación.* | **oo**-nah ah-bee-tah-thee-**ohn** |
| ...a ticket to ___. | *...un billete para ___.* | oon bee-**yeh**-tay **pah**-rah ___ |
| Is it possible? | *¿Es posible?* | ehs poh-**see**-blay |
| Where is...? | *¿Dónde está...?* | **dohn**-day eh-**stah** |
| ...the train station | *...la estación de trenes* | lah eh-stah-thee-**ohn** day **treh**-nehs |
| ...the bus station | *...la estación de autobuses* | lah eh-stah-thee-**ohn** day ow-toh-**boo**-sehs |
| ...the tourist information office | *...la oficina de turismo* | lah oh-fee-**thee**-nah day too-**rees**-moh |
| Where are the toilets? | *¿Dónde están los servicios?* | **dohn**-day eh-**stahn** lohs sehr-**bee**-thee-ohs |
| men | *hombres, caballeros* | **ohm**-brehs, kah-bah-**yeh**-rohs |
| women | *mujeres, damas* | moo-**heh**-rehs, **dah**-mahs |
| left / right | *izquierda / derecha* | eeth-kee-**ehr**-dah / deh-**reh**-chah |
| straight | *derecho* | deh-**reh**-choh |
| When do you open / close? | *¿A qué hora abren / cierran?* | ah kay **oh**-rah **ah**-brehn / thee-**ehr**-ahn |
| At what time? | *¿A qué hora?* | ah kay **oh**-rah |
| Just a moment. | *Un momento.* | oon moh-**mehn**-toh |
| now / soon / later | *ahora / pronto / más tarde* | ah-**oh**-rah / **prohn**-toh / mahs **tar**-day |
| today / tomorrow | *hoy / mañana* | oy / mahn-**yah**-nah |

# In a Spanish Restaurant

| English | Spanish | Pronunciation |
|---|---|---|
| I'd like / We'd like... | Me gustaría / Nos gustaría... | may goo-stah-**ree**-ah / nohs goo-stah-**ree**-ah |
| ...to reserve... | ...reservar... | reh-sehr-**bar** |
| ...a table for one / two. | ...una mesa para uno / dos. | **oo**-nah **meh**-sah **pah**-rah **oo**-noh / dohs |
| Non-smoking. | No fumador. | noh foo-mah-**dohr** |
| Is this table free? | ¿Está esta mesa libre? | eh-**stah** eh-stah meh-sah lee-bray |
| The menu (in English), please. | La carta (en inglés), por favor. | lah **kar**-tah (ehn een-**glays**) por fah-**bor** |
| service (not) included | servicio (no) incluido | sehr-**bee**-thee-oh (noh) een-kloo-**ee**-doh |
| cover charge | precio de entrada | **preh**-thee-oh day ehn-**trah**-dah |
| to go | para llevar | **pah**-rah yeh-**bar** |
| with / without | con / sin | kohn / seen |
| and / or | y / o | ee / oh |
| menu (of the day) | menú (del día) | meh-**noo** (dehl **dee**-ah) |
| specialty of the house | especialidad de la casa | eh-speh-thee-ah-lee-**dahd** day lah **kah**-sah |
| tourist menu | menú turístico | meh-**noo** too-**ree**-stee-koh |
| combination plate | plato combinado | **plah**-toh kohm-bee-**nah**-doh |
| appetizers | tapas | **tah**-pahs |
| bread | pan | pahn |
| cheese | queso | **keh**-soh |
| sandwich | bocadillo | boh-kah-**dee**-yoh |
| soup | sopa | **soh**-pah |
| salad | ensalada | ehn-sah-**lah**-dah |
| meat | carne | **kar**-nay |
| poultry | aves | **ah**-behs |
| fish | pescado | peh-**skah**-doh |
| seafood | marisco | mah-**ree**-skoh |
| fruit | fruta | **froo**-tah |
| vegetables | verduras | behr-**doo**-rahs |
| dessert | postre | **poh**-stray |
| tap water | agua del grifo | **ah**-gwah dehl **gree**-foh |
| mineral water | agua mineral | **ah**-gwah mee-neh-**rahl** |
| milk | leche | **leh**-chay |
| (orange) juice | zumo (de naranja) | **thoo**-moh (day nah-**rahn**-hah) |
| coffee | café | kah-**fay** |
| tea | té | tay |
| wine | vino | **bee**-noh |
| red / white | tinto / blanco | **teen**-toh / **blahn**-koh |
| glass / bottle | vaso / botella | **bah**-soh / boh-**teh**-yah |
| beer | cerveza | thehr-**beh**-thah |
| Cheers! | ¡Salud! | sah-**lood** |
| More. / Another. | Más. / Otro. | mahs / **oh**-troh |
| The same. | El mismo. | ehl **mees**-moh |
| The bill, please. | La cuenta, por favor. | lah **kwehn**-tah por fah-**bor** |
| tip | propina | proh-**pee**-nah |
| Delicious! | ¡Delicioso! | deh-lee-thee-**oh**-soh |

For hundreds more pages of survival phrases for your trip to Spain, check out *Rick Steves' Spanish Phrase Book*.

## Catalan Survival Phrases

Catalan may look similar to Spanish (*castellano*), but there are important variations in pronunciation. The letters **c** and **z** before vowels are pronounced as "s" (unlike the Spanish "th" sound). The letters **b**, **d**, **r**, or **t** at the end of a word are usually not pronounced (unless the final syllable is stressed). An **s** between two vowels sounds like a "z."

| English | Catalan | Pronunciation |
|---|---|---|
| Hello. | *Hola.* | **oh**-lah |
| Do you speak English? | *¿Parles anglès?* | **par**-luhs ahn-**glays** |
| Yes. / No. | *Sí. / No.* | see / noh |
| I (don't) understand. | *(No) entenc.* | (noh) ahn-**tehnk** |
| Please. | *Si us plau.* | see oos plow |
| Thank you (very much). | *(Moltes) Gràcies.* | (**mohl**-tehs) grah-**see**-ehs |
| I'm sorry. | *Ho sento.* | oh **sehn**-too |
| Excuse me. | *Perdó.* | pehr-**doh** |
| (No) problem. | *(Cap) problema.* | (kahp) proh-**blay**-mah |
| Good. | *Bé.* | bay |
| Goodbye. | *Adéu.* | ah-**day**-oo |
| one / two / three | *uno / dos / tres* | **oo**-noo / dohs / trehs |
| four / five / six | *quatre / cinc / sis* | **kwah**-trah / seenk / sees |
| seven / eight | *set / vuit* | seht / **voo**-eet |
| nine / ten | *nou / deu* | **noh**-oo / **deh**-oo |
| How much? | *¿Quant és?* | kwahn ehs |
| Write it? | *¿M'ho escriu?* | moh ah-**skree**-oo |
| Is it free? | *¿És gratis?* | ehs **grah**-tees |
| Is it included? | *¿Està inclós?* | ah-**stah** in-**klohs** |
| Where can I find / buy...? | *¿On puc trobar / compar...?* | ohn pook troo-**bah** / koom-**prah** |
| I'd like / We'd like... | *Voldria / Voldríem...* | vool-**dree**-ah / vool-**dree**-ahm |
| ...a room. | *...una habitació.* | **oo**-nah ah-bee-tah-see-**oh** |
| ...a ticket to ___. | *...una entrada per___.* | **oo**-nah ahn-**trah**-dah pehr ___ |
| Is it possible? | *¿És possible?* | ehs poh-**see**-blah |
| Where is...? | *¿On està...?* | ohn eh-**stah** |
| ...the train station | *...l'estació del tren* | lah-stah-see-**oh** dahl trehn |
| ...the bus station | *...l'estació d'autobuses* | lah-stah-see-**oh** dow-toh-**boo**-zehs |
| ...the tourist information office | *...l'oficina de turisme* | loo-fee-**see**-nah deh too-**rees**-meh |
| Where are the toilets? | *¿On estan els serveis?* | ohn eh-**stahn** ehls sehr-**vays** |
| men / women | *homes / dones* | **oh**-mehs / **doh**-nehs |
| left / right | *esquerre / dreta* | ehs-**keh**-reh / **dreh**-tah |
| straight | *dret* | dreht |
| At what time does this open / close? | *¿A quina hora obre / tanca?* | ah **kwee**-nah **oh**-rah **oh**-brah / **tahn**-kah |
| Just a moment. | *Un moment.* | oon moo-**mehn** |
| now / soon / later | *ara / aviat / més tard* | **ah**-rah / ah-vee-**aht** / mehs tahr |
| today / tomorrow | *avui / demà* | ah-**voo**-ee / deh-**mah** |
| Long live Catalunya! | *¡Visca Catalunya!* | **vee**-skah kah-tah-**loon**-yah |

# In a Catalan Restaurant

| English | Catalan | Pronunciation |
|---|---|---|
| I'd like / We'd like... | *Voldria / Voldríem...* | vool-**dree**-ah / vool-**dree**-ahm |
| ...to reserve... | *...reservar...* | reh-zehr-**vah** |
| ...a table for one / two. | *...una taula per una / dues.* | **oo**-nah **tow**-lah pehr **oo**-nah / doo-**ehs** |
| Is this table free? | *¿Està lliure aquesta taula?* | eh-**stah** yoo-rah ah-**kwehs**-tah **tow**-lah |
| The menu (in English), please. | *La carta (en anglès), si us plau* | lah **kar**-tah (ehn ahn-**glays**) see oos plow |
| service (not) included | *servei (no) inclós* | sehr-**vay**-ee (noh) in-**klohs** |
| cover charge | *preu d'entrada* | **preh**-oo dahn-**trah**-dah |
| to go | *per emportar* | pehr ehm-por-**tah** |
| with / without | *amb / sense* | ahm / **sehn**-seh |
| and / or | *i / o* | ee / oh |
| tapas (small plates) | *tapes* | **tah**-pahs |
| daily special | *plat del dia* | plah dahl **dee**-ah |
| tourist menu | *menú turístic* | mah-**noo** too-**ree**-steek |
| specialty of the house | *especialitat de la casa* | eh-spah-see-ah-lee-**tah** dah lah **kah**-zah |
| combination plate | *plat combinat* | plah koom-bee-**nah** |
| half portion | *mitja porció* | **meet**-yah poor-see-**oh** |
| appetizers | *entrants* | ehn-**trahns** |
| bread | *pà* | pah |
| cheese | *formatge* | foor-**mah**-jeh |
| sandwich | *entrepà* | ehn-trah-**pah** |
| soup | *sopa* | **soh**-pah |
| salad | *amanida* | ah-mah-**nee**-dah |
| meat | *carn* | karn |
| poultry | *aviram* | ah-vee-**rahm** |
| fish | *peix* | paysh |
| seafood | *marisc* | mah-**rees** |
| fruit | *fruita* | **froo**-ee-tah |
| vegetables | *verdures* | vehr-**doo**-rehs |
| dessert | *postre* | **poh**-streh |
| tap water | *aigua (de l'aixeta)* | **eye**-gwah (deh lah-**shay**-tah) |
| mineral water | *aigua mineral* | **eye**-gwah mee-nah-**rahl** |
| milk | *llet* | yeht |
| (orange) juice | *suc (de taronja)* | soo (dah tah-**rohn**-zhah) |
| coffee | *cafè* | kah-**feh** |
| tea | *te* | teh |
| wine | *vi* | vee |
| red / white | *negre / blanc* | **neh**-greh / blahnk |
| glass / bottle | *copa / ampolla* | **koh**-pah / ahm-**poy**-yah |
| beer | *cervesa* | sehr-**veh**-zah |
| Cheers! | *¡Salut!* | sah-**loo** |
| More. / Another. | *Més. / Un altre.* | mehs / oon **ahl**-treh |
| The same. | *El mateix.* | ahl mah-**taysh** |
| The bill, please. | *El compte, si us plau.* | ahl **kohmp**-teh see oos plow |
| tip | *propina* | proo-**pee**-nah |
| Delicious! | *Boníssim!* | boo-**nee**-zeem |

# INDEX

INDEX

# MAP INDEX

### Explore Europe

At ricksteves.com you can browse through thousands of articles, videos, photos and radio interviews, plus find a wealth of money-saving travel tips for planning your dream trip. And with our mobile-friendly website, you can easily access all this great travel information anywhere you go.

### TV Shows

Preview the places you'll visit by watching entire half-hour episodes of Rick Steves' Europe (choose from all 100 shows) on-demand, for free.

*your travel dreams into affordable reality*

## Radio Interviews

Enjoy ready access to Rick's vast library of radio interviews covering travel

tips and cultural insights that relate specifically to your Europe travel plans.

## Travel Forums

Learn, ask, share! Our online community of savvy travelers is a great resource for first-time travelers to Europe, as well as seasoned pros. You'll find forums on each country, plus travel tips and restaurant/hotel reviews. You can even ask one of our well-traveled staff to chime in with an opinion.

## Travel News

Subscribe to our free Travel News e-newsletter, and get monthly updates from Rick on what's happening in Europe.

# Audio Europe™

## Rick's Free Travel App

Get your FREE **Rick Steves Audio Europe**™ app to enjoy…

- Dozens of self-guided tours of Europe's top museums, sights and historic walks

- Hundreds of tracks filled with cultural insights and sightseeing tips from Rick's radio interviews

- All organized into handy geographic playlists

- For iPhone, iPad, iPod Touch, Android

With Rick whispering in your ear, Europe gets even better.

## Find out more at ricksteves.com

*Gear up for your next adventure at ricksteves.com*

## Light Luggage

Pack light and right with Rick Steves' affordable, custom-designed rolling carry-on bags, backpacks, day packs and shoulder bags.

## Accessories

From packing cubes to moneybelts and beyond, Rick has personally selected the travel goodies that will help your trip go smoother.

## Save time and energy

This guidebook is your independent-travel toolkit. But for all it delivers, it's still up to you to devote the time and energy it takes to manage the preparation and logistics that are essential for a happy trip. If that's a hassle, there's a solution.

## Rick Steves Tours

A Rick Steves tour takes you to Europe's most interesting places with great

## with minimum stress

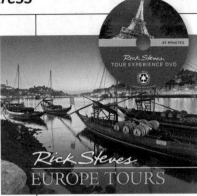

guides and small groups of 28 or less. We follow Rick's favorite itineraries, ride in comfy buses, stay in family-run hotels, and bring you intimately close to the Europe you've traveled so far to see. Most importantly, we take away the logistical headaches so you can focus on the fun.

customers—along with us on 40 different itineraries, from Ireland to Italy to Istanbul. Is a Rick Steves tour the right fit for your travel dreams? Find out at ricksteves.com, where you can also get Rick's latest tour catalog and free Tour Experience DVD.

### Join the fun

This year we'll take 18,000 free-spirited travelers— nearly half of them repeat

Europe is best experienced with happy travel partners. We hope you can join us.

## See our itineraries at ricksteves.com

## BEST OF GUIDES

*Full color easy-to-scan format, focusing on Europe's most popular destinations and sights.*

Best of France
Best of Germany
Best of England
Best of Europe
Best of Ireland
Best of Italy
Best of Spain

## COMPREHENSIVE GUIDES

*City, country, and regional guides with detailed coverage for a multi-week trip exploring the most iconic sights and venturing off the beaten track.*

Amsterdam & the Netherlands
Barcelona
Belgium: Bruges, Brussels,
  Antwerp & Ghent
Berlin
Budapest
Croatia & Slovenia
Eastern Europe
England
Florence & Tuscany
France
Germany
Great Britain
Greece: Athens & the Peloponnese
Iceland
Ireland
Istanbul
Italy
London
Paris
Portugal
Prague & the Czech Republic
Provence & the French Riviera
Rome
Scandinavia
Scotland
Spain
Switzerland
Venice
Vienna, Salzburg & Tirol

### THE BEST OF ROME

...me, Italy's capital, is studded with
...man remnants and floodlit-fountain
...ares. From the Vatican to the Colos-
...m, with crazy traffic in between, Rome
...onderful, huge, and exhausting. The
...ds, the heat, and the weighty history

of the Eternal City where Caesars walked
can make tourists wilt. Recharge by taking siestas, gelato breaks, and after-dark
walks, strolling from one atmospheric
square to another in the refreshing evening air.

...ed *Pantheon*—which
...est dome until the
...rly 2,000 years old
...day over 1,500).

...of Athens in the *Vat-
...dies the humanistic
...nce.

...gladiators fought
...another, entertaining

...is Rome *ristorante.*
...ds at St. Peter's
... seriously.

Rick Steves guidebooks are published by Avalon Travel,
an imprint of Perseus Books, a Hachette Book Group company.

## POCKET GUIDES

*Compact, full color city guides with the essentials for shorter trips.*

Amsterdam
Athens
Barcelona
Florence
Italy's Cinque Terre
London
Munich & Salzburg
Paris
Prague
Rome
Venice
Vienna

## SNAPSHOT GUIDES

*Focused single-destination coverage.*

Basque Country: Spain & France
Copenhagen & the Best of Denmark
Dublin
Dubrovnik
Edinburgh
Hill Towns of Central Italy
Krakow, Warsaw & Gdansk
Lisbon
Loire Valley
Madrid & Toledo
Milan & the Italian Lakes District
Naples & the Amalfi Coast
Northern Ireland
Normandy
Norway
Reykjavik
Sevilla, Granada & Southern Spain
St. Petersburg, Helsinki & Tallinn
Stockholm

## CRUISE PORTS GUIDES

*Reference for cruise ports of call.*

Mediterranean Cruise Ports
Northern European Cruise Ports

### Complete your library with...

## TRAVEL SKILLS & CULTURE

*Study up on travel skills and gain insight on history and culture.*

Europe 101
European Christmas
European Easter
European Festivals
Europe Through the Back Door
Postcards from Europe
Travel as a Political Act

## PHRASE BOOKS & DICTIONARIES

French
French, Italian & German
German
Italian
Portuguese
Spanish

## PLANNING MAPS

Britain, Ireland & London
Europe
France & Paris
Germany, Austria & Switzerland
Ireland
Italy
Spain & Portugal

# Credits

### RESEARCHER
To help update this book, Rick relied on...

### Amanda Buttinger

Amanda moved to Madrid in 1998, thinking she'd be there a year. Since then she's found many reasons to stay, from learning more Spanish to guiding for Rick Steves' Europe and travel writing to the best of all—sunny city walks with her boys.

## CONTRIBUTORS

### Cameron Hewitt

Born in Denver and raised in central Ohio, Cameron settled in Seattle in 2000. Ever since, he has spent three months each year in Europe, contributing to guidebooks, tours, radio and television shows, and other media for Rick Steves' Europe, where he serves as content manager. Cameron married his high school sweetheart (and favorite travel partner), Shawna, and enjoys taking pictures, trying new restaurants, and planning his next trip.

### Gene Openshaw

Gene has co-authored a dozen Rick Steves books, specializing in writing walks and tours of Europe's cities, museums, and cultural sights. He also contributes to Rick's public television series, produces tours for Rick Steves Audio Europe, and is a regular guest on Rick's public radio show. Outside of the travel world, Gene has co-authored *The Seattle Joke Book*. As a composer, Gene has written a full-length opera called *Matter* (soundtrack available on Amazon), a violin sonata, and dozens of songs. He lives near Seattle with his daughter, enjoys giving presentations on art and history, and roots for the Mariners in good times and bad.

Avalon Travel
An imprint of Perseus Books
A Hachette Book Group company
1700 Fourth Street
Berkeley, CA 94710

Text © 2016 by Rick Steves
Maps © 2016 Rick Steves' Europe. All rights reserved.
Transportation map, pages X-XI courtesy of Autoritat del Transport Metropolità
(ATM)
Printed in Canada by Friesens.
Second printing December 2017.

ISBN 978-1-63121-453-0
ISSN 2325-0542
Third Edition
For the latest on Rick's lectures, guidebooks, tours, public radio show, and public televi-
sion series, contact Rick Steves' Europe, 130 Fourth Avenue North, Edmonds, WA
98020, 425/771-8303, www.ricksteves.com, rick@ricksteves.com.

## Rick Steves' Europe

**Managing Editor:** Jennifer Madison Davis
**Special Publications Manager:** Risa Laib
**Editors:** Glenn Eriksen, Tom Griffin, Katherine Gustafson, Suzanne Kotz, Cathy Lu,
John Pierce, Carrie Shepherd
**Editorial & Production Assistant:** Jessica Shaw
**Editorial Intern:** Megan Simms
**Researcher:** Amanda Buttinger
**Graphic Content Director:** Sandra Hundacker
**Maps & Graphics:** David C. Hoerlein, Lauren Mills, Mary Rostad

## Avalon Travel

**Senior Editor and Series Manager:** Madhu Prasher
**Editor:** Jamie Andrade
**Associate Editor:** Sierra Machado
**Copy Editor:** Judith Brown
**Proofreader:** Janet Walden
**Indexer:** Stephen Callahan
**Production & Typesetting:** Rue Flaherty, Sarah Wildfang
**Cover Design:** Kimberly Glyder Design
**Maps & Graphics:** Kat Bennett, Mike Morgenfeld

## Photo Credits

**Front Cover:** © Getty Images/Peter Unger Sargada Familia
**Title Page:** View from Park Güell © Cameron Hewitt
**Additional Photography:** © 2016 Estate of Pablo Picasso / Artists Rights Society
(ARS), New York: Science and Charity (p 129, Album/Art Resource, NY), Bodego
la Desserte (p 132, INTERFOTO / Alamy), Els Quatre Gats, (p 132, Album/Art
Resource, NY), Las Meninas (p 134, Author's Image Ltd / Alamy), La Salhichona (p
134, Album/Art Resource), Still Life with Fruit (p 134, INTERFOTO / Alamy)
Dominic Arizona Bonuccelli, , Cameron Hewitt, David C. Hoerlein, Suzanne Kotz,
Gene Openshaw, Robyn Stencil, Rick Steves, Wikimedia Commons (PD-Art/PD-US)
(Photos are used by permission and are the property of the original copyright owners.)

# More for your trip!
## Maximize the experience with Rick Steves as your guide

**Guidebooks**
Spain and Portugal guides make side-trips smooth and affordable

**Phrase Books**
Rely on Rick's Spanish Phrase Book & Dictionary

**Rick's TV Shows**
Preview your destinations with 8 shows on Spain

**Free! Rick's Audio Europe™ App**
Hear Spain travel tips from Rick's radio shows

**Small Group Tours**
Take a lively Rick Steves tour through Spain